Introduction
to
Educational
Administration

Roald F. Campbell
Professor Emeritus
THE OHIO STATE UNIVERSITY

Edwin M. Bridges
STANFORD UNIVERSITY

Raphael O. Nystrand
THE OHIO STATE UNIVERSITY

INTRODUCTION TO EDUCATIONAL ADMINISTRATION

5th edition

ALLYN and BACON, Inc.
Boston, London, Sydney, Toronto

Photo Credits: page XII, Cary Wolinsky, Stock, Boston, Inc.; page 63, Ellis Herwig, Stock, Boston, Inc.; page 149, Jeff Albertson, Stock, Boston, Inc.; page 175, Boston University Photo Service; page 241, Anna Kaufman Moon, Stock, Boston, Inc.

LIBRARY OF CONGRESS CATALOGING IN PUBLICATION DATA

Campbell, Roald Fay, 1905–
Introduction to educational administration.

Fourth ed. entered under title: Introduction to educational administration.
Includes bibliographies and index.
1. School management and organization. I. Nystrand, Raphael O., joint author, II. Bridges, Edwin M., joint author. III. Titles.
LB2805•C25 1977 371.2 76–49658
ISBN 0–205–05678–4

Table of Contents

Preface ix

A PRELIMINARY LOOK AT ADMINISTRATION 1 **1**

Some Incidents 3
Some Understandings 20

Suggested Activities 24
Selected Readings 25

THE EVOLVING AMERICAN SCHOOL SYSTEM 26 **2**

Growth of Education in America 27
Basic Themes Affecting the Evolution of Our School System 33
The Emergence of Educational Administration 53

Suggested Activities 54
Selected Readings 55

THE SCHOOL SETTING 56 **3**

Background Factors 56
Education and National Development 62
The Contest to Shape Local Educational Policy 69

Suggested Activities 83
Selected Readings 83

DEVELOPMENT AND MEANING OF ADMINISTRATION 85 **4**

The Development of Administration 85

The Development of Educational Administration 94
An Overview of Educational Administration 102
Unique Aspects of Educational Administration 106
Theory in Administration 112

Suggested Activities 114
Selected Readings 115

5

ADMINISTRATIVE TASKS 116

School-Community Relationships 117
Curriculum and Instruction 122
Pupil Personnel 129
Staff Personnel 133
Physical Facilities 140
Finance and Business Management 144
Organizing to Achieve the Tasks 149

Suggested Activities 157
Selected Readings 157

6

THE WORK OF EDUCATIONAL ADMINISTRATORS 158

A Normative View of Managerial Work: The Administrative Process School 158
The Administrative Process and the Educational Administrator 165
A Descriptive View of Managerial Work: The Work Activity School 173

Suggested Activities 181
Selected Readings 181

7

THE SCHOOL AS A SOCIAL SYSTEM 183

The Conceptual Work 183
Some Empirical Studies 190
Limitations and Extensions of the Theory 197
Implications for Practice 202

Suggested Activities 208
Selected Readings 209

8

SYSTEMS PERSPECTIVES AND THE EDUCATIONAL ADMINISTRATOR 210

Systems Analysis: A General Framework 211
Input-Output Analysis 215
Planning-Programming-Budgeting Systems 219

Organizational Development (O.D.) 222
Network Analysis 226

Suggested Activities 231
Selected Readings 231

ROLES OF SCHOOL PERSONNEL IN ADMINISTRATION 232 **9**

The Role of the Superintendent 232
The Roles of Central Office Personnel 235
The Role of the Principal 240
The Teacher's Place in the Organization 244
The Teacher's Part in Decision Making 250
Planned Staff Participation 254

Suggested Activities 265
Selected Readings 266

ADMINISTRATIVE BEHAVIOR AND EDUCATIONAL ADMINISTRATION 267 **10**

The Administrator as an Initiator of Action 267
The Administrator as a Recipient of Action 279

Suggested Activities 288
Selected Readings 288

PERSONAL MOTIVATIONS FOR ADMINISTRATIVE BEHAVIOR 290 **11**

Factors Affecting Behavior 290
Perception of Others 292
Perception of Self 297
Values and Beliefs 301
Concept of Success 306

Suggested Activities 311
Selected Readings 311

CHOOSING EDUCATIONAL ADMINISTRATION AS A CAREER 313 **12**

Positions Available 314
Requisite Competencies and Traits 323
Rewards 329
Stresses and Strains 332

Suggested Activities 339
Selected Readings 339

13

QUALIFYING FOR EDUCATIONAL ADMINISTRATION 340

Creating a Plan 340
Using Teaching Experience 343
Expanding Experiences 346
Formal Preparation 347
Seeking the First Position 354
Continued Professional Growth 360

Suggested Activities 362
Selected Readings 362

14

CHALLENGE OF ADMINISTRATION 364

The Democratic Way of Life 364
The Educative Process 372
The Public School 376
Administrative Leadership 381
A Final Word 388

Index 389

Preface

The writing team has changed since the first edition of this book appeared in 1958. John Ramseyer passed away in 1968, and John Corbally has decided that his duties as President of the University of Illinois will no longer permit his participation. However, these colleagues helped shape the book and their influence is still recognized and appreciated in this fifth edition.

Primarily, we have prepared this book to help orient prospective educational administrators. Such people should get a view of the field, as well as a view of themselves, as possible workers in that field. With this information, we believe that they will be in better positions, to decide whether or not such a profession is for them. Should they decide in the affirmative, the book can help plan initial preparation for the job and for continued professional development.

A second purpose of this book is to help teachers understand the role of administrative personnel in the schools and participate more effectively in administration. Some of those teachers may also decide to become administrators.

Certain sections may also be useful to many practicing administrators, since the academic study of some administrators has included little material on the administrative process, administrative behavior, social systems, or systems analysis. The book may also be helpful to school board members and interested lay citizens who wish to know more about educational administration. By acquainting such people with the purposes and problems of the field, the book will give them a better understanding of administration in their own schools and school districts. Finally, the book may provide useful information for those administrators and educators who are working to improve programs for the selection and training of administrative personnel for the schools.

We have taken certain positions in this book. We believe that the field of educational administration is now too comprehensive to be surveyed adequately; thus, a first book should be an *introduction to,* not a *survey of,* the field. We are convinced that educational administration covers a wide range of positions in school systems and in other agencies. In order to provide an adequate concept of educational administration, we deal with the purpose of educational administration and then present several ways of viewing the field. In addition to considering the internal operation of schools, we examine the external forces in society that impinge upon school operation. Finally, we take the position that competent administrative leadership is crucial to the perpetuation of the democratic way of life in America.

The most complete treatment in the book deals with the actual job of administration: the tasks that comprise it, the steps in the administrative process, administrative behavior, systems analysis, and administration of the school as a social system. We then deal with the administrators as individuals in terms of the demands made on them by the job and the qualifications necessary to meet these demands. We also suggest methods of determining one's potential for the job and ways of preparing oneself for an administrative position. Finally, we discuss the field of educational administration as a whole—its opportunities and challenges as a profession—and emphasize the role of administrative leadership in a democratic society.

The book is built upon the conviction that one develops an understanding of educational administration as one examines concepts and relates them to actual experiences. This posits a partnership between the campus and the field. Each chapter of the book should be seen as part of the whole rather than as a separate entity. Thus, the reader will obtain maximum meaning from the book if the content of these chapters is seen as aspects of a developmental process of concept building.

How may this book be used? As we see it, the book can be useful as a text in the beginning course in educational administration. In many institutions such a course is available to students early in the graduate program. Actually, the material in the book has been used with many groups of such graduate students. The questions, concerns, and reactions of these people have helped shape the book into its present form. We are grateful for their help.

Changes in schools and society over the past few years suggest that a new edition of this book is desirable. Developments within society itself have been responsible for much of this change. Social issues related to economic recession, unemployment, race, pollution, and other problems demand attention. Concerns in the larger society inevitably affect the program and operation of the schools. The critical nature of relationships between teachers, both as individuals and as organized groups, and boards of education and administrators has come into sharp focus. The role of the federal government in education has been somewhat reduced, while for state governments the role has increased. Responding to these and other changes the entire book has been updated, some materials have been deleted, and new sections have been added.

The number of women in educational administration is growing; nonetheless, the majority of administrators being men combined with the awkwardness of expressions like "he or she" has influenced our using the masculine pronoun when referring to administrators throughout the book. This is done for convenience and clarity only and is by no means intended to deny or discount the presence and valuable contributions of women in educational administration.

We have tried here to give frank expression to our convictions about the book and our aspirations for it. We want it to make a contribution to the growing professionalism of an important calling. We know that the extent to which this proves to be the case now rests in the hands of those who use this book.

R. F. C.
E. M. B.
R. O. N.

Introduction to Educational Administration

1

A PRELIMINARY LOOK AT ADMINISTRATION

What is the function of administration in the modern school? Does it have a counterpart in business, government, the military, and other established organizations? How does educational administration differ from, and in what ways is it similar to, administration in these other organizations? What are the best modern theories and expert opinions with regard to the art or science of administration? What contributions do administrators make to help organizations become more efficient and effective? What should the role and responsibility of the educational administrator be in working with civic and other leaders to solve the many complex problems that confront communities and people in today's rapidly changing, high-pressure, pluralistic society? What are the duties of the principal, the supervisor, and the superintendent of schools? If I were to be employed in one of these positions, what would be expected of me? Could I live up to those expectations? These are a few of the questions asked by those who are anticipating educational administration as a career.

Teachers, too, are concerned about the roles of administrators in the schools they work in. The beginning teacher, for example, wants to know what the principal of the school "will be like." How much will he (or she) help? Will he understand that I may have certain difficulties in getting started? May I go to him with my questions? How much administrative support can I expect if parents and others are somewhat critical of my beginning efforts? Experienced teachers may have similar questions, but they know that teachers have a part in decision making. They have worked with parent-teacher organizations, some of them have participated actively with lay groups in educational planning, and some have negotiated for their local association with the local board of education. Teachers are asking for a clarification of their roles, and the roles to be played by others, in the important decisions that are to be made about school matters.

This book is designed to help both the prospective administrator and the teacher answer the basic questions: Why is administration necessary? What is it? How does it affect me? What role do I play in the administration of schools today? The student's problem is to answer these questions and others that come to mind as facts, issues, and propositions are presented in this and following chapters.

This book is not intended as handbook of ready answers for administrators faced with particular problems. Indeed, it does not deal with very many such problems in detail. Students with interests in particular topics will want to read more advanced materials in areas such as school finance, personnel, law, and organization. The purpose of this book is to serve as a general introduction to the understanding and application of administration in education. The approach taken is to provide some background and contextual material about schools and then to suggest some alternative perspectives for viewing educational administration.

The various perspectives addressed in the book are suggested by the respective chapter titles. We present this diversity out of the conviction that an administrator who conceives of more than one way to view a problem situation is likely to think of more than one way to solve it. Moreover, these perspectives are not mutually exclusive conceptual tools. For example, administrators may find it useful to think about achieving particular tasks in terms of particular process or system approaches. In short, the book provides a variety of conceptual glasses for viewing the full range of administrative activities and problems. The student and practitioners should find these perspectives helpful in devising personal approaches to such matters, but they will not be a substitute for actual experience or more detailed information in particular areas.

An important set of perspectives which any administrator brings to a particular situation are those based upon his or her own experience. The following pages describe some interesting incidents that have occurred in certain schools and school districts.[1] Similar happenings could certainly be cited by the readers. It is suggested that these incidents be read largely for the purpose of identifying the problems which are presented and suggesting approaches for dealing with them. We further suggest that readers take time to discuss the cases with other persons in order

1. Names and places cited in these cases are fictitious.

to appreciate the different perspectives which their respective experiences may have provided them. The reader later may find these cases useful examples for testing some of the perspectives discussed in subsequent chapters. The fact that a variety of ways can be identified for looking at particular problem situations underscores the likelihood that no single "right" solution exists for these or many other administrative problems. A particular solution at any point in time depends upon a number of things including the objectives of the problem solvers, the resources available to them, and the relationship of this particular problem to others.

SOME INCIDENTS

Jimmy Is Promoted

Jimmy was in the eighth grade. He had been a good citizen of the Midland schools since the time he enrolled as a pupil in the fourth grade. Although slow to learn, he was cooperative with his teachers and liked by his classmates. When the boys chose sides to play ball, Jimmy was always among the first selected. His friends admitted that he was "a little dumb, but a nice guy."

When Jimmy transferred to the Midland schools in the fourth grade, his report cards showed that he had received failing marks in reading and arithmetic several times. Because these failures persisted, his teachers thought it best that he repeat the fourth grade. In the two ensuing years his progress was fair; it appeared that he had found about the right level of learning for him. After all ,he had an I.Q. of only about 90 and, with considerable help from his teachers, he had managed to pass the fifth and sixth grades. In the seventh grade he failed arithmetic and history. Again he was required to repeat the grade. Now, in the spring of the year, he was one of six eighth-graders whose promotion was a subject of deep concern among the faculty members.

A faculty meeting was called by Superintendent Jones. The teachers of both the elementary and secondary divisions of the school were present, since the business of this meeting seemed to concern both groups. The first item on the agenda, "Promotions," had been discussed many times in the lunch room, the halls, and any place where a few teachers chanced to meet.

"This year, as has been true in years past, we have a number of pupils who, the elementary school teachers think, should be admitted to high school even though their work in the elementary grades has not been too satisfactory. According to board policy these teachers have the authority to promote them, but knowing that some of you would be displeased, I thought that we should discuss the matter together," was Superintendent Jones's opening remark.

Mr. DeMuth, the high school mathematics teacher, asked, "Who are the kids being passed this time?"

Mrs. Wirth, the head teacher for the elementary school, read off the list of names.

"Well, take Jimmy Keith, for example. We all like him and all of that, but from what I've heard of him, he just can't do high school work," said DeMuth.

A number of teachers joined in the discussion. Most of the elementary school teachers took the position that these pupils were working almost to the limit of their individual capacities. High school teachers, on the other hand, reflected the feeling that grade school teachers "were not tough enough."

DeMuth, the most outspoken member of the high school staff, said, "I don't suppose that there is anything we can do about it now, but I'm warning you, if he comes into my algebra class, he's a dead duck."

After a few minutes of this kind of talk, Superintendent Jones broke into the conversation with, "Now that Jim has been pointed out as our example, I guess we would have to admit that he might not get as much out of high school as most of our students. Let's keep in mind, though, that he is only one of six pupils that we are talking about."

One of the high school teachers expressed his point of view this way: "It isn't Jim. I like him. But you know what people are saying. 'High school graduation doesn't mean anything any more.' How can we make it mean something if we keep graduating these morons all the time? The elementary teachers don't have to take the rap for this, but we do. I'm against it."

Miss King, a teacher in the elementary school, said, "Isn't the policy on matters of promotion clear? I thought we settled all of this two years ago. Now, here we go again."

Sensing that this was the time to channel the meeting into a more objective course, Superintendent Jones agreed that a policy had been adopted by the board of education two years ago. He then read from the Teacher's Handbook this statement of board policy on promotions:

1. When the work of any child has been below the minimum level of achievement commonly accepted for promotion, the case may, upon recommendation of the grade teacher, be referred to the appropriate faculty to be acted upon in terms of their judgment as to what is best for the child and the school.

2. No child shall be retained in any grade more than one year, or in either the elementary or secondary school more than two years beyond the normal number of years for pupils to complete this work.

"Although I was not superintendent at the time this policy was adopted," he continued, "I would interpret this last statement to mean that when a child has been retained in any grade for one year or in either division of the school for the two years, the faculty has no choice in the matter. Promotion is automat. . . ."

"That's just it. You said it!" shouted DeMuth. "Promotion is automatic. What do the teachers have to say about it? The kids know that. Do you think that makes them respect us any more? They know they'll pass. Why should they care. . . ."

Superintendent Jones interrupted to say, "I wasn't finished with my statement, Mr. DeMuth. The policy statement does give the faculty the right to decide at least four times in a pupil's career—twice in the elementary grades and twice in high school—whether or not to promote him.

"I'm not saying that I agree with the policy. I'm merely stating that according to the policies we inherited—those statements in your handbook—the elementary teachers have acted within their rights as nearly as I can determine. The high school teachers have a similar privilege—or responsibility—for the pupils in that division."

Another high school teacher, seemingly resigned to accepting the decision in part, commented, "O.K., we get Jim! But I thought we were going to consider. . . ."

What do you suppose the last teacher had in mind?

Is there some alternative to the present policy that might be considered?

Whose responsibility it is to mention alternatives?

What should the superintendent do now?

Given the action of the teachers of the elementary school, the dissatisfaction of the high school teachers, and the board policy, what course of action would you recommend?

Negotiations in Bigtown

The Bigtown Board of Education and the teachers' union began negotiations for a new contract. In each of the preceding two years, imminent strikes had been avoided at the eleventh hour when the Bigtown mayor mediated settlements. In each instance, the board of education had granted salary increases that would require an increase in revenues if they were to be met. The first year, a voted increase in the local property tax and action of the state legislature had provided the necessary funds. However, the second year, funds the board had believed it would receive when it had negotiated the contract were not forthcoming. While teachers had received their promised raises, the board had been forced to make severe program cutbacks and had begun the school year anticipating a large deficit. Remembering this experience, several board members resolved not to grant raises in the current negotiations unless the necessary funds were in hand.

The president of the Bigtown Teacher's Union announced that program improvements rather than pay raises would have top priority in the forthcoming negotiations. He specifically mentioned class size, teacher aides, preparation periods for elementary teachers, and in-service training for inner city teachers as items of importance to the union. He added that some effort would also be made toward raising salaries and called upon the state to make more money available for schols.

On the following day, the chairman of the school board negotiating team announced that the system simply had no money available to meet any of the union proposals. Shortly thereafter, the superintendent made public the proposed budget and indicated that the schools might be forced to dismiss six thousand teachers in September unless added revenues were received. The union president responded that the state must help and that the teachers' union and the board should work together to find more money for Bigtown's schools.

By mid-December, union spokesmen were listing salary demands ahead of, rather than after, the educational matters that they had given top billing earlier. The president explained this as response to the fact that police and firemen had just been given raises that would make them better paid than teachers. However, it was also clear that the union leadership was confronted with two differing factions—one that believed higher pay should have top priority and another that stressed educational improvements. By this time, one reporter noted that "neither side seems optimistic about averting a strike" and that some board members were saying they would not seek mediation help from the mayor again.

Also at this time, the union house of representatives resolved that a contract offer would have to be ready for their consideration by January 6. Another source of temporal pressure was the fact that the school budget had to be presented to the City Council in mid-January.

As the month wore on, it became apparent that talks were deadlocked. The union president made statements indicating that strike preparations were underway and speculated about the effectiveness of selective strikes "where teachers don't want to work anymore because they say conditions are intolerable." The chairman of the board negotiating committee responded that such talk was premature and that no strike would be effective because the board lacked money. The union leader replied that the purpose of the strike would not be to get money but to "simply call attention to the plight of the Bigtown school system."

On January 6, a proposed contract, which did not include provisions for salary increases, was placed before the union. Although the president recommended acceptance of this contract, claiming it was the best that could be achieved under the circumstances, the union (with less than 15 percent of its members voting) rejected it and authorized a strike. This rejection reportedly came because of feelings that the proposed educational improvements were not "substantial enough" and because some members demanded a cost-of-living salary increase. The union leadership made some effort to obtain a second vote on the proposal through a membership referendum but abandoned this when it became evident that the membership would demand a salary increase.

The union then announced that it would present a new contract proposal and called upon the board to reenter negotiations. The union president referred to the earlier membership vote as a "mandate" to include a salary increase in any proposal he might make. The board of education, however, held fast to its position that no more money was available and that it had already done the best it could. At this point, the mayor stated at a press conference that although he had no plans to mediate the disagreement, his office was "always available to try and resolve questions that confront the community. But unless the people involved want to come in," he said, "I've never been one to force them."

Negotiations resumed on January 10. The union and school board leadership agreed to extend the prior contract for six months without a salary increase and to add a few minor educational improvements to those offered earlier. The union president and his executive board endorsed this proposal "not because it is adequate, or satisfactory, but only because it contains as much as we can get at this time without an immediate strike." The union membership sustained this agreement by a margin of nearly two to one and authorized the president to negotiate on salaries after July 1, when the amount of aid forthcoming from the state legislature would be known.

Now the issue shifted to the state legislature, where both the board and the union had made known their intention to seek more funds. Both sought an increase in the basic state aid formula from $400 to $600 per pupil. The governor proposed a figure of $500 and a group of legislators urged $550, which officials said would provide sufficient funds to meet the Bigtown budget deficit but not to increase teacher salaries as well. Approximately two thousand Bigtown teachers journeyed to the state capital in late April to lobby for the $600 figure. The governor responded by urging them to marshal legislative support for the state income tax he was proposing, and many legislators referred them back to the governor.

According to one news account, "The teachers came back to Bigtown, bitter, frustrated, and inclined to strike." At an early May meeting, the union voted to strike later that month, with the president claiming that the board had reneged on some contract features and had not worked hard enough for the increase in state aid. The strike date was subsequently set for May 22.

Reaction was quickly forthcoming. The board negotiating committee chairman again said the board had done all it could. The superintendent of schools warned that a strike would "immediately lose support for the schools" and urged that the legislature decide on funding levels soon. The governor referred to the proposed strike as "the most ridiculous action that any group of people has ever taken at any time" and warned that "if . . . [the teachers] walk out, they're going to stay out because I'm not going to give them any help." The union president said this statement was "unfortunate" and referred to the governor as "a very frustrated and excited man."

In a last-ditch effort to avoid a strike, the mayor arranged for both sides to meet in his office on May 21. Nonetheless, preparations for the strike proceeded because, the union president stated, it would not be possible to hold the membership vote needed to call off the strike until the next day at the earliest. The superintendent announced that if the strike were held, the schools would be open to teachers but closed to students. The daylong negotiations did not produce a settlement, and the first teacher's strike in Bigtown history began the next day.

Approximately 85 percent of the teachers participated in this walkout, which lasted two days. Significant opposition to the strike was apparent among a coalition of black teachers who announced that their action had two goals—"to protest the board of education's closing of the schools and its failure to educate black children" and to protest against the union, which "has not addressed itself to the needs of black schools." Negotiations continued under auspices of the mayor. The strike was settled over the weekend when the board of education agreed by a one-vote majority to a contract that met most of the union demands. As in the previous two years, full implementation of the contact would require acquisition of funds (presumably from the state legislature) that the board did not yet have. The union membership voted overwhelmingly in favor of the new contract but stipulated that unless it was fully implemented in September another strike vote would be taken.[2]

This case points up some important questions about the scope of negotiations and about participants in them.

What is negotiable?

Who decides this?

Who should participate in negotiations?

What effect does disagreement within the teachers' union or the board of education have upon the negotiating process?

Officials of the city and state government were involved in this particular case. What are the implications of such involvement for school administrators?

Motivating Students in Northton: A Study in Frustration

Northton is the capital of an important industrial and agricultural state in the Midwest. The population of the Northton metropolitan area is slightly over 1,000,000 persons. This population is largely middle class, native born, and politically conservative. About 4 percent of the core city population of 600,000 persons has recently immigrated to Northton from the Appalachian area, and about 14 percent is black.

The Northton City School System has a total enrollment of just over 100,000 pupils. There are nine senior high schools (grades 10–12), 24 junior high schools (grades 7–9), and 132 elementary schools (grades K–6) in the system.

Much of the southeastern section of Northton is comprised of low-value slum or slum clearance dwellings. A large percentage of the city's black, chronically unemployed, and "on-relief" citizens live in this section. Most of the teen-age

2. This account is based on a paper prepared by Francis Landwermeyer.

children living within this part of the city are sent to the four junior high schools and the one high school (Tower Park) which are found in the eight-square-mile area.

A survey of the Tower Park enrollment area revealed that most of the homes are either in low-cost public housing projects or in somewhat higher cost (in terms of rent) crowded, semislum apartments. Less than 10 percent of the residents of the area own their own homes. Over 12 percent of the family units in this area have no male head of family present in the home. A large percentage of the female heads of family are unwed mothers, others have been deserted by their husbands, or the husbands are in prison. Of the family units with male heads of family present, 27 percent of the men are unemployed. In 11 percent of these families, *both* parents are unemployed.

Over 40 percent of all family units are dependent upon some form of welfare or unemployment payments. A rough breakdown of the welfare picture is as follows: 24 percent of all family units receive Aid to Dependent Children, 9 percent receive Poor Relief, 7 percent are drawing Unemployment Compensation, and less than 1 percent receive Aid for the Blind and Aged. No matter what instruments are used for evaluation, there is little question that Tower Park High School and its feeder junior high schools qualify as depressed or underprivileged area schools.

The crux of this case involves the frustrations experienced by Mrs. Beck, a teacher of commercial subjects at Tower Park, as she attempted to help some of her students help themselves to overcome some of the disadvantages and deprivations under which they lived.

Mrs. Beck was in her eighth year as a teacher at Tower Park during the months when the incidents described took place. She invariably had a warm relationship with her students; she was understanding, firm, and fair. Her students recognized that Mrs. Beck was a teacher who respected them, was interested in them, and wanted to help them.

As a result of her experience over the years at Tower Park, Mrs. Beck was convinced that one of her pupils' most important needs was that of "gaining a feeling that they have a chance in life," a feeling that "they are not destined to spend their lives living on the relief rolls as most of their parents have." In short, despite her occasional feelings of hopelessness about the school, she believed that the students needed personal accomplishments and success experiences in order to demonstrate to themselves that there was some opportunity to move out of the environment in which they lived.

Mrs. Beck spent a great deal of her off-duty time trying to find ways to provide these experiences for her pupils. She had learned long ago that success in class work and activities was not enough for these children—this kind of success motivated them for a very short time. The culture from which her students came recognized more tangible gains, such as success in athletics or making money. She could not, of course, do much to help her students become star athletes, so she attempted to provide for achievement through teaching wage-earning skills.

For the past five years Mrs. Beck had been helping students in her advanced typing, bookkeeping, and general office practice courses obtain part-time employment in business offices throughout the city. She had been able to develop many contacts with employers in Northton, most of whom were sympathetic to the problems her students faced. Students recommended by Mrs. Beck were, in almost every case, found to be dependable, honest, and, for their age and experience levels, competent. Thus the relationship between Mrs. Beck, the employers, and the student-workers gradually but steadily improved over the years. Most of the students enrolled at Tower Park were aware of the opportunity to "prove that they could do something" and to "earn some money" which Mrs. Beck tried to provide. Consequently, her classes were always full to capacity, and motivation was high. Mrs. Beck felt that, although her efforts fell far short of solving all the problems of all her students, her work was a promising step in the right direction. During the previous four years, increasing numbers of students had been placed annually in part-time positions. The program seemed to be developing very well; student morale and motivation, while still not high enough, were definitely improving. But far from being content with her efforts, Mrs. Beck's constant concern was to find more jobs—and better jobs, if possible—for more of her students.

On Thursday, November 12, Mrs. Beck was asked to stop in at the principal's office after school. The principal, Mr. Gordon, was aware of and appreciated Mrs. Beck's efforts to help her students. He had offered her constant support and encouragement and had tried to see that she received all the teaching materials and supplies that she requisitioned. Many times Mr. Gordon had helped Mrs. Beck find positions for her students, and he felt a personal concern for the progress of her program. After her last class, Mrs. Beck stepped into Mr. Gordon's office. After they exchanged greetings and some small talk, the following conversation took place:

Gordon: Mrs. Beck, I feel badly about having to tell you, but it looks like we may be in trouble with your job program.

Mrs. Beck: Oh, Mr. Gordon, what do you mean! The children are all old enough to work, they all have work permits, their parents approve, and I've had no complaints from any of the employers. Do you mean that the people downtown at the central office don't think that I should be getting jobs for the students?

Gordon: No, that's not it at all. I wish it were that simple. You see, this afternoon I had a call from Mr. Bartholemew of the County Welfare Department. He told me that he had received a complaint from an 'interested citizen' with regard to 'chiseling' by relief recipients. The 'chiselers' involve the families of the children in your program, or so he said.

Mrs. Beck: But Mr. Gordon, I don't understand! What have welfare and 'chiseling' to do with the work of my students? What are they trying to do?

Gordon: Well, Bartholemew said that he probably shouldn't have called at all, but he wanted to let us know that because of this complaint he would be *forced* to make an investigation of the incomes of some of the relief recipients who have children in Tower Park. I don't quite understand it myself, but it seems that there is a standard allotment set by the state and county for the monthly amount to which a family receiving Aid to Dependent Children or other welfare funds is entitled. Bartholemew said that if *any* family receiving welfare funds has any income at all from any member, this income *must* be reported to the Welfare Department and it *must be deducted* from the amount of aid to which the family is entitled.

Mrs. Beck: Do you mean to tell me that the tiny bit of income that these children make must be reported? The *kids* aren't on relief!

Gordon: That's exactly what I said to him. But his answer was that the law is clear—the income must be reported, and no matter how little it is, or who makes it, it has to be deducted from the sum the family usually gets from the Welfare Department. Bartholemew said that it was a state law and that if anyone pushed the matter further the parties involved could lose their welfare benefits entirely. They could even be prosecuted for fraud.

Mrs. Beck: But it's not fair! Isn't there anything we can do? How can I face the children when they find out about this? How can I explain to them why they can't get anything for their work? Think of all the work in school that they've done so that they could get these jobs, and that doesn't include all the work I've done to get this thing going. I don't care if it is the law, how can we be expected to help these children become self-respecting, productive members of the community if this is what the community is going to do to them as soon as they begin to try to help themselves? Actually, it's forcing them *not* to try. What sort of person would do such a thing? Who could have complained?

Gordon: I know how you must feel, I feel the same way. I think it's one of the most unjust situations I've heard of in a long time. Mr. Bartholemew couldn't tell me who lodged the complaint, but from the way he talked I got the impression that it was someone from a family in our area; someone who is envious because his child does not have a job. He didn't say that the kids would have to quit their jobs, only that they would have to declare their earnings, so that they could be deducted. I pointed out to him that this was rather a poor way to help these kids—the families' total income would be the same whether the kids worked or not. They would be, in effect, working just for the sake of working. These children aren't stupid. They can see that they will be just as well off to stay home and watch T.V. I'm sure their parents won't be able to see any reason for them to continue working for nothing when they could be home to help around the house. Bartholemew said that he recognized the problem that we face, but that his hands were tied—he must see to it that the law is followed. He pointed out that any students from families not receiving welfare aid would not be affected by the law. I felt like saying, 'Thanks a lot,' but he was only doing what he had to do, and I don't think he likes doing this at all.

Mrs. Beck. Well, about one-third of the children we have on jobs will not be affected, but the ones that will be hurt are the very ones who need the jobs and the self-respect that goes with them most. Isn't there anything we can do? I mean, after all, if we can't get any more help and cooperation than this, then what's the use?

Gordon: Well, I've tried to think of what we might do. We can try to talk Bartholemew into looking the other way on this. I'm willing to go with you to speak with him. We know that what we're trying to do for these children is right, but we have to consider what might happen if looking the other way backfires and these families lose all their welfare aid because of us. If this happens the parents are going to blame us, the schools, and their children for the loss of the little money they get—and rightly so, since we have been warned of how the law reads. I don't know if we have the right to risk the parents' much-needed income in spite of the need we see for continuing our program.

Mrs. Beck: No, you're right, we can't risk other people's money or take the chance of being the agency that involves them in legal difficulties. But isn't there anything we can do . . . what am I going to say to the children? I've been trying for years to instill in them the belief that effort will pay off for rich man, poor man, white man, or black man. Now this happens and makes a lie of all that I've said as far as they're concerned.

Gordon: The only other thing that I can think of is to take this problem to the superintendent and to the board of education. Perhaps we can get support from the public if our case is presented to them. The Urban League and the NAACP should be willing to help us. The newspapers may help, but you know how the city is 'down' on relief recipients. The newspapers are continuously

> crying about 'chiselers' and reliefers who drive in cabs or Cadillacs to pick up their money—some of those reporters should spend a week with us just seeing how these people really live. The problem of explaining to the students is going to be a tough one. I'll try to help you. We've going to have to do some fancy talking to keep this from destroying their morale completely.

In this case, an interpretation of parents' legal rights seems to thwart the efforts of the teacher and principal, who are attempting to help their disadvantaged students. What might have been done to resolve problems resulting from such restrictions?

Should the principal take the problem to the superintendent?

What might the superintendent do?

How far should schools be expected to go in solving this kind of problem?

What other community agencies should schools be working with on problems of this kind?

How would you explain what had happened to the students involved in this situation?

What are some other factors that tend to limit the schools' efforts to help such children?

Shutdown at Lincoln Junior High School

Lincoln Junior High School was attended by nearly nine hundred students who resided in an urban ghetto. Almost all of these students were black, as was approximately half the faculty. Less than ten years earlier, the neighborhood was predominantly white and lower middle class. Now it was nearly all black and had been declared a "target area" in the "war on poverty." Almost one-third of neighborhood families had an annual income of less than $3000. Fifteen hundred of the neighborhood's five thousand housing units had been declared substandard, and there were six hundred welfare cases in the area. The Wilson County Community Action Agency maintained a neighborhood center to serve residents of the area.

Early in October, Marty Phillips, a youth worker from the neighborhood Community Action office, appeared at the school to speak with the principal, Mr. Owens. Phillips expressed concern about youngsters in the community who were potential dropouts and stated his desire to work with a small number of these students. The principal agreed to have the school guidance counselor identify some of these youngsters and to provide the youth worker access to records of the students he would be working with. He also made a room near the school office available to him for talking with these students on the assumption that he would arrange to interview them out of school. No official agreements were made regarding the limits of Mr. Phillips' activities or the duration of his stay.

The principal later commented that he had assumed that Mr. Phillips would need only a few days to collect his information and that he then would leave. However, Phillips remained in the school for approximately three weeks, during which time the original group of twelve students with whom he worked expanded considerably. At this point, Owens, with the backing of his central officer superiors, asked Phillips to bring his work at school to a close and leave the building. The principal explained that Phillips had begun to counsel students in school and maintained that he had no authority to allow persons other than certificated employees of the board of education to do this. Some persons also took exception to some of Phillips' methods. For example, criticism was offered of an incident in which Phillips and some students sat and talked in an office which was dark except for a candle burning on a table.

Phillips maintained, on the other hand, that he was simply using different situations to establish communication with the youngsters and that he did not consider this to be counseling. At least some of the students he worked with believed him to be effective. They said that Phillips knew how to talk with them and that they would rather meet with him than "sit up in some dumb class." He also received support from some adults in the community. The local black newspaper referred to him as a "counselor who cracked the wall of hopelessness for some students" and quoted one parent as saying, "He used the candle in a dark room as a way to get through to kids; he used innovative methods and helped raise one boy's grade from F to B in a short time. The issue of Marty brought to light the fact that a different type of counseling is necessary."

Phillips was asked to finish up his work on a Wednesday, and he did not return to the school after that day. By the end of the week some of the students he had been working with began circulating petitions protesting his removal. On the following Monday, the principal met with officials from the Community Action office and Marty Phillips. The outcome of their discussion was that the school would maintain its position and continue to disallow Phillips the use of school facilities to work with youngsters. Reports of these events spread through the community. On Tuesday, school staff members began to sense tension as indicated by an unusual amount of lateness to class, disrespect to teachers, and horseplay in the halls.

On Wednesday morning a group of approximately thirty parents and leaders from community groups arrived at the school to discuss the developing unrest. This meeting lasted for quite some time. Many students were aware of the fact that it was taking place and began milling around in the halls in anticipation of what they thought was to be some kind of decision about the status of Marty Phillips. As the number of youngsters who gathered around the room where the meeting was taking place continued to increase, the meeting was moved to the auditorium so more people could hear what was happening. However, as news spread, an estimated two hundred students filled the halls and refused to go to class.

Student tension heightened further when a neighborhood resident reported to the police that there was trouble at Lincoln, with the result that six police cruisers were dispatched to the scene. Although no acts of violence had actually occurred inside the school (there were reports of thrown erasers and chanting in the halls), the principal felt that the situation endangered the safety of students. He therefore asked for and received permission from the central office to dismiss school for the remainder of the day. Students left the school without serious incident shortly after noon. The school was also closed early on the following day when a number of students refused to return to class after an assembly.

While school remained in session all day Friday, it too was tension-filled. Police patrolled the halls, and one teacher was reported by the press to have said that teachers feared their safety without such protection. The principal reportedly told his teachers at a Thursday evening meeting that they must take a stand against outside agitators and that the student demonstrators were being directed by leaders of various social agencies. Approximately 150 students boycotted Friday classes following a Thursday evening meeting of parents. (Some parents said they kept children home for their safety rather than in support of the boycott.) At the meeting, parents called for curriculum changes, improved counseling services, parent and student involvement in decision-making, amnesty for student demonstrators, review of discipline procedures, and evaluation of teachers.

The director of the Community Action agency took a middle ground position. He agreed that his staff member should not be counseling students at Lincoln ("That's what school counselors are for.") but that he could work with them at the center. This, however, was not the real issue. In his view, "What the parents really are saying is that they are concerned about the quality of education their children are getting. This was a chance to get a foot in the door. Now they are going to speak."[3]

Might this incident have been anticipated?

What is the responsibility of the building administrator in the face of student unrest?

How would you respond to the student boycott and the demands set forth by the parent group?

What guidelines would you suggest for working with the police when disruptive incidents occur?

What do you think of the implication in the CAA director's comments that student activism provides adults with a "foot in the door" to change schools?

Local School Support in Edgewood

Edgewood is an upper middle class suburb of a major midwestern city. In 1970, it had more than forty thousand residents, and the average family income was in excess of $21,000. Approximately 9,000 students attended the six elementary, two junior high schools, and one high school in the district. The community had a strong tradition of pride in its schools, bolstered by what interested residents considered the phenomenal successes of local athletic teams and the fact that most graduates went on to college. Many of them returned to pursue business or professional careers in Edgewood or neighboring Big City.

Despite the pride and prosperity of Edegwood citizens, the public schools operated on relatively low budgets. This became a particular problem in 1969 when proposed tax levies were twice defeated by voters. As a result, class sizes increased substantially, textbook purchases fell behind schedule, major maintenance needs were deferred, and teacher salary levels fell behind those of most other school districts in the county. Moreover, the district had just erected a new elementary school in an area of new homes and was depending upon revenues from the anticipated levy to make it possible to staff that building.

In the wake of the second levy failure a "blue ribbon"

3. This account is based upon a paper prepared by Charles E. Taylor.

citizens' committee was commissioned by the board of education to present a report on the financial status of the district to local voters. This report indicated that a millage increase would be necessary to just maintain current programs and that an additional amount would be required to support any program improvements. The report also pointed out that Edgewood citizens were taxing themselves at a level below the state average for schools and suggested that residents could afford to do more. With the help of a well-organized citizens' campaign, a resubmitted levy passed by a narrow margin in the spring of 1970. Further good news for the schools came in the form of a substantial increment in state aid in 1972. The combined effect of these new resources was to permit school officials to reduce class size once again, increase teacher salaries to a level competitive in the area and make some modest program improvements.

An unintended side effect, however, was to convince many voters that school financial problems had been finally solved and would not recur. Particularly important in this regard was the increased state aid which was accompanied by much fanfare and achieved after a highly partisan battle to enact a state income tax and subsequently unsuccessful effort to repeal it via public referendum. The most prominent rallying cry of those who supported the income tax across the state was that it was needed to support schools. Many citizens in Edgewood and elsewhere took the view that this new and not particularly popular tax should be ample to support the schools in perpetuity.

This was not to be the case. By early 1973, it was apparent that additional local taxes would be required to sustain the current Edgewood school program into 1974 and 1975. A number of factors made this necessary according to both the board of education and another citizens' committee established to review the school financial picture. Among them were negotiated contractual increases with teachers and other employees and rapidly escalating costs of such things as educational supplies, insurance, electricity, and fuel. A further complication was that state aid to the district was projected to decline in 1974 and 1975 because local enrollments had crested in 1972 and were beginning to decline. While school officials noted this fact and reduced the size of the teaching staff accordingly, many citizens found it hard to comprehend how the schools could need more money when the number of students to be served was actually decreasing.

The 1973 citizens' committee found that a tax increase of more than 5 mills would be required to merely sustain current programs and recommended that the board of education request a total amount somewhat more than 5 mills to remedy some particular maintenance needs and add some new programs. Accordingly, the board of education asked voters to approve a new levy of approximately 7.5 mills at the November 1973 general election. However, local voters defeated it by a margin of approximately 8100 to 6800.

This defeat forced the board of education to make some adjustments in its 1974 budget. Among those were reductions in transportation services, the establishment of fees for use of school facilities, drastic reductions in allocation for supplies, maintenance, and other nonpersonnel expenses, and the making of auxilliary programs such as adult education and summer school completely self-sustaining. Feeling that the community would not accept a levy of the magnitude proposed in November but still cognizant of the need for additional resources, the Board also voted to place a levy of slightly less than six mills on the ballot in the spring election of 1974. Considerable publicity as well as media support was given to this proposal, and no organized opposition was apparent. Nevertheless the measure failed again, although this time the vote was close—5241 against and 5213 in favor.

After careful deliberation, the board of education decided to put the same proposal before the voters again in a special election during the third week of September. Again, the proposal received favorable publicity, and no organized opposition appeared. Moreover, a very carefully designed procedure was established to canvass every house in the district for the purpose of identifying both positive and negative voters. Supportive voters were helped to register or obtain absentee ballots if necessary. In addition, every possible effort was made to answer questions of prospective voters who indicated ambivalence on the issue. On the day before the election, all of the persons who had been identified as positive voters were called and reminded to vote. This campaign was so extensive that more than 800 persons took part in it. Nevertheless, the issue was defeated again, this time by a vote of 5610 to 5300.

Parents and other school supporters were naturally disheartened and somewhat mystified by these events. Many found it hard to believe that such a prosperous community would continually refuse to increase school support. This was especially true of residents who moved to Edgewood from other parts of the country and found the total tax burden to be very much lower than where they had lived previously. Nevertheless, surveys conducted in the wake of and in preparation for the various tax elections found that economic matters headed the concerns of persons who opposed the levy. The four reasons most often given by those persons who opposed the levy were: (1) taxes were too high, (2) the schools contained too many frills, (3) people on fixed income found it hard to support higher taxes, and (4) the schools needed to tighten their belts like everyone else in a period of inflation. Post election analyses indicated that the highest levels of voter support came from areas with the highest school enrollments. A perhaps related fact was that of the approximately 17,000 registered voters in the district, only about 8,000 had children enrolled in the schools.

This case reflects a situation that is common across the nation. School districts are finding it increasingly difficult to win taxpayer support for levies and bond issues. Why is this?

What are the implications of declining enrollments, inflation, and reliance on local property taxes for this issue?

What alternatives are available to a superintendent and board of education when local voters decline to support financial issues?

Some school people have argued in recent years that the growing rate of voter rejections at money elections are reason enough to change the system so that citizens no longer have this opportunity. What is your opinion of such proposals?

SOME UNDERSTANDINGS

We hope that discussion of the preceding incidents has fostered individual awareness of personal and other perspectives which come to bear upon problem situations. We suspect too that such discussion helps make the point that all administrative situations have a past history. Even when an entirely new district has been formed and new schools are built, there remain from the former districts certain perceptions of what schools should do and how they should be operated. Often there remain, also, certain habits or ways of making decisions that are characteristic of the people who live there. Some of the teachers who are selected for the new school have built their expectations of an administrator out of past experiences. However much the administrator would like to start anew, these remnants of past situations are real and must be reckoned with. Even the administrator is a product of his past experience and cannot escape some influence from it. So the usual administrative problem is to "move from where we are," not to "start from scratch."

PROBLEM MAKER OR PROBLEM SOLVER

Each of the administrative incidents described above has been lifted from context. There are additional factors and circumstances affecting all of them. It could scarcely be said that these factors are unrelated to other circumstances of the same situation. Undoubtedly the causes for incidents such as these are more complex than they appear on the surface. Occurrences of this kind represent problem situations that require solutions. To ignore them is an abdication of leadership responsibility which often allows an already serious problem in school affairs to grow worse.

It would be naïve of any administrator to expect to find a position devoid of problems. But situations do differ in the kinds of problems they present. Often problems differ in complexity and ease of solution. The questions of concern here are: What are the causes for problems that arise? Are these causes inherent in the situation itself? Is a climate being created which is conducive to problem making or to problem solving?

WHAT LABEL IS APPROPRIATE?

The manner in which problems are solved often determines the label with which people characterize the administrator of their schools. Pupils might call him a *dictator* because of their perception of his rigidity in solving problems that concern them. Yet the same behavior might cause parents to speak of this administrator as a *good disciplinarian.*

Sometimes teachers refer to the principal or the superintendent as *the boss.* The term may connote a feeling of warmth and kindliness toward a person whom they fondly call the boss, or it may be a sign of disrespect for one who treats his teachers as underlings rather than as professional equals. Usually the latter interpretation results from the feeling on the part of teachers that the administrator does not consider their opinions, that he tells them what to do and does not seek their cooperation. If they feel that he asks for but does not really consider their opinions, teachers may consider him a *manipulator* determined to have his own way while appearing to do what others wish. Noting that the principal is often sensitive to the views of parents and other citizens and that he spends much time with these people, some teachers may consider him more of a *public relations specialist* than an educator.

A *good manager* is a label that often goes along with efficiency. An administrator who is economical in the use of funds, who organizes his time wisely, or who manages to have appropriate facilities ready and handy is said to solve management problems effectively. Good equipment, clean school buildings, well-organized services, accounts in good condition, buses running on time and in good order, funds available when needed, and smoothly running schedules represent some of the more apparent evidence of effective management.

The *coordinator* is one who sees relationships and organizes events so that they appear to work in harmony. He is contrasted with the person who solves each problem as though it were unrelated to any others, for whom activity is a series of separate acts. Management problems are solved without reference to their relation to program development; public relations is the strategy employed for passing bond issues or special levies. The coordinator, however, relates these activities so that all administrative tasks are linked together in a meaningful chain of events that promote the instruction of boys and girls. Activity interrelated in a meaningful way is his objective.

Two abilities, at least, characterize *the leader.* He has a goal for the future and a plan for achieving it. In addition to this, he understands that effective planning for the achievement of goals involves the people who are affected by those goals. The leader marshals the intelligence of these people to get a job done. The leader is expected to furnish ideas. He in turn expects to receive ideas from his associates. He inspires people to cooperate in dealing with these ideas, so that the purposes of education are served.

In all problem situations, administrators face the decision of when to suggest, when to urge, and when to require people to act. A leader must make up his mind about who should help make a decision—the lay public, the board of education, the teachers, the pupils. What will the circumstances permit in this case? Is this the appropriate time? What are we waiting for? How will this decision affect the educational program? Will this answer make it easier or more difficult to answer questions or solve problems in the future?

Pondering such questions may render some people inactive altogether. These people are not the administrative type. An administrator must act with the full knowledge that the manner in which he acts, the way in which he involves other people in action, and the way people perceive the results of the action will determine the label that people place upon him.

DEVELOPING A CONCEPT OF ADMINISTRATION

To look at administration in terms of the problems that arise and the manner in which the administrator goes about the solution of problems, as we have done in this chapter, is just one of many ways of beginning to think about the subject. Certainly administration has a problem-solving dimension. For some people this may be the most challenging aspect of administration as a profession. Others may find it tiresome to be forever facing the prospect of solving problems created by people and the circumstances that surround them. Can administration be defined as the process of solving problems such as those presented in the incidents above? Or is it more than that? Perhaps a consideration of the following questions will be helpful in building a concept of administration.

What is the purpose of administration? Nations, states, and municipalities have their executive officers and branches of government. The armed forces, business, the church, and social, governmental, and professional organizations, like schools, have some administrative arrangement with an executive officer at the head. The duties and functions of an administrative officer and the staff that assists him must be determined by the organization to be served. A major task before the prospective administrator is that of determining how to serve the functions for which the group is organized in the way in which the group intended. This question is treated in some detail in chapter 4.

What is educational administration? In recent years we have become increasingly conscious of the problems of human relations in all sorts of organizations. There is also a burgeoning science and technology of administration which cuts across many fields. Public administration, business administration, church administration, social welfare administration, and educational administration have many common elements. Some studies have been made of military organization, procedure, and strategy in the search for clues to improve administrative behavior in other areas. Undoubtedly there is much to be learned by a transfer of knowledge from one field of administration to another. But in an attempt to get help from research in a related field, one could make a grave error by incorporating practices designed to accomplish a mission different from that of the public schools.

Big business deals in production of goods. It is prompted by the profit motive. Although it is the aim of our country and others to limit war to a protective measure to permit freedom to flourish, this is not the usual military motive. In waging war a nation must be prepared to kill and destroy if necessary. Education, on the other hand, promotes the enrichment of living. The strategies employed for the accomplishment of these various objectives may be quite different. Later we shall consider the elements which educational administration may have in common with other kinds of administration. It is sufficient for our purposes at this time to point out that in some respects educational administration is unique.

What do people expect of the educational administrator? Research findings indicate that expectations differ. Studies have shown that the board of education, the faculty, and the citizens of a town differ in what they expect of their school administrators. Differences of opinion exist even within each group. Sometimes individuals hold two or more expectations, which are opposed and cannot be fulfilled, as a realization of one would deny the achievement of the other. The problem of the administrator is to determine how to deal with various expectations, however different or similar they may be.

Do I have an adequate concept of the job? Probably not. Most prospective administrators in education come to the job through teaching. They view the administrator's job from the viewpoint of the teacher; their sympathies are with the teacher. In many respects this is good, because administrators may often be accused of failure to appreciate the teacher's point of view. But that is only one of the points of view to be considered. The pupils, the parents, the board of education, other patrons of the school, the state as a whole, and even the nation have a stake in the school. Administrative decisions must be made with due consideration for all parties concerned. To broaden one's own outlook to encompass all viewpoints, and yet not lose the vividness of each, is indeed a task of high order.

How can I gain a more adequate understanding of educational administration? This book is the beginning. It is designed, first, to provide the student with some *perspectives* from which to view administration. In this chapter, one's own experience furnished the setting in which to think about problem situations similar to those encountered in many public schools.

It is our intention that as students build their own concepts of educational administration, moving progressively from one consideration to the next, they will continue to draw upon their own experience, the experience of their associates, and that of other writers in this field. Hence, at the close of each chapter, the suggested activities and selected readings provide guides for obtaining greater depth and breadth of meaning. Our purpose will have been served if this book alerts the student to the need for a more critical analysis of the nature of administration, the competencies required for it, and the professional obligations and challenges which it provides, and if it helps him or her make personal decisions about administration as a career.

SUGGESTED ACTIVITIES

1. For one of the incidents reported in this chapter:
   a. Identify the problem or problems confronted by the administrator.
   b. List the facts in the case which might be useful in solving the problems.
   c. State the unknowns in the incident that complicate the solution to the problem.
   d. State your idea of some next steps to be taken. Upon what do you base your projected solution?
2. Write about an incident that occurred in a school in which you were a member of the professional staff. Give your anal-

ysis of the problem presented in the incident and the procedure you would employ in its solution.

3. Read one of the cases presented in Gorton or in Culbertson, *et al.* (see Selected Readings). How does this case differ from the incidents presented in this chapter? Identify the administrative problems in the case you selected.
4. Attend a meeting of a board of education. Briefly describe what happens at the meeting. List your criteria for the effectiveness of such a meeting, and evaluate this meeting in terms of them.

SELECTED READINGS

Culbertson, Jack A.; Jacobson, Paul B.; and Reller, Theodore L. *Administrative Relationships: A Casebook.* Englewood Cliffs, N.J.: Prentice-Hall, 1960.

English, Fenwick W. *School Organization and Management.* Worthington, Ohio: Charles A. Jones Publishing Co., 1975.

Gorton, Richard A. *Conflict, Controversy and Crisis in School Administration and Supervision: Issues, Cases and Concepts for the 70's.* Dubuque, Iowa: Wm. C. Brown Co., 1972.

Hack, Walter G.; Ramseyer, John A.; Gephart, William J.; and Heck, James B. *Educational Administration: Selected Readings,* 2nd ed. Boston: Allyn and Bacon, 1970.

Hodgkinson, Harold L. *Educational Decisions: A Casebook.* Englewood Cliffs, N.J.: Prentice-Hall, 1963.

Kimbrough, Ralph B.; and Nunnery, Michael Y. *Educational Administration: An Introduction.* New York: Macmillan Publishing Co., 1976.

Knezevich, Stephen S. *Administration of Public Education,* 3rd ed. New York: Harper and Row, 1975.

Miller, Van; Madden, G. R.; and Kincheloe, J. B. *The Public Administration of American School Systems,* 2nd ed. New York: The Macmillan Co., 1972.

Morphet, Edgar L.; Johns, Roe L.; and Reller, Theodore L. *Educational Organization and Administration,* 3rd ed. Englewood Cliffs, N.J.: Prentice-Hall, 1974.

Sarason, Seymour B., *The Culture of the School and the Problem of Change.* Boston: Allyn and Bacon, 1971.

THE EVOLVING AMERICAN SCHOOL SYSTEM

It is important for every school administrator to realize that America's school system is in a constant state of change. The present chapter is designed to acquaint the administrator with the broad dimensions of this evolutionary process. Contemporary controversy about "community control" notwithstanding, it has often been said that what makes American schools different from other educational systems is the extent of local autonomy in their operation. Perhaps it is this same characteristic of American education that accounts for what many critics call "lack of system." But on one point protagonists and antagonists of American schools agree: These schools have a quality of uniqueness that distinguishes them from schools in countries with a national system of education. Americans generally believe that this quality is something to be maintained.

While the dynamics of the evolutionary process have urged more comprehensive organization and a more effective system of education, the American people have been reluctant to give up a large measure of the local control of education in order to achieve such aims. Yet the interdependence of our several communities and states is irrevocable, and the mobility of our population is a trend that is seemingly irreversible. Not only is this interdependence evident among our communities and states, but it increasingly permeates international relationships as well. Thus a national tension exists between the ideology of local control and pressures toward uniformity and comprehensiveness.

School districts throughout the nation are now in the position of having to face up to several questions: What can and should they do alone? What can and should they do in cooperation with other districts? What must they do as parts of a larger educational unit—that is, the state and the nation? The fact that in recent times the number of basic school districts has been greatly reduced suggests that people find that the school districts which were in existence in the first part of the twentieth century are no longer adequate for the educational program needed in the last third of the century. At the same time, it is clear that people sometimes believe their school districts are too large. This concern has led to the decentralization of some city school systems.

To gain perspective on contemporary leadership demands and opportunities, let us briefly review some of the steps through which the American school system has passed. Notice that throughout much of the development of American education, the lay people, through town councils, directors, and boards of education, along with much state legislation and litigation over various disputes, provided much direction for the American system of education. This degree of citizen involvement in education is unique to the United States. It is incumbent upon the school administrator and other educators to build upon it as they supply professional leadership necessary to wise decision making in the future.

GROWTH OF EDUCATION IN AMERICA

DECISIONS MADE IN COLONIAL AMERICA

Even while the early American settlers, lacking the conveniences of the homes and towns from which they came, struggled for existence amidst the hardships of remaking a wilderness into a fit place to live and raise their children, their concern for education was manifested by the steps which they took to develop an educational system. When we remember that the Boston Latin Grammar School, the first secondary school in America, was established in 1635, and that Harvard University was founded in 1636, we realize that education was recognized as important to the future development of the country, even at that early date in American history.

The New England common school. Attitudes toward education differed throughout the colonies. In New England people began to teach their children in the home. At the elementary level the objective of this instruction was to help children understand and participate in religious ceremonies at home and at church. This proved to be inadequate, however, and by 1642 Massachusetts passed a law requiring all children to be taught to read and write and to know the principles of religion.[1]

This was the beginning of compulsory education in America. The law did not require that children attend a school, but it did place pressure on each town or community to see that parents provided for instruction in the home. Enforcement was difficult because of different interpretations of the meaning and effect of the law. A notable consequence, however, seemed to be that, although the law did not require instruction *other than* by parents, there was an increase in the amount of teaching done by masters of apprentices, by private tutors, and by town school masters. Latin grammar schools were established in the larger towns to prepare boys for college. This educational plan, of course, was dominated by the church. In the law of 1642, the people of the Massachusetts Colony had merely recognized the state as servant of the church. In this case, the civic body became the legislative and enforcement agency of the church. Thus, the New England educational pattern began as part of the program of the religious state—a pattern much like that of England.

Colonial America, however, was not entirely like the mother country. Colonial towns and communities were made up of people who had to carve out their own way of life in a land where precedents were lacking. Ideas about many things, including education and schools, differed. By 1647, the enforcement of compulsory education in the home had proved to be inadequate; but faith in education persisted, and a new law was written in Massachusetts ordering:

1. That every town having fifty householders should at once appoint a teacher of reading and writing, and provide for wages in such manner as the town might determine; and
2. That every town having one hundred householders must provide a grammar school to fit youths for the university, under a penalty of five pounds (afterward increased to twenty pounds) for failure to do so.[2]

While these laws did not enforce attendance, they clearly established the precedent for compulsory schools. The Massachusetts Colony, by passing the laws of 1642 and 1647, had pioneered the common-school concept in America.

Parochial school concept. In the middle colonies, particularly New York, Pennsylvania, and Maryland, where Baptists, Catholics, German Lutherans, German Reformed, Mennonites, Moravians, Presbyterians, Quakers, and other religious denominations were represented, the concept of the paro-

1. Ellwood P. Cubberley, *The History of Education* (Boston: Houghton Mifflin, 1920), p. 363.
2. Ibid., p. 365.

chial school developed. In these colonies each church wanted to teach the children of its denomination according to its own beliefs and doctrines. Instruction carried on in the homes was under the direction of clergymen. Private schools, which developed in the larger centers of population, were church schools, supported by church funds and by the tuition paid by families who could afford the cost of this kind of education.

Even though such a program of education obviously favored families of means, the churches stubbornly resisted any move toward the establishment of a state system of education. They wanted to preserve at all costs the right of each church to educate its children and youth. Representing many different denominations, the churches of these colonies supported each other in this position and thus established the private school. Today such schools are recognized as essential elements of our total educational system.

This is not to say that the right of attendance at private schools has never been questioned. In 1922, the people of the state of Oregon passed an initiative measure that, in effect, required that children attend the public schools. The law was to become effective in 1926, but two private corporations—the Sisters of the Holy Names of Jesus and Mary, and the Hill Military Academy—sought a restraining injunction against the enforcement of the law and received favorable action from the District Court. In 1925, the state of Oregon appealed to the Supreme Court of the United States, which ruled in favor of the two corporations. The *Oregon Case* stated in part:

> We think it entirely plain that the Act of 1922 unreasonably interferes with the liberty of parents and guardians to direct the upbringing and education of children under their control. . . . The fundamental theory of liberty upon which all governments of this Union repose excludes any general power of the state to standardize its children by forcing them to accept instruction from public teachers only. The child is not the mere creature of the State; those who nurture him and direct his destiny have the right, coupled with the high duty, to recognize and prepare him for additional obligations.[3]

This seems to make it clear that parents have the right to educate their children in private schools as long as these schools meet the state's educational requirements.

The pauper school. One of the problems that disturbed the consciences of people who developed these early concepts of education was that of making adequate provision for orphans and children of the poorer classes. This problem plagued the people of the middle colonies more than it did

3. *Pierce* v. *Society of Sisters of the Holy Names of Jesus and Mary* (and *Pierce* v. *Hill Military Academy*), 268 U.S. 510, 45 Sup. Ct. 571 (1925).

their neighbors to the north, due partly to the fact that the private school pattern established in the middle colonies definitely favored people of some means. Then too, the poorer classes immigrated in greater numbers to the middle colonies than to the New England colonies.

The Southern colonies had an even larger number of poor immigrants. While the church and state made some provisions for schooling the paupers and orphans, these were temporary measures. People of means resisted proposals to extend such provisions into some kind of permanent remedy for the lack of educational opportunity for all. Some historians believe that the need to extend education to the many who were being denied the opportunity during colonial days was a powerful force in promoting legislation leading to the tax-supported educational program now existing in all of the states.

A dual program emerges. To students of American education it is quite apparent that by the time the colonies were ready to declare their independence, two patterns of education had emerged—*public schools,* having their beginnings in Massachusetts and the other New England colonies, and *private schools,* still largely under the direction of church groups.

Throughout our history as a nation we have practiced the separation of church and state. From the laws which have been enacted and the court decisions that have been made in reference to this principle as it affects education, it appears that the people have reserved the right to educate their children in either a public or a private school, but that they have conceded to the state the right to enforce a minimum standard in private and in public schools. The Oregon Case, to which reference has been made, and the Hawaiian Cases, which established the right of parents to send children to foreign-language schools,[4] give evidence that the courts agree that the interest of the state in an education for all children can be served in both private and public schools. At the same time, however, tension has developed over the question of whether and how the public interest is served by providing public financial support to nonpublic schools.

EDUCATION AS A STATE RESPONSIBILITY

The time between the Declaration of Independence and the War of 1812 is generally regarded as a period in which American education deteriorated. As a matter of fact, because of the impoverished condition of the nation at that time, schools and colleges did suffer severe setbacks. People could not afford the advantages of private education and they were reluc-

4. *Farrington* v. *Tokushige,* 273 U.S. 284, 47 Sup. Ct. 406 (1927) and *Stainback* v. *Mo Hock Lok Po,* 336 U.S. 368, 69 Sup. Ct. 606 (1949).

tant to increase their tax burdens to support public education. Nevertheless, this period is important in the development of our schools because it was the time when the first state constitutions were written.

State responsibility grew out of colonial action. By 1800, sixteen states had joined the new Union. Of these, seven had incorporated in their state constitutions provisions concerning the state's responsibility for education. The New England states, having gone through a long colonial period during which state responsibility for education was being developed, incorporated in their constitutions the most comprehensive provisions for public education. The middle states, which had espoused the parochial school concept, were less emphatic in placing state responsibility. The Southern colonies and the new states of Kentucky and Tennessee ignored the matter entirely.

Federal recognition of state control. By the time the ordinance for the organization of the Northwest Territory had been adopted (1787), the theory of education as a state function had been quite generally accepted. Article 3 of the Ordinance of 1787 is significant in this regard as it provides that:

> Religion, morality, and knowledge being necessary to good government and the happiness of mankind, schools and the means of education shall be forever encouraged (in the states to be formed from this territory).[5]

When Ohio was admitted to the Union, Congress gave the new state land to establish and maintain a state system of schools, a practice continued by the federal government as states were admitted to the Union. General state school laws began to be adopted by the older states in the Union. In 1784 the University of the State of New York, an administrative organization similar to present-day state departments of education, was formed to supervise secondary and higher education in New York.

No provision was made in the Constitution of the United States for federal support or control of education. Article X of the Bill of Rights, passed by Congress in 1789 and ratified by three-fourths of the states in 1791, stated that "The powers not delegated to the United States by the Constitution, nor prohibited by it to the States, are reserved to the States respectively, or to the people." This clause indicated that the growth of state control of education was acceptable to the founders of our federal government.

General acceptance of state regulation. Many of the early state laws on education were permissive. Such laws provided that people had a right

5. Quoted in Ellwood P. Cubberley, *Public Education in the United States* (Boston: Houghton Mifflin, 1934), p. 92.

to establish schools in their own communities if they so desired. The people were also permitted to tax themselves for school purposes if they wished. The fact that legislation was permissive left many communities without adequate provision for education, and it can be readily understood that in time of stress the school program deteriorated. Gradually, however, permissive legislation gave way to mandatory provisions. The adoption of state financial aid for public schools completed a series of actions and regulations which now made it mandatory that the powers of the state be defined. Thus, in each state we witnessed the development of a school code that provides a framework by which the school districts of the state are regulated.

All state constitutions now have sections devoted to education. It should be noted that the states reserve to themselves the authority and power over education. The school district is a subordinate creation of the state and is established for purposes of local administration. The districts—towns, townships, villages, cities, or counties—derive their powers from the state legislature. Thus, the people of the state, acting through their state legislature and not in small competing groups representing individual communities, have given their sanction to such a system. The courts have upheld this action and have repeatedly ruled that the state may establish standards below which the district programs of education may not fall.

Delegation to local districts. An examination of the educational programs of the several states reveals, however, that much power has been delegated by the state to the local district. In the beginning, such a practice was necessary just to get schools started; now all states (except Hawaii, which has a unitary district) find it necessary for public approval and efficient administration of the schools. The states differ, however, in the degree of delegation of powers and in the size and number of districts to which such power is delegated. The tendency in recent years has been to provide a greater amount of state aid, to enforce minimum standards more rigidly, and to increase the size of school districts.

The movement to reduce the number of administrative units has been encouraged by state governments not only to take better advantage of the taxable wealth, but also to provide an educational program to meet more adequately the needs of children in diverse communities. Some people have interpreted this movement as a gradual revocation of delegated powers. They would argue that there is not only an increasing amount of state control, but also a tendency toward centralization of administration of schools at the district level; and these schools are becoming more and more remote from the people. Even so, the school district reorganization movement gained momentum in the mid-twentieth century. In New York the number of school districts was reduced from 9,500 in 1925 to 1,932 in 1955. In Illinois the major reorganization took place in a period of 10 years, 1945 to 1955, and reduced the number of school districts from approximately 12,000 to 2,349. In the United States the number of districts reached a peak of about 127,000 in the 1930s, was reduced to approximately 80,000 by 1950, and by 1975 the number of operating districts was only about 16,000.

During the 1960s and 1970s, substantial interest developed in two other types of reorganization: The first was the establishment of special purpose or supplementary service districts which serve a number of local school districts. In some instances, this involved the creation of new units to administer programs in areas such as vocational education. In other states, the movement has been one of restructuring the boundaries and functions of existing intermediate school districts. The second type of reorganization which has achieved recent popularity is the decentralization of large city school systems into semi-independent operating districts. The best known example is New York City where the city-wide board of education retained jurisdiction over some functions (e.g., establishing teacher salaries) and other operating responsibilities (e.g., assignment of personnel) were given to thirty-one local boards of education. Public pressure for decentralization also has been apparent in other cities including Chicago, Detroit, Los Angeles, and Philadelphia.

BASIC THEMES AFFECTING THE EVOLUTION OF OUR SCHOOL SYSTEM

As we review the evolution of the American school system, it is apparent that several basic themes have recurred in its development. In some instances the resolution of questions related to these themes has been so consistent that their legacies can be viewed as principles to guide us in the further development of schools. They have withstood and continue to withstand severe tests of both public and legal opinion. In other instances, the questions have a quality of perennialism; educators and citizens alike remain divided in opinions about them. In both cases, it seems prudent for educational leaders to be mindful of the way in which these themes have developed, to weigh the evidence regarding them, and to provide leadership to help people in their school districts understand the background and ramifications of such themes as they grapple with local issues. With this in mind, let us turn our attention to eight historical themes that still have meaning for the administration of local schools.

UNIVERSAL EDUCATION

One of the basic issues in the history of America has been the determination of whether or not education should be universal. That is, should it be required of all? Is education basic to our way of life? Many developments in American history have suggested that the answer to these questions is *yes*. On the other hand, there have always been persons who have taken a more limited view, choosing to believe that education is a privilege rather than a right or that public funds cannot be stretched to provide a required education for all.

The early settlers of America had great faith in education. They proceeded earnestly and quickly to provide educational opportunity. Although at first the purpose was largely to create understanding of religious doctrine, secular concerns and interests soon modified this purpose. The fact that some educational provisions were made for paupers and orphans suggests a feeling that all children had a right to receive some education. The unwillingness to develop an adequate tax base to help make education generally available may suggest, on the other hand, that education did not receive top priority on the colonists' list of essentials. Or it may suggest that the purposes of education differed so much from community to community, church to church, and colony to colony that no uniform practice could be developed.

Later, however, these purposes did become clearer. Some of the founders of America eloquently expressed their belief that ignorance and freedom are incompatible. Thomas Jefferson expressed it well when he said, "If a nation expects to be ignorant and free, in a state of civilization, it expects what never was and never will be." To develop a nation of free people—free to think, to express their thoughts, to remold these thoughts in the melting pot of ideas, and finally to put them to work for the betterment of society—that was an ideal of the founders of America and an ideal for which many struggle today.

The elimination of the pauper school was a big step in the movement to provide education for all because of the prospect which it holds for the betterment of society. The chief battle was waged in Pennsylvania and New Jersey, two of the states in which the idea of the pauper school had developed. Political statesmen approved the new plan for free schools on the principle that "all men are created equal, and endowed by their Creator with certain inalienable rights." People caught the spirit of this concept and saw the obvious implication: The continuation of private schools for those able to pay, and of public schools at state expense for the poor, could lead only to the emphasis of class distinction.

The separation of the population into upper and lower classes was to have no place in American educational law. The Pennsylvania Free School Act of 1834, together with subsequent legislation in that state and in New Jersey, eliminated the pauper school from the northern states. The West had never tolerated it. Although the idea of pauper schools lingered somewhat longer in a number of the middle and southern states, it was almost entirely eliminated in the reorganization that took place in these states following the Civil War. More recently, attention has been drawn to the de facto class distinctions which sometimes occur in schools because of the way district boundaries or attendance areas are established or, in some instances, as a result of tracking or homogeneous grouping procedures. However, support for such practices remains strong in many quarters and their advocates seldom view them as impediments to general education.

With the decision that schools are a responsibility of the state and pauper schools should be eliminated, much of the battle for universal education had been won. However, education was still considered a privilege, not an obligation. It was not until 1852 that the first compulsory school attendance law was passed. Here again, it was the state of Massachusetts that led the way. More than 200 years had elapsed since the passage in Massachusetts of the school law of 1647.

We know, of course, that prior to this time some of the states could not have supported an educational program that would have been adequate to meet the requirements of compulsory school attendance laws. This is one of the reasons why such laws appeared so late in our educational development. Without doubt, the reluctance to force education upon those who did not wish it was also a deterring factor. Here was a problem of democracy that required some real thinking. In a freedom-loving country, do we have the right to force people to do something against their will? Or, in reality, is the education of all essential to the freedom that people desire to achieve and maintain? The history of legislation from 1852 to the present time indicates that the American people have answered the latter question in the affirmative because, by 1918, all forty-eight states had enacted some form of compulsory education law. Alaska and Hawaii have enacted like statutory provisions, but some southern states repealed them following the *Brown* decision. For example, Mississippi repealed its law in what has been described as an effort "to preserve racial segregation".[6] More recently, there has been pressure to restore the law (as other states did) in recognition that many poor Mississippians, both black and white, have dropped out of school and not found a suitable place in society.[7]

Current compulsory education laws vary considerably. The most common practice is to require children to attend school between the ages of seven and sixteen years. In some states the age range is eight to sixteen years and in others eight to eighteen. Most of the states have regulations that deal both with school attendance and with employment of children between the ages of fourteen and sixteen, or fourteen and eighteen. Under these regulations, permission to accept employment may be granted a pupil when it is believed that the child can profit more from employment than from attendance at school.

Parents are held responsible for the attendance of their children in school during the age range for compulsory education adopted by the state in which they live. The recent tendency, however, has been to place some responsibility on the school for meeting the wider range of needs of

6. Stephen Arons, "Compulsory Education: America in Mississippi", *Saturday Review/World* (November 6, 1973), p. 154.

7. Ibid.

the children and youth. Increased provisions for vocational education, education for children with special problems, programs to meet individual differences of all children, cooperative work and school arrangements, and many pupil personnel services are incorporated into our educational program to meet this obligation.

Despite the range of programs offered by the public schools, many young people become disinterested in school programs and drop out of school at their first legal opportunity—often after a period of absenting themselves illegally. In some high schools, so many students are absent on any given day that school officials therein despair of enforcing attendance regulations. Noting these developments and questioning the amount of formal education required by all, a growing number of educators have called for abolition or revision of compulsory education laws to permit adolescents greater latitude in moving to adulthood.[8] Thus the theme of universal education faces a contemporary challenge from within the profession.

A significant external threat is the refusal of taxpayers in many locales to approve requests to increase tax support for schools. Continued voter refusals in the face of escalating costs has brought some school districts to the brink of financial collapse. The belief in public schools for all children supported by taxes upon nonparents as well as parents appears to be under severe challenge in many communities. Indeed, it is sometimes difficult to get parents in general to support expanding educational opportunities for particular groups of children such as those who are physically or emotionally retarded or foreign speaking. Recent court decisions[9] have expanded the legal concept of universal education to include public school responsibility to make education available to children with special educational handicaps and to provide foreign language instruction for large numbers of pupils who do not speak English. More public money will be required to implement such decisions, thereby requiring voters to face the issue of universal education once again.

FREE EDUCATION

Despite the many reforms made in the educational system throughout the first half of the nineteenth century, many states were unable to raise sufficient money to support the system. Thus was prolonged the undesirable practice, held over from colonial days, of adjusting costs above those paid by taxation on a pro rata basis according to the number of children per family. This so-called *rate-bill* had an effect similar to that created by the

---

8. For discussion of this issue, see the series of articles in the December, 1973 *Phi Delta Kappan* Vol. LV, No. 4.

9. See for example *Lau* v. *Nichols,* 414 U.S. 563 (1974) and *Mills* v. *Board of Education of the District of Columbia,* 346 F. Supp. 866 (D.D.C. 1972).

pauper school. Wealthy districts voted local taxes, which together with state funds were sufficient to provide free schools for their children. Poor districts, unable to do so, struggled along with shorter school terms and inferior programs of education.

By the middle of the century, however, the fight for free schools was being waged. Cities led in the battle by securing legislation to form school systems operated apart from city governments under the administration of local boards of education. Boards of education were given power to levy taxes at the local level for educational purposes. Pennsylvania was the first of the northern states to eliminate the rate-bill (1834).

After a stormy battle and much agitation over this subject in New York State, the legislature, in 1849, submitted the problem to the people who overwhelmingly voted in favor of "making the property of the state educate the children of the state." Immediately, opponents of the action organized in sufficient strength to convince the legislature to turn again to the people for their voice in the matter. The action of the previous year was sustained, and the battle for free schools in this state was won. Indiana, Ohio, and Illinois passed similar legislation in the years immediately following that in which New York made its decision. Other northern states were going through similar struggles at about the same time; in a five-year period they too had won the battle for free schools. In the southern states free education was provided in the reorganization that took place following the Civil War.

The story just related is a very brief description of the struggles which the people of America have undergone to provide free schools. This statement should not be mistaken to mean that we now have free education. The problem that remains with us is, how much education should be free? For the most part, we seem agreed that it should include the elementary and the secondary school, with college education at nominal cost. Kindergarten and junior colleges represent extensions in public educational opportunity provided in some parts of the country. As noted in the preceding section, the courts are extending the concept of free education to include special programs for children who are handicapped or do not speak English.

How much instructional material is to be included in "free" education? Should laboratory fees be charged? What special services are to be provided? Do the schools that are free to the children provide them equal educational opportunity? Should schools attempt to provide extensive vocational-technical training, perhaps including the thirteenth and fourteenth years for pupils who do not intend to work for a college degree? Should college or a part of it be free? Might the schools provide free programs for school drop-outs who wish to resume their education? Should free education be provided for adults who are unemployed or underemployed simply because their particular skills are no longer needed in our highly automated society? Is free education for adult avocational and leisure time activity a proper function of the schools? Finally, should the schools provide free preschool programs for three- or four-year-old children? Inferior programs, programs inadequate to the special needs of some children, and the hidden costs imposed by activities sponsored by the school are just a few of the problems that remain to be solved in providing free education.

STATE RESPONSIBILITY

A consequence of the actions related so far has been to place the state in control of education. The process of extending education to all children and youth, and providing public funds to support an adequate educational system required that the issue of state versus local control be settled over and over again throughout the entire nation. The previous discussion indicates many problems which arose in this area.

Authority for education was left to the people of the several states when our national Constitution was formed. The people, in turn, in attempting to solve their problems, found the state to be the logical agency for the final resolution of issues. Along with this recognition of the authority of the state came its obligation to control the educational program. Towns, cities, villages, and rural areas were organized into school districts and were asked to meet state requirements in providing schools. In the early days this problem was much greater than it is today.

One way to meet the problem was to appoint a state officer to supervise the schools of the state. New York was the first state to create such a position, and in 1812 it enacted legislation providing for the appointment of the first State Superintendent of the Common Schools. Gideon Hawley, the first superintendent, apparently was so vigorous in his enforcement of state law that local pressures on the legislators caused the position to be abolished for a period of time. However, the secretary of state acted ex officio in this capacity for some time. Some states, fearing that they might have similar difficulties with a chief state school officer, used the ex officio arrangement as a temporary solution to their problem.

Another means of exercising state control was through the formation of a state board of education, with a secretary who performed the same functions as a state superintendent of schools. Horace Mann, as secretary of the Massachusetts Board of Education, became a vigorous leader in school organization. Mann and Henry Barnard, secretary of the Connecticut State Board of Commissioners for the Common School, and later State Commissioner of Public Schools in Rhode Island, became the nation's outstanding campaigners for educational reform. They were not merely officers who controlled schools through the enforcement of legislation. These were men of vision who helped the people define their problems, visualize new prospects for their schools, and develop new interest and enthusiasm for public education and its support.

Now all states in the United States have chief state school officers, and virtually all of them have state boards of education in each of which the chief state school officer is the executive officer of the board.[10] State control is not always as enlightened as was that exemplified by Horace Mann and Henry Barnard. Nevertheless, all states recognize an obligation to enforce state school regulations and have state departments of public instruction with extensive staffs consisting of personnel who carry out specialized regulatory, research, or leadership functions to improve schools throughout the state. Adjustments are constantly being made concerning the relative amount of state and local tax funds to be used for school purposes. The functions of state departments of education are redefined periodically. What state control exists and how it functions changes from time to time and from state to state.

There seems to be little controversy over the states' right to fix minimum standards for the schools. Questions do arise concerning the nature of the standards and the means that shall be used for enforcing them. Likewise, the use of public monies for schools is a privilege of the state which has general acceptance, but considerable controversy ensues when these monies are used for purposes of regulation. School administrators and local boards of education usually display an active interest in these matters and often are responsible for the initiation of legislation that will determine what the state does toward improving education at the local district level.

Other groups also recognize state responsibility and authority in education and sometimes seek legislation which affects the schools. For example, state teachers associations have sought statewide negotiations and benefits legislation, and civil rights advocates have sought state mandates for racial balance. More recently, legislators and state board members have responded to citizen concerns regarding school expenditures by instituting various accountability measures. The concept of state responsibility also has been dramatically underscored in legal efforts to reform state arrangements for financing schools which rely heavily upon local property taxes. As these examples indicate, the location of state level responsibility for education provides an avenue of appeal for those who wish changes in local policies and procedures. It also poses continuing problems of regulation, coordination, leadership, and mediation of local tensions for state officials.

LOCAL OPERATIONS

The recognition that the state has an obligation for the education of its children and youth does not imply that the state is the most appropriate

10. For analysis of state policy making processes in education see Roald F. Campbell and Tim L. Mazzoni Jr., *State Policy Making for the Public Schools* (Berkeley, Calif.: McCutchan Publishing Corp., 1976).

agency to administer the schools. The history of the reorganization of school districts within states indicates that the people hold very zealously to their local schools and to their desire as citizens to participate in decisions about what the schools shall do. State governments, early in our history, accepted from the people the obligation to regulate the formation, support, and standards of the school program. These are still the functions exercised through state governments. It seems probable that the people will never permit the regulatory framework that is established by the state to become so rigid that some local initiative in educational program development is eliminated.

The number, size, and types of school districts vary from state to state. In some states the town or township is the basic unit. For twelve states the basic unit is the county. One state (Hawaii) is organized as a single statewide district. In most states, whatever the classification of basic units may be, there are exceptions by which certain towns or cities have been constituted as independent or separate districts. The movement for district reorganization has been an effort on the part of the states to improve local schools and equalize educational opportunity for all of the children of the state.

For purposes of operation, the state delegates most of its powers to the local district. A district board of education is elected or appointed to represent the people in formulating the policy by which their local school is to operate within the framework established by the state. Sometimes members of these boards of education find themselves in a quandary because they are officers of the state and at the same time elected officials of the local district. Where local interests conflict with state regulations, the course of action to follow may become complicated. If the regulation in question is a state law, the most common course of action is to submit to it. But, as we have seen from the previous discussion, there may be times when state regulations should be challenged. Many court actions have actually clarified the regulatory powers of the state, because someone challenged the interpretation of a regulation as it was being enforced. In some instances, local feelings have been so strong that officials have defied state and federal laws and/or court rulings. Particularly conspicuous examples have been some refusals to adhere to desegregation and school prayer guidelines. Thus the delegation of operating responsibility to local levels can pose dilemmas of complying with more general regulations or responding to local citizen interests.

A different problem related to local operation is that citizens sometimes choose not or are unable to participate in school affairs to the extent that the local control ideology suggests. Particularly in large school districts, this may be because they lack access to decision makers. Several of our larger cities have been concerned with this problem for some time. New York and Chicago, for instance, developed at least the first stage of regional administrative areas under the jurisdiction of the general administrative organization of the city school system by the middle 1960s. Public demand for citizen participation has intensified since that time and led to more extensive decentralization in some cities, notably New York and Detroit.

We find ourselves at a stage in our history where we are seeking an optimum size of local operating school districts. Undoubtedly the size will vary with many conditions, but we can be fairly certain that the principle of local initiative has been so firmly established in the minds of both the educator and the layman that efforts will continue to make it effective in determining the role of the school in the community.

FEDERAL PARTICIPATION

An issue of historical importance to people throughout the nation is to what extent the federal government should support the public schools. Most advocates of additional support for schools base their case essentially on two arguments: (1) that there is great need for equalization of educational opportunity among the states; and (2) that since about two-thirds of the tax dollar now goes into the federal coffers, there is little chance that an appropriate part of our total wealth will be spent for educational purposes unless this source of revenue is used.

Compared with a few years ago, relatively few persons now argue against federal aid to schools. However, the traditional arguments have been that federal control would be the inevitable result and that the states can meet their school needs if they so desire. Some of the opponents of federal support have claimed that a recognition of the possibility of federal control was the reason why the framers of the Constitution made no mention of education, and also the reason for the Tenth Amendment, which reserves to the states and to the people all powers not expressly delegated to the United States. It is difficult, of course, to document the motives that prompted the founders of our government to leave education to the states and to the people. Whatever the reason may have been at that time, the Congress representing the people of the United States has not interpreted the Tenth Amendment to mean that the federal government cannot participate in the improvement of educational opportunity.

As a matter of fact, the people have been using all of the levels of government for the support of their schools for a long time. The participation of the federal government began immediately after the ratification of the Tenth Amendment, when the government made land grants to aid the states in the establishment of public schools and colleges. Additional ways in which the educational program of the country has been assisted by the federal government include: grants for special education, particularly in the field of vocational education; maintenance of certain types of schools for special purposes, notably the military schools and military programs in our colleges and universities; financial support of schools in the District of Columbia, in the territories, and for the Indians; authorization and maintenance of welfare programs having certain educational benefits, such as the Civilian Conservation Corps, the National Youth Administration, and the Works Progress Administration; aid to school districts affected by war-incurred federal activities; support for the education of veterans and subsequent mass support for special programs thought to be in the interest of national defense under the National Defense Education Act; support of the United States Office of Education; the Vocational Education Act of 1963; the Economic Opportunity Act of 1964; and the Elementary and Secondary Education Act of 1965. Generally speaking these aids have been "categorical" in that they have been available to support only those activities designated by the legislation.[11]

In all of these instances, it seems fair to say that the fear of undue federal coercion has not been borne out by the facts. The great bulk of the activity that affects the program of general education has been carried on with a minimum of federal control and with much of the responsibility delegated to the states. At the same time, however, it is clear that federal participation in education has produced substantially increased paper work for state and local school agencies and that compliance with federal laws and guidelines has affected local policies and procedures. As the scope of federal guidelines and paperwork has increased, concern about the extent of federal control has mounted among many school officials.

The most prominent philosophical question now surrounding federal aid is not whether it should be provided but in what form. Some persons who are skeptical of federal intentions or strong supporters of state and local initiative advocate federal "block grants" or "revenue sharing" to the states. The states, in turn, allocate these funds to whatever educational purposes they might specify instead of administering "categorical" requirements. Despite the appeal of the "block grant" approach in some quarters, we believe that its expansion on a large scale is unlikely. It does not seem reasonable to expect the federal government to appropriate funds "to promote the general welfare" without providing some direction for its achievement.

The mobility of our population being what it is, inequities in educational opportunity become increasingly apparent. Economists tell us that the trend toward the collection of the large bulk of our taxes at the national level will not be reversed. If schools are to receive a greater portion of the tax dollar, and if these monies are to be used to provide our children and youth with comparable opportunities for education, it seems imperative that we move toward even greater federal financial participation in education. While declining enrollments and national inflation probably limit the political feasibility of such development, its desirability and importance remain clear.

11. For discussion of the federal role in school affairs, see Roald F. Campbell, *et al., The Organization and Control of American Schools,* 3rd ed. (Columbus, Ohio: Charles E. Merrill Publishing Co., 1975).

EXTENDING THE SCHOOL SYSTEM

The trend toward continuing education beyond the high school raises the old question of how far the public school program should go. Many school districts now provide for kindergarten and preschool programs. Some people have raised the question of whether or not there should be any limiting age. Adult education is serving a useful purpose and will be more and more necessary. Many school systems have realized this and provide extensive adult offerings on credit and noncredit bases. Should the state make some provision for education at all age levels?

The answer lies squarely within our system of values. How much do we value education and where do we place it on our scale of wants? While it is impossible to compare meaningfully the relative expenditure for education in Russia and the United States, we do know that, by edict from the Kremlin, Russia can spend for education that portion of its national income that its leaders deem necessary to meet the desired ends. In the United States, on the other hand, the decision to increase expenditures for education depends in large part upon the intelligence, the insight, and the understanding of need on the part of the citizenry.

The common school, our first division of publicly supported education, provided the rudiments of the 3 *R*'s. The extension of this school into the primary age brackets permitted extensions of the curriculum. The next problem to be faced was the addition of high schools. Up to about 1850, most of what we now call high school education was taught in the Latin Grammar School. Later, the academy, a semiprivate school depending largely upon tuition and grants of money from churches and other benevolent organizations and groups, became the popular "high" school.

The academy was not simply a college preparatory school like the Latin Grammar School. It was open to both girls and boys, and its curriculum contained a variety of subjects not unlike those found in many of our secondary schools today. Although the Boston Latin Grammar School admitted boys at the secondary school level, its single aim of college preparation rules it out as the real forerunner of the modern secondary school. Perhaps the Massachusetts Law of 1827 really marks the beginning of the high school movement as we know it.

The Latin Grammar School movement was not widespread. Very few schools were established, and most of them died out when the academy grew in popularity. This new kind of secondary school spread throughout the eastern half of the United States and reached its peak of popularity about 1850. Its decline in number after 1850, however, was almost as spectacular as its rise in the preceding fifty years.

Massachusetts and New York were leaders in the development of the high schools as an upward extension of the common school system. Legislation permitting districts to tax themselves for this purpose was passed in a number of states, but progress came slowly because many schools had to be supported solely by local taxation.

The enactment of permissive legislation is an illustration of a device that has been used by the states over and over again, one which gives the people a chance to try out the idea. Where the legislation is seriously questioned, it is tested in the courts. The famous Kalamazoo Case,[12] in which the Supreme Court of the state of Michigan upheld the right of the state to enact such legislation, is an illustration of the impetus given by such legislation to extend public education to include the secondary school. The speed with which the states incorporated the high school as a part of the common school system was greatly accelerated after the settlement of this case.

The growth of the state university is still another chapter in the history of the upward extension of our school system. The earlier colleges and universities were private institutions, supported by tuition, church, and endowment funds. By 1800 there were about two dozen of these institutions, with not over a hundred professors and no more than two thousand students in all. By 1860, the total number of colleges and universities had grown to 246, of which seventeen were state universities. In this case, as well as at the lower levels of the school program, great effort was made to change church-dominated colleges into state schools. The idea did not work out in practice, but the movement to establish state universities persisted. Weak at first because of inadequate state support, state universities have grown in strength and have now become the institutions of higher learning in which the great majority of our youth receive their college education.

RELIGION AND THE PUBLIC SCHOOLS

There can be little doubt that religion played a large part in the early development of American education. In New England, it was the concept of the Calvinistic religious state, the state as servant of the church, which gave the state the power to regulate the schools. All churches throughout the several colonies continued many of their European habits, one of which was education for the furtherance of the church. They could not break away from this idea, even though a strong motive for many of the early settlers to come to America had been to break away from religious oppression.

When we recall that, in the beginning, schools were controlled by the church and maintained largely to promote religious purposes, we recognize how much the public schools as we know them now have changed. History supports the conclusion that this change has not been easy, but that people gradually have come to support the principle of separation of church and state. Religious instruction became a private concern and a right which the state has always protected on that basis.

The parochial school of the middle colonies has withstood the test of time and has established itself along with the public school as a

12. *Stuart* v. *School District No. 1 of Kalamazoo* (1874) 30, Mich. 69.

recognized agency in which children and youth may receive the education prescribed by the state. Many of the court cases cited below indicate that the principle of separation of church and state gets much of its support from church groups. Hence, even today, the protection of the minority from religious domination and the right of different denominations to provide religious instruction as they see fit influences the kind, the place, the time, and the responsibility for instruction in the community.

The public school, however, became an educational agency that reached many different church groups, hence the parochial interests of each could not be protected. Public monies, collected as they were by different forms of taxation and paid by individuals and groups with vastly different concepts of religion, could not be spent in such manner that each of these interests was appropriately served. Cubberley points out two factors that he says served to bring about the secularization of the public schools. They were:

> 1. The conviction that the life of the Republic demanded an educated and intelligent citizenship, and hence the general education of all in common schools controlled by the State; and
> 2. The great diversity of religious beliefs among the people, which forced tolerance and religious freedom through a consideration of the rights of minorities.[13]

Not only did this principle of secularization of the public schools serve to shift the control from the church to the state, it also eliminated the practice of using state funds to support church and other private schools. There was a bitter battle in most of the eastern states because such a principle required almost a complete reversal in policy and practice. Horace Mann was a leader in the struggle in Massachusetts while he served as secretary of the Board of Education. Pennsylvania, New Jersey, and New York were the states where the problem seemed to be unusually difficult to solve. New Hampshire, as early as 1792, was the first state to settle the issue by a constitutional amendment. The matter was resolved generally throughout the country by the adoption of constitutional amendments forbidding a division or a diversion of public funds for the support of parochial or private schools. Most of the states joining the Union after 1850 had this provision in the original constitutions. Butts reminds us that

> from 1876 onward all new states added to the Union were required by Congress to include in their basic laws an irrevocable ordinance guaranteeing religious freedom in line with the principles of the First Amendment. . . .[14]

---

13. Cubberley, *The History of Education,* p. 692.

14. Freeman Butts, *The American Tradition in Religion and Education* (Boston: Beacon Press, 1950), pp. 103–104.

Also, that

> the principle of separation of church and state in education was almost completely accepted through the United States by 1900.[15]

There is still another aspect of the problem that plagues us. This is the use of the school for religious instruction. "Released time" programs of religious education, a practice whereby a portion of the school day is set aside for religious instruction, have been ruled by the courts to be unconstitutional. The case of *McCollum* v. *Board of Education of School District No. 71, Champaign, Illinois*[16] is just one example of many such cases where released time was seen as a violation of the principle of separation of the church and state. In this case, the interpretation of the court was that the use of school buildings for religious instruction resulted in making the school "an establishment of religion." Thus, the practice of providing religious instruction within the school building, even on time released from public school responsibilities, was ruled illegal.

On the other hand, in 1952, the Supreme Court of the United States in *Zorach* v. *Clauson*[17] upheld the school board of the city of New York in providing that children may be released from school for religious instruction off the school premises.[18] The combined effect of these two actions seems to be that children may be excused from regular classroom activities for religious instruction that is conducted off the school premises.

In 1961, when federal participation in the financial support of public education was proposed by President Kennedy, the religious issue again reached a peak. The President saw public support of nonpublic schools as unconstitutional, a violation of the principle of separation of church and state. One of the arguments used in the defeat of his program for federal financial aid to the public schools was that aid to the public schools without aid to private schools was in violation of the principle of equal educational opportunity for all. This argument prevailed with the passage of the Elementary and Secondary Education Act of 1965.

In 1963, the United States Supreme Court ruled against religious exercises and required Bible reading in the public schools. This ruling in *Abington Township* v. *Schempp*[19] and *Murray* v. *Curlett*[20] is considered of major significance because it appears to indicate a basic shift in the Court's

15. Ibid., pp. 137–138.
16. *McCollum* v. *Board of Education,* 333 U.S. 203, 68 Sup. Ct. 461 (1948).
17. *Zorach* v. *Clauson,* 343 U.S. 306, 72 Sup. Ct. 679 (1952).
18. Clark Spurlock, *Education and the Supreme Court* (Urbana, Ill.: University of Illinois Press, 1955), pp. 126–133.
19. *Abington Township* v. *Schempp,* 374 U.S. 203 (1963).
20. *Murray* v. *Curlett,* 374 U.S. 203 (1963).

interpretation of the First Amendment. While previous decisions of the Court placed great stress on the concept of the "wall of separation between church and state" the *Abington* decision set forth a "neutrality" concept. This concept means that the state (and the schools) must be neutral in its impact upon religion. In effect, the opinion makes the "wall of separation" illegal, for if the schools erect a wall they are not being neutral in their impact upon religion.

The chief administrative problem in communities where the issue of religious instruction is raised is to help people understand that the principle of separation or of neutrality is intended not to prohibit religious instruction in the community by a church or private enterprise, but to protect the right of all by restricting the use of public school funds and property to that which is a public and not a private concern.

Despite some assistance provided nonpublic schools through the Elementary and Secondary Education Act of 1965,[21] many of these schools face serious financial problems. The number of nonpublic schools and the number of students in them has decreased somewhat since the late 1960s because of this factor. The financial plight of nonpublic schools had led to considerable pressure for providing state financial aid to them. Legislation to provide such assistance has been introduced in many states and passed in some including Ohio, Connecticut, New Jersey, and Pennsylvania. Moreover, the list of functions for which such aid is requested is growing. The principle of state support for benefits which go directly to children rather than schools (e.g., textbooks and transportation) has been well-established.[22] However, efforts to provide public support for teacher salaries (either lay teachers or teachers of nonsectarian subjects) have been held to be unconstitutional.[23] A subsequent case struck down a Pennsylvania law which provided auxiliary services such as counseling and speech and hearing therapy to pupils in nonpublic schools.[24] In the same decision, however, the court continued to allow the state practice of loaning nonreligious textbooks to nonpublic school students.

Another proposal which would aid nonpublic schools and have important consequences for public schools would be the widespread implementation of a "voucher system." A number of plans of this type have been suggested. In general, they would provide government aid in the form of vouchers to be given directly to students and their parents rather than the schools. The students would then be able to cash their vouchers in return for education at a school of their choice. If adopted, such plans would have the effect of putting the schools, public and private, in competition with each other.

---

21. Provisions of this legislation are discussed in chapter 3.
22. *Cochran* v. *Louisiana State Board of Education*, 281 U.S. 370 (1930).
23. *Lemon* v. *Kurtzman*, 403 U.S. 602 (1971) and *Sloan* v. *Lemon*, 413 U.S. 825 (1973).
24. *Meek* v. *Pittinger*, 95 S.Ct. 1753 (1975).

THE MELTING POT INFLUENCE

The growth of public education in America reflects the development of a pattern of values which are thought of as distinctively American. Gunnar Myrdal, a Swedish student of the American way of life, has observed that "America, compared to every other country in Western Civilization, large or small, has the *most explicitly expressed* [italics in original] system of general values in reference to human relationships." He goes on to say that "this body of ideals is more widely understood and appreciated than similar ideals are anywhere else."[25] He refers, of course, not only to the Bill of Rights and other formal documents in which these ideals have been expressed, but also to the struggles through which we have gone as a nation to realize them.

While the majority of the people who first settled America were of Anglo-Saxon origin, coming from England, Wales, and Scotland, these settlers were soon joined by Dutch, Swedish, French, Spanish, Irish, and German nationals and people of other races and nationalities. By and large, these were common people—people of the middle or lower classes. The Beards tell us "it seems probable that at least one-half the immigrants into America before the Revolution, certainly outside New England, were either indentured servants or Negro slaves."[26] Religious and political dissenters, a few English adventurers and French aristocrats, some people who sought wealth and power, others who withstood the misery of illness and poverty to be free, carved out their fortunes together. To them, coming to America meant the hardships of frontier life; but it also meant freedom to shape their way of life as they saw fit. Immigrants to the United States in the past two centuries have been assimilated into the American culture but have also contributed to the distinctiveness of this culture.

The notion that America is a great melting pot where persons of diverse cultures have come to create a new one has been a prominent theme in American history. The assimilation of early settlers and the working class immigrants of the late nineteenth and early twentieth centuries provide the best examples of this theme. As noted earlier in this chapter, schools played an important part in these developments particularly as the pauper schools were eliminated and other steps were taken to extend educational opportunities to middle and lower class citizens.

However, interpretations of American educational history which stress the melting pot concept must also acknowledge at least two fundamental challenges to this ideal. The first has been reluctance on the part of some citizens to extend equal educational opportunities to particular minority groups. The second has been insistence by some school commu-

25. Gunnar Myrdal, *An American Dilemma,* Vol. 3 (New York: Harper & Brothers, 1944), p. 3.

26. Charles A. Beard and Mary R. Beard, *The Rise of American Civilization,* Vol. 1 (New York: The Macmillan Company, 1927), p. 103.

nities that minorities forsake their particular cultures in favor of majority values and practices. These conditions have been most apparent in the struggles to provide equal educational opportunities for black Americans, but they have impinged upon Mexican Americans, American Indians, Puerto Ricans, and other minorities as well.

The effort to achieve school desegregation has been a long and conflict-filled episode in the struggle to achieve equal educational opportunity. In the early history of our country, blacks did not have many educational opportunities. In the Northern states some of them attended the pauper schools of colonial times. As free schools were provided, blacks were gradually accepted in them. But in the South black education began to be accepted much later. Philanthropic interests and agencies assisted in its development until the separate public schools were established.

After the Civil War, the principle of *separate but equal* was established to meet the standards for racial relationships which had been set forth by the thirteenth, fourteenth, and fifteenth amendments to the Constitution. Although the principle was contested in the courts, the case of *Plessy* v. *Ferguson* in 1896, in which the Supreme Court ruled that "separation did not necessarily mean inferiority,"[27] gave it support sufficient to establish the principle as the legal basis for the development of a dual school system in the South. It was not until the mid-thirties of the present century that this principle was challenged successfully. At this time there were a number of court cases in which blacks were granted the privilege of attending graduate schools in certain southern colleges and universities.

The following excerpts from the Supreme Court decision of 1954 clarify, for our purposes, the position of the court which has been the cornerstone for subsequent desegregation efforts:

> The doctrine of "separate but equal" did not make its appearance in this Court until 1896 in the case of *Plessy* v. *Ferguson, supra,* involving not education but transportation. American courts have since labored with the doctrine for over half a century. In this Court, there have been six cases involving the "separate but equal" doctrine in the field of public education. In *Cumming* v. *County Board of Education,* 175 US 528, and *Gong Lum* v. *Rice,* 275 US 78, the validity of the doctrine itself was not challenged. In more recent cases, all on the graduate-school level, inequality was found in that specific benefits enjoyed by white students were denied to Negro students of the same educational qualifications. *Missouri ex rel. Gaines* v. *Canada,* 305 US 337; *Sipuel* v. *Oklahoma,* 332 US 631; *Sweatt* v. *Painter,* 339 US 629; *McLaurin* v. *Oklahoma State Regents,* 339 US 637. In none of these cases was it necessary to reexamine the doctrine to grant relief to the Negro plaintiff. . . .

27. *Plessy* v. *Ferguson,* 163 U.S. 537 (1896).

> Segregation of white and colored children in public schools has a detrimental effect upon the colored children. The impact is greater when it has the sanction of the law: for the policy of separating the races is usually interpreted as denoting the inferiority of the Negro group. A sense of inferiority affects the motivation of a child to learn. . . .
>
> We conclude that in the field of public education the doctrine of "separate but equal" has no place. Separate educational facilities are inherently unequal.[28]

Despite a number of advocates (black and white) who state otherwise, we continue to believe that racial segregation should be eliminated from our schools. The unresolved issue, however, centers about the means of enforcement which in some areas is looked upon as either unfortunate and unnecessary or demographically impossible.

A number of attempts have been made to set aside or to ignore the decision of the Supreme Court. An early incident was in Little Rock, Arkansas, in which the state government opposed the federal government in the desegregation of the public high schools on the basis that public education is a state, not a federal, function. Nevertheless, the basic rights of all people of the nation, the principle upon which the Supreme Court decision was rendered, have held firm. Desegregation of the schools is far from universal, but states are gradually moving toward compliance with Supreme Court decisions in this area. In October 1969, the Supreme Court provided a strong prod in this direction by holding that time for "deliberate speed" toward desegregation of dual school systems had passed and ordering that thirty Mississippi school districts desegregate immediately.[29] Subsequent decisions have established busing as a legitimate means to achieve desegregation[30] and established tests for de jure segregation in northern cities.[31] In what many viewed as a landmark but controversial decision, however, the Supreme Court ruled that states were not compelled to order metropolitan district reorganization to combat segregation in the central city.[32]

In the years immediately following 1954, it was common to view school desegregation as a southern problem. Observers noted that the dual school systems dealt with in the *Brown* decision were located in southern states and produced de jure segregation. This condition was contrasted with what came to be termed de facto segregation in the North. A significant change that has implications for the schools has been the

28. *Brown* v. *Board of Education of Topeka, Kansas,* 347 U.S. 483 (1954).
29. *Alexander* v. *Holmes County Board of Education,* 396 U.S. 1218 (1969).
30. *Swann* v. *Charlotte-Mecklenburg Board of Education,* 402 U.S. 1 (1970).
31. *Keyes* v. *School District N. Denver, Colorado,* 413 U.S. 189 (1973).
32. *Bradley* v. *Milliken,* 94 S. Ct. 3112 (1974).

massive migration of southern blacks into northern cities. The black population in some of these cities has more than doubled as the result of this migration. The influx of blacks into the central core of the northern cities has precipitated an out-migration of many whites to the suburbs. The net result of this in-and out-migration has been to create a stable or even an increasing amount of residential segregation for blacks, while other ethnic groups have continued a pattern of desegregation. In addition, national economic growth has outpaced the blacks' economic advance. High unemployment among blacks, particularly the black youth, has aggravated the problems associated with inability ot provide for one's economic needs.

These factors have led to de facto segregation in a number of school districts in the North. Such districts usually have schools in which the enrollment is largely, if not totally, black, while in the same districts there are schools in which the enrollment is largely, or totally, white. Indeed, the population shifts which have created Northern ghettos are probably the principal reason that more black students attended segregated schools in 1965 than in 1954.[33] While the schools may be innocent victims of larger social problems and conditions which have created segregation, the adverse effects and racial antagonisms are no different than those encountered in de jure segregation. Moreover, some northern school districts have gerrymandered attendance boundaries and otherwise contributed to maintaining segregated schools. As a consequence, legal remedies are being sought with increasing frequency and success in the North. As this occurs, desegregation as an issue achieves the volatility formerly associated with it in the South.

Debate over the importance of school desegregation and means of achieving it has intensified in recent years both academically and in the streets. Evidence that school desegregation could help improve education for lower class and minority group children was presented by Coleman[34] in a widely discussed report commissioned by the U.S. Office of Education. A subsequent report of the United States Commission on Civil Rights[35] extended the Coleman findings and suggested means to achieve desegregation. These reports have been subjected to powerful criticism. For example, Henry Levin[36] asserted that the methodological bias of the Coleman study underestimated the importance of school factors and gave undue prominence to contextual variables such as social class in predicting student achievement. Later research indicated that the achievement effects attributed to desegregation may not be as great as the Coleman study indi-

33. U.S. Commission on Civil Rights, *Racial Isolation in the Public Schools,* Vol. 1 (Washington, D.C.: U.S. Government Printing Office, 1967), pp. 2–10.

34. James S. Coleman et al., *Equality of Educational Opportunity* (Washington, D.C.: U.S. Government Printing Office, 1966).

35. U.S. Commission on Civil Rights, *Racial Isolation in the Public Schools.*

36. Henry Levin, "Do Schools Make a Difference?" *Saturday Review* (January 20, 1968): 57–58, 66–67.

cated.[37] More disturbing yet to advocates of desegregation was the work of Arthur Jensen[38] which revitalized the argument that achievement differences between black and white students can be explained genetically.

While scholars have explored the ramifications of these and other studies, administrators faced with the task of desegregating school systems have encountered strong public feelings.[39] Demonstrators who charge school officials with reluctance, if not ill will, toward desegregation have registered protests in school systems across the nation. On the other hand, when school officials have taken steps to desegregate, they often have met counter-protestors whose militance equals that of civil rights advocates.

A notable and widespread form of counter protest has been white flight from city to surrounding suburban school districts. A 1975 study by Coleman and others found that city school desegregation may intensify white flight to the suburbs. Noting his belief that ". . . achievement benefits do exist; but they are not so substantial that in themselves they demand school desegregation, whatever the other consequences," Coleman asserted that the white flight phenomenon suggested "two opposing kinds of policy implications." The first would be judicial encouragement of metropolitan wide school desegregation. The second would be action to retard white flight from cities and increase black mobility to the suburbs. This would call for court action to reduce residential segregation. Coleman further suggested that any child in a metropolitan area be allowed to attend any school in the area so long as it "had no higher proportion of his race than his neighborhood school" and would not be overcrowded as a consequence.[40]

During the late 1960s the pressure for school desegregation slackened somewhat. It was replaced, however, by strong demands that minority groups and communities be given more control over schools in their neighborhoods including the right to make decisions about curriculum and to employ and dismiss teachers and administrators according to their sensitivity and dedication to neighborhood children and objectives.

These developments have reflected the second kind of challenge to the melting pot ideal. In cases where minority group children have entered white schools and classrooms, they sometimes have been confronted with pressure to conform to majority values and reject elements of minority culture. Examples are legion: they have included insistence that minority

---

37. See Nancy St. John, *School Desegregation* (New York: John Wiley and Sons, 1975).

38. Arthur R. Jensen, "How Much Can We Boost IQ and Scholastic Achievement?" *Harvard Educational Review,* 29 (Winter 1969): 1–123.

39. For a series of cases which illustrate and analyze this problem, see Robert L. Crain, *The Politics of School Desegregation* (Chicago: Aldine Publishing Co., 1968).

40. James S. Coleman, "Racial Segregation in the Schools: New Research With New Policy Implications," *Phi Delta Kappan* vol. 57, no. 2 (October 1975): 75–78. The article is based upon James S. Coleman, Sarah D. Kelly, and John Moore, *Trends in School Segregation: 1968–1973* (Washington, D.C.: Urban Institute, 1975).

group pupils adopt majority standards for dress and hair styles; observance of Christian but not Jewish religious days; and neglect of minority group contributions to literature, art, and history. Thus the melting pot ideology has placed so much emphasis on the commonalities of American heritage as defined by the majority that some persons have interpreted it to include the discouragement of diversity. Recent emphases upon cultural pluralism have stimulated new thought about the meaning of the melting pot ideal and its implications for our society.

It presently appears that the melting-pot tradition in American education is also being threatened by public insistence upon neighborhood schools at a time when neighborhoods are increasingly homogeneous. Such demands come from both minority advocates of community control and white proponents of the status quo. Schools continue to face the perplexing problems of providing equal opportunity for persons who are unequal in many ways. Moreover, they have the task of helping individuals to understand and accept others who are unlike themselves. The dilemma posed by the continuing need to work for an integrated society based upon a balance between shared values and respect for diversity on the one hand and the likelihood of growing separation among citizens in ideological and geographical terms on the other must be of concern to contemporary educators.

THE EMERGENCE OF EDUCATIONAL ADMINISTRATION

In the early years of our national history, schooling was a relatively simple enterprise. Children walked to school—first, to learn to read the Bible, and, later, to learn the 3 R's for broader secular purposes. The school buildings they attended were not elaborate structures. Furnishings were meager. Permissive rather than mandatory legislation was largely the governing role of the state. Local autonomy permitted people to have good schools or poor ones.

Probably the little red schoolhouse, which has only recently passed from the American scene, is the most characteristic symbol of the local school operation that was so jealously guarded. There was little need here for administration in the sense that we know it today. The teacher taught the children of grades one through eight, made out the attendance records, took care of his own discipline, made the fires and did other janitorial work, all as a part of the day's activities. A local board of laymen hired the teacher and made a record of the financial affairs of the district. Usually the local board "opened the school" in the fall of the year. It was the responsibility of the board to see that the school house was cleaned and painted, that the roof was repaired, that the stove was in order, that the floors were oiled, that the seats and desks were repaired and varnished, and that the coal and other supplies needed for the year were purchased. The teacher assumed the responsibility for the children while in school. The board of directors—school committee or otherwise designated local board of education—managed the business affairs. When the office of county superintendent was created in the nineteenth century, the county superintendent became the arm of the state through which local schools were regulated.

In the cities, however, the development of administration took place somewhat differently. Here, school buildings were needed to house more pupils than could be handled by a single teacher. Thus in the multiple-teacher school, someone, usually the teacher of the highest grade, became the "head teacher" or the "principal teacher." Early Latin Grammar schools of sufficient size to require more than one teacher, and later the academies, often referred to the head teacher as the "head master," a name still used commonly in private schools. Head teachers, head masters, or principals "had charge of the building," usually kept all records, and had general responsibility for the discipline of the pupils. Before the establishment of the superintendency, these building heads were responsible to the local school committee, or some other similarly named body, which had legal responsibility for the schools and performed any necessary administrative functions.

As schools took on more complex responsibilities, and as the population of the nation congregated in the urban centers, a greater number of managerial tasks needed to be performed. The sheer weight of these responsibilities caused lay boards of education to see the wisdom of employing an administrative officer to assume such obligations. Throughout the growth of this American school system, then, there has developed an increasing awareness of the need for professional leadership and administration. This chapter has provided some of the historical setting for the educational challenges to present and future school administrators. The following chapter describes the contemporary setting in which he functions.

SUGGESTED ACTIVITIES

1. List a few important decisions which the American people should be making about the public schools and show how these decisions would affect the schools in which you work.
2. Select one school problem about which decisions need to be made at the present time. In solving the problem, what decisions should be made at the district level? The state level? The national level? Why?
3. As an administrator, what part do you think you should play in the decisions to be made in 2 above?

SELECTED READINGS

American Association of School Administrators. *Religion in the Public Schools.* Washington, D.C.: The Association, 1964.

Berke, Joel S., and Kirst, Michael W. *Federal Aid to Education: Who Benefits? Who Governs?* Lexington, Mass.: D.C. Heath and Co., 1972.

Campbell, Roald F. et al. *The Organization and Control of American Schools,* 3rd ed. Columbus, Ohio: Charles E. Merrill Publishing Co., 1975.

Cremin, Lawrence A. *The Transformation of the School.* New York: Alfred A. Knopf, 1964.

Hogan, John C. *The Schools, The Courts and the Public Interest.* Lexington, Mass.: D.C. Heath and Co., 1974.

Katz, Michael B. *Class, Bureaucracy, and Schools: The Illusion of Educational Change in America.* New York: Praeger, 1971.

Kirp, David L., and Yudof, Mark G. *Educational Policy and the Law: Cases and Materials.* Berkeley, Calif.: McCutchan Publishing Corp., 1974.

Sexton, Patricia C., ed. *School Policies and Issues in a Changing Society.* Boston: Allyn and Bacon, 1971.

Silberman, Charles E. *Crisis in the Classroom.* New York: Random House, 1970.

THE SCHOOL SETTING

Our intention in this chapter is to describe some characteristics of the setting in which the contemporary administrator works, particularly in relation to the way in which policy is made. What happens within schools is often influenced by conditions and events which are not subject to the direct control of the administrator. Policy decisions are not a product of the people of the local school community alone, but often reflect the desires of the people of the school district, the state, and in some sense the world beyond. In like manner, program decisions are not made by the professionals of a single school in isolation. The administrator is sometimes constrained and advantaged by outside factors as he works toward objectives. The successful administrator will be aware of such factors and their particular implications for his assignment. In this chapter, we will consider some general background factors, the place of education in national development, and the contest to shape educational policy at the local level.

BACKGROUND FACTORS

Four general characteristics of American society which have implications for schools are urbanization, economic growth, socioeconomic diversity, and tension regarding national issues. The expectations which citizens have for schools and their willingness and ability to support them are associated with these factors.

URBANIZATION

The United States is primarily a nation of cities and suburbs. The percentage of the American population residing in urban areas increased from 45.6 in 1910 to 56.1 in 1930 to 73.5 in 1970. Most of these people are concentrated in large metropolitan areas. Approximately 73 percent of the total population resided in 266 Standard Metropolitan Statistical Areas in 1970. The latter figure is somewhat misleading because Standard Metropolitan Statistical Areas are defined to include total counties. Thus approximately 8 percent of the total population in 1970 lived in rural areas within Standard Metropolitan Statistical Areas.[1]

The growth of metropolitan populations has not been uniform. Suburbs have grown at a much faster rate than central cities which in many instances have actually declined in population. Seventy of the 257 cities which were centers of the 212 Standard Metropolitan Statistical Areas in 1960 declined in population from 1950–1960.[2] Hauser and Taitel projected a continuation of this trend and estimated that 100 million of the projected 170 million metropolitan area residents of 1980 will live in suburbs.[3]

Population shifts from rural to urban areas have had important consequences for schools and educators. Most obviously, they have brought about a redistribution of schools and students on the American landscape. The one-room rural schoolhouse, which occupies a prominent spot in the history and hearts of many Americans, is fast disappearing. Less than two percent of American students are enrolled in school districts of less than three hundred pupils, and nearly two-thirds of them attend schools in districts of more than five thousand pupils.[4] However, many of these larger districts have experienced great fluctuations in enrollment in recent years. During the 1960s, the lack of classroom space forced many schools to operate double sessions. Many cities mounted large scale building programs to keep pace with expanding enrollments. The Columbus, Ohio, public schools, for example, opened a new classroom on the average of every three and one-half days between 1950 and 1968. More recently, however, declining enrollments have permitted many districts to discontinue double shifts and have presented some of them with the problem of finding new uses for vacant classrooms and buildings.

As most knowledgeable persons are aware, the impact of urbani-

---

1. Figures in this paragraph are from U.S. Bureau of the Census, *Statistical Abstract of the United States: 1975,* 96th annual ed. (Washington, D.C.: 1975), pp. 17–19.

2. Philip M. Hauser and Martin Taitel, "Population Trends—Prologue to Educational Programs." In Edgar L. Morphet and Charles O. Ryan, eds., *Designing Education for the Future, No. 1: Prospective Changes in Society by 1980* (New York: Citation Press, 1967), p. 34.

3. Ibid., p. 36.

4. Based upon figures in U.S. Department of Health, Education and Welfare *Digest of Educational Statistics,* 1973 ed. (Washington, D.C.: Dept. of Health, Education and Welfare, 1973), p. 36.

zation upon schools goes considerably beyond the need to provide classrooms. The popular as well as professional literature has discussed such problems as teaching large numbers of students who have serious educational deficiencies, fiscal inequities related to city schools, the impersonality of large school bureaucracies, and the lack of coordination among schools and other public service agencies. While most acute and obvious in largest cities, such problems often exist in smaller school systems as well. Many educators and national policy makers believe the amelioration of urban educational problems should have top priority in American education.

It is important to note that urbanization also affects the task of schools which are not in urban areas. This is true because urbanization is a style of life as well as a clustering of people.[5] The central feature of urban life is the interdependence of individuals and institutions. Rural as well as city residents are affected by this life style in our predominantly urban society. As institutions charged with helping prepare young people for life in an urban society, schools must teach the skills and values essential to urban living.

ECONOMIC GROWTH

The United States is a wealthy nation. Since 1929, the gross national product has increased more than twelve times to an estimated $1397.3 billion in 1974.[6] Some of this gain was due to inflation. When standardized on a 1958 price base, the gain was from $203.6 billion in 1929 to $821.1 billion in 1974. On the same basis, personal consumer expenditure increased from $139.6 billion to an estimated $539.5 billion, federal purchases from $3.5 billion to an estimated $56.5 billion, and state and local government purchases from $18.5 billion to an estimated $89.5 billion. Also on the basis of 1958 prices, per capita disposable personal income rose from $1236 in 1929 to an estimated $2845 in 1974. We can summarize these data by saying that although prices have increased over the last forty years, the real levels of government services and personal consumption have increased even more.

For the most part, the economy has expanded at such a rate that the availability of jobs has kept pace with population growth. The rate of unemployment in relation to the total civilian labor force has not often exceeded 5 percent since 1942. Economic growth has provided the resources necessary to finance the new schools and expanded programs required by the growing population. To be sure, few school systems are financed at the

5. Urbanization is analyzed in this context by Scott Greer, *The Emerging City* (New York: The Free Press of Glencoe, 1964).

6. Figures in this paragraph are from *Economic Report of the President* (Washington, D.C.: U.S. Government Printing Office, 1969), and U.S. Bureau of the Census, *Statistical Abstract,* p. 380–383.

level which their strongest supporters advocate. Nevertheless, it can be said with confidence that the expansion of American education has depended upon economic development.

It should be noted, however, that economic growth is not a steady and all-encompassing process. It is often accompanied by serious dislocations for particular regions or occupational groups. For example, the decision of a large corporation to close a plant in a particular town cannot only leave its own employees without work, but will simultaneously reduce the income potential of merchants and professional persons in that community. Such a community is unlikely to feel it can afford an increase in school tax rates until the local economy is revitalized. Similarly, inflation can be a deterrent to increased levels of school support, particularly when citizens believe that taxes are already high. Such was the case in many areas during the mid 1970s. The high levels of unemployment characteristic of this same period had similar effect.

There is at least one other aspect of this subject worth noting here. Continued economic development depends upon educational development. Industrialization and technology have revamped the American occupational structure. We are no longer a nation of farmers and factory workers. The number of white collar workers has grown steadily larger than the number of blue collar employees in the nation since 1956.[7] Many jobs which were common a decade or two ago (locomotive fireman, streetcar conductor) no longer exist and a host of new positions (key punchers, computer operators, air-conditioning and television repairmen) have emerged. A large percentage of young people now in school will work at jobs that are not yet existent. This changing nature of the occupational structure means that schools should provide students with the background needed to adapt to changing vocational opportunities.

SOCIOECONOMIC DIVERSITY

Our comments about economic development notwithstanding, a large part of the American population is not prosperous. The Bureau of the Census reported that, in 1974, median family income in the U.S. was $12,836. However, 13.0 percent of all families and 29.5 percent of non-white families had incomes of less than $5000 annually.[8] Although rural poverty has continued to be a problem in some areas, notably the South, most of the poor are concentrated in central cities. At the other end of the spectrum, the Census Bureau reported that, in 1974, nearly 40 percent of American families enjoyed incomes of more than $15,000.

As noted in chapter 2, it has been traditional to refer to the public

7. Joseph W. Garbarino, "The Industrial Relations System." In Edgar L. Morphet and Charles O. Ryan, eds., *Designing Education for the Future,* p. 162.

8. U.S. Bureau of the Census, *Statistical Abstract,* p. 390–91.

school as a "melting pot," where children of varying ethnicity and socioeconomic status come together for common education. Indeed much of the argument in favor of neighborhood schools derives from the presumed benefits of such intergroup experiences. Today the neighborhood school is less likely to provide such experiences. Neighborhoods, particularly those in large metropolitan areas, have become progressively more segregated in terms of ethnic and socioeconomic characteristics. Continued adherence to neighborhood school policies has meant that schools are segregated as well. Race is not the only variable by which urban residents have segregated themselves. The newcomer to most metropolitan areas quickly learns which neighborhoods are high-income suburbs; which are working-class communities; and which are inhabited mainly by Poles, Irish, Jews, or some other ethnic group.

The reality of a pluralistic society living in relatively homogenous neighborhoods affects school administrators in several ways. If his school is in a particularly high or very low income area, it is unlikely that either he or members of his staff will have the first-hand sensitivity to local concerns which comes from experiencing them. Whether he lives in the community or not, he and his staff will need to give careful thought to ways in which the school can help its clients become more knowledgeable about and understanding of the broader society. Finally, many of the concerns and decisions which come to the attention of administrators will depend upon the neighborhood in which their school is located. We would expect the demands upon an elementary school principal in a very wealthy suburb to differ in many respects from those of his counterpart in a school which draws all of its students from a public housing project.

A TIME OF TENSIONS

Because America is a pluralistic and democratic society in which freedom of expression is a fundamental value, disagreement among citizens has been commonplace in our history. At times the issues have been so fundamental and the feelings so intense that the very fabric of society has been threatened. The classic examples, of course, center around the periods of the Revolutionary and Civil wars. Schools were not ignored during these conflicts, as citizens sought education for their children which was consistent with their own beliefs. The same has been true at other times in history, although the issues have been less dramatic. For example, many citizens in the middle decades of this century divided over the nature of steps which schools should take to indoctrinate students against Communism. Divisiveness regarding the appropriateness of sex education in the schools has been apparent more recently. These issues and others have generated periodic conflict about the content of textbooks.

Although contemporary administrators need to be aware of tensions surrounding the anti-communist and sex-education issues, two other conflicts in American society seem even more basic to school operation: The first deals with the role of youth in society; the second is race relations.

Student unrest became a national concern in the late 1960s.[9] Although the movement began at colleges and universities, it spread to the point that more than two thousand elementary and secondary schools experienced some form of unrest during 1968. These protests were violent in some instances. Students demanded and sometimes won a variety of changes in school policies and procedures ranging from dress codes, to criteria for selecting principals and assigning teachers, to expanded curricula. This series of protests raised fundamental questions about the role of students in their own education. Educators and laymen alike have diverse views on this subject, and often hold these views very strongly. While the tide of militant protest apparently has ebbed, many youths continue to challenge not only school procedures but also other institutions in society.

Despite the challenges posed by youth to older generations, the most basic tensions in American society continue to be racial. Following the disastrous riots during the summer of 1967, the National Advisory Commission on Civil Disorders issued a report which declared "Our Nation is moving toward two societies, one black, one white—separate and unequal.[10] The commission's allegation that "white racism" was fundamentally responsible for the disadvantaged status of black Americans became a topic for heated debate. A national survey in July, 1968, by CBS News gave some indication of public attitudes toward this conclusion. Seventy-four percent of blacks but only 31 percent of whites agreed with the statement "white racism is essentially responsible for the conditions in which Negroes live in American cities."[11] Racial tensions have gained further visibility recently as a result of efforts to desegregate many northern school districts.

A detailed examination of the implications of racial issues for schools is not in order here. Suffice it to say that schools have been confronted with many demands to improve educational opportunities for minority group students. Both the presentation of such demands and efforts to respond to them have frequently generated tension in school communities. It seems likely that such tension will continue not only until equality is achieved in the broader society but also until persons in the majority accept this condition.

---

9. For more discussion of this subject, see Kenneth L. Fish, *Conflict and Dissent in the High Schools* (New York: The Bruce Publishing Co., 1970) and Jerome A. Skolnick, *The Politics of Protest: Violent Aspects of Protest and Confrontation: A staff report to the National Commission on the Causes and Prevention of Violence* (Washington, D.C.: U.S. Government Printing Office, 1969), pp. 63–69.

10. Report of the National Advisory Commission on Civil Disorders. (New York: Bantam Books, 1968), p. 1.

11. CBS News, *White and Negro Attitudes Towards Race Related Issues and Activities* (Princeton, N.J.: Opinion Research Corp., 1968), p. 5.

EDUCATION AND NATIONAL DEVELOPMENT

We noted in chapter 2 that the state has responsibility for education and that operating decisions are generally made at the local level. However, there are many developments which make it clear that the public has a stake in education at the national level and that some decisions and activities have nationwide implications.

EDUCATION AS PUBLIC INVESTMENT

Economists[12] have suggested that expenditures for education can be viewed in either or both of two ways. From one perspective, they can be treated as personal consumption in which individuals or governments spend their money for education instead of other goods or services because they enjoy the result. On the other hand, Theodore W. Schultz[13] and others have argued that expenditures for education can be considered investments in human capital. Conventional wisdom has acknowledged this view for individuals for some time. Thus many parents have advised their children to attend school to increase their earning power. However, it has also been shown that national levels of education are associated with gross national product and other indicators of economic health. Therefore, it is argued that investment in public education can enhance prosperity on national as well as individual bases.

We believe that the interest which many federal policy makers have shown in extending vocational education as well as improving other opportunities for schooling can be attributed at least partially to acceptance of this "investment perspective." During the middle 1960s, the extent of poverty in an affluent nation was documented by researchers and deplored by the American public. Passage of the Economic Opportunity Act of 1964 and the Elementary and Secondary Education Act of 1965 was achieved in this atmosphere.

During the early and middle 1970s federal investment in education was subjected to greater scrutiny. Many citizens and legislators felt that the federal investment in education during the 1960s did not have the desired effects. Concern about escalating school costs in a time of declining enrollments, societal divisiveness about school purposes and programs, and lack of empirical evidence regarding school effectiveness diminished enthusiasm for further federal investment in education. Influenced

---

12. For review of research on the economics of education, see John Vaizey, *The Economics of Education* (London: Faber and Faber, 1962) and Maureen Woodhall, "The Economics of Education." In *Review of Education Research* 34: (October, 1967), pp. 387–398.

13. T. W. Schultz, *The Economic Value of Education* (New York: Columbia University Press, 1963). Also see Frederick Harbison and Charles A. Myers, *Education, Manpower and Economic Growth* (New York: McGraw-Hill, 1964).

Teachers need to support Families
NEW-BOSTON IDEAS
SUPPORT BETTER SCHOOLS
Media
PROMISES?

by two studies[14] widely cited to support claims that investments in education have little return, federal support for elementary and secondary schools was cut back. Despite the increasingly articulate protests of the education lobbies, both the President and Congress pursued this course. As a result, it seems clear that even stronger efforts and/or new evidence will be required to persuade federal officials to return to the "investment perspective" held earlier.

THE PUBLIC AND ITS SCHOOLS

More than one-fourth of the American population is directly involved with the schools in some way. There were in 1973 an estimated 45 million students enrolled in public elementary and secondary schools. More than two million teachers were employed in these schools and their efforts were supplemented by approximately 120,000 administrators. These persons worked in approximately 90,000 different schools located in approximately 16,000 different school districts.[15]

Approximately five million other students attended nonpublic elementary and secondary schools during the same year. These schools were staffed by approximately 209,000 teachers and an additional 20,000 administrators. There were approximately 18,000 nonpublic schools operating at this time.

Public and nonpublic school expenditures for current operation and capital outlay were more than $61 billion in 1974. Public school expenditures alone were approximately $56 billion. Only national defense accounted for a greater proportion of government expenditure.

The above figures do not reflect the large and growing number of persons and amount of resources related to the schools in a supportive or supplementary way. Business and industry have shown interest in relating to schools in a variety of ways. The traditional relationship has been profit-oriented. Schools have long depended upon private firms to provide the books, furniture, and materials which they need. Few would deny that business has had substantial impact upon school curricula in the design, production, and supply of these materials.

During the 1960s, several large firms made known their interest in developing new and improved materials for schools and also in providing services heretofore not available from commercial sources. Among the early leaders in this area were General Learning Corporation (a new firm formed by Time-Life and General Electric) and subsidiaries of other major

---

14. James Coleman et al., *Equality of Educational Opportunity* (Washington, D.C.: U.S. Government Printing Office, 1966) and Christopher Jencks, *Inequality: A Reassessment of the Effect of Family and Schooling in America* (New York: Basic Books, Inc., 1972).

15. Most of the data in these paragraphs are drawn from U.S. Bureau of the Census, *Statistical Abstract of the United States: 1974,* 95th ed. (Washington, D.C.: U.S. Government Printing Office, 1974), pp. 108–128.

corporations such as IBM, Westinghouse, and Litton Industries. While the exact nature of the contribution which these and similar firms can make to education remains undetermined, the extent of their interest establishes the fact that education is big business in the United States.

NATIONALIZING TENDENCIES

Campbell and others[16] studied nationalizing influences upon education during 1961 and 1962. In particular, they examined the impact of the National Science Foundation, the National Merit Scholarship Program, the National Defense Act of 1958, and The College Entrance Examination Board (CEEB) upon secondary schools. They reported nine general findings:

> 1. National programs have changed substantially the courses offered in science, mathematics, and foreign languages in our high schools.
> 2. National programs have altered the guidance programs of our high schools.
> 3. National programs have created a vast external testing program for our high schools.
> 4. National programs have changed college admissions procedures.
> 5. National programs have established a new pattern for the inservice education of teachers.
> 6. National programs have altered school plant planning and construction.
> 7. There has been differential use of national programs. . . . Rural schools appeared to be the low users of the most programs. Suburban users were high users of NSF and the College Board and most NDEA programs.
> 8. National programs have given the public a new measuring stick with which to evaluate schools.
> 9. Apparently many people do not recognize or will not acknowledge the impact of the national programs on the schools.

The programs which Campbell and his colleagues studied have expanded considerably since they viewed them. For example, more than three million tests were administered by the College Entrance Examinations Board

---

16. Roald F. Campbell and Robert A. Bunnell, eds., *Nationalizing Influences in Secondary Education* (Chicago: Midwest Administration Center, 1963).

(CEEB) in 1966–1967 whereas an estimated 750,000 students took such tests in 1960. During the same period, the number of colleges and universities which were members of the CEEB climbed from 427 to more than 600. It is also likely that both rural and city schools participate more actively in these programs than they did in 1961–1962, and that the American public is more aware of them now than at that time.

In addition, there have been other developments since the early 1960s which have augmented the nationalizing influences already discussed. Funds from the United States Office of Education and some private sources made it possible to expand the curriculum development projects originally supported by the National Science Foundation. Some of the research and development centers and regional educational laboratories initially supported by the U.S. Office of Education have been important in this regard.

The activities of national foundations have also been a nationalizing influence. Much of the national interest in improving urban schools by strengthening their relationships with citizens and community agencies can be attributed to the efforts of the Ford Foundation. First through support of the "Grey Areas Projects" and later by their involvement in plans to decentralize the New York City schools, the foundation provided stimuli in this direction. Similarly, the Carnegie Corporation supported the studies of James B. Conant, which most thoughtful observers believe have had enormous influence on educational practice throughout the nation. Carnegie has also supported the early years of the national assessment program, which has developed an abundance of data pertinent to planning on a national basis. The Mott Foundation provided national impetus for the community school movement, and the Kettering Foundation has also become an active supporter of educational projects including the Individually Guided Education (IGE) program. In recent years, private as well as public support for many such developments has been decreased.

Even so nationalizing tendencies have been enhanced by what we might term the "multiplier factor of public interest." Citizens believe that schools are important and seek expanded educational opportunities for their children. At the same time the national media have made more knowledge about educational developments available to the population. Thus citizens can often read stories in national magazines and see television programs about informal classrooms in elementary schools, individualized instruction, community control, or other developments. They often become a source of support to introduce similar programs in their own locale. This tendency is strengthened by the fact that approximately 20 percent of the population moves annually and brings expectations for schools which are based upon their prior experiences.

The federal government has been a consistent and significant influence upon educational development in the nation. The notion that federal influence is relatively new in education is widely held but inaccurate. As noted in chapter 2, federal participation dates back to the earliest days of the nation. It is also true, that the federal government became much more active during the 1960s, particularly through the Office of Education. For example, Allen reported in 1950 that the annual federal expenditure for education was more than $3 billion and that less than 1 percent of these funds was allocated by the Office of Education.[17] By 1968, estimated federal expenditures for education had increased to more than $11 billion, of which nearly one-third was expended through the Office of Education.[18] By 1974, Congress had cut back; legislation was passed which limited the amount which could be appropriated "for all educational purpose including higher education and vocational education" to not more than $7.5 billion in fiscal 1975, $8 billion in fiscal 1976, and $9 billion in fiscal 1977.[19]

The cornerstone of current federal aid to education remains the Elementary and Secondary Education Act of 1965 (ESEA). Although the primary focus of this measure is upon improving educational opportunities for children from low-income families, most local school districts qualify for aid under its provisions. The core of ESEA, in terms of both Congressional intent and the proportion of funds allocated to it, is Title I. More than $1 billion annually has been authorized by this Title for educational programs to benefit children from families with poverty-level incomes.

Title II authorized federal assistance to school districts for the purchase of textbooks and other instructional materials. Title III authorized the creation of supplementary educational centers which would engage nonpublic as well as public schools in collaborative programs with other educative agencies. A variety of remedial and supplementary services has been provided through such centers. Proposals for Title III projects were originally reviewed at the federal level, but control over Title III funds was subsequently transferred to state departments of education. Title IV of ESEA authorized additional funds for the cooperative research program as well as the establishment of research and development centers and regional educational laboratories. Title V authorized funds to strengthen state departments of education. These programs have been modified by Amendments or incorporated in other legislation since their original authorization.

A study[20] of the 1965–68 period assessed the impact of eight major federal programs across six states. These programs which together comprised more than 95 percent of federal revenues going to local school districts were Titles I, II, and III of ESEA, Title III of the National Defense Education Act (providing support for instruction in certain subjects including science, mathematics and modern foreign language) Title V-A of NDEA (guidance, counseling, and testing), Vocational Education; School Lunch

---

17. Hollis P. Allen, *The Federal Government in Education* (New York: McGraw-Hill, 1950).

18. *Digest of Educational Statistics 1967* (Washington, D.C.: U.S. Government Printing Office, 1967), p. 165.

19. James R. Kirkpatrick, ed., "D.C. Dateline." In *The School Administrator* (September 1974), p. 9.

20. Joel S. Berke and Michael W. Kirst, Federal Aid to Education: Who Benefits, Who Governs? (Lexington, Mass.: Lexington Books, D.C. Heath and Co., 1972).

and Milk Program and School Assistance in Federally Affected Areas. Among the major findings were that except for ESEA Title I, programs often provide more aid to suburban than city districts; nonmetropolitan areas generally receive more aid per pupil than metropolitan areas; ESEA Title I funds tend to be used for supplementary rather than core curriculum programs; and the total amount of federal aid available is inadequate to the needs of school districts.

Federal legislation affecting schools has had objectives which go beyond provision of funds for particular purposes or the stimulation of new programs. For example, Title IX of the education amendments for 1972 included provisions against sex discrimination which have required many school districts to provide new interscholastic activities for girls. In 1974, Congress reacted to public opposition to school bussing for purposes of achieving racial balance by enacting legislation stating that children may not be required to be bussed beyond the school closest to their neighborhood school unless ordered by a court. In the same year, the Family Educational Rights and Privacy Act was passed. This opened school files of students to their parents (or the students themselves once they reach eighteen years of age) and limited the access of other parties to these files.

Federal influence upon local school districts is not limited to legislative action. Both the executive and judicial branches exert considerable influence. The participation of the executive branch is evident in several ways. Government administrators are often influential in shaping the nature of legislation which is enacted. For example, this was true in the case of the Elementary and Secondary Education Act.[21] Once legislation is passed, government officials draw up the guidelines for its administration and hold delegate agencies such as school districts responsible for compliance. In this way, government officials may serve as a source of appeal for citizens who believe that federal programs are not being administered appropriately at the local level. Moreover, administrators of federal agencies other than the Office of Education sometimes call upon school officials to assure compliance with particular guidelines and coordination with other federal programs. For example, the Department of Justice has sued school systems for noncompliance with civil rights laws. Local schoolmen have also been called upon to coordinate some of their programs with certain model cities and Office of Economic Opportunity efforts.

The federal courts have had significant influence upon local school districts through a number of decisions. Some of these decisions have involved interpreting parts of the Bill of Rights such as freedom of speech or religion as they apply to public education. Many other decisions have been based upon interpreting the due process and equal protection clauses

21. C. Philip Kearney, "The 1964 Presidential Task Force on Education and the Elementary and Secondary Education Act of 1965" (Ph.D. diss., Department of Education, University of Chicago, 1967).

of the Fourteenth Amendment. Most of the desegregation cases have involved interpretation of the Fourteenth Amendment.

Areas in which federal courts have made decisions of great impact upon local public school practice include desegregation, relationships with nonpublic schools, and religious observances. Some of the most important cases in these areas were discussed in chapter 2. Another area in which recent decisions of importance were made is that of student rights. Following its tradition of upholding civil liberties, the Warren Court held in 1967 that rights of due process must be observed in dealing with students charged with delinquency.[22] In a subsequent case, *Tinker et al.* v. *Des Moines Independent Community School District et al.,* the Court upheld the right of students to wear black armbands to school in peaceful protest of the Vietnam War. The Court stated:

> First Amendment rights, applied in light of the special characteristics of the school environment are available to teachers and students. It can hardly be argued that either students or teachers shed their constitutional rights to freedom of speech or expression at the schoolhouse gate. . . . School officials do not possess absolute authority over their students. Students in school as well as out of school are "persons" under our Constitution. They are possessed of fundamental rights which the State must respect, just as they themselves must respect their obligations to the State.[23]

The *Tinker* decision has provided the basis for much subsequent litigation regarding student rights. Many of these cases turn upon whether or not it can be shown that the alleged exercise of such rights is or may reasonably be presumed to be disruptive of the school program. In the latter instance, of course, school officials do possess authority to regulate student behavior. The Court has subsequently spoken to procedures which may be used to regulate student behavior. In a controversial 5–4 decision, it was held that schools may not suspend students without first providing them a hearing.[24]

THE CONTEST TO SHAPE LOCAL EDUCATIONAL POLICY

Our theme thus far in this chapter has been that external factors influence decisions made at all levels, including that of the local school or school district. We shall now deal a bit more specifically with local processes. It

22. *In the Matter of Gault,* 387 U.S. 1 (1967).
23. *Tinker* v. *Des Moines Independent Community School District,* 390 U.S. 942 (1968).
24. *Goss* v. *Lopez,* 419 U.S. 565 (1975).

appears that policy making for local schools has become more controversial in recent years, as a wide range of parties has become involved in decisions. Our focus here will be to identify parties who are often involved in the political action and formal enactment stages of policy making and then to examine some issues of contemporary importance at this level.

PARTICIPANTS IN LOCAL POLICY MAKING

A logical place to begin the consideration of parties involved in local school policy making is with boards of education, sometimes called school committees or school trustees. Such bodies have legal responsibility for enacting local school policy within the guidelines established by the state constitution and school codes. As noted in chapter 2, board of education members are state officials and must carry out state laws. The board has legal status only as an entity (individual members cannot act for the board), and enjoys only those powers expressly or implicitly delegated to it by the state constitution or statutes. However, boards of education enjoy considerable "discretionary authority" (although exact conditions vary from state to state) because the wording of state codes is often permissive rather than mandatory and quite general in many areas. To cite only a few examples, boards of education generally make formal decisions to hire and dismiss particular employees; determine salaries and other budgetary allocations; and establish when, where, and in what style new schools will be constructed. Even where boards are guided in such areas by state requirements (personnel certification requirements and salary minimums), they can exercise a wide range of alternatives.

Boards of education ideally exercise their discretionary powers in the best interests of the citizens they represent. Most board members are elected at large in nonpartisan elections. However, in some locales, they are appointed by the mayor, the city council, or other public official often upon the nomination of another body such as a "blue-ribbon" citizens committee. Regardless of how they achieve office, most board members do not acknowledge indebtedness to a particular local constituency. The general view is that each member represents "all of the people." McCarty and Ramsey[25] have noted that exceptions to this view do exist. In a study of fifty-one school districts, they found that some board members serve as representatives of special interests and for self-oriented motives, and that such motivations affect the behavior of their respective superintendents.

Middle-class businessmen and professional persons have been

25. Donald J. McCarty and Charles E. Ramsey, *The School Managers: Power and Conflict in American Public Education* (Westport, Conn.: Greenwood Publishing Corp., 1970).

traditionally over-represented on boards of education.[26] Similarly, board membership is most widely held by persons who tend to be in middle or upper-middle social strata according to such indicators as education and income. Neither the poor nor the extremely rich serve very often as board of education members. Similarly, representatives of minority groups have generally been under-represented on school boards in the past. There are indications that the latter circumstance may be changing, particularly in large cities where a growing number of blacks have achieved election or appointment to these positions. Similarly, there is some evidence that recent events, particularly the civil rights movement and the concomitant increase in the visibility of school affairs, have associated some board members with particular racial, ethnic, or neighborhood constituencies.

Some scholars[27] have suggested that the actual influence of boards of education upon school decisions is somewhat less than their formal responsibility would indicate. Pointing out that board membership is a part-time and avocational activity, they note that members must rely heavily upon information and recommendations from professional administrators. On the other hand, Crain[28] found that boards of education in eight Northern cities tended to remove the decision of how to respond to civil rights demands from administrators, and that the attitudes of board members were important determinants of these responses.

Minar[29] studied the decision-making relationships between boards of education and superintendents in suburban communities. He found that boards of education comprised of persons who are experienced managers and directors in professional life tend to give administrators more latitude in making operating decisions about the schools than do boards with less managerial expertise among their members. He also reported that such variations in style were associated with community factors. School boards are more likely to give administrators wide decision-making latitude in communities where there is relatively little conflict in school affairs (defined as the percent of negative vote in school board and school tax elections).

The research summarized above points out the importance of the

---

26. Cf. George S. Counts, *The Social Composition of Boards of Education* (Chicago: University of Chicago Press, 1927) and L. Harmon Ziegler and M. Kent Jennings, *Governing American Schools: Political Interaction in Local School Districts* (North Scituate, Mass.: Duxbury Press, 1974), pp. 25–37.

27. For example, see Norman D. Kerr, "The School Board as an Agency of Legitimation," *Sociology of Education* 38 (Fall 1964), pp. 34–59, and Ziegler and Jennings, *Governing American Schools.*

28. Robert L. Crain, *The Politics of School Desegregation* (Chicago: Aldine Publishing Co., 1968). A follow-up study attributed more importance to outside pressures in desegregation decisions. See David S. Kirby, Robert T. Harris, and Robert L. Crain, *Political Strategies in Northern School Desegregation* (Lexington, Mass.: D. C. Heath and Co., 1973).

29. David W. Minar, *Educational Decision-Making in Suburban Communities* (Washington, D.C.: U.S. Office of Education, Cooperative Research Project No. 2440, 1966) and *Idem.* "The Community Basis of Conflict in School System Politics," *American Sociological Review,* vol. 31, no. 6 (December 1966), pp. 822–835.

relationship between the school board and the superintendent in policy making. It suggests that the popular notion whereby the school board makes policy and the superintendent carries it out is an oversimplification. Both parties make contributions to this process and they function most effectively when a sense of mutual trust and responsibility exists among them. In exercising their respective legal authority and professional judgment, the successful board and superintendent must show respect for each other and sensitivity to community interests.

The school board-superintendent relationship is the focal point for local policy development. However, many other groups and individuals attempt to influence decisions made at this level. Several years ago, Gross[30] asked superintendents and board of education members from approximately half the school districts in Massachusetts who exerted pressure upon them. The responses to this question are summarized in Table 3–1. Table 3–2 summarizes the kinds of pressures to which these persons said they were exposed.

The data reported by Gross are fairly old, and the nature of local

TABLE 3–1 Percentage of Superintendents and School Board Members Who Said They Were Exposed to Pressures from the Specified Individuals and Groups

INDIVIDUALS OR GROUPS WHO EXERT PRESSURE	*SUPERINTENDENTS (N = 105)*	*SCHOOL BOARD MEMBERS (N = 508)*
1. Parents or PTA	92	74
2. Individual school board members	75	51
3. Teachers	65	44
4. Taxpayers' association	49	31
5. Town finance committee or city council	48	38
6. Politicians	46	29
7. Business or commercial organizations	45	19
8. Individuals influential for economic reasons	44	25
9. Personal friends	37	37
10. The press	36	19
11. Old-line families	30	26
12. Church or religious groups	28	18
13. Veterans' organizations	27	10
14. Labor unions	27	5
15. Chamber of Commerce	23	5
16. Service clubs	20	11
17. Fraternal organizations	13	9
18. Farm organizations	12	4
19. Welfare organizations	3	1

Source: Neal Gross, *Who Runs Our Schools?* (New York: John Wiley & Sons, 1958). p. 50.

30. Neal Gross, *Who Runs Our Schools?* (New York: John Wiley & Sons, 1958).

TABLE 3–2 Percentage of Superintendents and School Board Members Exposed to Specified Pressures

PRESSURE	*SUPERINTENDENTS (N = 105)*	*SCHOOL BOARD MEMBERS (N = 508)*
1. Demands that the schools should place more emphasis on the three *R*'s	59	53
2. Demands that the schools should teach more courses and subjects	64	47
3. Protests about the use of particular textbooks	19	19
4. Protests about the views expressed by teachers	49	41
5. Demands that teachers should express certain views	13	12
6. Protesting school tax increases or bond proposals	73	70
7. Demanding more money for the general school program	66	52
8. Protesting the introduction of new services (in addition to academic instruction) for pupils	39	35
9. Demanding the introduction of new services (in addition to academic instruction) for pupils	63	49
10. Demands that school contracts be given to certain firms	46	24
11. Demands that teachers be appointed or dismissed for reasons other than competence	46	24
12. Demanding the introduction of new teaching methods	29	35
13. Protesting the introduction of new teaching methods	43	28
14. Demanding that greater emphasis be placed on the athletic program	58	52
15. Demanding that less emphasis be placed on the athletic program	40	38

Source: Neal Gross, *Who Runs Our Schools?* (New York: John Wiley & Sons, 1958), p. 49.

issues has probably changed some in recent years. Nevertheless, his research illustrates the wide range of groups and individuals who attempt to influence school decision making. In our judgment, current pressures are at least as diverse in origin as they were when Gross did his study. Moreover, it is clear that the intensity with which some groups advocate their views has increased appreciably since then. Many of what the persons interviewed by Gross reported as pressures were no doubt requests, opinions, or demands made quietly by individuals. To be sure, these expressions frequently were not devoid of sanctions, as Gross makes clear.[31] At the present time the quiet demands of individuals are often augmented or opposed by public demands and sophisticated tactics of organized groups.

Certainly the most visible and probably the most powerful of such groups are the teacher organizations. The National Educational Association and the American Federation of Teachers emerged as strong advocates of teacher interests during the 1960s. Both groups predate this decade, however. The National Education Association was formed in 1857 as the National Teachers Association, a confederation of ten state teachers' associations. The name of the organization was changed in 1879, and it has grown to the point that in 1975 it had more than one and one-half million members. These members are served through a large bureaucracy which in 1975 had a budget of nearly 42 million dollars.[32] Although the Department of Classroom Teachers has been the largest division of the association since it was formed in 1942, its internal influence was exceeded until recent years by other departments, notably those which represented administrators. The organization reorganized in 1972 and is now guided by a representative assembly which included delegates from more than 9,000 state and local associations. At least until recently, the NEA showed more concern for the establishment of national goals and standards through bodies such as the Educational Policies Commission, advocacy of increased state and federal aid to education, and dissemination of research and statistics than it did for direct teacher benefits and expanded teacher participation in policy-making.[33] Among national goals in 1975 were a federal bargaining bill, increased practitioner control over certification, and assistance to teachers in implementing desegregation policies.[34]

The American Federation of Teachers was founded in 1916 as an affiliate of the American Federation of Labor. This organization, which in 1976 had approximately 475,000 members in thirty-six state federations and 2000 local affiliates, has emphasized teacher rights and welfare since its origin. As Rosenthal[35] points out, the relative significance of the two organizations is belied by simple comparison of membership figures. The Federation has strong support in large cities, and there is little doubt that its activities have prodded the NEA and its affiliates into a more militant position than they formerly held.

What many observers note as the most significant turning points

31. Gross defines pressure as "a request, demand, or expressed opinion behind which lies a threat for failure to conform to the request, demand, or opinion, whether this threat is intended or unintended, implicit or explicit." *Who Runs Our Schools?,* pp. 47–48.

32. NEA Handbook, 1975–76 (Washington, D.C.: National Education Association, 1975), p. 32.

33. Alan Rosenthal, *Pedagogues and Power: Teacher Groups in School Politics* (Syracuse, N.Y.: Syracuse University Press, 1969), p. 5.

34. NEA Handbook, pp. 29–31.

35. Ibid., p. 23.

to increased teacher militancy took place in New York City during 1960–1962.[36] In November of 1960, the United Federation of Teachers (an AFT local) held a one-day strike to back its demand that the board of education designate a collective bargaining agent for teachers. The UFT won the subsequent election held to select such an agent, and struck again for a day in April, 1962, to back contract demands that were settled after Mayor Robert Wagner and Governor Nelson Rockefeller intervened in the negotiations. More than 20,000 teachers participated in the second strike, which served notice to the NEA and the nation at large that substantial teacher benefits could be won through collective bargaining. The same event was the first to demonstrate that the New York State law and others like it, which call for heavy penalties such as dismissal for public employees who strike, are virtually unenforceable in the face of large-scale walkouts.

The UFT victory in New York encouraged AFT leaders in other cities to press for representative bargaining status or negotiated contracts in their own locales. In response, the NEA at its 1962 convention adopted resolutions which employed the terms "professional negotiation" and "professional sanctions" for the first time. Lieberman and Moscow note that these acts by the NEA were significant, but considered them less so than the speech by the NEA executive secretary at the same convention. He "identified unionization as a threat to education and the NEA" . . . [and] "went on to explain that the newly established Urban Project would direct the NEA fight against unionization of teachers."[37]

The competition between the two organizations continued throughout the decade. There were noteworthy differences between the groups at the outset of this period. The most prominent of these was the AFT perspective and affiliation which identified teachers with "labor" in opposition to "management." This contrasted with the NEA claim to "professional" status and affiliation with administrators in a common organization. A second difference was AFT support of strikes, continued negotiation, and mediation in the event of bargaining impasses. In contrast, the NEA spoke of professional sanctions (ranging from public notice of an undesirable teaching situation to urging teachers not to seek employment in a particular school district until such conditions are remedied) and advocated written agreement upon procedures for resolving impasses preferably through educational rather than labor channels.[38]

These differences led to considerable variation in the rhetoric employed by organizational leaders. A structural difference which has been reflected in the membership dues of the two groups has been the greater emphasis by the NEA upon activities of the state and national levels. The

---

36. For a review of these events, see Myron Lieberman and Michael H. Moskow, *Collective Negotiations for Teachers* (Chicago: Rand McNally, 1966), pp. 35–47.

37. Ibid., p. 45.

38. Ibid., pp. 319–320.

NEA and its state affiliates have continued to provide numerous publications, to hold conferences, and to work actively for legislation. For the most part, the AFT has concentrated on supporting local affiliates in quest of local benefits.

Differences between the organizations have lessened as their competition has increased. The most noticeable trend in this direction has been the increasingly militant pursuit of welfare objectives by NEA affiliates. Early steps in this direction were the imposition of statewide sanctions in Utah and Oklahoma in 1964 and 1965. More recently, NEA affiliates have moved away from their earlier aversion to strikes or other forms of work stoppages. The Kentucky Education Association held a one-day "professional study day" in 1966, and the Florida Education Association staged a three-week walkout to support salary demands in 1968. Some persons might consider it surprising that a total number of 114 teacher strikes occurred during the 1967–1968 school year and that seventy of these were waged by NEA affiliates (two others were joint union-NEA affiliate actions).[39] Another difference between the two organizations was obviated when the association and various administrator groups which were formerly affiliates established their independence. Against the backdrop of these developments, the president of the AFT, David Selden, called for a merger of his group and the NEA. While this has occured at some local levels, it continues to be a national issue largely because of NEA refusal to affiliate with the AFL-CIO.

It is apparent that teacher organizations have become a formidable force in local policy making. The most obvious evidence has been their ability to win substantial salary gains from local school boards. Indeed, they have sometimes won contracts (as in the Bigtown case described in chapter 1) which call for more revenue for salaries than is available to the local board, and require additional funds from state sources. But teacher power has also been effective on issues other than salaries. A long and bitterly contested strike by the UFT in New York City had substantial effect upon the "community control" debate there.[40] Likewise, Detroit teachers went on strike to avoid an accountability policy urged by local officials.

Further evidence that teachers are a force to be reckoned with in local policy making is the growing formalization of negotiating procedures. Several states have enacted legislation which acknowledges the legitimacy of or specifically requires school boards to negotiate with teacher organizations. Moreover, the range of items subject to negotiation has expanded beyond salaries and working conditions. A 1968 NEA publication[41] which summarized provisions contained in 1,540 negotiations agreements

---

39. "Teacher Strikes in Perspective," *NEA Research Bulletin* 46 (December 1968), pp. 113–116.

40. See Martin Mayer, *The Teacher's Strike: New York, 1968* (New York: Harper & Row, 1969) and Marilyn Gittell and Maurice Berube, *Confrontation at Ocean Hill-Brownsville* (New York: Praeger, 1969).

41. "What's Negotiable?" *NEA Research Bulletin* 46 (May 1968), pp. 42–43.

indicated that various aspects of the instructional program were often negotiated. Included were such items as class size, selection and use of instructional materials, parent conferences, and pupil discipline. An item subject to negotiation in at least one state (Michigan), which can further strengthen teacher groups, is the "agency shop." In effect, an agency-shop provision "requires all employees in the negotiating unit who do not become members of the representative organization to pay service charges or the equivalent of membership dues as a condition of continued employment."[42]

Finally, and perhaps most indicative of teachers' enhanced bargaining status, there is the position of the National School Boards Association. This group, which strenuously opposed collective negotiations for some time and which continues to oppose strikes, boycotts, and sanctions, stated as a matter of policy:

> In determining general policies relating to the operation of the schools, handling of personnel problems, and the general welfare of all professional personnel, each local school board should set up satisfactory procedures for communication with all professional [personnel]. Such procedures should recognize that the function of the professional practice of teaching requires that individual teachers have and exercise full freedom of association, expression, organization, and designation of representatives of their own choosing for the purpose of conferring with school boards concerning the terms and conditions of their employment.[43]

The emergence of militant teacher organizations has forced superintendents to reexamine their roles vis-à-vis the board of education and teachers in their district. Several roles have been suggested for them in the negotiations setting—including negotiator for the board, negotiator for the teachers, and impartial advisor to both parties. According to our judgment, the effect of events in most districts has been to identify the superintendent as management and on the side of the school board in negotiations. This does not necessarily mean that he, himself, should be negotiator for the board. This is often a time-consuming and technical responsibility which can be delegated to someone with special preparation for it.

Negotiated agreements with teachers have also limited administrative prerogatives in some areas. For example, where contracts specify that class sizes must be kept below a certain figure, constraints are placed upon the way classrooms are organized. Similarly, contracts which specify that teachers need not remain at school for more than a short time after

---

42. "Teachers and the Agency Shop," *NEA Research Bulletin* 47 (December 1969), p. 110.

43. "Beliefs and Policies of the National Association of School Boards." In *New Dimensions in Leadership*, Proceedings of the 1968 Convention (Evanston, Ill.: The Association, 1968), pp. 88–89.

students are dismissed can limit administrative plans to hold faculty meetings.

Teachers have not been the only group to organize in order to have an impact upon school affairs in recent years. Parent and neighborhood groups have often done likewise.[44] Demands associated with school desegregation, improved education for minority group children, and, later, "community control" appeared to be the most frequent stimuli to such activity in the 1960s. Protestors were sometimes associated with civil rights groups such as the NAACP or CORE and were sometimes organized independently. Protests have also been mounted by urban whites in opposition to black demands, and by suburbanites or small town residents, over various questions dealing with curriculum, school finance, and other subjects. For example, a group of parents in one city recently protested and attempted court action in opposition to a school board decision not to allow a high school band to march in an out-of-town holiday parade.

In some instances, teacher and citizen groups have been on opposite sides of issues. A well-known case was the Ocean Hill-Brownsville controversy (Brooklyn, N.Y.). However, there have been similar but less visible instances in other cities; and the interest in community control and accountability among some Americans suggests that further confrontations may be in the offing. Citizen groups have often employed tactics similar to those of militant teacher organizations in dealing with school officials. These include insisting upon "negotiations" (sometimes to the point of written agreements) and threatening or sometimes bringing about "work stoppages" in the form of school boycotts, demonstrations, and other disruptions of normal activities.

One other point should be noted about participation in local policy making. The demands of militant teacher and citizen groups have sometimes been so threatening to the established order or so far beyond the capacity of school officials to respond, that school authorities have turned to other levels of government for assistance. Several examples can be cited. One is disruptive activity by adult or student protestors for which schoolmen seek police assistance. Another is the example of teacher negotiations discussed in chapter 1, in which school officials sought additional funds to meet teacher demands through the mayor and the state legislature. Another was the Ocean Hill-Brownsville dispute, in which New York officials sought help in resolving their crisis from the state commissioner of education and other officials.

In addition, aggrieved citizens who feel they are making little headway in direct negotiation with school officials sometimes petition other governments to intervene. For example, desegregation advocates in many locales have petitioned state and federal courts and executives to withhold funds from their school districts until greater desegregation can be achieved.

44. See Luvern L. Cunningham and Raphael O. Nystrand, *Citizen Participation in School Affairs* (Washington, D.C.: The Urban Coalition, 1969).

The point of the preceding examples is that power to establish educational policy is diffuse and can be checked or augmented by numerous actors in a variety of ways. Moreover, there are signs that the involvement of noneducation officials in school matters is increasing. A survey of mayors of big cities revealed that 60 percent of them believed their participation in educational affairs would increase in the future.[45] School administrators work in a very pluralistic setting and must act frequently as brokers who encourage coalitions among diverse groups including citizens, teachers, and sometimes politicians in support of particular policies and programs.

CONTEMPORARY ISSUES

An indication of the wide range of issues which face schoolmen was presented in Table 3–2. Another listing was provided by Goldhammer, who interviewed a number of superintendents across the nation. He categorized many of their problems as follows:

> 1. *Educational change* . . . Superintendents feel that many of their problems arise from shifting expectations for the schools within the community as well as from the interventions of agencies outside of the school. They are equally concerned with the fact that there are pressures for change within the organization itself.
> 2. *Teacher Militancy* . . . These problems [dealing with teacher groups] change the nature of the school organization and create new definitions of the limitations and potentialities of public school programs.
> 3. *Instruction* . . . [The superintendent] is deeply involved in and concerned with problems of curriculum, instructional services of all sorts, evaluation, adaptation, and learning outcomes.
> 4. *Administrative Leadership* . . . The times require changes in the nature of the leadership functions of the superintendency and new demands on his competency. He seems to be forced to consider not only these issues and their impacts upon the schools, but also the major role he is required to play within the community and the school organization because of these issues.
> 5. *Critical Social Issues* . . . The issues of church and state, of desegregation, of the more equitable distribution of economic resources, of the reduction of social distance among cultural and racial groups—all involve the schools and create new demands not only upon the programs of the schools

45. Richard W. Saxe, "Mayors and Schools," *Urban Education* 4 (October, 1969), 243–251.

but also upon the nature of the decisions which have to be made in the maintenance and operation of the schools.

6. *Finance* . . . The traditional role of the administrator as the procurer of resources for the school organization has not been greatly changed . . . financial worries still plague the superintendent and are a primary problem for him.[46]

The problems identified by Goldhammer have not been resolved since he reported his research. Indeed they have probably intensified in at least some areas. Another perspective was provided by a national poll of citizens in 1975. Asked to identify the major problems confronting the schools, citizens mentioned the following most often: lack of discipline; integration; segregation; bussing; lack of proper financial support; difficulty of getting "good" teachers; size of school/classes; use of drugs; poor curriculum; crime/vandalism/stealing; lack of proper facilities; pupils' lack of interest.[47] The overlap with some of the categories set forth by Goldhammer is apparent. Also interesting, however, is the strong citizen concern for pupil behavior as shown by the items dealing with discipline, drugs, crime and lack of interest. The same survey indicated that while a large majority of citizens continue to give their local schools a grade of *A*, *B*, or *C* (on a scale of *A*, *B*, *C*, *D*, *F*, don't know), the level of public confidence in schools declined from 1974 to 1975 particularly among young adults and the college educated. The authors point out that this may be associated with a general decline in public confidence in public institutions but add that it should be regarded as a "warning signal."[48]

We judge there are at least four general issues which crosscut the problems mentioned here. Each of them calls for the kind of administrative leadership Goldhammer mentions in response to social change.

The first issue is the one discussed in the preceding section of this chapter: Who should participate in school decision making? As already noted, the changing roles of teachers seem particularly important in their implications for administrators.

A second and related issue which became quite controversial in the late 1960s deals with the nature of local control. In a series of encounters which began in New York City, citizens in minority group communities have challenged the representativeness of city boards of education. Frustrated by what they see as the failure of school systems to educate their children to the extent they wish, these citizens have demanded that city boards of education surrender their jurisdiction to a number of neighborhood or community governing boards.

---

46. Keith Goldhammer et al., *Issues and Problems in Contemporary Educational Administration* (Eugene, Ore.: Center for the Advanced Study of Educational Administration, University of Oregon, 1967).

47. George H. Gallup, "Seventh Annual Gallup Poll of Public Attitudes Toward Education," *Phi Delta Kappan,* vol. 57, no. 4 (December 1975), pp. 227–241.

48. Ibid.

Community control proposals have come from and are attractive to citizens who believe the schools have not served them well and who feel they cannot achieve redress of their grievances through existing structures. Through community control, many persons seek a means of holding school personnel accountable for educational outcomes. By the 1970s, school reformers were urging expanded community or citizen control for all public schools on the premise that traditional governance structures had led to professional dominance. For example, a Commission on Educational Governance of the National Committee for Citizens in Education recommended that a school council be elected for each school and ". . . share authority and responsibility for curriculum, school program budgeting, school progress reports, and personnel evaluations."[49]

It is clear that community or citizen control proposals challenge more than the traditional prerogatives of school boards. Also under fire are the ability of teacher organizations to negotiate system-wide contracts, administrative procedures for making many kinds of operating decisions including the assignment of personnel and the selection of instructional materials, and procedures for evaluating personnel and programs.

A third contemporary issue deals with what the schools should teach. This question has been controversial for centuries, and there is no reason to predict its final resolution. The specifics of the issue change rather frequently. Prominent at the present time are questions about whether or not the schools should make special efforts to teach the culture and history of minority groups and, if so, to whom and how. Another controversial issue, mentioned above, is what—if anything—the schools should do about teaching sex education. In a more general sense, there has been considerable disagreement about the role of the school in combating social problems. The most visible controversy has been related to desegregation proposals. However, matters such as free lunches or dental examinations, placement of special remedial programs in some schools but not others, and even matters related to the dress and grooming of students have touched off public debates of major proportion.

A fourth issue deals with how schools should be financed. There are two general dimensions to the problem. One is determining how the funds available to schools should be allocated. If *X* dollars are available to a school system in a given year, what part should be allocated to teacher salaries, introduction of new programs, instructional materials, and other items? This dimension clearly overlaps the issues discussed above inasmuch as controversies about who should make what decisions at what levels about what programs can be defined operationally as questions of resource allocation. As discussed here, these are questions about allocations within particular schools or school districts.

The second dimension of the finance problem relates to the

49. National Committee for Citizens in Education, *Public Testimony on Public Schools* (Berkeley, Calif.: McCutchan Publishing Corp., 1975), p. 221.

sources of revenue available to individual school districts and consequent inequalities of expenditure among them. Levels of expenditure vary widely among school districts, and the level of financial support available to school districts influences the range of educational opportunities available to students in the respective districts.[50]

Public schools depend upon local, state, and federal governments as sources of revenue. Although federal aid has been present for some time variation exists in the levels at which the respective states aid local schools and schools in most states have depended primarily upon local revenues in the past. Table 3–3 shows there has been little change in this situation during the past two decades.

TABLE 3–3 Percent of Total School Revenues Received Annually from Various Government Sources

	GOVERNMENT LEVEL		
YEAR	*FEDERAL (%)*	*STATE (%)*	*LOCAL (%)*
1940	1.8	30.3	68.0
1950	2.9	39.8	57.3
1960	4.4	39.1	56.5
1970	8.0	39.9	52.1

Source: U.S. Bureau of the Census. *Statistical Abstract of the United States* (Washington, D.C.: U.S. Government Printing Office, 1969), 90th ed., p. 115 and 96th ed. p. 132.

The primary source of local school revenues is the property tax. Much of the variation among local district expenditures therefore can be attributed to differences in the amount of taxable property per pupil in given school districts and the level of tax rates, respectively.

The constitutionality of state plans which allow such variations has been challenged in the courts. Although the U.S. Supreme Court held that a state plan for financing education which permits such inequities is not unconstitutional, the court also noted the need for state school finance reform and urged that state legislatures take such steps.[51] Moreover, a series of efforts in state courts has produced decisions which hold that state plans of this type violate state constitutional guarantees to education and therefore must be modified.[52] Thus it would appear that basic changes in school financing arrangements may be forthcoming.

The likelihood of such change illustrates the nature of the policy process. This process may be summarized in terms of four steps: Basic

50. See, for example, J. Alan Thomas, *School Finance in Michigan* (Lansing, Mich.: State Department of Education, 1968).

51. *San Antonio Independent School District* v. *Rodriguez*, 411 U.S. 1 (1973).

52. See, for example, *Robinson* v. *Cahill*, 62 N.J. 473 (1973).

forces, Antecedent Movements, Political Action, and Formal Enactment.[53] The impetus for it can be traced to the concerns for equality which emerged during the middle of this century. Important antecedent movements included both the civil rights movement and an emergent tendency on the part of citizens to pursue their rights through the courts. In addition, foundations provided support for studies which documented the extent of fiscal inequities among school districts within particular states. Political action has included efforts by various educational and other groups to file and defend suits related to the issue. In response, some state legislatures have considered adopting new programs of school support. Formal enactment in these instances will come from both courts and legislatures and will have profound effects upon subsequent policy decisions made in local school districts.

SUGGESTED ACTIVITIES

1. Examine the 1950, 1960, and 1970 census figures for your school district or attendance areas. What changes have occurred, and what are their implications for schooling?
2. Spend a day visiting a school and social agencies in a neighborhood different from your own. How are neighborhood characteristics reflected in these institutions?
3. Determine what federal assistance programs are in operation in your school district.
4. Interview a principal or superintendent about the processes he employs to be sensitive to community expectations.
5. Compare two or more contracts or professional negotiations agreements developed in the same school district over a period of time. What do these documents indicate about teacher participation in district affairs?

SELECTED READINGS

Berke, Joel S. and Kirst, Michael W. *Federal Aid to Education: Who Benefits, Who Governs?* Lexington, Mass., Lexington Books, D.C. Heath and Co., 1972.

Burkhead, Jess. *Public School Finance: Economics and Politics.* Syracuse, N.Y.: Syracuse University Press, 1964.

Campbell, Roald F., and Bunnell, Robert A., eds. *Nationalizing Influences on Secondary*

53. This view of the policy process is discussed in Roald F. Campbell, "Process of Policy Making Within Structures of Educational Government as Viewed by the Educator." M. W. P. McClure and Van Miller, eds., *Government of Public Education for Adequate Policy Making* (Urbana, Ill.: Bureau of Educational Research, University of Illinois, 1960), pp. 59–76.

Education. Chicago: Midwest Administration Center, University of Chicago, 1963.

——— and Layton, Donald H. *Policy Making for American Education.* Chicago: The Midwest Administration Center, 1969.

——— and Mazzoni, Tim L., Jr. *State Policy Making for the Public Schools.* Berkeley, Calif.: McCutchan Publishing Corp., 1976.

———, et al. *The Organization and Control of American Schools,* 3rd ed. Columbus, Ohio: Charles E. Merrill Books, 1975.

Crain, Robert L. *The Politics of School Desegregation.* Chicago: Aldine Publishing Co., 1968.

Goldhammer, Keith, et al. *Issues and Problems in Contemporary Educational Administration.* Eugene, Oregon: Center for the Advanced Study of Educational Administration, 1967.

Havighurst, Robert J., ed. *Metropolitanism: Its Challenge to Education.* Sixty-seventh Yearbook, Part I, National Society for the Study of Education. Chicago: University of Chicago Press, 1968.

Kirst, Michael W., ed. *The Politics of Education at the Local, State, and Federal Levels.* Berkeley, Calif.: McCutchan Publishing Corp., 1970.

National Committee for Citizens in Education, *Public Testimony on Public Schools.* Berkeley, Calif.: McCutchan Publishing Corp., 1975.

Rosenthal, Alan. *Pedagogues and Power: Teacher Groups in School Politics.* Syracuse, N.Y.: Syracuse University Press, 1969.

Skolnick, Jerome A. *The Politics of Protest: Violent Aspects of Protest and Confrontation.* Washington, D.C.: U.S. Government Printing Office, 1969. Also available from Simon and Schuster and Ballantine Books, New York.

Thompson, John Thomas. *Policy Making in American Education.* Englewood Cliffs, N.J.: Prentice Hall, Inc., 1976.

Ziegler, L. Harmon, and Jennings, M. Kent. *Governing American Schools: Political Interaction in Local School Districts.* North Scituate, Mass.: Duxbury Press, 1974.

4

DEVELOPMENT AND MEANING OF ADMINISTRATION

In chapter 1, we were confronted with some brief exposures to the reality of administration. In chapter 2, we noted certain historical developments that appear to have had relevance to the evolution of schools and to the emergence of the function of administration in those schools and school systems. In chapter 3, we considered some characteristics of the current setting in which administration operates. We shall now examine more explicitly the development and meaning of administration—first in its general sense and, second, in its application to education. We shall conclude this chapter by suggesting the place and limitations of theory in administration and by indicating specific ways in which administration will be viewed in chapters 5 through 8.

THE DEVELOPMENT OF ADMINISTRATION

Educational administration, like many other branches of administration, has suffered from too much emphasis on the adjective and too little on the noun. To understand educational administration, one must acquire some sense of the development of administration generally. This may be found in treatises on public administration, business management, industrial psychology, military leadership, and in other writings. Analysis in all of these settings has dealt with mobilizing the efforts of a number of people toward the achievement of a common goal.

Activating members of a group toward a common objective is as old as history itself. Whether we look at the public regulation of the waterways in ancient Egypt, the duties of the magistrates in the far-flung Roman Empire, or the efficient use of resources in the German states more than 200 years ago—growing largely from the work of the Cameralists—the significance of administration becomes clear. While other sources must be consulted for a history of administration,[1] we would mention that both Alexander Hamilton and Woodrow Wilson made contributions to the understanding and practice of the field.

Some aspects of the conflict between Hamilton and Jefferson—both members of Washington's cabinet—are well known. It may not be as fully appreciated that Hamilton became the chief Federalist philosopher and perhaps its most brilliant practitioner. The Federalists must be credited with creating an administrative system from practically nothing. White explains that the system they created included an independent chief executive, a plan of effective delegation by the chief executive to the department heads, an administrative organization separate from the several states, canons of personal integrity on the part of public officers, and approval of the right of public criticism.[2]

This centralization of power and responsibility was often opposed by Jefferson, who was disposed to place confidence in legislative as opposed to executive action, and who emphasized states' rights more than federal responsibility. Hamilton, however, continued to stress the need for an energetic executive, and the customs service in his own department was perhaps the best example of his ideal of government. This page in our history serves to highlight some of the persistent issues found in administration.

In 1887 Wilson attempted to distinguish between politics and administration. He said:

> . . . administration lies outside the proper sphere of politics. Administrative questions are not political questions. Although politics sets the tasks for administration, it should not be suffered to manipulate its offices.[3]

What appears to be a clear differentiation between policy and administration is probably intended for quite another purpose. The cue is in Wilson's last sentence; he was greatly concerned lest special interest groups manipulate public officeholders and thus prevent them from serving the general

---

1. For example, see chapter 4 in Albert Lepawsky, *Administration* (New York: Alfred A. Knopf, 1949).
2. Leonard D. White, *The Federalists* (New York: The Macmillan Co., 1948), p. 512.
3. Woodrow Wilson, "The Study of Administration," *Political Science Quarterly* 41 (December 1941), p. 494. Reprinted from 1887 issue.

welfare. Even so, the relationship between policy and administration was raised, and the question is still being vigorously debated.

RECENT HISTORICAL EMPHASES

Let us turn from this brief exploration of the emergence of the concept of administration and look more specifically at some of the recent historical emphases in administration. In each case, we shall deal with a major emphasis by citing the work of a few contributors. These contributors were in reality students of administration; they described or rationalized what was being said about administration and, at least to some extent, what was being practiced in administration. Some of them were also practicing administrators themselves, and all of them had many direct relationships with practitioners.

Job analysis. The first approach to administration was that of job analysis. We shall note the work of two major contributors to this approach. Frederick Taylor, often called the father of the scientific management movement, was born in 1856. He studied in France, Germany, and Italy in his youth, and later earned an M.E. degree at Stevens Institute. From 1878 to 1889, he was employed by the Midvale Steel Company; first as a laborer, then as clerk, machinist, foreman, chief draftsman, and finally chief engineer. Taylor noticed that workers were in charge of both planning and performing their jobs, a situation that led, he thought, to much waste and inefficiency. His experience at all levels of industry led him to formulate his principles, which were condensed in *The Principles of Scientific Management,* published in 1911.[4]

His essential points have been summarized by Villers as follows:

1. *Time-study principle.* All productive effort should be measured by accurate time study and a standard time established for all work done in the shop.
2. *Piece-rate principle.* Wages should be proportional to output and their rates based on the standards determined by time study. As a corollary, a worker should be given the highest grade of work of which his is capable.
3. *Separation-of-planning-from-performance principle.* Management should take over from the workers the responsibility for planning the work and making the performance physically possible. Planning should be based on time studies and other data related to production, which are scientifically determined and systematically classified; it

4. This and other works appear in Frederick W. Taylor, *Scientific Management* (New York: Harper & Brothers, 1947).

should be facilitated by standardization of tools, implements, and methods.

4. *Scientific-methods-of-work principle.* Management should take over from the workers the responsibility for their methods of work, determine scientifically the best methods, and train the workers accordingly.
5. *Managerial-control principle.* Managers should be trained and taught to apply scientific principles of management and control (such as management by exception and comparison with valid standards).
6. *Functional-management principle.* The strict application of military principles should be reconsidered and the industrial organization should be so designed that it best serves the purpose of improving the co-ordination of activities among the various specialists.[5]

Taylor and other spokesmen of the scientific management movement were influential in seeing many of their principles applied to such firms as the Midland Steel Company, Bethlehem Steel Company, Santa Fe Railway, and Acme Wire Company. Labor, on the other hand, resisted time and motion studies, and other activities which were perceived as treating men as though they were machines. The whole movement became the object of an investigation by the Social Committee of the House of Representatives in 1912. Following extended hearings, Congress attached a rider to the military appropriations bill prohibiting the use of such funds for time and motion studies.

From the perspective of our day, we find that Taylor took a narrow view of management, and that, moreover, he tended to ignore the psychological or personal aspects of mobilizing human effort. At the same time, he did demonstrate that many jobs could be done more efficiently. Even more important, his work stands as a monument to the concept that management can be studied scientifically. No aspect of administration has remained immune to this idea.

Henri Fayol was another major contributor to the job analysis approach to administration. He was born in 1841 of a family of the French *petite bourgeoisie.* At the age of nineteen, he graduated from the national School of Mines at St. Etienne. In a sense, he had four careers: twelve years as a mining engineer, sixteen years as a geologist, thirty years as the very able managing director of a large metallurgical firm, and seven years—after retirement at age seventy-seven—as a teacher of administration. In the fourth period, he undertook two main tasks: the first was the formation of a Centre of Administrative Studies; the second was an effort to persuade the French government to pay some attention to the principles of administration.

Although Fayol wrote his book, *Administration Industrielle et Gén-*

5. Raymond Villers, *Dynamic Management in Industry* (Englewood Cliffs, N.J.: Prentice-Hall, 1960), p. 29.

érale, in 1916, it did not appear in an English translation until 1929, and it was not made generally available in the United States until 1949.[6] Containing the first two parts of the eventual treatise Fayol planned to write, it describes the necessity and the possibility of teaching the principles and elements of management. The now famous elements were planning, organizing, command, coordination, and control.

In the early stages of the popularization of Fayol's work, attempts were made by some to represent his approach as antithetical to that of Taylor. But at the Second International Congress held at Brussels in 1925, Fayol himself made clear that such interpretations were false. Actually, both men applied the scientific method. Taylor worked primarily at the operative level, or the bottom of the hierarchal structure, while Fayol began with the managing director at the top of the hierarchy. The work of Fayol has been reflected in the thinking and writing of Gulick, Urwick, Sears, and other students of administration. A more detailed treatment of this approach to administration will be found in chapter 6.

Both Taylor and Fayol were concerned with industry; both believed that the processes involved in production could be analyzed and studied scientifically. While Taylor concentrated on the worker and Fayol on the manager, both had as an ultimate objective the increased efficiency of industry. To be sure, in his later years Fayol extended the application of his administrative principles to government as well as to industry. Even so, both men tended to stress organizational processes and to ignore individuals as such. The time was ripe for a new emphasis, and Mary Parker Follett helped to supply it.

Human relations. Human relations constituted the second major approach to administration. Again the work of two major contributors will be noted. Mary Parker Follett was born in 1868. She graduated from Radcliffe College, where she followed a course devoted to economics, government, and philosophy. Throughout her life, she worked to help bring about a better-ordered society in which the individual might live a more satisfying life. This motivation was expressed when she served on the Boston Committee on the Extended Use of School Buildings from 1909 to 1911, in the help she gave to establish the Department of Vocational Guidance in Boston in 1912, in her service on the Massachusetts Minimum Wage Board for many years, and in her great interest in the League of Nations.

Her book, *Creative Experience,*[7] has been characterized by Metcalf and Urwick as follows:

> . . . mainly psychological in interest and content, [it] marks a definite advance both in the crystallization of thought and in style and phraseology. Its thesis is the reciprocal character—the

6. Henri Fayol, *General and Industrial Management* (London: Sir Isaac Pitman & Sons, 1949).

7. Mary Parker Follett, *Creative Experience* (New York: Longmans, Green, 1924).

> interpenetration—of all psychological phenomena, from the simplest to the most complex. Human relationships—the ways and work of society and of industry—are at their best when difference is solved through conference and cooperation, when the parties at interest (1) evoke each other's latent ideas based upon the facts of the situation, (2) come to see each other's viewpoints and to understand each other better, and (3) integrate those viewpoints and become united in the pursuit of their common goal.[8]

Follett contended that the fundamental problem of any enterprise, whether it be local government, national government, a business organization, or an educational system, is the building and maintenance of dynamic, yet harmonious, human relationships. She tended to reduce her principles of organization to four in number, all aspects of what she termed *coordination.* The principles were:

1. Coordination by direct contact of the responsible people concerned.
2. Coordination in the early stages.
3. Coordination as the reciprocal relating of all factors in the situation.
4. Coordination as a continuing process.[9]

Mary Parker Follett might be characterized as a social philosopher with deep psychological insights. She came onto the scene when the process and organizational aspects of administration had been emphasized to the exclusion, perhaps, of the values to be cherished for society and for the most adequate development of individuals in that society. As an academician Miss Follett made a contribution in both the United States and England; but she was also a woman of action. She found much stimulation in the observation of governmental and industrial organizations, and she was welcomed as a consultant by many such enterprises.

While Mary Parker Follett became the first great exponent of the aspect of human relations in administration, it remained for Elton Mayo and his colleagues to supply empirical data in support of such a view. Mayo was born in Adelaide, Australia, in 1880, and received A.B. and M.A. degrees from the University of Adelaide. For twenty years, he served as the senior professor in the Department of Industrial Research of the Harvard Business School. From 1923 to 1932, he and his associates were connected with the now famous experiments done at the Hawthorne plant of the Western Electric Company, near Chicago.

8. Henry C. Metcalf and L. Urwick, eds., *Dynamic Administration* (New York: Harper & Brothers, 1942), p. 14. The collected papers of Mary Parker Follett with an introduction by the editors.

9. Ibid., p. 297.

Industry had long assumed that wages and physical working conditions were the chief factors in employee motivation. The first experiment at Hawthorne, 1923–26, was quite simply designed to test the effect of one of these physical conditions—illumination—on worker production. It was found that illumination was not significantly related to production. In the true scientific spirit, the results of the experiment were accepted as proof that the basic assumption needed reconsideration.

A second inquiry was conducted to explore the problem more fully. A group of six girl operatives was selected for study to determine what factors might be related to their job productivity. It was found that whatever factors were changed—whether rest periods, length of day, or methods of payment—and whatever way they were changed, even if the change meant returning to the original conditions, production continued to increase. Moreover, the girls were more and more satisfied with their jobs, and their attendance continued to show greater regularity. Findings of this nature were secured almost without exception over a five-year period of meticulous experimentation between 1927 and 1932.

Mayo has explained the findings as follows:

> . . . What the Company actually did for the group was to reconstruct entirely its whole industrial situation.
>
> . . . the consequence was that there was a period during which the individual workers and the group had to re-adapt themselves to a new industrial milieu, a milieu in which their own self-determination and their social well-being ranked first, and the work was incidental.
>
> . . . The Western Electric experiment was primarily directed not to the external condition but to the inner organization. By strengthening the "temperamental" inner equilibrium of the workers, the Company enabled them to achieve a mental "steady state" which offered a high resistance to a variety of external conditions.[10]

Clearly, this and similar experiments demonstrated that economic and mechanistic approaches to human relations in industry were inadequate. While wages and working conditions are important to the worker, they rank second to what Mayo called "a method of living in a social relationship." Apparently, the girls in the Hawthorne experiment had gained a sense of playing an important part in a project instead of being mere cogs in a large productive enterprise.

Mayo's work has been subjected to much examination, and some students find two major biases in his experiments.[11] He may have had a

10. Elton Mayo, *The Human Problems of an Industrial Civilization* (Boston: Graduate School of Business Administration, Harvard University, 1946), pp. 73, 75.

11. See Delbert C. Miller and William H. Form, *Industrial Sociology,* 2nd ed. (New York: Harper & Brothers, 1964), pp. 78–83.

management bias, since he was employed by business to help business solve its problems. He may also have had a clinical bias, in that he began with observation and not with theory. Apparently, Mayo did have some disdain for theory and had more faith in empiricism. Regardless of these criticisms, however, one must recognize that through long and meticulous experimentation Mayo and his associates collected a large body of data that make it clear that what goes on inside the worker is even more significant for production than what goes on outside.

Were one to accept the work of Follett and Mayo uncritically, he might assume that adequate human relations is the sum total of administration. Indeed, the so-called "democratic" emphasis in administration of the 1940s and 50s may have sprung from the work of these contributors or, more likely, the inadequate interpretations of some of their disciples. Fortunately, Chester Barnard had turned his great talent to the examination of administration.

Behavioral science and administration. Chester Barnard appears to have been the first to relate administration to the behavioral sciences. Born in 1886, Barnard attended Harvard College from 1906 to 1909. He served for many years as the president of the New Jersey Bell Telephone Company and for four years as president of the Rockefeller Foundation. During this time he demonstrated an unusual capacity to deal with theoretical abstractions and with practical problems of management. He found himself consulting with clergymen, military men, government officials, university officials, and leaders of widely diversified businesses on problems of organization.

In 1937, he prepared eight lectures for the Lowell Institute in Boston. These lectures, revised and expanded, became his very important book, *The Functions of the Executive.*[12] Barnard himself suggests that the book has two parts: ". . . an exposition of a theory of co-operation and organization" and "a study of the functions . . . of executives in formal organizations." The book emphasizes the universal character of formal organizations and stresses the need for a theory to explain their behavior.

The development of an appropriate theory, Barnard suggested, has been retarded because of a misconception about the nature of authority, a misconception growing out of interpretations of the church, and because of the unwarranted emphasis given to the economic motivation of man. He saw an organization as a complex social organism—an organism whose peripheral aspects had been dealt with by the various social sciences, but whose core had never been analyzed. His own work did much to promote analyses of organizations as such.

A formal organization, Barnard maintained, is

12. Chester I. Barnard, *The Functions of the Executive* (Cambridge, Mass.: Harvard University Press, 1938).

> . . . an impersonal system of co-ordinated human efforts; always there is purpose as the co-ordinating and unifying principle; always there is the indispensable ability to communicate, always the necessity of personal willingness, and for effectiveness and efficiency in maintaining the integrity of purpose and the continuity of contributions.[13]

While Barnard dealt mainly with formal organizations, he also pointed out that in each formal organization there are informal organizations. He characterized informal organization as the contacts or interactions of people without a specific conscious joint purpose. While these organizations may not be governed by joint purposes, such informal interactions do change the experience, knowledge, attitudes, and emotions of the people affected. Since informal organization may perform important roles in a formal organization by way of communication and even in terms of helping build self-respect in organization members, Barnard thought that informal organization could not be ignored.

One of Barnard's major contributions was the concept of effectiveness and efficiency. Effectiveness is system oriented and has to do with the achievement of the organization goals. Efficiency, on the other hand, is person oriented and has to do with the feelings of satisfaction a worker derives from membership in an organization. For the first time, the interrelationship of organization achievement and individual satisfaction was noted. This conception did much to put the work of Taylor and Fayol, who had concentrated on organization achievement, and Follett and Mayo, who had tended to emphasize individual satisfaction, in appropriate perspective.

A second contributor to the science of administration was Herbert A. Simon. Simon was born in 1916 and received A.B. and Ph.D. degrees from the University of Chicago. His graduate work was in political science and he became particularly interested in public administration. His Ph.D. dissertation became the basis for *Administrative Behavior,*[14] the book that established him as a scholar in the field. Simon has spent much of his professional career at Carnegie Institute of Technology as a professor of administration.

Simon contended that he wrote *Administrative Behavior* in an attempt to develop a set of tools—a set of concepts and a vocabulary—suitable for describing an organization. He did give meaning to such terms as administrative behavior, decision making, organization, rational behavior, and many others. He relied not only on political science to develop his concepts, but on economics, psychology, and sociology as well. In a very real sense he used the behavioral sciences to explain organizations and the behavior of people in them. In a number of books and journal articles, Simon has continued to provide additional insight into the field of administration.

13. Ibid., pp. 94–95.
14. Herbert A. Simon, *Administrative Behavior* (New York: The Macmillan Co., 1945).

Following Barnard and Simon, a great many behavioral scientists have turned their attention to the study of organizations. In a review of much recent work having to do with organizational models, particularly as they apply to education, Corwin has classified organization analyses in broad categories as rational versus natural systems, open versus closed models, and derivative models. He suggests that "social scientists are all groping for ways to deal simultaneously with whole organizations, their *complex* components, and their environments."[15]

Roughly speaking, the three periods in the development of administration might be established as follows: job analysis, 1910–1930; human relations, 1930–1950; and behavioral science, 1950–1970. This is not to suggest that we have seen the last of any of these approaches. Actually, we have a new birth of efficiency in such a movement as program budgeting. As well, the human relations approach has been given new emphasis in such formulations as organizational development and sensitivity training. Nor do we suggest that the application of the social sciences to administration has come to an end. We seem to be looking toward more of the social sciences than ever before. Whereas social psychology provided many initial insights, we are now employing political science and economics as sources of basic concepts. It seems that we are coming to recognize that administrative behavior is a complex phenomena; perhaps no single approach will provide us with adequate explanation. A number of these newer approaches use the word "systems" to capture their central thrust. The systems approach is treated in chapter 8.

THE DEVELOPMENT OF EDUCATIONAL ADMINISTRATION

We have examined some of the major developments in the general field of administration. We shall turn now to developments in educational administration.

EARLY SCHOOL ADMINISTRATION

It seems appropriate to recall that for most of our history the organization and management of schools has been a function of laymen and not of

15. Ronald G. Corwin, "Models of Educational Organizations." In Fred N. Kerlinger and John B. Carroll, eds., *Review of Research in Education* 2 (Itaska, Illinois: Peacock Publishers, 1974), p. 286.

professional administrators. Suzzalo has traced, with consderable care, the supervision of the schools in Massachusetts.[16] For almost two hundred years, the school committee was, in one way or another, made up of the town selectmen. It was 1827 before school government was differentiated from general government, and it was some years later before the lay school committee or board of education was ready to employ a school administrator. Thus school administration did not evolve as a field of practce until the latter part of the nineteenth century, nor become a field of study until the twentieth century.

While much of our discussion above has dealt with major concepts and ideas about administration, any consideration of the development of educational administration must deal chiefly with its practice. The development of concepts about educational administration and the testing of those concepts empirically is at best a relatively new and unexplored field.

State and county school administration have both played important parts in the development of educational administration in America, but the major surge has been at the local level, chiefly in the growth of the school superintendency and of the school principalship. This phenomenon is largely a result of the decentralization of education in this country. The usual connotation of school administration to this day is local school administration. Any other meaning requires an adjective such as state school administration or county school administration.

Leadership in local school administration came first in our cities. Gradually, as multiple school districts within a single city were merged, the board of education found itself in need of a full-time executive. The first cities to establish the office of the superintendent of schools were Buffalo and Louisville in 1837, and St. Louis and Providence in 1839.[17] The practice soon spread throughout the country. Although a number of cities were unsuccessful in their experimentation with the office and abolished it for a while, they eventually returned to it as the best solution to meet the need for district-wide administration. Duties varied from city to city, with some stressing the examining and visiting function while others placed emphasis on business and clerical functions.

In the beginning, the variations in the duties to be performed, the uncertainty regarding the competence needed for the position, and the lack of any specific preparation for it made it difficult to secure people who could serve satisfactorily. Adams spoke disparagingly of the early superintendent, saying that "the ordinary superintendent is apt to be a grammar school teacher run to seed, or some retired clergyman or local politician

16. Henry Suzzalo, *The Rise of Local School Supervision in Massachusetts.* Teachers College Contribution No. 1 (New York: Teachers College, Columbia University, 1906).

17. Theodore Lee Reller, *The Development of the City Superintendency of Schools in the United States* (Philadelphia: published by the author, 1935), p. 7.

out of a job."[18] Northend, writing of the situation in Connecticut, described the candidates for the position as follows:

> Lawyers, whose business could not "wane" because it never "waxed"; doctors, whose patients were not troublesomely numerous; clergymen, afflicted with bronchitis or some other malady, or not overburdened with hearers; office seekers of various kinds and all sorts of "do nothings" all become suddenly and wonderfully impressed with the importance of common schools, accompanied by a sort of feeling that in themselves was the only power for truly elevating those schools.[19]

But this was not the general evaluation of the superintendency, or the position would not have survived. The outstanding contributions of some of the early superintendents—such as Gove of Denver, Jones of Cleveland, Philbrick of Boston, and Harris of St. Louis—are recorded as examples of the sort of leadership that was being sought for the schools. However, the controversy over the need for the position and the brilliance of a few people holding the office had caused a thorough examination and study of the superintendency.

The growth of cities not only created populous school districts, but also populous attendance areas for single schools. The increased size of schools, in conjunction with the new practice of classifying pupils by grades, led to the need for an executive or principal for each school building. This official was first called a principal teacher, and we learn that Cincinnati had designated principal teachers for each school within that city as early as 1838. Quincy School in Boston in 1847, however, was probably the first school to have a full-time executive or supervising principal.[20] St. Louis reported in 1859 that all schools of that city had been placed in charge of full-time administrators. This practice is now common in many schools over the country.

To begin with, the work of the principal—particularly while he was still the principal teacher—was largely clerical in nature. Reports on enrollment and attendance, and other matters, were needed in the central office. With the increase in enrollments, pupils had to be classified—by grade and otherwise—and assigned to teachers and rooms. As time went on, instruction, particularly in the upper grades, was departmentalized. These and other developments tended to highlight the organization and management functions of the principal. In recent decades, these clerical and management functions of the principal have received less stress, and

18. Charles Francis Adams, quoted in J. D. Philbrick, "Which Is the True Ideal?" *Education* 1 (January 1881), pp. 300–302.

19. *Connecticut Common School Journal and Annals of Education* 8 (August 1960).

20. Paul R. Pierce, *The Origin and Development of the School Principalship* (Chicago: University of Chicago Press, 1934).

his instructional leadership role more. With the current emphasis on decentralization, the place of the principal in community relationships is under scrutiny.

While educational administration has tended to focus on the superintendent of schools as the chief executive officer of the school system and on the principal as the executive officer of a single school within a school system, it should be clear, as will be made explicit in chapter 9, that there are many other administrative positions in education. All of these administrative personnel have unique and complementary roles to perform.

FEW SCHOLARS

We can find in the history of American education a number of notable administrators. On the other hand, there are relatively few notable scholars of administration. Yet the contributions of such men as Cubberley of Stanford, Strayer of Columbia, Reavis of Chicago, Hart of California, and Reeder of Ohio State should not be overlooked. These and a number of other men had a hand in shaping the organization and management of public education in this country. Each of these men, moreover, had hundreds of students who became school administrators and occupied major administrative posts at all levels of education.

Many of these early professors of educational administration approached school administration through the school survey. The surveys of Boise, Idaho, in 1910, and of Montclair, New Jersey, and Baltimore, Maryland, in 1911 appear to be the first.[21] Such surveys provided some of the first literature in educational administration; and indeed, some of the early ones are still very useful reading.

Since the chief purpose of the survey, however, was to improve practice, the approach often dealt with what *ought* to be, in place of determining basic relationships. The surveys tended to reflect the value judgments of the surveyors and, as such, often proved most useful in pointing the way to improved practice. At the same time, such surveys were not designed to deal with basic concepts or to test such concepts in an empirical setting.

More than anything else, these early students of educational administration approached the field from the standpoint of job analysis. They observed administrators at work, noted the tasks they were required to perform, and then suggested how these tasks might be performed more effectively. Consciously or unconsciously, perhaps both, this attitude was a reflection of the work Taylor was doing in scientific management. In 1913,

---

21. Dan H. Cooper, "School Surveys," *Encyclopedia of Educational Research* (New York: The Macmillan Co., 1960), pp. 1211–1216.

Bobbitt devoted a long article to principles of management and their applications, as he saw them, in school systems.[22]

The faithful application of Taylor's principles to school operation is illustrated in the following statement from Bobbitt:

> The primary functions of educational directors and supervisors, as relating to methods, are therefore: first, the discovery of the best methods of procedure in the performance of any particular educational task; and second, the giving of these discovered best methods over to the teachers for their guidance in securing a maximum product. Since so few methods, demonstrably the best, have yet been discovered with entire certainty, it is impossible yet to devote any very large amount of time to the function of distribution of this information to the teachers. This leaves the major work at the present moment in the realm of discovery of best methods, it would appear.[23]

The early textbooks in educational administration written by Cubberley, Strayer, Reeder, and others may not have followed Taylor as faithfully as did Bobbitt, but their approach was essentially that of job analysis. Callahan[24] has made a penetrating analysis of how the schools, particularly during the period from 1910 to 1930, responded to the cult of efficiency that appeared to characterize the business ideology, and perhaps the entire American culture, of that time.

A somewhat similar approach or theory of educational administration is found in the work of Sears—for many years a professor at Stanford University. He was familiar with the work of Fayol, Gulick, Urwick, and other students of public administration. In a notable book, he attempted to adapt the administrative process—first suggested by Fayol—to the administration of the public schools.[25] Sears saw the process as including the following activities: planning, organization, direction, coordination, and control. After developing each aspect of the process, he related the whole to such concepts as authority, delegation, and policy-making. Further treatment of the process will be given in chapter 6.

While Sears appears to have been one of the early scholars of educational administration, his contribution created no great stir—a lack of general recognition that may be due to a number of circumstances. First, since Sears' major treatment of the administrative process appeared after

---

22. Franklin Bobbitt, "Some General Principles of Management Applied to the Problems of City School Systems," *The Supervision of City Schools,* Twelfth Yearbook of the National Society for the Study of Education, Part I (Chicago: University of Chicago Press, 1913), pp. 7–96.

23. Ibid., p. 53.

24. Raymond E. Callahan, *Education and the Cult of Efficiency* (Chicago: University of Chicago Press, 1962).

25. Jesse B. Sears, *The Nature of the Administrative Process* (New York: McGraw-Hill, 1950).

his retirement, he had little opportunity to work directly with other students of administration. Second, and perhaps more significant, only in recent years have professors and some practitioners of educational administration become interested in theoretical approaches to the field. Third, the process is a useful concept in administration, but it has not stimulated the formulation of many hypotheses to be tested.

Taylor's concept of scientific management in industry, we have seen, had a counterpart in education given its clearest expression by Bobbitt; likewise the formulation of Fayol became a major inspiration to Sears, who adapted it to educational administration. In both cases there was an attempt at job analysis—Bobbitt concentrating on the work of the teacher and supervisor, Sears concentrating on the work of the administrator. The emphasis on human relations supplied by Follett and Mayo has also influenced educational administration. This emphasis was reflected in the "democratic administration" movement. Democratic administration had many exponents,[26] but for the most part they dealt in hortatory expositions and did little to give greater insight into the realities of school organizations and their operation. The more recent emphasis on behavioral sciences and administration, reflecting the work of Barnard and others, likewise has been applied directly to educational administration, as can be noted in a yearbook of the National Society for the Study of Education.[27]

SOME RECENT DEVELOPMENTS

Scholarship in educational administration, generally meager during the first part of the present century, seems to be getting some genuine bolstering in the last two or three decades. A number of events have been part of this dramatic development.

In 1947, the first meeting of a group later to be known as the National Conference of Professors of Educational Administrators was held at Endicott, New York. This meeting was largely the idea of, and was made possible through the influence of, Walter D. Cocking. The succeeding annual meetings of NCPEA have permitted those who teach educational administration to become acquainted with each other, have encouraged an examination of what is known in the field, and have helped shape the other events noted here.

Another event of great importance to educational administration was the Cooperative Program in Educational Administration underwritten, to a large extent, by the W. K. Kellogg Foundation. From its beginning in 1950 until most projects were closed out about a decade later, Kellogg

26. For instance, see G. Robert Koopman et al., *Democracy in School Administration* (New York: Appleton-Century-Crofts, 1943).

27. National Society for the Study of Education, *Behavioral Science and Educational Administration,* Sixty-Third Yearbook, Part II (Chicago: University of Chicago Press, 1964).

spent about $7 million on the program. This money was supplemented by the funds of many universities, state departments of education, and local school districts. Eight Kellogg centers were established in the United States and one in Canada; each of them was encouraged to develop a regional program devoted to the improvement of educational administration.

Initially, CPEA placed more emphasis on the improved practice of administration than on its study. It soon became apparent, however, that improved practice was dependent, in part, upon more knowledge about administration. Some participants in the CPEA program found substantial stimulation in studies done in public and business administration, and in the concepts and research findings of the social sciences. Thus, in the closing period of CPEA, theory and research in educational administration emerged as the most important concern in several of the centers.[28]

One of the CPEA centers, Teachers College at Columbia University, proposed that the major universities with programs in educational administration form an organization for the purpose of continuing the work thus started. Hence, in 1956, representatives from thirty-three universities organized the University Council for Educational Administration. At first the Council was located at Columbia University; in 1959, UCEA was incorporated under the laws of Ohio and moved to the campus of The Ohio State University. The W. K. Kellogg Foundation made substantial initial and subsequent grants to UCEA to help the new organization get established.

UCEA has three major purposes:

1. To improve the pre-service and in-service training of school administrators.
2. To stimulate and produce research in educational administration.
3. To disseminate materials growing out of research and training practices.

Among its activities, UCEA has organized career seminars for professors of educational administration, participated in large-scale research projects, set up a number of task forces on particular problems in administration, sought foundation and government assistance for fellowships and other aspects of training programs, alerted member institutions to possible sources of support for research and training projects in administration, and published a number of books and monographs growing out of its many activities.

From the beginning, UCEA has maintained a small but competent central office staff. Staff members have visited member institutions, have

28. More information about the influence of CPEA may be found in Hollis A. Moore, Jr., *Studies in School Administration* (Washington, D.C.: American Association of School Administrators, 1957); and Roald F. Campbell and Russell T. Gregg, eds., *Administrative Behavior in Education* (New York: Harper & Brothers, 1957).

ascertained much about the interests and strengths of those institutions, have helped bring professors of similar interests in different institutions into touch with each other, and have in general, served as an important communication link among some fifty universities now belonging to the organization. UCEA, like CPEA and NCPEA, continues to be useful in helping students of administration define the field and learn more about it.

Related to these efforts was the funding in 1964 by the U.S. Office of Education of a research and development center in educational administration at the University of Oregon, site of one of the earlier CPEA centers. In 1973 the Center for the Advanced Study of Educational Administration (CASEA) became the Research and Development Division of a larger organization, the Center for Educational Policy and Management, at the University of Oregon. The Research and Development Division is still funded largely by the National Institute of Education as is the ERIC Clearinghouse on Educational Management, also part of the larger unit at the University of Oregon. The nature and level of NIE funding in the past few years appears to have made it difficult for both of these units to operate as initially planned. Even so, CASEA and its recent successor have produced a number of papers, monographs, and books designed to increase knowledge about and improve the practice of educational administration and to improve its practice.[29]

Still other efforts to improve educational administration include programs supported by the Ford Foundation and the U.S. Office of Education. Ford support permitted seven universities to organize a Consortium for Educational Leadership to promote innovative programs for the training of administrators. Under the auspices of the U.S.O.E. the National Program for Educational Leadership was established and again a consortium of institutions, including universities, a state department of education, and a community college, was formed. A unique feature of this program was the effort to recruit proven leaders in fields outside of education and to provide them with a flexible training program in educational administration for a year or more prior to placement in leadership positions in education throughout the country.[30]

Recent developments in educational administration have affected both students and practitioners. Many who would teach administration are becoming more conscious of the place of theory and careful research in the field. Selection and training, moreover, are also receiving additional attention. Criteria for selection are being established, and selection procedures developed and evaluated. New approaches in instruction, such as the case method and the use of simulated material, are being used and

---

29. One of the more notable of these documents is R. A. Schmuck and P. J. Runkel, *Handbook of Organizational Development in Schools* (Palo Alto, Calif.: National Press Books, 1972).

30. Beverly Gifford, "A New Path to Educational Leadership," *American Education* (December 1971).

appraised. A recognition that good training and research programs are expensive is also dawning. But one can become too optimistic about the impact of scholarship on educational administration. In recent years, with schools subject to extensive criticism, many practicing administrators have found that scholarly formulations do not provide ready made answers to their problems. This realization, even though it be an unwarranted expectation, has caused some administrators and some of their professor-colleagues to reject scholarly approaches and to over romanticize the place of field experience as the source of wisdom and the place for training. Some of the recent experimental training programs also appear to rely more heavily on field experience than on contributions from theory and research. We do not deny the place of field experience in a training program for administrators; we do question that field experience alone, often overly burdened by the need to cope with the status quo, is adequate.

While the profession may debate the relative merits of research based and field based preparation programs for administrators, social conditions generally have deepened the concerns about the role and effectiveness of administrators. Even though decreases in school enrollments make education a declining industry, as March[31] has suggested, the field is still characterized by challenge and excitement.

AN OVERVIEW OF EDUCATIONAL ADMINISTRATION

PURPOSE AND ACTIVITIES OF ADMINISTRATION

As we see it, the central purpose of administration in any organization is that of coordinating the efforts of people toward the achievement of its goals. In education these goals have to do with teaching and learning. Thus, administration in an educational organization has as its central purpose the enhancement of teaching and learning. All activities of the administrator—whether working with the public, the board of education, or the professional staff—should ultimately contribute to this end.

To enhance teaching and learning, administrators are required to perform five major functions: (1) to discern and influence the development of goals and policies; (2) to stimulate and direct the development of programs designed to achieve the goals and purposes; (3) to establish and coordinate an organization concerned with planning and implementing the programs; (4) to procure and manage resources, money, and material nec-

31. James G. March, "Analytical Skills, University Training in Educational Administration" *Journal of Educational Administration* 12 (May 1974): 17–44.

essary to support the organization and its program, and (5) to evaluate the effectiveness and efficiency by which all of these functions are being achieved.

While all five of these administrative functions have the improvement of teaching and learning as their end purpose, more than the classroom is, clearly, involved. In order to influence goals and policies, the administrator must work with the board of education and the lay community, as well as with the school organization itself. To stimulate the development of programs, the efforts of many persons in and out of the organization must be brought into productive relationships. To establish the organization, the administrator must see that the proper personnel are selected for it; then he must see that the efforts of these personnel are coordinated. To secure resources, the administrator must secure approval from three sources—the board of education, the voters of the school district, and the appropriate state and national agencies. Evaluation requires an appraisal of both outcomes and the process used to obtain those outcomes.

Clearly, the managerial decisions of administrators may be pointless unless they are geared to the implementation of programs that have, in turn, grown out of the goals. Or, to put it differently, administrators who raise money, build buildings, institute accounting procedures, set up computer programs, organize transportation systems, and do many other things without visualizing a clear relationship between these activities and the teaching and learning programs they are to enhance, may forget that administration is always instrumental, not primary. For administrators to relate managerial acts to program decisions requires some knowledge of education—its purposes and procedures. It is at this point that the school administrator transposed from business or the military may encounter some difficulty.

In suggesting that the administrator not only discern but influence goals and policies, we recognize that we have departed from the formulations of some students of administration. But this is more than a mere difference of opinion. In a study of 272 school districts in Illinois, Allison[32] found that boards of education rely heavily on the recommendations of their superintendents on both policy and implementation matters. In effect, we are suggesting that the division between policy making and administration is not a clear one, and that inevitably the administrator influences policy even as he attempts to discern and clarify policy. This influence is a function of both the knowledge and the values of administration. To the extent that the administrator knows something about education, he can supply information, note alternatives, and suggest probable outcomes. His professional orientation or values permit him to prefer one alternative above another and to explain the reasons for his choice. At this point he is speak-

32. Howard C. Allison, "Professional and Lay Influences on School Board Decision-Making" (Ph.D. diss., Department of Education, University of Chicago, 1965).

ing as a professional and giving professional information, which any lay group needs if policy is to be well conceived.

To be sure, the administrator may find it desirable to use other professionals more expert than he in many aspects of education. Thus the contributions of the philosopher, the sociologist, the psychologist, the curriculum theorist, and the able teacher may all be used. Even so, someone must serve as the generalist to suggest how these various specialties are to be related to the problem at hand. While this function may be shared with able laymen, it is also a role that administrators cannot escape.

Obviously, it is at the level of policy-making that professional knowledge and values must make sense to laymen. With knowledge exploding in every field of study, this juncture of special and general understanding is becoming fraught with more and more difficulty. In every public endeavor, however—whether foreign affairs, public health, or public education—there seems to be no alternative to the forging of policy decisions by laymen who have been enlightened by the experts. We are suggesting that foreign affairs are too important to be left to the army, public health too important to be left to the medical profession, and public education too important to be left to the educators. However, we are also insisting that laymen would make even more blunders in these areas if they refused to use the specialized knowledge available to them.

ADMINISTRATION IN A COMPLEX WORLD

As was noted in chapter 3, one cannot understand the administration of any organization in isolation; there is always a context within which the administrative process operates. In the first place, the world is an ever-expanding one geographically. Although we may begin with an attendance area in which we have a single school, we soon discover that this attendance area is part of a school district, that the district is part of a state, that the state is part of the nation, and that the nation is part of the world; and we are now in a period in which we are constantly reminded that this world is part of a mammoth universe.

The administrator of the attendance area, the principal, cannot perform his major administrative functions without reference to the larger world. Policy decisions are not a product of the people of the local school community alone, but often reflect the desires of the people of the school district, the state, and in some sense the world beyond. In like manner program decisions are not made by the professionals of a single school in isolation. The professionals at the district, state, and national levels have an influence on these decisions.

Second, the administrator's world is most complex sociologically. Many people and groups of people performing different roles are involved. In a school district, for instance, there are lay citizens who hold expectations for schools and school administrators, who determine the membership of the board of education, and to some extent the expenditure level of the district. The board of education becomes a major interstitial body between school and community and also determines, within limits, the policies of the school district. The superintendent of schools finds that he must deal with the aspirations and expectations of the people and serve as executive officer and professional adviser to the board of education. But the superintendent also has a professional staff composed of supervisors, principals, and teachers. Groups of staff members, notably teachers, organize themselves into associations or unions to protect their interests. In face of complex and often conflicting personal dispositions and group pressures, persons are assigned to perform different roles in the school system, and somehow their activities must be coordinated toward common objectives.

Third, the adminstrator's world is complex in terms of the many public services to be provided by government. In addition to public education, there are health and welfare, fire and police protection, public roads, and other public services. This means, particularly at district and state levels, that support for public education is always in competition with support for other public services. Inevitably, such a condition places the school administrator within all the complexities of the political world.

Not only must schools compete with highways and welfare; all public services must compete with private services. In government there is the perennial question: Shall we leave matters to individual initiative, or shall we use tax resources to provide the service for all? Clearly there is need to do some of both, a concept Galbraith has called social balance.[33] With growth in any private realm (let us say the manufacture of more automobiles) there is also need for growth in the public realm—in this case the bulding of more highways.

We have shown that the world of the administrator is a complex one geographically, socially, and politically. Let us now examine a little more carefully the legal relationships between state and school district. The legal responsibility for education rests with the state. The state through the legislature has established school districts to help the state perform its educational function. The legislature has also created boards of education to preside over these districts, and the boards have the powers delegated to them by the legislature. In legal theory the districts are the creatures of the state, not the product of local autonomy. When there is need to alter districts or school boards, the state can take such action.

It is within this legal framework that the school district and legislature interact, that the superintendent of schools and the state superintendent interact, that the professional staff of a school district and the professional staff of the state department interact. But these legal relationships cannot ignore the geographical, sociological, and political relationships we have already noted. We must recognize, too, as will be

33. John K. Galbraith, *The Affluent Society* (Boston: Houghton Mifflin, 1958).

demonstrated in later chapters, that the psychological needs and dispositions of people provide still another dimension in the complex world of the administrator.

The major functions of administration must go forward within this complex geographical, social, political, legal, and psychological world. Not all administrators perform all of these activities. We suspect that an able superintendent of schools actually performs at all five levels—he discerns and influences goals and policies, stimulates and directs the development of programs, establishes and coordinates an organization, and procures and manages resources, and evaluates process and outcomes. Most school principles, on the other hand, probably concentrate more on coordinating the efforts of staff members in building a total program and somewhat less on seeking resources to support the program. Supervisors of instruction, even more than principals, probably devote most of their efforts to coordinating staff activities as they relate to instructional programs.

But whether differentiated by position or by level of operation, administration operates in a complex and interdependent world. To approach administration in terms of one set of dimensions yields only a partial view of the phenomenon. He who concentrates, for instance, on intraorganizational behavior will soon run aground, for extraorganizational influences are also inevitable.[34]

UNIQUE ASPECTS OF EDUCATIONAL ADMINISTRATION

As noted earlier, educational administration has much in common with public administration, hospital administration, business administration, and administration in other organizational settings. This recognition represents a gain, for the insights and research findings thus available to educational administration have been multiplied many times.

Still, this new-found knowledge has caused some uneasiness. Perhaps dwelling on common elements in administration, useful as such an approach is, oversimplifies the picture. Instead of trying to define either common or unique elements, it might be useful to develop some continua on which administration in a variety of organizational settings might be placed.

Parsons has suggested three levels of systems within organizations—the technical, managerial, and institutional levels.[35] In schools, for example, teaching is at the technical level of operation, action to direct the

34. This point is elaborated in Roald F. Campbell, Luvern L. Cunningham, Raphael O. Nystrand, and Michael D. Usdan, *The Organization and Control of American Schools,* 3rd ed. (Columbus, Ohio: Charles E. Merrill, 1975).

35. Talcott Parsons, "Some Ingredients of a General Theory of Formal Organizations." In Andrew W. Halpin, ed., *Administrative Theory in Education* (Chicago: Midwest Administration Center, University of Chicago, 1958), pp. 166–185.

efforts of groups of teachers toward a common goal or program is at the managerial level, and moves to seek financial support for the school from the larger society are at the institutional level. In the study of administration, according to Parsons, we have dealt mainly with the managerial level and have neglected the technical and institutional levels somewhat.

As we think of various kinds of organizations in our society and realize that all organizations, whether public or private, must be legitimized by that society, we find questions that might be asked regarding any organization:

1. What is the service that the organization is designed to provide?
2. What is the nature of the activity in which the organization will engage to perform this service?
3. What are the characteristics of the people who work in the organization?
4. How may the activities of the organization be appraised?

These considerations led us to develop six continua. Two of these, cruciality and visibility, were in response to our first question on the service to be rendered. Two others, complexity and intimacy, were in response to the second question on the nature of the activity. Staff professionalization grew out of question three on characteristics of the people. Difficulty of appraisal seemed to be a part of the general appraisal problem found in question four. While other continua may have been developed, these six will be discussed as one way of suggesting what may be unique about educational organizations and their administration. The organizations cited are for illustrative purposes only and organizational activities have been oversimplified to make the major point.

CRUCIALITY TO SOCIETY

Cruciality to society, as a continuum, obviously rests at the institutional level. We are suggesting that important as the making of ping-pong balls is to some people, this activity is not as crucial to society as fire protection. Likewise, important as fire protection is, we suspect that if a choice had to be made between schools and fire departments, society, particularly our kind of society, would choose schools. Or, to put it differently, we suspect that our society would settle for minimum fire protection before it would settle for minimum school programs.

The crucial place of the school in our society has been suggested by Thelen and Getzels:

> But education as a system is also unique in certain respects. It is a system whose major functions seem to be delegated to it by the other systems, and, to a degree, the effective functioning of the other systems depends directly on the effective functioning of the educational system. Our geographer, for example, wants education to prepare us for the wise utilization of natural resources; in this sense the school is very much part of the geographer's domain. Our political scientist wants education to prepare us for the wise exercise of political power; in this sense the school is part of *his domain.* Our economist wants education to prepare us for the wise selection of economic alternatives; in this sense the school is also part of *his* domain. In short, the educational system seems unique in the range of its functions and the centrality of its relationship, at least theoretically, to the other social institutions. It is the institution that is charged with responsibility for the "socialization," "politicalization," "acculturation," and so on of the child (and other newcomers) in our society.[36]

The cruciality continuum has interesting implications for the fiscal dependent-independent argument in education. To place all public services at the same point of cruciality to society seems unrealistic. Thus, those who would have all purpose government, or fiscal dependence for education, whether at local, state, or national levels, should also devise ways by which services thought by citizens to be most crucial to society can be given priority. Similarly, those who would have special purpose government, or fiscal independence for education, should recognize that some mechanism for weighing the need of various public services is necessary. Under either system, cruciality to society ought to determine the allocation of public financial resources.

PUBLIC VISIBILITY AND SENSITIVITY

The continuum of public visibility and sensitivity seems to reside at the institutional level. Here the factory as an organization, particularly in its internal operations, is far less visible than the college and the school. Furthermore, the management of the factory need not be particularly sensitive to public opinion except as that opinion is connected with the product of the factory. To be sure, in times of labor crises, management must tell its story to the public; but such circumstances are the exception, not the rule.

36. Herbert A. Thelen and Jacob W. Getzels, "The Social Sciences: Conceptual Framework for Education," *School Review* 65 (Autumn 1957), p. 346.

LEAST VISIBILITY AND SENSITIVITY →		**MOST VISIBILITY AND SENSITIVITY**
FACTORY	*COLLEGE*	*SCHOOL*

In contrast, the school, particularly the public school, highly visible at all times, must be sensitive to its many publics. The high visibility is connected in part with the intimacy of relationships discussed below. Even more important is the fact that most schools are public, not private, enterprises. But, as school administrators soon discover, there is not one but many publics, which often hold sharply different views about the task of the school. In spite of the high visibility of the school, it is only in recent years that school administration has begun a serious examination of the relationship of the school to the broader society and the implications of that relationship to administrative behavior.

COMPLEXITY OF FUNCTION

The continuum of complexity of function applies to the technical level of the organization. Some organizations perform more complex technical functions than others. The exact placement of the four organizations on the continuum might be argued, but the process of teaching and learning, at least to one who knows little about making bolts, seems to be complex. In teaching and learning, for instance, the teachers who are charged with the responsibility of guiding the process are not in complete control of it. The learners may or may not respond to the stimulation provided. In contrast, workers who guide the process of bolt making seem to be more nearly in control of their materials.

LEAST COMPLEX →	→	→	**MOST COMPLEX**
FACTORY	*GOVERNMENT*	*SCHOOL*	*PSYCHIATRIC STAFF*
Making Bolts	Collecting Taxes	Teaching and Learning	Changing Personality

Still, the task of teaching and learning is probably not so complex as the task that confronts a psychiatric staff. Perhaps a more explicit way of making the point would be to say that in terms of results acceptable to the organization, the teaching-learning task is less complex than personality change as attempted in the psychiatrist-patient relationship. Learning and bolt making, for that matter, may both be highly complex processes, but we are concerned here with results acceptable to the respective organizations.

The main point seems to be that in each organization the administrator must have some knowledge of the complexity of the task acceptable to his organization if he is to function as coordinator of the organization.

INTIMACY OF NECESSARY RELATIONSHIPS

The continuum of intimacy, too, may be applied to the technical level of the organization. Exact placement of various organizations on the continuum is unnecessary to illustrate the point that relationships necessary to achieve organizational goals vary in intimacy from organization to organization. They are least intimate in a bolt factory, somewhat more intimate in tax collecting by a government agency, appreciably more intimate in a school, and perhaps even more intimate in a hospital.

LEAST INTIMATE ————→————→ MOST INTIMATE

FACTORY	*GOVERNMENT*	*SCHOOL*	*HOSPITAL*
Making Bolts	Collecting Taxes	Teaching Children and Youth	Treating the Ill

It should be noted that school organizations involve the relationship of teacher to pupil, pupil to pupil, teacher to teacher, teacher to parent, and pupil to parent. Nor are school relationships confined to the formal learning of skills or knowledge. Because all human behavior is interrelated and much learning is concomitant in nature, these relationships often spill over into problems of personal adjustment, family membership, and social acceptance. Only in medical practice, in hospital care, and perhaps in the church, are personal relationships more intimate.

STAFF PROFESSIONALIZATION

Staff professionalization seems to be part of a managerial continuum. We are using the term professionalization to represent competence that requires specialized preparation through which the individual acquires in marked degree the knowledge and values of his colleagues. Factories have relatively fewer professionals than skilled and unskilled workers. In a hospital, doctors and nurses are professionals, but practical nurses, nurses aides, and attendants of various kinds are not.

LEAST PROFESSIONALIZATION ————→ MOST PROFESSIONALIZATION

FACTORY	*HOSPITAL*	*SCHOOL*	*COLLEGE*

In a school, however, teachers and administrative personnel make up two-thirds to three-fourths of all employees. They at least tend to be, and many are, professional in education and outlook. On this continuum, the college ranks higher than the school only because, on the average, college teachers possess more specialized knowledge than school teachers.

To the extent that personal dispositions of the staff are affected by professional values, superior intelligence, and articulate communication, it seems clear that administrators in schools must pay greater attention to personal dispositions than administrators in factories. Conversely, school administrators can rely less on standard operating procedures than can administrators in industrial plants.

DIFFICULTY OF APPRAISAL

The appraisal continuum also seems to reside at the technical level of the organization. While we do not wish to underestimate the difficulty of the process of appraisal in sales organizations and manufacturing concerns, it does seem that sales and production are fairly simple indexes of performance.

LEAST DIFFICULT ⟶ **MOST DIFFICULT**

SALES ORGANIZATION	*MANUFACTURING ORGANIZATION*	*SCHOOL*	*CHURCH*
Sales	Products	Change in Behavior	Inner and Outer Change

The school, in contrast, must be concerned with change in behavior, to use behavior in a broad sense. The change may involve knowledge, skills, or attitudes—all of which, presumably, influence behavior itself. But these changes are not immediately or easily perceptible. Often procedures or instruments have to be devised to measure change. But even when special instruments or procedures are used, students may, particularly in short-run evaluation, give what they believe to be appropriate responses. Sustained changes in behavior can be determined only over a period of years and by the accumulation of evidence from many sources. Obviously, the delay and the complexity of the evidence make useful feedback to the school for the purpose of revising practices most difficult.

Evaluation of a church program may be even more difficult than evaluation of a school program, for faith adds a transcendental dimension. The appraisal of school and college programs seems to be fraught with problems. Perhaps only the problems of appraising church programs are more difficult.

The six continua shown here offer a way of analyzing the common and the unique features of administration in various institutional settings. It is significant that three of the dimensions reside at the technical level, two at the institutional, and only one at the managerial level of organizations. This analysis suggests that the common elements in administration tend to be found at the managerial level, and the differentiations at the technical and institutional levels.

THEORY IN ADMINISTRATION

Some of the concepts dealt with above illustrate the quest for administrative theory characteristic of the last decade or two. In attempting to answer the question, "What is theory?" we have two alternatives. We can go full distance and side with Halpin[37] and Griffiths,[38] who both rely on Feigl[39] for a hypothetico-deductive definition. Or we can follow Walton, who suggests that we approach theory through such steps as observation, identification, definition, systematic classification, analysis, and finally, a hypothetico-deductive system.[40]

Our favorite definition of theory comes from Einstein:

> In our endeavor to understand reality we are somewhat like a man trying to understand the mechanism of a closed watch. He sees the face and the moving hands, even hears it ticking, but he has no way of opening the case. If he is ingenious he may form some picture of a mechanism which could be responsible for all things he observes, but he may never be quite sure his picture is the only one which could explain his observations. He will never be able to compare his picture with the real mechanism and he cannot even imagine the possibility or the meaning of such a comparison. But he certainly believes that, as his knowledge increases, his picture of reality will become simpler and simpler and will explain a wider and wider range of his sensuous impressions.[41]

Perhaps Einstein provides the most significant cue in what has been said up to now—"our endeavor to understand reality." In this context, the development of theory is the process whereby we describe reality more and more accurately.

Since the social sciences are newcomers to the scientific field, administration deals with most complex problems, and any theory seems to deal with but a few of the variables found in these phenomena, we are willing to keep the definition broad at this time. In the development of theory careful observation is a step above careless observation. Systematic classification is superior to no classification. To be sure, a series of related

---

37. See chapter 1 in Andrew W. Halpin, ed., *Administrative Theory in Education* (Chicago: Midwest Administration Center, University of Chicago, 1958).

38. Daniel E. Griffiths, *Administrative Theory* (New York: Appleton-Century-Crofts, 1959).

39. Herbert Feigl, "Principles and Problems of Theory Construction in Psychology." In *Current Trends in Psychological Theory* (Pittsburgh: University of Pittsburgh Press, 1951), p. 182.

40. John Walton, *Administration and Policy Making in Education,* rev. ed. (Baltimore: Johns Hopkins Press, 1969).

41. Albert Einstein and Leopold Infeld, *The Evolution of Physics* (New York: Simon and Schuster, Inc., 1938), p. 33.

concepts from which we may derive testable hypotheses is theory of a higher order.

In any case, let us note some of the characteristics of theory. Theory is conceptual; it exists only in one's mind. Theory is not right or wrong; it is useful or not useful. At best, theory explains what is—never what ought to be. Theory, if it be useful, has within it the seeds of its own destruction and reconstitution. In other words, theory suggests a process of thinking, not a recipe for action.

Recent interest in theory has led both students and practitioners of administration to expect a full-blown, grand theory of educational administration. Certainly no such manifestation is currently available, and we suspect that its formulation is a long way off.[42] On the other hand, a number of stimulating and useful theories are available. March and Simon have assessed the literature on organizational theory. They suggest that back of every proposition about organizations is a set of assumptions regarding the behavior of people. They grouped these propositions as follows:

1. Propositions assuming that organization members, and particularly employees, are primarily *passive instruments,* capable of performing work and accepting directions, but not initiating action or exerting influence in any significant way.
2. Propositions assuming that members bring to their organizations *attitudes, values,* and *goals;* that they have to be motivated or induced to participate in the system of organization behavior; that there is incomplete parallelism between their personal goals and organization goals; and that actual or potential goal conflicts make power phenomena, attitudes, and morale centrally important in the explanation of organizational behavior.
3. Propositions assuming that organization members are *decision-makers and problem-solvers,* and that perception and thought processes are central to the explanation of behavior in organizations.[43]

The view of Taylor, described briefly earlier in this chapter, appears to be based on the proposition that people are rather passive instruments. Barnard, as noted earlier, tended to accept the proposition that members bring to an organization their attitudes, values, and goals. Simon, as noted above, appears to have been the first person to suggest decision-making as a central proposition.

As Getzels and others[44] have suggested, to avoid theory leads to

42. For development of this point, see Joseph J. Schwab, "The Professorship in Educational Administration: Theory—Art—Practice." In chapter 4 *The Professorship in Educational Administration* (Columbus, Ohio: University Council for Educational Administration, 1964).

43. James G. March and Herbert A. Simon, *Organizations* (New York: Wiley, 1958), p. 6.

44. J. W. Getzels, J. M. Lipham, and R. F. Campbell, *Educational Administration as a Social Process* (New York: Harper & Row, 1968), chap. 1.

a number of untoward consequences. The first of these is factualism, the collection of facts with little or no purpose in mind about how they are to be used. A second consequence is unwarranted respect for the authority of experts, principles, and techniques; in other words, there is no framework for accepting one authority over another. Perhaps even more pernicious is another consequence—emotional identification with one's own personal views. It is fully as important for practitioners as for students of administration to avoid the consequences of lack of theory. Dewey was right many years ago when he contended that "theory is in the end . . . the most practical of all things."[45]

For the practitioner, theory is perhaps most useful in furnishing a number of concepts, or sets of spectacles, with which to view his situation. Such concepts were noted in the work of Taylor, Fayol, Follett, Mayo, Barnard, and Simon. In a thoughtful treatment on the state of the art in theory development in educational administration Willower[46] suggests the contributions as well as the limitations of applying theory to field problems.

In this chapter we have presented an overview and have suggested the meaning of administration. In chapters 5 through 8 we shall describe four different ways of viewing administration. Perhaps only chapter 7 can be seen, in any sophisticated sense, as a theory of administration, but each of the other approaches is a useful way of viewing the field. Taken together, these chapters illustrate the difficulty of subjecting a most complex phenomenon to a single theoretical formulation.

SUGGESTED ACTIVITIES

1. For one school district, suggest practices that seem to be related (a) to the scientific management or job analysis movement and (b) to the human relations emphasis in administration.
2. Note the duties suggested for the superintendent, principals, supervisors, and teachers in the rules and regulations of a city school district. How would you improve the statement? What assumptions are back of your recommendations?
3. Interview a superintendent of schools concerning his major activities. Interview five teachers concerning their view of the major activities of the superintendent. Analyze similarities and differences in perceptions.

45. John Dewey, *Sources of a Science of Education* (New York: Liveright, 1929), p. 17.

46. Donald J. Willower, "Theory in Educational Administration." *Journal of Educational Administration* 13 (May 1975): 77–91.

SELECTED READINGS

Barnard, Chester I. *The Functions of the Executive.* Cambridge, Mass.: Harvard University Press, 1938.

Callahan, Raymond E. *Education and the Cult of Efficiency.* Chicago: University of Chicago Press, 1962.

Fayol, Henri. *General and Industrial Management.* London: Sir Isaac Pitman & Sons, 1949.

Getzels, Jacob W.; Lipham, James M.; and Campbell, Roald F. *Educational Administration as a Social Process.* New York: Harper & Row, 1968.

Griffiths, Daniel E., ed. *Developing Taxonomies of Organizational Behavior in Education Administration.* Chicago: Rand McNally, 1969.

Halpin, Andrew W. *Theory and Research in Administration.* New York: The Macmillan Co., 1966.

Katz, Daniel and Kahn, Robert L. *The Social Psychology of Organizations.* New York: John Wiley & Sons, 1966.

Lawrence, Paul R. and Lorsch, Jay W. *Organization and Environment.* Homewood, Ill.: Richard D. Irwin, Inc., 1969.

March, James G., and Simon, Herbert A. *Organizations.* New York: Wiley, 1958.

Mayo, Elton. *The Human Problems of an Industrial Civilization.* Boston: Graduate School of Business Administration, Harvard University, 1946.

Metcalf, Henry C., and Urwick, L., eds. *Dynamic Administration.* New York: Harper & Brothers, 1942. The collected papers of Mary Parker Follett with an introduction by the editors.

Mintzberg, Henry. *The Nature of Managerial Work.* New York: Harper & Row, 1973.

Monahan, William G. *Theoretical Dimensions of Educational Administration.* New York: The Macmillan Co., 1975.

National Society for the Study of Education. *Behavioral Science and Educational Administration,* Sixty-Third Yearbook, Part II. Chicago: University of Chicago Press, 1964.

Simon, Herbert A. *Administrative Behavior,* 2nd ed. New York: The Macmillan Co., 1957.

Taylor, Frederick W. *Scientific Management.* New York: Harper & Brothers, 1947.

5

ADMINISTRATIVE TASKS

If administration is to facilitate teaching and learning, as we maintained in the preceding chapter, it becomes necessary to examine the major tasks necessary for the achievement of such a purpose. In this chapter we shall suggest the nature and scope of these tasks. We shall show something of the interrelationships among these tasks, though we cannot treat the detailed techniques to be employed in the achievement of them. Such a treatment requires books, not a single chapter!

The task approach to administration is not characterized by any highly developed theory. At best, the organization of the tasks into operational areas is a taxonomy. This classification, however, brings a certain order to the field which will prove useful to both student and practitioner of administration.

The administrative tasks or operational areas of administration may be grouped into categories. We think the six categories shown below represent a convenient grouping:

1. School-community relationships.
2. Curriculum and instruction.
3. Pupil personnel.
4. Staff personnel.
5. Physical facilities.
6. Finance and business management.

The principal of a school and the superintendent of a school system ordinarily have many tasks to perform in each of these operational areas. In large schools or school systems, assistants to principals and superintendents may be given limited responsibilities in one or two of the operational areas. For example, a high school principal may have a vice-principal in charge of pupil activities, discipline, and attendance, to assist him. Or a superintendent of schools may have a director of curriculum and a business manager to assist him. Or a county superintendent may have an elementary supervisor as a major staff member. In these cases a team of administrators has been formed to work at the administrative tasks.

The organization and treatment of administrative tasks in this chapter should in no sense imply that one administrator or even a team of administrators can or should do these things alone. Other people are nearly always involved. These people may be citizens, school board members, or members of the teaching or nonteaching staffs of the school. In some cases the tasks are achieved with the assistance of these people, in other cases entirely by them, and in still other cases these people advise the administrator regarding the tasks. It should be clear, however, that the responsibility for seeing that these jobs are done rests with the administrator. The nature of each of the major operational areas will now be suggested.

SCHOOL-COMMUNITY RELATIONSHIPS

Because education in our country is largely a public venture, and because in the final analysis it can be no better than the citizens of a community will have it, school-community relationships represent both a point of beginning and a continuing concern for any school administrator. As suggested in chapter 4, we are defining community in operational terms only as the attendance area for a single school or the school district for a school system. We recognize that in some ways the state or even the nation might be thought of as a community. Moreover, we are aware that the politics of education has emerged in recent years as an important area of study. Clearly many aspects of school community relationships are caught up in the political arena. But that arena includes local, state, and national concerns and their various interrelationships, a topic too comprehensive to be treated here. We shall limit this treatment to local school units. While the tasks incident to school-community relationships are numerous, we shall limit our discussion to what seem to be certain focal points.

CHARACTER OF THE COMMUNITY

School communities may be characterized as urban or rural, as farm or nonfarm, as industrial or residential, as middle class or lower class. In large city school districts, such as New York and Detroit, efforts have been made over the past decade or so to decentralize school operation and provide the community surrounding a single school more control over school matters. This movement has been treated in some detail by Cronin[1] and can only be noted here. Whether a school community be conceived in terms of a single school or a school district, the characteristics of that community provide some working clues to the school administrator. The voting behavior of citizens is one such characteristic to be noted.

Piele & Hall[2] have recently summarized and analyzed the research on the voting behavior of citizens in school elections. The authors found that the normal participants in school elections, about 30 percent of those eligible, were those citizens who were property owners, parents, had higher incomes, and had more schooling. They also point out that the evidence suggests that when participation of citizens beyond the normal group is increased that some level of community conflict probably exists. Even more significant, they note that as participation increases the percentage of unfavorable votes tends to increase.

In terms of democratic theory this is a shocking finding. Such evidence prompts a number of questions: Are our cherished beliefs about democracy unfounded? Or, do school leaders place propositions on the ballot which make little sense to a wide range of citizens? Or, are school leaders quite inept in their support of propositions placed on the ballot? Or, do school elections often ignore the social and economic circumstances which surround many citizens and provoke a negative response as their most effective form of protest? We suspect that any one or more of these conditions may characterize school elections in a particular place at a particular time. In any case, it seems most important that the school administrator understand the composition and character of his school community and the conditions which pertain in that community at a particular time.

DESIRES AND ASPIRATIONS OF CITIZENS

Some of what was said above has implications for the assessment of the desires and aspirations that citizens have for their schools. We need to note specifically, however, that this is another important aspect of school-community relationships. There are many ways by which assessment might be made, such as through informal conversations with citizens and through the use of rating scales like those developed by Bullock and referred to above.

A number of studies done at the University of Chicago have dealt

1. Joseph M. Cronin, *The Control of Urban Schools* (New York: The Free Press, 1973).
2. Philip K. Piele & John S. Hall, *Budgets, Bonds, and Ballots* (Lexington, Mass.: D. C. Heath & Co., 1973).

with the task of the public school as perceived by various sub-publics.[3] Occupation and amount of schooling were found to be the best predictors of educational belief. Fair predictors were also geographic region in which one lives, age, race, and religion. Interestingly enough, the type of community in which a person lives, income, sex, and participation in school programs did not prove to be closely associated with educational viewpoint. Some useful instruments for the assessment of public perceptions were also developed as part of these studies.

The building of a realistic expectation of what the public schools can and should do in a community represents one of the major tasks of any school administrator. Only with such understanding can school procedures make sense to citizens and lead to significant advances in school programs.

INFORMATION ABOUT THE SCHOOL

We do not subscribe to the public relations concept of "selling" the public schools to the people. Actually, the people already hold title to the public schools. We do believe, however, that after school and community representatives reach agreement on programs and those programs are put into operation, there must be full and frequent reporting to the community on their progress. Thus, dissemination of information about the school to the community is an important obligation of any administrator.

Indeed, information needs to be disseminated on many subjects. It might pertain to a new emphasis in mathematics, a new method of reporting pupil progress, a program for the in-service education of teachers, the extension of the school plant, changes in the tax resources of the school district, the development of school board policies, or any number of other items. Of great importance to many school patrons, as the accountability movement has emphasized, are the results of instructional programs, their strengths and their weaknesses.

Just as there are many things to report, there are many ways of reporting. Inevitably school pupils become conveyors of school news. Teachers, too, have many community contacts and are often sources of information about schools. Many schools have found letters to parents, room meetings for parents, and regular P.T.A. sessions useful aids in reporting. Some central offices print short brochures about school matters to be included with the report cards of pupils. Other school districts issue annual reports either as booklets or as special editions of the local newspaper. A few school districts have prepared summaries of achievement test results, broken down by grade and building, for distribution to parents

3. Lawrence W. Downey, *The Task of Public Education* (Chicago: Midwest Administration Center, University of Chicago, 1960), p. 88. Also see, George H. Gallup, "Sixth Annual Poll of Public Attitudes Toward Education." *Phi Delta Kappan* 56 (September 1974): 20–32.

and other school patrons. Coverage of school news by newspaper, radio, and television is, of course, a common and important means of disseminating information about the school.

A nine year study on "the structure and process of school-community relations" undertaken at Stanford University provided a great deal of information on this topic.[4] Some of the more important findings of the study were that informal citizen communication about the schools is scanty and ineffective, that mediating agencies between the schools and citizens, such as the school board and parent organizations, are little used by citizens, and that consumer orientations of citizens toward the schools and nonissue related concerns tend to influence support for the schools in general and, specifically, voting in school tax and bond referenda.

ROLE OF THE SCHOOL

Another aspect of school-community relations is the development of a consensus on the role of the school in the community. That the establishment of such a consensus is not so simple as it once was is attested by a statement from the White House Conference on Education:

> The basic responsibility of the schools is the development of the skills of the mind, but the over-all mission has been enlarged. Schools are now asked to help each child to become as good and as capable in every way as native endowment permits. The schools are asked to help children to acquire any skill or characteristic which a majority of the community deems worthwhile. The order given by the American people to the schools is grand in its simplicity; in addition to intellectual achievement, foster morality, happiness, and any useful ability. The talent of each child is to be sought out and developed to the fullest. Each weakness is to be studied and, so far as possible, corrected. This is truly a majestic ideal, and an astonishingly new one. Schools of that kind have never been provided for more than a small fraction of mankind.
>
> Although it is new, this ideal of schools which do everything possible for all children was a natural development in the United States. The moving spirit of this Nation has been from the beginning a sense of fairness. Nowadays equality of educational opportunity for adults means little without equality of educational opportunity for children. Ignorance is a greater obstacle than ever to success of most kinds. The schools have become a major tool for creating a Nation without rigid class barriers. *It is pri-*

4. Richard F. Carter and William R. Odell, *The Structure and Process of School-Community Relations: A Summary,* vol. 5, U.S. Department of Health, Education and Welfare, Office of Education, Cooperative Research Project No. 1039 (Stanford, Calif.: Institute for Communication Research and School of Education (Stanford University, 1966).

> *marily the schools which allow no man's failure to prevent the success of his son.*[5] [Italics in original]

Jencks[6] contends that the evidence to date suggests that schools make less of a contribution to the economic well-being of people generally than do their families or their personal characteristics. While this conclusion has not gone unchallenged, it may be that school influence is only one of a combination of factors that make a difference in the earning capacity of individuals. Moreover, schools do not exist for economic ends only.

The social, as well as the educational, purpose of the school is also emphasized in a study of the Chicago schools:

> The future of the city is bound up with the program of the public schools in two basic ways.
>
> First, the schools help to give the next generation and the present generation of citizens and workers the knowledge and the understanding and the attitudes that make them good, bad, or indifferent citizens, workers, and parents.
>
> Second, the program of the schools is the greatest single factor in the decision of middle-income people to live in the central city or to live in the suburbs, and to live in one section of the city or another.[7]

The administrative task suggested here is two-fold. There is first of all the stimulation of school workers and lay citizens in thinking about the role of the school in a particular attendance area or school district, with, of course, the clear recognition that state, regional, national, and world forces also impinge upon every locality. Second, this consideration must be continued until agreements can be reached which will serve as operating bases for the schools.

ROLE OF OTHER COMMUNITY AGENCIES

As lay citizens and school people work together to determine for a particular school community the role of its school or school system, they will inevitably have to give attention to the roles to be played by other community agencies and organizations. These organizations and agencies include the home; the churches; the city or county government; farm, labor, or business associations; public libraries; newspapers, radio, and television sta-

---

5. The Committee for the White House Conference on Education, *A Report to the President* (Washington, D.C.: U.S. Government Printing Office, 1956), p. 9.

6. Christopher Jencks et al., *Inequality; A Reassessment of the Effect of Family and Schooling in America* (New York: Basic Books, 1972).

7. Robert J. Havighurst, *The Public Schools of Chicago* (Chicago: Board of Education, 1964), p. 28.

tions; and many others. In the total development of a community each of these agencies has a part to play.

Goldman examined the perceptions held by educators, noneducators, and high school students regarding the roles of the high school, the family, and the church in the development of a number of qualities in the high school graduate.[8] Educators and noneducators agree that the family should hold primary responsibility for developing most of the qualities of the ideal graduate. To the high school was assigned the responsibility for developing the theoretic and political qualities, while the family was seen as having primary responsibility for developing the religious, economic, altruistic, hedonistic, social, æsthetic, and ethical qualities. While the students themselves saw the church as having primary responsibility for the religious quality, neither educators nor noneducators were of that opinion.

These findings suggest that more work needs to be done in assessing the perceptions people hold regarding the role of the school and the roles of other community agencies in the total program of education. Moreover, current perceptions in any particular community, we suspect, need not be ultimate perceptions. Again, the need to work out community understandings and programs becomes apparent.

In the operational area of school-community relations, we have suggested that the administrative tasks include those of ascertaining the composition and character of the community, and of determining the desires and aspirations the people have for the public school. We have also indicated that with such data at hand administrators must stimulate the development of some agreements in a community regarding the roles of the public school and of other community agencies. In large city school districts with the current emphasis upon decentralization, the principal of a single school will be increasingly challenged to work within this context for his own attendance area.

CURRICULUM AND INSTRUCTION

A second, and in a sense the basic, operating area for the school administrator is that of curriculum and instruction. By curriculum and instruction we mean those activities in which school workers, sometimes assisted by lay citizens, engage to plan, implement, and evaluate an instructional program. Since curriculum design and instructional procedures are so central to school operation, any dissatisfaction with the school often centers in this area. In recent years recommended changes have run the entire gamut

8. Samuel Goldman, "Sub-Public Perceptions of the High School Graduate and the Roles of Institutions in His Development" (Ph.D. diss., Department of Education, University of Chicago, 1961); see also George H. Gallup, "Sixth Annual Gallup Poll of Public Attitudes Toward Education." *Phi Delta Kappan* 56 (September 1974): 20–32.

from "deschooling" or the elimination of schools altogether as advocated by Illich[9] through a host of changes recommended by school reformers of whom Silberman[10] in *Crisis in the Classroom* is one of the best known, to modest changes to be made on the basis of research and experience.[11]

While these treatments of needed reforms cannot be ignored, in the final analysis change in instructional content or method does not come through mere talking about it. Actually, changes occur when the understanding and skills of teachers and other workers change. To be effective, therefore, curriculum development activities should provide ways by which school workers may acquire new insights or develop new skills. Such insights and skills are related to the following curriculum categories: determination of objectives, the development of a program of instruction, the use of instructional procedures, and the appraising of instruction. Each of these will be treated briefly here.

DETERMINING OBJECTIVES

Each school staff needs to develop, in the light of all the evidence available, a concept of the specific objectives of the school or school system in a particular community. Setting the conditions so that this procedure can be carried out effectively is another important administrative task.

General statements of policy, like those found in *Goals for Americans,* are provocative.[12] Gardner suggested, it will be recalled, that "our schools must prepare all young people, whatever their talents, for the serious business of being free men and women."[13] These broad objectives seem acceptable enough until one tries to spell them out in more specific terms. For instance, in the interest of intellectual development, are youngsters going to be free to examine controversial issues such as the energy shortage and our dependence on the Arab nations for oil?

In the moral realm, to what extent can and should representatives of religious denominations be used in the school program? In what ways do we challenge the gifted and still provide for their participation in social situations with pupils of a wide range of abilities? The administrator must be concerned with these and similar questions as he tries to develop a plan whereby the professional staff can get at the objectives of the school.

What are some of the elements of such a plan? Basically, two things are necessary: to provide opportunity to learn more about the culture and its demands upon the school, and to provide opportunity to learn

9. Ivan Illich, *Deschooling Society* (New York: Harper & Row, 1971).

10. Charles E. Silberman, *Crisis in the Classroom* (New York: Random House, 1970).

11. For instance see several articles in *Phi Delta Kappan* 57 (January 1976) no. 5.

12. John W. Gardner, "National Goals in Education." In Report of the President's Commission on National Goals, *Goals for Americans* (New York: Prentice-Hall, 1960), chap. 3.

13. Ibid., p. 100.

more about the growth and development of children and youth. These are the foundations of any kind of curriculum study.

Teachers and other school workers, to be sure, already know a great deal about the culture which determines, in part, what the school ought to be about. In a society as complex and pluralistic as ours, however, such knowledge may be fragmentary, incomplete, and even in error. For instance, Coleman and his colleagues have recently analyzed the complex conditions surrounding youth as they attempt to become adults in our society.[14]

Any plan for helping professional workers to make a continuous assessment of the social scene requires that they have an opportunity to examine the culture both first hand and vicariously. To examine first hand, people must have an opportunity to travel in their own locality, in the nation, and the world at large. Such travel can, of course, be supplemented by reading or by hearing the reports of other observers, provided such observers have the ability to see and to report.

Opportunity for extending the knowledge of teachers about human growth and learning is readily at hand. Pupils can be seen not only as people to be taught but as subjects to be studied. Actually, the challenge of teaching is probably not fully appreciated until both approaches are used. To study children and youth, however, certain conditions seem necessary. Teachers need a little time for reflection. They may also need the help of a person who is more capable in study and research approaches if their own studies are to be well conceived and executed. The studies suggested here need not conflict with recent concerns about the protection of student privacy.

PROGRAM OF INSTRUCTION

After the objectives of an instructional program are formulated, the job of actually determining a program to achieve these objectives still remains. Facilitating the development of such a program is also the task of the administrator. To the extent that programs are district-wide in character, the superintendent and his staff should take major responsibility to facilitate the process. To the extent that each building has autonomy in developing its own program, the building principal and his staff should take major responsibility to facilitate the process.

Many of the conditions suggested above for administrators to promote in the determination of objectives pertain also to the development of instructional programs. It seems desirable, however, to look more specifically at the behavior of administrators, particularly as such behavior may affect the work of teachers and other professional personnel as they engage in program development.

14. James S. Coleman et al., *Youth: Transition to Adulthood.* Report of the President's Science Advisory Committee (Chicago: University of Chicago Press, 1974).

In an older but still useful study, Jenkins and Blackman examined the relationship between the behavior of elementary school principals and the curriculum development activities of their staff members in a large city school district.[15] While many of the findings were suggestive only, the data do indicate rather clearly that there was no significant relationship between the verbalization of democratic attitudes by administrators and the effectiveness of those administrators in putting democracy into action. Or to put it another way, administrators may say they involve teachers in curriculum planning—they may even think that they do involve them—and at the same time this condition may not exist.

In the same study it was also found that the most effective administrators used approaches that were neither strongly "staff-centered" nor strongly "task-centered." Rather, principals who had some facility to help teachers define jobs and who at the same time were able to exhibit warmth toward teachers were the ones who, in general, had the most effective staffs in terms of developing curriculum programs.

A number of investigators have focused on the single school as opposed to a school district, as potentially the most significant unit in effecting change or improvement in the instructional program. Goodlad,[16] after years of experience with a league of cooperating schools, offers a number of postulates pertaining to school improvement, the first of which suggests the single school as the optimal unit. Earlier, Sarason[17] noted the key role of the principal in affecting the culture of the school and thus providing an environment in which change might go forward. But innovation or improvement is not an easy process, even at the building level, as Smith and Keith[18] have shown in their perceptive analysis.

NATIONAL CURRICULUM PROGRAMS

Development and implementation of the program of instruction is no longer an activity carried on chiefly by a school district or a single school. Under the auspices of the National Science Foundation and other groups, national curriculum programs have been developed, and they have had decided impact upon the instructional practices of many schools.[19] Beginning

15. David H. Jenkins and Charles A. Blackman, *Antecedents and Effects of Administrator Behavior,* SCDS Monograph No. 3 (Columbus, Ohio: College of Education, The Ohio State University, 1956).

16. John I. Goodlad, *The Dynamics of Educational Change* (New York: McGraw-Hill Book Co., 1975), chap. 7.

17. Seymour B. Sarason, *The Culture of the School and the Problem of Change* (Boston: Allyn & Bacon, 1971).

18. L. M. Smith and P. M. Keith, *Anatomy of Educational Innovation: An Organizational Analysis of an Elementary School* (New York: Wiley & Sons, 1971).

19. Roald F. Campbell and Robert A. Bunnell, eds., *Nationalizing Influences on Secondary Education* (Chicago: Midwest Administration Center, University of Chicago, 1963).

in 1956 with the Physical Science Study Committee, with headquarters at the Massachusetts Institute of Technology, extensive programs have also been developed in mathematics, biology, and chemistry.[20] The United States Office of Education has also supported projects in English and social studies whose results may have national impact.

These national programs raise several important issues. For one, control of education in this country has, in the past, been assumed to be a state and local matter. Legally, this is still the case for the most part, but actually the influence of the national programs is widespread and pervasive. At one time, extensive teacher participation was considered essential to the development of curriculum programs. But today relatively few teachers take part in the development of most national programs; in fact, they find that they are, rather, the consumers of these programs. Although very limited resources were once available for curriculum development, the national programs had at their disposal millions of dollars for holding conferences, developing instructional materials, hiring consultants, and organizing institutes wherein teachers might become acquainted with the programs. During the 1970s funds from national agencies for curriculum revision were reduced or dried up completely.

Even so, these programs created new responsibilities for the administrator who had to acquire some knowledge of them in order to consider them with his staff. Moreover, those involved in curriculum development at the local level cannot ignore the ideas growing out of the national programs, nor can they ignore the instructional materials these programs made available.

INSTRUCTIONAL MATERIALS

Another closely related task for which the administrator takes responsibility is the selection and procurement of instructional materials. The teacher, to be sure, is central to adequate instruction, but even good teachers can do better when they are provided with appropriate tools.

The first task in this area is that of budget provision. Budget building at its best assumes that program development, discussed briefly above, has gone forward, and that the materials needed to implement such a program will now become the basis for the budget request. For instance, if it has been decided that every biology student should have actual experience using laboratory equipment and supplies, the budget request will be quite different from one based upon a course that is to be taught with the textbook-demonstration-lecture approach.

20. John I. Goodlad, ed., *The Changing American School.* Sixty-Fifth Yearbook of the National Society for the Study of Education, Part II (Chicago: The University of Chicago Press, 1966), chap. 2.

Even assuming this kind of budget approach, however, it will usually be the administrator who must convince the superintendent's staff, the board of education, and finally the community that expenditures for instructional materials are indispensable to an adequate program of instruction. Sometimes elaborate plant and grounds—the outside façade of the school—win out over books, maps, and other instructional aids when budgets become tight. Without deprecating adequate programs of plant operation and maintenance, administrators need to be able to hold the line for budget items intimately related to the instructional program.

In the actual selection of instructional materials, teachers should play a large part. It has been found that teachers feel strongly the need to assume responsibility for those activities which have to do with instruction. It behooves administrators, therefore, to devise ways by which teacher participation in instructional matters, including the selection of instructional materials, can be encouraged. It should be recognized, however, that since such participation does take time, it must be regarded as a part of the total load of the teacher.

But teachers and administrators, with what seems to be increasing frequency, are finding that other actors insist on having a hand in the selection of instructional materials. One such example is found in *Man: A Course of Study,* a widely used middle school course of study. Even though this material was prepared by an eminent scholar under the sponsorship of the National Science Foundation, some parents and other persons object to the program because they feel that the treatment of some topics fails to take into account the maturity level of the pupils, and that it represents unwarranted interference in curriculum matters by the federal government. This controversy is treated by Peter Dow and George Weber in an issue of *Phi Delta Kappan.*[21]

When budget provision for instructional materials has been made and when teachers have assisted in the actual selection of materials, there still remain the problems of procurement and delivery. These are tasks which the administration of a school district should perform with the greatest possible dispatch. Nothing is as exasperating to a teacher as to participate in a budget building or a materials selection program and then have purchase or delivery of materials delayed indefinitely by administrative red tape. The principal and the superintendent must cut through any such maze or avoid creating it.

APPRAISING INSTRUCTION

Another major responsibility confronting any administrator in the area of curriculum development is that of appraising instruction. Some industries allocate as much as one-sixth of their manpower to quality control. In edu-

21. *Phi Delta Kappan* 57 (October 1975) 2, pp. 79–82.

cation, unfortunately, evaluation has tended to be done with the left hand, if at all.

Space here will not permit a full treatment of evaluation. It does seem appropriate to suggest, however, that evaluation as a process has the following steps:

1. The formulation of objectives.
2. The definition of these objectives in behavioral terms.
3. Determination of places where these behaviors may be observed.
4. Selection or development of instruments upon which to record these behaviors when observed.
5. Appraisal and interpretation of the evidence thus collected.

Perhaps this formulation places too much stress on final outcomes, whereas recent treatments of evaluation[22] stress the need to appraise the processes employed as well as the final outcomes. In any case, evaluation is a laborious activity. All aspects of an instructional program probably cannot be submitted continuously to such a careful procedure. On the other hand, the spirit of the evaluative approach can be applied much more generally than is now the case. Essentially, such an approach stresses careful formulation of purposes and collection of evidence in terms of those purposes.

Administrators need to help school workers and lay citizens alike to see that evaluation is a necessary complement to planning and doing. If we devise a new program for the teaching of reading, we must, of course, try it out, and we must evaluate, as best we can, how effective the program has been. Planning, doing, and evaluating are, in a real sense, just parts of a whole.

If this view is taken, it becomes clear that teachers must have time to participate in planning and evaluating as much as in doing. Such a statement has implications for teacher selection, job expectation, and teacher load. Moreover, the assistance of specialists in evaluation should probably be made available to teachers and others in the school system if the process is to be done well. It seems clear that only with regular and adequate evaluation can the administrator fulfill his responsibilities to his staff, his board of education, and his community. Recent demands for accountability and the application of cost-benefit analyses make it clear that citizens insist on knowing "how we are doing."

We have suggested that, in the operational area of curriculum and instruction, administrators have the responsibility for setting conditions that will promote the determination of objectives, the development of instructional programs, and the procurement of instructional materials. We

22. For instance, see Daniel L. Stufflebeam et al., *Educational Evaluation and Decision Making* (Itaska, Ill.: Peacock Publishers, 1971).

have also indicated that, as programs are planned, plans for their evaluation should be formulated.

PUPIL PERSONNEL

Curriculum and instruction as discussed above had to do essentially with that part of the school program which is concerned with regular classroom instruction. Activities included within the operational area of pupil personnel embrace those services to pupils that supplement regular classroom instruction. Except in schools with very small enrollments, the chief role of the administrator in the pupil personnel area is one of integrating the personnel functions with instruction and of coordinating the various kinds of personnel services. Developments, such as special programs for the talented and the growth of external testing, have placed even more emphasis on pupil personnel services. A discussion of a few of the major tasks in pupil personnel follows.

PUPIL INVENTORY AND ORGANIZATION

Some staff member in a school district must first of all determine how many youngsters there are of school age in the attendance area or district. He does so by means of a school census, by the keeping of enrollment and attendance data, and by other means that will be discussed later. It is usually necessary that the number of pupils be determined by grade level and by school or attendance area.

With this information in hand, the administrator is in a position to determine to what extent school rooms in the existing buildings will house the pupils of the district. If certain buildings appear to be overcrowded and others have capacity to spare, the administrator may find that attendance boundaries need to be altered. In recent years, with charges of de facto segregation in many cities, the establishment of attendance areas has taken on new significance. The social and racial composition of the attendance area is fully as important as the consideration of number of pupils to be enrolled in the school.

The continual or yearly enumeration of pupils also furnishes one of the bases for determining new building needs. Often this enumeration furnishes data having to do with the direction of growth in a school district. In city school districts, particularly, population growth is usually toward the outskirts or even beyond the boundaries of the district to the suburbs. In recent years, enrollments in many school districts, particularly in schools near the center of cities, have decreased dramatically and many schools have had to be closed.

Enrollment data also furnish the administrator with the best single index of teaching personnel needed by grades, by subject area, and by school or attendance area. For example, if the projected enrollment data for a new elementary school indicated that 456 pupils would attend, and if the district had a policy of providing a teacher for each 28 elementary pupils, it is clear that the new school would require no fewer than 16 teachers.

Up to this point we have spoken of gross enumeration of pupils. It is also necessary that much be known about the characteristics of the pupils found within a school district. How many are gifted, how many are slow learners, how many are hard of hearing, how many are orthopedic cases? Ordinarily census or enrollment data will not, of course, provide the kind of information suggested here. The identification of pupils with special problems will require the cooperation of teachers, parents, and specially trained personnel. Again, however, such information is necessary in order that a school or school system can plan a program of services for all, including its deviate pupils.

PUPIL ACCOUNTING

We have already alluded to the first task of pupil accounting, the enumeration of pupils. Ordinarily a school census system is established to help with this task. There is a compulsory education law in nearly every state, and a school census is a necessary step in the enforcement of such laws. While census taking was once seen as a yearly task, many school systems now use the continuing census approach. Specific procedures to be followed have been described in detail elsewhere.[23]

Another task facing every school system is the development and the operation of a pupil accounting system. A plan for dealing with pupil absence and tardiness must be developed. If such a plan is to be followed by teachers and principals as part of their regular duties, it needs to be relatively simple. If specialized attendance personnel are to be employed, the plan may be somewhat more ambitious. In any case, teachers should have some voice in deciding upon the plan, and their own part in its operation will need to be clearly understood.

It seems appropriate to say at this point that the "hooky cop" approach to attendance leaves much to be desired. There is usually substantial cause back of nonattendance of school pupils. The school needs personnel who can both determine these basic causes and work toward their alleviation. Such causes often reside in the family, or the culture of which the family is a part, and thus non-attendance may actually be a social symptom toward which school workers, social agencies, and society itself ought to be directing their efforts.

Another duty common in pupil accounting is the issuance of work

23. Dean L. Hummel and S. J. Bonham, *Pupil Personnel Services in Schools: Organization and Coordination* (Chicago: Rand McNally, 1968).

permits. In most states pupils may be excused at age fourteen or sixteen if they are needed to help support a family or if they can benefit no further from school attendance. These are important decisions in the life of a child and should be made only after facts are ascertained and appropriate counseling has been given the pupil and the family. In small school districts, principals and superintendents ordinarily perform these functions. In larger districts, specialized personnel are usually employed.

PUPIL PERSONNEL SERVICES

A very important aspect of the pupil personnel area is the provision of appropriate pupil personnel services. Large school districts may have services such as the following:

1. Child study.
2. Guidance and counseling advisement.
3. Testing.
4. Visiting teacher and social worker.
5. Speech and hearing therapy.
6. Medical and nursing.
7. Special education
   a. Physically handicapped
   b. Emotionally disturbed
   c. Mentally handicapped
   d. Gifted.

To some of these services we have already alluded. For instance, tests and measurements would be helpful in any program of evaluation; the school social worker might be skilled in getting at causes behind nonattendance of pupils. Some school systems see special education as a part of the curriculum program, but even so the workers in special education need to have close affiliation with the workers in the pupil personnel area.

Recently, another consideration has been injected into pupil personnel services. Mounting concern about the kinds of data appearing in student records, such as test results and teacher judgments about student behavior, provoked the U.S. Congress to pass the Federal Family Educational Rights and Privacy Act of 1974. While the impact of the act is not yet fully determined, it seems clear that students or their parents will have the right to inspect confidential records kept by the school and approve their external use.

If pupil personnel services are really going to supplement regular classroom instruction, it seems quite clear that some specialized personnel will be necessary. The welfare federation of a large city has suggested that a minimum staff for pupil personnel services should be composed of specialized people for each of the following:

1. Director (or coordinator) of pupil personnel services.
2. Health service.
3. Secondary school counseling service.
4. Speech and hearing therapy.
5. Child study service (psychological service and psychiatric consultation).
6. School social work service.

To be sure, small school districts cannot ordinarily employ all of the specialists suggested above. Such districts might start by getting one guidance counselor and by determining where the other services could be obtained on a part-time basis. For instance, in many states the county or intermediate school district is becoming a service unit to smaller school districts. In such cases most of the services noted above can be provided on a cooperative basis. Again, the job of the administrator is that of seeing that these services are made available and coordinated.

CONTROL OF PUPIL BEHAVIOR

While schools should attempt to determine the cause of misbehavior in pupils, and to treat the cause and not the symptom of such actions, there are times when pupils must be corrected or disciplined. Policies governing these matters should be clear, and the responsibilities of teachers and other staff members in this area should be understood. Competent teachers can and should exercise appropriate controls over their pupils. Actually, and contrary to the views of some beginning teachers, pupils prefer those teachers who are seen as fair, helpful, setting high standards, and allowing no "monkey business."

Even with the best of teachers, however, there are times when the principal, guidance counselor, or some other nonteaching staff member is placed in the role of disciplinarian. Many contend that guidance counselors and other pupil personnel workers should have no disciplinary function; that function, they insist, should be carried by the principal or some other administrative officer. The logic behind such an argument is that the guidance counselor should be individual- and not group oriented—or, perhaps better stated, pupil centered in place of school centered.

In general, we accept this position; but carried to its extreme it would mean that both guidance counselors and principals would become less effective than they should be. When it is necessary for a principal to take part in a discipline problem, he should ascertain, if possible, the circumstances surrounding the misbehavior prior to arriving at a plan of action. Some of this information he may get from the pupil, some he should get from those workers who have specialized knowledge and the competence to place such knowledge in its appropriate context. The best diagnosis possible is needed if the principal is to be effective in helping youngsters toward the ultimate goal of self-discipline.

Recent developments require a reexamination of the traditional concepts of pupil control. The student activist movement, first prominent among college students, acquired many adherents among high school students. Westin[24] surveyed 1,800 newspapers over a four-month period and found reports of 239 serious episodes such as strikes, sit-ins, riots, and other forms of violence in high schools located in 38 states. Westin categorized the causes of these disturbances in order as follows: racial, political, dress, discipline, and educational reform. While there are no ready made panaceas for dealing with student demands, it seems clear that high school administrators should hear what the students are saying. Some of their contentions are sound, a position supported by the U.S. Supreme Court in the Tinker case[25] in which the right of students to wear black armbands to protest the Vietnam war was affirmed. Other student contentions may not require reform but some firmness in making boundaries clear may be in order.

We have suggested that in the area of pupil personnel the major administrative tasks have to do with pupil inventory and organization, pupil accounting, provisions for pupil services, and control of pupil behavior. These services should complement the program provided all pupils through regular classroom instruction.

STAFF PERSONNEL

To implement any of the programs suggested above under curriculum development or pupil personnel, appropriate staff must be provided. Here, therefore, we should like to examine staff personnel as one of the major operational areas in administration. Our discussion will be focused on certificated personnel such as teachers, guidance workers, and administrators. Many of the approaches suggested also have application to non-certificated personnel (custodians, lunchroom workers, and bus drivers). Some additional comments regarding non-certificated personnel will be made when business management is discussed.

PERSONNEL POLICIES

In personnel administration, as with all other aspects of administration, one of the first tasks is the development of appropriate personnel policies.

24. Alan F. Westin, *The New York Times,* May 9, 1969.

25. *Tinker* v. *Des Moines Independent Community School District,* 393 U.S. 503 (1969); see also *Goss* v. *Lopez,* 95 S. Ct. 729 (1975).

Often school districts recognize the necessity for personnel policies even before they see the need for more general policy statements. Perhaps a word should be said here about the meaning of policy. As we use the term here, and as it might be applied more broadly to school administration, policies refer to a set of guiding principles that establish a framework to give consistency to a school board's actions. In a sense, then, a policy statement represents the framework, in terms of law and of the philosophy of the board, upon which action is to be based.

To be sure, many boards of education will need help in thinking through possible alternatives if they are to express what we would deem sound personnel policies. This means that the administrator will think with both staff members and lay citizens concerning policy matters, and from such deliberation will gain assistance in arriving at policy statements to be recommended to his board of education. These policies will probably most often pertain to working conditions and to the salary program.

Personnel policies pertaining to working conditions, we believe, should meet the following criteria:

1. Appear reasonable and not capricious.
2. Have a positive and not a punitive flavor.
3. Be suggestive and not merely prescriptive.
4. Establish the fact that full information on school operation is available to teachers.
5. Provide clear channels of communication.
6. Make plain the bases for promotion.
7. Provide for staff participation in the formulation and operation of policies.

A decade or so ago board of education personnel policies often contained provisions pertaining to ways by which teachers might participate in policy making having to do with personnel matters. As teacher negotiations have become more formalized those voluntary provisions have ordinarily been superceded by a formal contract between the board of education and the teachers organization. For instance, the contract between the Salt Lake City Board of Education and the Salt Lake Teachers Association is included as an appendix in the published Board Policies and is over fifty pages in length. Many topics are dealt with in the contract including the following: recognition, negotiations, grievance procedure, salaries, teacher evaluation, and termination procedures.[26]

It will be noted that the place of the committee system has been made clear. Participation of staff members in discussing major school problems is given official endorsement, and the need for face-to-face communication among the superintendent, professional staff members, and board of trustees is recognized.

---

26. Salt Lake City, "Board Policies" (October 2, 1973).

The increasing militancy of teachers and teachers' organizations has added a new dimension to the problem of formulating personnel policies. The day when school boards and administrators could take a rather paternalistic attitude toward teachers seems to be drawing to a close. Teachers' associations and unions are ever more frequently demanding some type of collective relationship with the board of education.

Lieberman and Moskow[27] have dealt extensively with the evolving field of collective negotiations. They suggest that there are at least three approaches: the marketplace or short-range approach, the professional approach, and the problem-solving approach. They deal extensively with each of these approaches, with the procedures involved in collective negotiations, and they include samples of many documents which have been evolved in actual negotiations. One of these documents is the agreement between the New Haven Board of Education and the New Haven Teachers' League.[28] The agreement is twenty-five printed pages in length and includes the following major items: recognition of the league, teaching hours and load, teaching assignments and transfers, promotions, teacher facilities, class size, textbooks, specialists, teacher aids, summer school programs, protection, accident benefits, sick leave, leaves of absence, salaries, grievance procedures, dues deduction, and negotiation of successor agreement.

Collective negotiations have changed the world of most school administrators. At its worst, negotiated agreements can negate any leadership role the administrator may attempt to play. At its best, negotiated agreements can clarify the roles of teachers and administrators and provide for each. In these situations, much can be made of the ground that is common, and the bases for working out differences will probably be more easily established. In shifting from school board domination of teachers, we should not accept teacher domination of school boards. Negotiations imply bargaining in good faith, with recognition of the constraints operating on both sides.

SECURING PERSONNEL

The administrator must also determine the kinds and numbers of people needed to man the various programs of the school and must then proceed to secure the people. While the end of the teacher shortage may ease this task somewhat, it is still a critical one. Schools will continue to confront such factors as competition in the labor market for highly trained people,

---

27. Myron Lieberman and Michael H. Moskow, *Collective Negotiations for Teachers* (Chicago: Rand McNally, 1966); see also Myron Lieberman, "Negotiations: Past, Present, and Future." *School Management* 17 (May 1973): 14–19.

28. Ibid., pp. 594–618.

expanded occupational opportunities for women, and the fact that teaching in some situations is a most difficult task.

These circumstances suggest at least two courses of action for the administrator. He must find ways of helping lay citizens understand the need for specialized and competent personnel. Only as citizens become convinced that levels of compensation should be adequate and working conditions desirable will they support projected school budgets.

A second task for the administrator is the establishment of employment, assignment, induction, and supervision procedures which will attract and hold capable people. Teachers prefer to work in schools and school systems where they feel wanted, where they believe the program is on the move, where they think their contribution is important, and where they feel that the "boss" is understanding and fair. Important as adequate pay is, a number of studies have shown that work conditions are even more significant.[29]

In essence the personnel policies of boards of education and the personnel practices of administrators can do much to encourage teachers not to drop out of the profession after they have entered it. Moreover the personnel policies and practices that tend to keep teachers in the profession are the same factors that help teachers perform at their highest levels. In short, the relationships an administrator establishes with his staff to achieve the purpose of the school may well be the essence of administration.

Perhaps brief mention should be made of the procedures to be followed in the selection and assignment of personnel.[30] The first task confronting the administrator is the preparation of a job description. Ordinarily, responsibility for the preparation of this statement will be given to the building principal. He may, of course, consult his staff in the process of deciding just what is needed for a particular job. Moreover, it must be assumed that job openings are determined within the framework of personnel policies that have been previously formulated.

With job descriptions in hand the superintendent is in a position to seek candidates from a file of applicants, from college placement bureaus, and from other sources of supply. The objective will be to find the best possible people for each of the openings. Often good people must be approached in terms of professional opportunities present in the school system and not merely in terms of an available vacancy and salary to be paid. In other words, selection of personnel is a two-way process: the prospective teacher is appraised by the school system, and the school system is appraised by the teacher. In this kind of approach the superintendent will often find that principals and teachers in the school where the teacher may be placed are key people in the exploration.

29. For instance, see Daniel Katz and Robert L. Kahn, *The Social Psychology of Organizations* (New York: Wiley, 1966), pp. 368–373.

30. For more detail, see William B. Castetter, *The Personnel Function in Educational Administration* (New York: The Macmillan Co., 1971).

When the candidate and the school system have reached agreement, the superintendent is in a position to recommend the prospective teacher to the board of education for employment. It should be quite clear that seeking out and selecting candidates is a professional task. Actual employment of the teacher is, of course, the prerogative of the board of education.

SUPERVISING PERSONNEL

After personnel have been employed and assigned to various positions of responsibility within a school system, there is still the need for the administrative leader—be he called superintendent, principal, or supervisor—to supervise the work. Three terms—supervision, curriculum development, and in-service education—are closely related. Each suggests that teachers and administrators need to work together to decide what the program ought to be, how it should be implemented, and how it is to be evaluated.

Activities related to supervision ordinarily focus on the educational program and incidentally upon teachers and others who implement such a program. Thus supervision may include, as Burton and Brueckner suggest, such activities as the following:

1. An appraisal of the educational product.
2. A study of the learner; diagnosis of learning difficulties.
3. A study of instruction.
4. A study of curriculum in operation.
5. A study of materials of instruction, including the socio-physical environment.[31]

More recently, Cogan has dealt with what he calls clinical supervision. He maintains:

> that clinical supervision is conceptualized as the interaction of peers and colleagues. It is *not* unilateral action taken by the supervisor and aimed at the teacher. On the contrary, the teacher is called on to assume almost all the roles and responsibilities of a supervisor in his interaction with the clinical supervisor. He initiates action, proposes hypotheses, analyzes his own performance, shares responsibilities for devising supervisory strategies, and is equally responsible for the maintenance of morale in the supervisory processes.[32]

The older formulation by Burton and Brueckner places the emphases on the tasks to be performed, while Cogan emphasizes the interpersonal rela-

---

31. W. H. Burton and Leo J. Brueckner, *Supervision—A Social Process* (New York: Appleton-Century-Crofts, 1955).
32. Morris L. Cogan, *Clinical Supervision* (Boston: Houghton Mifflin Co., 1973), p. xi.

tions involved in the process. We believe that both are essential in a supervision program.

APPRAISING TEACHER EFFECTIVENESS

Administrators who have been given responsibility for the operation of a school or a school district must develop some plan of appraising the work of the certificated and noncertificated personnel who work in the school or the district. We suggest that the appraisal be based on the work or performance of the teachers or other personnel rather than on their personal characteristics. The latter involves looking at traits in isolation, an approach that has been largely discredited. Moreover most of us can look more objectively at our performance than we can at our persons.

The major objective of any plan designed to appraise the work of teachers and other personnel should be that of improving performance. It seems clear that when teacher and principal, both of whom comprehend the teaching-learning process, can discuss quite frankly the performance of the teacher, some ways of improving that performance can be determined.

While the primary purpose of performance appraisal should remain that of improving such performance, certain secondary purposes may also need to be served. Decisions pertaining to the retention or dismissal of teachers must be made. Decisions to place or not to place teachers on tenure status are required in many school systems. Many school districts also have a policy of promotion from within the system. Such a plan is based upon the assumption that some teachers have the competencies for such jobs as assistant principals, pupil personnel workers, and other posts, and that those competencies can be recognized. If all of these purposes are to be served well, there must also be appraisal of performance.

In recent years lay citizens and school board members in many school districts have demanded that teaching performance be evaluated in relation to salary. This issue has been debated more than it has been studied. We are convinced that if merit performance is to become a factor in salary determination, most school districts have a long process of "getting ready" for such a program. This eventuality, however, does suggest an additional reason for appraising teaching performance.

Several approaches have been made to the appraisal of teacher performance. One of these might be termed the change-in-pupil-achievement approach. Notable experimentation along this line was first carried out by Barr and his students.[33] It rests on the assumption that the effectiveness of teaching performance can be determined by the growth in achieve-

33. A. S. Barr et al., "The Measurement of Teaching Ability," *Journal of Experimental Education* 14 (September 1945): 1–100.

ment of pupils while under the direction of the teacher. While there is much to support such an assumption, influences on pupil learning other than the teacher's do not seem to be adequately recognized.

A second approach to the appraisal of teaching performance might be termed the pupil-rating method, to which Bryan has been a major contributor.[34] This plan rests on the assumption that pupils know when they are being well taught. Again, there seems to be some truth in such a contention, but it is doubtful that pupils are acquainted with all of the expectations which most school systems have for teachers. Then too, pupils in the early years of school seem less able than older pupils to make a judgment about the quality of teaching performance.

If both of the approaches noted above have limitations, what approach can an administrator use in appraising teaching performance? In our judgment the evaluation approach discussed earlier in this chapter seems to be the most fruitful one. It includes the following steps:

1. The characteristics or criteria of good teaching will be determined.
2. These characteristics will be defined in behavioral terms.
3. A method of observing and recording these behaviors will be evolved.
4. The evidence collected will be appraised.

If these four steps seem formidable, the essence of this approach might be reduced to two major points: (1) there is joint decision as to what good teaching is and (2) a procedure for collecting and appraising evidence concerning good teaching is evolved.

A series of articles in *The National Elementary School Principal*[35] dealt with the question of teacher evaluation. Conceptual approaches, actual experience with evaluation programs, and studies of evaluation procedures were reported. The problem is a complex one but apparently in some schools a cooperative definition of good teaching has been developed and acceptable procedures have been established.

In the discussion above we have suggested that the major administrative tasks in the area of staff personnel include developing personnel policies, securing personnel needed to man programs of instruction and pupil services, providing appropriate stimulation and encouragement to staff members as they work at their jobs, and appraising the performance of staff members in terms of their assigned responsibilities in the school system.

---

34. R. C. Bryan, *Student Reactions and Merit Salary Schedules* (Kalamazoo, Mich.: School of Graduate Studies, Western Michigan University, 1958), p. 67.

35. *The National Elementary School Principal* 43 (November 1963): 3–67.

PHYSICAL FACILITIES

Most programs of instruction and of pupil services require some physical facilities. We include under such a term school buildings, school grounds, and equipment needed in instruction and incidental to instruction. We have also chosen to include school buses and other transportation equipment under the general term of physical facilities. The major tasks of school administration in this area are what we turn to next.

SCHOOL PLANTS FOR INSTRUCTION

We would like to emphasize the point that school plants exist to facilitate the instructional program. To be sure, these plants may be impressive or they may be beautiful, but neither monumental character nor artistic expression should be achieved at the expense of functional arrangement. Actually, we would suggest that artistry and impressiveness be achieved through assigning function its highest type of physical expression.

Perhaps we can illustrate the relationship we see between program and plant. If the program calls for self-contained classrooms, these rooms must be large enough to permit a variety of activities. If the program includes gardening or camping, clearly the plant must provide for these activities. If television is to be used extensively in instruction, the plant must be designed to permit closed circuit hookups or other necessary arrangements. If part-time farmers are to be given help with their problems, land for agricultural demonstration should be provided. If the school is also to serve as a center for many community activities, it must be so located and so constructed as to permit such use.

Prediction of the educational program of tomorrow is hazardous, but it seems clear that education will undergo change. Hence modern designers attempt to make school plants highly flexible. The problem facing planners is well put by a commission report:

> If the educational program never changed; if the culture were static and scientists had ceased probing into the unknown; if inventors had gone on a long holiday and discoveries and innovations were at a standstill; if population mobility had ceased and the birth rate had become a constant factor; if community life always remained the same; if towns and cities were all alike; if there were no differences in school sites; if no new jobs were being created; if no new educational needs were emerging and the specific purposes of the school were rigidly defined; if the researchers had concluded that all the answers to the problems of teaching and learning had been found; if there were no more content to be added to the curriculum; if the producers of instructional materials and equipment had ceased to experiment and had settled down to producing a standard product; if people were

> entirely content with present accomplishments; if the dynamic forces of society had all been securely grounded and had ceased to function, then school-building planning would be a simple matter. Stock plans and standard classrooms would be the answer to the school districts' needs for building space. But such is not the case nor is it likely to be.[36]

PLANT DEVELOPMENT PROGRAM

The many problems involved in developing a plant to house a school program are dealt with in the report mentioned above.[37] This volume details the steps to be taken in the development of a school plant program. In order to determine what school plants are needed, an administrator must have data of four kinds: a picture of the educational program to be housed, a projection of the school population to be served, a plan for usage of the existing plant, and an indication of money available for plant expansion. The character of the data needed in each of these areas will be noted briefly.

The school program is a matter of prime importance. For instance, are schools to be organized on a K6–3–3 basis or on a K8–4 basis? Are elementary schools to be designed for 300 pupils or 1,000 pupils? Are rooms to be designed to house 25 pupils or 40 pupils? Is the seventh grade to be organized largely on a self-contained basis or on a departmental plan? Is science to be taught by the laboratory or by the demonstration method? Is team teaching, where large and small rooms are needed, to be a part of the program? Is closed-circuit TV to be provided?

These questions suggest that the plant should be built to house a program. In a report[38] on educational change and architectural consequences,

> Educators have pointed out how innovative approaches as disparate as nongradedness and televised instruction are handicapped by facilities that block groups of students and teachers off from one another, making mobility onerous, impose a tight-ship kind of discipline and a custodial attitude toward resources, and prohibit full use of technology. . . . The school program should dictate school space and not the other way around.

---

36. Report of the AASA School-Building Commission: *Planning America's School Buildings* (Washington, D.C.: The Association, 1960), p. 5.

37. Ibid., 229.

38. *Educational Change and Architectural Consequences* (New York: Educational Facilities Laboratories, 1968), pp. 15–16. Also, the entire issue of the *Harvard Educational Review* 39, 4 (1969), is devoted to an exploration of the reciprocal relationships between architectural values and educational goals, particularly at a time when the basic values of society are undergoing change.

The report concludes that what is needed are flexible school facilities that provide for five general kinds of settings for learning: the conventional classroom, independent study facilities, teacher-pupil one-to-one dialogue, small group discussions, and large group lecture presentations.

The second area of concern has to do with the pupils to be served, and in this case the administrator is dealing in futures. Such questions as the following must be answered: What changes are anticipated in the school population? How do these changes affect each grade level? How do these changes affect each part or attendance area of the district? What are the prospects of changes in district boundaries, and how are they likely to affect pupil population, including racial composition? What housing developments are in prospect, and what effect are they likely to have on pupil population? For decades answers to these questions were based on the assumption of growth in the student population. Now with decreases in student population in many school districts the data may have quite different implications for school plant programs.

A third body of data necessary in planning for the school plant has to do with the proposed use of the existing plant. Again, key questions must be answered. Are the present buildings safe? Are they located where they will be needed? Can they be adapted to serve the educational needs of the district? What capacities do the existing buildings have in terms of the educational program and pupil population of the future?

Results of these three types of studies begin to suggest the kind, amount, and location of school plants needed by the district. At this point the financial resources available for capital outlay must be examined. Since most districts must rely on a bond issue for capital outlay, the bonding possibilities of a district, usually limited by statute, must be noted. Moreover, practical considerations usually require that attention be given to tax levies already in effect for capital outlay and for current operation of the school. These considerations may require that the relative cost of reconditioning existing buildings as opposed to costs of constructing new buildings be determined. All in all, the financial data help answer the big question of whether or not the needed plant expansion is practicable.

In a school district of any size the four kinds of data mentioned above are necessary to a program for the development of the school plant. In a small school district the superintendent will work directly with principals, teachers, and citizens on the problem. In a larger school district he may have one or more staff members who will assist with these studies. In some cases, the help of outside consultants can be secured to guide or supplement the work of local people. In any case, however, the superintendent must see that these studies are made. With such information in hand the board of education and the people of a community are in a better position to make decisions regarding the modification of the existing plant, the securing of additional plant facilities, or the disposal of some plant facilities. If new construction or remodeling of old construction is needed, the superintendent will have other tasks as he works with architects and contractors, but his basic responsibility lies in the tasks enumerated above. Unless the administrator and his staff have given attention to the program to be housed, the planning aspect of the plant program will not be adequate. If plants are to be closed, tasks inherent in community relations may become most demanding.

In addition to a program designed to expand the physical facilities of a school district, administrators are confronted with the operation and maintenance of the existing school plant. Operation, as the word implies, has to do with the day-to-day running of the plant. The major objectives of operation are to keep the plant safe, sanitary, attractive, and in readiness for teaching and learning. All of this is to be done as efficiently as possible. Extravagance in plant operation may mean that less money is available for those aspects of the program which are more directly related to teaching and learning.

School plants, like other physical facilities, require a constant program of maintenance. Equipment wears out and must be replaced. Paint deteriorates and must be replaced. Mortar loosens and must be repaired. Roofs eventually leak and require repair. A hundred other examples could be given. Most maintenance jobs require skilled craftsmen, including plumbers, painters, electricians, masons, roofers, and many others.

A perennial issue in the plant maintenance field is how to get these skilled workmen. Should the school set up a maintenance department and employ many of these craftsmen on an annual basis so as to have them available when needed? Or should maintenance work be let out on contract at times when there is work to be done? This problem and many allied problems will require administrative attention in any school district.

As suggested above, we have made transportation a part of our discussion of physical facilities, a decision which seems to be logical for two reasons. First, the transportation service is carried on with a rather high capital investment in equipment, for which the problems of procurement and maintenance are somewhat similar to the procurement and maintenance of other equipment. Second, the transportation program is auxiliary to the instructional program in somewhat the same manner as are building facilities. Pupils are housed or transported so as to be available for instruction.

In rural areas the transportation function has become so extensive as to require in some places as much as 25 percent of the school budget. In such instances administrative responsibility for establishing the transportation program, for purchasing equipment, for securing bus drivers and mechanics, for supervising their work, and for maintaining relationships with parents of transported pupils is a major task. In all but the very small districts, supervisors of transportation are usually added to the administrative staff.

FINANCE AND BUSINESS MANAGEMENT

In a money economy such as ours, the services of personnel, the buildings, the equipment, the supplies, and the other items necessary to the operation of a school or a school system must be paid for. Thus another operational area of administration, that of finance and business management, is indicated. The administrative tasks included in this area, whether they have to do with securing revenues or making expenditures, are instrumental, not primary, in character. In other words, money is useful only as it is used to purchase a program of teaching and learning. The details of both finance and business management have been described elsewhere.[39] For our purposes, we shall deal with budget making, securing revenue, managing expenditures, and managing noncertificated personnel.

BUDGET MAKING

The school budget is often defined as a school program expressed in fiscal terms. Actually, a good budget will have three major aspects: the proposed program of the school district, the expenditures necessary to support such a program, and the anticipated revenues to cover such expenditures.

Again, the basic position of the instructional program is stressed. The budget should not provide simply for personnel, but rather for particular personnel to carry out particular parts of the program. The budget should not call simply for new or remodeled buildings, but rather for particular buildings with particular facilities to permit particular parts of the program to go forward. The budget should stipulate not simply money for equipment, but money for particular equipment to facilitate teaching and learning for particular parts of the program.

If the budget is to reflect the school program to the extent here indicated, it is clear that budget building becomes a most important process within a school system. We would like to comment upon some aspects of that process.

It is important that the people within the school system who actually operate the program have a large part in budget building. This means that teachers will have a real voice in suggesting what is necessary by way of working conditions, equipment, supplies, books, and other items to make instruction more effective. This means also that noncertificated employees who clean floors, repair roofs, or do other tasks will also have a voice in suggesting what is needed to do these jobs efficiently. To be

39. For instance, see Roe L. Johns and Edgar L. Morphet, *Economics and Financing the Education,* 2nd ed. (Englewood Cliffs, N.J.: Prentice-Hall, 1969), and W. G. Hack & F. O. Woodard, *Economic Dimensions of Public School Finance: Concepts & Cases* (New York: McGraw-Hill, 1971).

sure, all of these suggestions may not be accepted, but they should be considered.

Budgetmaking is also a continuous process. It has both short-range and long-range aspects. Filling out a budget estimate for the ensuing year may be essentially a short-range task. On the other hand, teachers may work for a year or two in projecting an improved program for the teaching of the social studies. We submit that such planning is long-range budget making as truly as it is curriculum development. In brief, we suggest that all planning for program improvement, whether it be for instruction or for services, should also be considered as budget making.

In recent years, largely based on experience in the Department of Defense, the federal government has stressed program planning and budgeting systems (PPBS). Such systems are seen as methods which require long-range planning, the choice of alternatives, and the relating of costs and benefits. While such procedures are most difficult when applied to an enterprise as complex as education, the concept behind PPBS, and similar formulations, seems worthy of further scrutiny. James[40] has provided one of the more insightful analyses of the movement. We have treated PPBS as one expression of systems analysis in chapter 8.

The concept of the budget suggested here means that it is a major policy statement in any school district. Unfortunately, there are still many school districts in which the budget is seen only in its short-range aspects, where the deliberations of staff members are seldom reflected, where the program which the budget proposes to buy is meagerly portrayed, and where the format is unattractive. Such an important document deserves better treatment.

SECURING REVENUE

Another important administrative task in the area of finance and business management is securing of revenue. The financing of schools is, of course, but one aspect of public finance. Numerous governmental services at local, state, and national levels must be financed. The securing of money for these services, chiefly through taxation, is intimately related to the general economy of the nation. These interrelationships are often not fully appreciated by citizens, or for that matter by school administrators. Benson[41] has dealt extensively with school finance as an area of public finance, and he has applied economic analyses to a comprehensive selection of topics in the financing of education.

School districts ordinarily receive revenues from local, state, and

40. H. Thomas James, *The New Cult of Efficiency and Education* (Pittsburgh: University of Pittsburgh Press, 1969).

41. Charles S. Benson, *The Economics of Public Education,* 2nd ed. (Boston: Houghton Mifflin, 1968).

federal sources as was shown in chapter 3. There is great variability among the states with regard to the percentage of school revenues received from each level of government, as can be seen in Table 5–1.

TABLE 5–1 Estimated Percent of Revenue for Public Elementary and Secondary Schools for Selected States by Levels of Government (1972–1973)

	LOCAL	*STATE*	*FEDERAL*
Alabama	18.9	63.6	17.6
California	56.5	36.7	6.8
Illinois	55.2	38.6	6.2
Nebraska	75.8	17.4	6.7
New Mexico	18.9	63.0	18.2
New York	52.6	41.4	6.0
Ohio	61.2	33.1	5.7
Texas	43.0	46.3	10.7
United States	51.2	41.0	7.7

Source: Research Division, National Education Association, *Ranking of the States, 1973.*

At the local level, the source of school revenue is almost entirely the property tax. At the state level, legislative appropriation from the general fund is the usual practice. While revenues accruing to the states upon which legislative appropriations may draw are from several sources, the retail sales tax, the state income tax, or both, have become major sources of such revenue in most states.

Over recent decades, the federal government has become the chief tax collector. Whereas in 1929 approximately 75 percent of the taxes were collected at local and state levels, and the remaining 25 percent at the federal level, during World War II these percentages were almost reversed, thus making the federal government the chief tax collector. This shift has, of course, been accompanied by a great increase in total taxes collected and by unprecedented expenditures on the part of the federal government for services at home and abroad.

Large sums of federal money have been allocated for such services as hospital construction and road building. Because state and local sources have been shown to be inadequate for these and other public services, many doubt that public schools can be supported adequately from state and local sources alone. Certainly the flow of goods, services, and money tends to be national and international rather than local and state in character.

With the clear recognition that the various states must play a major role in financing public education, and with the likelihood that the federal government will also share to some extent in such financing, school administrators must be prepared to give leadership in public school finance at both state and federal levels. The administrator cannot see his responsibilities in the finance realm as limited to his own school district.

At the state level this means that the whole plan of state support for public education must come under the purview of the school administrator. Most states have some kind of foundation program for the financial support of schools, an arrangement which is supposed to guarantee a minimum educational program for every district of the state. School administrators must be able to help state boards of education, state legislatures, and citizens generally to understand the purposes and operations of such a foundation program. Without such study and vigilance, state aid, as recent court cases demonstrate, may equalize neither educational opportunity nor tax burden. School administrators should join in school finance reform already underway in many states.

At the federal level, too, administrators should have insights based upon the economic realities of a highly industrialized and interdependent economy. With such insights, and with facts based upon careful research, the appropriate role of the federal government in school finance might be determined. While federal aid expanded during the 1960s, such aid has been subjected to reexamination and reduction since that time. The task ahead seems to be the evolution of an appropriate local-state-national partnership in the financing of the schools.

Though school administration should provide statesmanship in school finance at both state and federal levels, the concern with the revenues available to one's own school district must also have attention. For instance, the superintendent or members of his staff must check to see that taxes levied for the school district are properly calculated and distributed. In many states this will require close working arrangements with the county assessor and the county auditor.

In similar manner the superintendent or members of his staff must ascertain all ways by which the school district might become eligible for state funds; and when the district is eligible, he must check to see that allocations due the district are being made. Ordinarily, then, the local superintendent must have a working relationship with the state department of education.

While federal funds are a minor part of total school revenue, they are exceedingly important to many school districts. Public Laws 874 and 815, for instance, have provided federal funds for operation and capital outlay to school districts where enrollments have been increased due to population movements caused by federal installations. Recent congressional action has also authorized appreciable revenues for the improvement of vocational education and for the education of the disadvantaged. As with local and state revenues, the administrator has the obligation to determine the eligibility of the school district for federal funds and then to see that such funds are made available.

MANAGING EXPENDITURES

The management of expenditures made by a school district is another administrative responsibility. There are many tasks in this aspect of administration, including purchasing, payroll operation, supply management, accounting and reporting, insurance management, and the keeping of a property inventory. The adequate performance of each of these tasks requires considerable knowledge and skill.[42] In small school districts, the superintendent will be expected to perform many of these functions. In larger school districts specialized help may be secured, but it is still the superintendent's responsibility to see that these jobs are performed.

One important part of the accounting procedures of a school district is the budget control record. As will be recalled, we advocated that the budget be formulated in considerable detail so as to depict the educational program for which the money was to be spent, and the sources from which the money was to come. With such a budget as a beginning point, a budget control system should be developed so that at least once a month the conditions of expenditures and revenues might be ascertained. Such a report can both help the superintendent and his staff in their administration of the budget, and prove an indispensable aid to a board of education in its efforts to understand how the school enterprise is going forward. For budget control, bookkeeping, and other aspects of business management, a machine technology, including the use of computers, has been developed.

MANAGING NONCERTIFICATED PERSONNEL

Ordinarily the management of noncertificated personnel is made a part of business management. In small school districts the distinction is of little consequence. In larger districts, however, the business management function, including responsibility for noncertificated personnel, is delegated by the superintendent to a business manager or assistant superintendent in charge of business. Noncertificated personnel include a wide variety of workers such as custodians, skilled craftsmen, cafeteria employees, bus drivers, and secretaries. In many school districts, these employees number approximately one-half the number of instructional or certificated workers.

For each of these categories of workers, a plan of personnel management needs to be evolved. In many respects the details of such a plan are similar to those which were developed at some length in the discussion of staff personnel above. For each group of workers, appropriate personnel policies must be developed, suitable people must be selected

42. Hack & Woodard, *Economic Dimensions of Public School Finance.*

The management of expenditures is another administrative responsibility.

and employed, supervision must be provided, and appraisal of work performance made.

The components of job satisfaction for noncertificated workers are similar to those of certificated workers. People like to feel wanted, they like to feel that the institution has a desirable program, and they like to feel that their contribution is valued.

We have suggested that administrative activities in finance and business management are instrumental to the achievement of the major purpose of the school. The major tasks of this area have been presented as budget making, securing revenues, managing expenditures, and directing noncertificated personnel.

ORGANIZING TO ACHIEVE THE TASKS

Achievement of the tasks enumerated above requires an organization or structure. The establishment of this structure represents, in a sense, an additional task area. However, we have chosen to view the development of such a structure as a way of implementing the tasks already suggested rather than as a set of additional tasks.

By structure we refer to the relationships of people as they work to achieve a common goal, and it is these relationships with which this section will deal. In this connection it is necessary to discuss briefly the meaning of formal organization, the controlling board, administrative organization, and channels for communication and participation.

MEANING OF FORMAL ORGANIZATION

Most people belong to both formal and informal organizations. A group of women may get together regularly to play bridge, a group of men may become a golf foursome, children on a particular street may become a play group, or a half-dozen members of a high school faculty may meet frequently for lunch. All of these are examples of informal organizations.

On the other hand, a business corporation, a military battalion, a church congregation, and a school district are examples of formal organizations. What are the basic differences between these two kinds of groups? There are several worthy of mention. With respect to origin, informal groups tend to be voluntary while formal groups are usually official. An informal organization may terminate when the present membership leaves, while a formal organization persists beyond its immediate membership. The task or purpose of an informal group is probably not known or, at least, not clear to outsiders, while the task of a formal group is usually adequately perceived by people out of the organization. An informal organization ordinarily has no assigned status hierarchy while a formal organization does. In an informal organization there may be little regular differentiation of assigned work (or play), while in a formal organization there is definite allocation of work responsibilities.

The people who work in a school or school district are definitely members of a formal organization. The school or school district came into being by official governmental act. The organization will go on beyond the lives of the present members. The task of the school or school district is clear to those outside the organization. In all except the smallest schools, there is a recognized hierarchy of position. The work of administrators, teachers, custodians, and other workers is clearly differentiated. This concept of the school as a formal organization is relevant to the remainder of this discussion.

We are well aware of the fact that a school or school district, in addition to being a formal organization, may have one or more informal organizations within it. A clique within a faculty, for instance, may greatly influence decisions of the faculty or of the administrator, entirely outside the formal organizational channels. It is not our purpose here to explore the ramifications of informal organizations within formal organizations. Suffice it to say that formal organization cannot replace informal organization.

We also recognize that the formal organization established by the school district will often be called upon to deal with one or more other formal organizations established by the teaching employees, and in many cases by the nonteaching employees of the district.

CONTROLLING BOARD

As with most other formal organizations, workers of a school district are subject to the direction of a controlling board, in most states known as the board of education. In some states the terminology is board of trustees or board of directors. In all cases these boards are created by the respective state legislatures and given by them broad grants of power to organize and conduct schools within their respective school districts. In addition to the specified powers enumerated in the respective state codes, boards of education also have the powers implied as necessary to the proper exercise of the specified powers. The breadth of these responsibilities is illustrated by two sections of the laws of Wisconsin relating to the public schools:

> . . . the school district board shall have the possession, care, control, and management of the property and affairs of the district. (40.29) The board may make rules for the organization, graduation, and government of the schools. . . . (40.30)

While the language shown above makes clear the fact that the board of education has complete legal control, within the limitations of state and federal law, to operate a school district, the board of education has found it necessary in actual practice to create an organization to operate the schools. In a small school district this may be a very simple organization of a few teachers and a custodian with the board itself attempting to retain the administrative function. In most school districts, however, the board of education employs a superintendent of schools as its chief administrator. In turn, the superintendent is expected to organize separate schools under the direction of building principals, and to secure instructional and non-instructional personnel, usually subject to approval of the board, to man the school enterprise.

With the employment of a superintendent of schools, the differentiation of function between the controlling board and its chief executive officer becomes a matter of importance. In general, a board of education does or should become chiefly a legislative and judicial body, while the administrative function is or should be given to the superintendent. This distinction is not as simple as it sounds and many boards and superintendents have difficulty in establishing their respective roles. Since legal control, even for administration, rests finally with the board. The superintendent cannot exercise an executive role except as his board permits.

To assist in this kind of understanding, the role of the board is often defined as part of the rules and regulations of the school district. An excerpt from the *Administrative Guide*[43] for the Columbus, Ohio schools is shown below:

> 108.01. The Board . . . shall appoint a qualified person to act as Superintendent of the Columbus City School District for a term not longer than five years . . .

Other duties of the Columbus Board are organized under mandatory duties and permissive duties. Sample mandatory duties are shown below:

> 201.01 The Board shall provide for the free education of the youth of school age within the district under its jurisdiction, at such places as will be most convenient for the attendance of the largest number thereof.
>
> 201.02 The Board shall have the management and control of all the public schools, of whatever name or character, in the Columbus City School District. (R.C. 3313.47)
>
> 201.06 The Board shall employ teachers in accordance with the provisions of Section 3319.08 of the Revised Code, and fix their salaries . . .
>
> 201.13 The Board shall make such rules and regulations as are necessary for its government and the government of its employees and the pupils of the schools. (R.C. 3313.20)

Sample permissive duties follow:

> 202.01 (1) Issue bonds for the purpose of acquiring or constructing any permanent improvement. (R.C. 133.24)
>
> 202.02 The Board may build, repair, furnish, and enlarge school buildings . . .

To perform the duties enumerated above in a few meetings per month—all the time lay citizens can ordinarily devote to the school board—it is clear that the Columbus Board of Education would have to deal with questions of policy and not with the details of operation. Often the establishment of policy, upon the recommendation of the superintendent and his staff, constitutes the legislative activity of the board of education. Examination of how that policy has worked in practice, often with the help of rather complete reports supplied by the superintendent and his staff, permits the board to exercise its judicial function.

This discussion has already implied much concerning the role of the superintendent, but let us look more specifically at that matter. Columbus has also defined the superintendent's job as follows:

43. Columbus Public Schools, *Administrative Guide* (1975).

108.02. The Superintendent

(1) Shall be in all respects the chief executive officer of the Board for the management of all the departments of the school system, except as otherwise provided by law. He shall have the power to make rules not in conflict with the law or with the rules of the Board and to decide all matters of administration and supervisory detail in connection with the operation and maintenance of the schools.

(2) Shall be directly responsible to the Board: he shall possess the power to initiate and to direct the development of policies for the approval of the Board, and the power to delegate such responsibilities to associates and subordinates as he may desire.

(5) Shall have the sole power to appoint, assign, transfer, promote and demote, or suspend all employees of the Board, except as otherwise provided by law and by the rules of the Board. All appointments, promotions, demotions, and suspensions which shall be made by the Superintendent shall be reported in writing to the Board for approval and confirmation.[44]

We believe that the superintendent should serve as the chief executive officer and as the chief professional adviser to the board of education. Zeigler[45] contends that superintendents have gone beyond these two roles and that they dominate boards of education even in the area of policy making. In short, he suggests that boards tend only to legitimize the policy proposals of the superintendent. We see some merit in Zeigler's position but we suspect that he has given too little attention to the phenomena of "anticipated consequences." Most superintendents probably recommend policies in keeping with the values held by the board and the community. Nonetheless, Zeigler has provided a warning which superintendents and boards should consider as they review their complementary roles and strategic relationships.

ADMINISTRATIVE ORGANIZATION

The school enterprise of many school districts is of such magnitude that a single administrator cannot give it adequate direction and supervision. In these cases an administrative organization must be established. In some districts this organization may include only the superintendent and three

44. Ibid.

45. L. Harmon Zeigler et al., *Governing American Schools* (North Scituate, Mass.: Duxbury Press, 1974).

or four building principals; in others a much more complex structure becomes necessary.

While we maintain that no form or amount of administrative organization will, per se, guarantee an effective school system, we do believe that appropriate administrative organization can facilitate the achievement of the goals of a school system. There are some telltale signs that betray ineffective administrative organization. Some of these are: a large proportion of administrative time spent on "emergencies," unexplained delays in carrying out plans, or frequent complaints that "no one told me." These and similar breakdowns warn that the concepts and principles of administrative organization should be examined.

Let us mention some of the concepts that require attention. One of these is the question of centralization versus decentralization. In the centralized plan the superintendent's office exercises tight control over all of the schools of the district. In the decentralized arrangement building principals and their staffs are given considerable autonomy with regard to many aspects of school operation. Centralization requires a relatively large central office staff of directors and supervisors, whereas decentralization may mean that each principal will be given administrative assistance. Centralized control usually requires considerable uniformity of practice among the various schools; decentralized control ordinarily results in more diversity of practice among the schools. Decentralization in major cities received new impetus from demands for community control during the 1960s but that movement seems to have decreased in recent years.

Another concept in organization is that of line and staff. Line officers are usually thought of as those responsible for the operation of the major units of an organization, i.e., school district or school attendance area. Staff officers usually serve in a fact gathering or advisory capacity or perform a specialized function for line officers, i.e., director of research or school psychologist. Since these terms have a military connotation, some educators have been prone to condemn them, a rejection which seems rather foolish, for in relatively large school organizations some line and some staff officials seem necessary. Ordinarily building principals are thought of as line people, since they are responsible for the operation of a school. On the other hand, a director of research and a director of in-service education would usually be designated as staff people. Their function is that of assisting the superintendent either by supplying him with research findings or performing some tasks in his name. While staff people do not have the responsibility for a school, they do have functional responsibility.

In any organization there is also the matter of a flat or a pyramidal arrangement. A superintendent working directly with principals represents a flat or a two-level arrangement, while a plan of organization which includes assistant superintendents and directors may mean a pyramid, or a four-level arrangement. More levels seem to increase the feeling of distance between the chief administrator and the teachers, and may easily lead to such remarks as, "Oh, I know nothing about that, for it is handled downtown."

Closely related to flat and pyramidal organization is the concept of span of control. This refers to the number of people reporting directly to a single administrator, usually the chief administrator or superintendent of schools. Often the superintendent is torn between wishing a flat organization, and having so many subadministrators reporting directly to him that he cannot do justice to those relationships. Some students of organization think that the chief administrator should not have more than five to eight administrative assistants reporting directly to him.

Still another concept is that of horizontal and vertical organization. Assistant superintendents in charge of elementary and secondary education respectively represent a horizontal arrangement, while assistant superintendents in charge of functions or operational areas such as instruction or staff personnel represent a vertical plan.

Griffiths and others have suggested that the establishment of an administrative organization is one of the basic functions of administration. They suggest that the steps necessary in this process are as follows:

1. The purposes of the school should be stated clearly and in operational terms.
2. The conceptual framework on which the organization will be constructed must be agreed upon.
3. The functions of administration necessary to the achievement of the stated purposes must be listed.
4. The present administrative structure must be surveyed to determine which functions are being performed by whom.
5. A plan of organization must be developed consistent with the conceptual framework of organization.
6. The functions of administration must be related to specific administrative positions.
7. Job descriptions must be developed for the administrative positions to which functions are assigned.
8. The administrative positions and the job descriptions must be related to the incumbent administrators.
9. A timetable must be set up to implement the reorganization.[46]

COMMUNICATION AND PARTICIPATION

In any formal organization it becomes necessary to establish channels for communication and participation. Only through adequate communication can members of the organization remain aware of organizational goals,

46. Daniel E. Griffiths et al., *Organizing Schools for Effective Education* (Danville, Ill.: Interstate Publishers, 1962), p. 309.

keep clearly in mind how their own work contributes to those goals, understand how the work of others contributes to the goals, and make suggestions for the improvement of operational procedures in the organization. The conditions suggested above make it clear that communication in an organization must flow up, down, and across.

Culbertson points out that there are many barriers to communication in an organization.[47] These barriers may include the words used in the communication, many of which carry different emotional overtones to different people; or the barrier may rest with the administrator as the communicator, particularly if he is inclined to emphasize the aspects of his office related to status; or the barrier may rest with members of the organization as communicatees, if their values and motivations are different from those of the communicator.

Erickson and Pedersen[48] reviewed a number of studies having to do with communication within schools, focusing particularly upon impediments to such communication. Some of these impediments were found in the situation such as the hierarchical structure of the school, the large quantity of information needing transmission, the lack of collegial interaction, and the cultural influences on interpretations of the messages.

Impediments were also found in the persons, and included such factors as inept transmission and reception, failure to respond, misplaced quest for power, and aversion to threat. Much of the responsibility for removing these impediments to the communication rests with the administrator.

As part of the conclusion of their comprehensive volume on organizations, Katz and Kahn[49] suggest that the conflict between rising expectations of involvement and the difficulties of communication and participation can have several maladaptive effects such as a feeling of apathy at being outside the system, blind conformity to the system, and ferment without form. Katz and Kahn continue by suggesting that most organizations can profitably move toward decentralization, that there can be some shift of authority from officials to members, that distinctions between classes of citizenship can be reduced, and that role enlargement can often give a sense of greater participation.

We have concluded our overview of the administrative tasks in education administration by a consideration of organization and structure. We have suggested that organization and structure imply arrangements designed to facilitate the other administrative tasks; and all administrative tasks, it will be recalled, have their *raison d'être* in improving the programs for teaching and learning in a school or school district.

---

47. Jack Culbertson, "Recognizing Roadblocks in Communications Channels," *Administrator's Notebook,* 7 (March 1959), pp. 1–4.

48. Donald A. Erickson and K. George Pedersen, "Major Communication Problems in the Schools," *Administrators Notebook* 14 (March 1966) 7, pp. 1–4.

49. Daniel Katz and Robert L. Kahn, *The Social Psychology of Organizations* (New York: Wiley, 1966), pp. 470–471.

SUGGESTED ACTIVITIES

1. Compare the operational areas of this chapter with those suggested by Miller. Which categorization do you prefer? Why?
2. In the light of the criteria suggested for personnel policies in this chapter, appraise the personnel policies of your district.
3. Determine what percentage of the budget of your school district over the past ten years has been allocated for (a) instruction and (b) capital outlay and debt service.
4. Taking account of recent legislation enacted by the Congress, project the school revenues from federal sources for your state during the next three years.

SELECTED READINGS

Benson, Charles S. *The Economics of Public Education,* 2nd ed. Boston: Houghton Mifflin Co., 1968.

Campbell, Roald F.; Cunningham, Luvern L.; Nystrand, Raphael O.; and Usdan, Michael D. *Organization and Control of American Schools,* 3rd ed. Columbus, Ohio: Charles E. Merrill, 1975.

Castetter, Wm. B. *The Personnel Function in Educational Administration.* New York: The Macmillan Co., 1971.

Frost, Joe L., and Rowland, G. Thomas. *Curricula for the Seventies.* Boston: Houghton Mifflin Co., 1969.

Hack, W. G., and Woodard, F. O. *Economic Dimensions of Public School Finance: Concepts and Cases.* New York: McGraw-Hill, 1971.

Hummel, Dean L., and Bonham, S. J. *Pupil Personnel Services in Schools.* Chicago: Rand McNally, 1968.

Iannaccone, Laurence. *Politics in Education.* New York: Center for Applied Research in Education, 1967.

Johns, R. L., and Alexander, K. *Alternative Programs for Financing Education.* National Education Finance Project, University of Florida, Gainsville, 1971.

Miller, Van; Madden, G. R.; and Kincheloe, J. B. *The Public Administration of American School Systems,* 2nd ed. New York: Macmillan, 1972.

Stufflebeam, Daniel L., ed. *Educational Evaluation and Decision Making.* Itaska, Ill.: Peacock Publishers, 1971.

6

THE WORK OF EDUCATIONAL ADMINISTRATORS

Thus far we have examined administration from the standpoint of its development and meaning, and in terms of the major tasks confronting a school organization. We shall now look at the work of an administrator from two perspectives. First, we shall view administration in normative terms and suggest how an administrator should behave if he wishes his activity to result in the greatest attainment of objectives with available resources. Second, we shall focus on what administrators actually do as they seek to achieve the organization's goals. We shall conclude our discussion by identifying a major problem which is suggested by the normative and descriptive views of administration.

A NORMATIVE VIEW OF MANAGERIAL WORK: THE ADMINISTRATIVE PROCESS SCHOOL

DEVELOPMENTS OF THE ADMINISTRATIVE PROCESS CONCEPT IN BUSINESS AND PUBLIC ADMINISTRATION

As noted in chapter 4, Fayol, as early as 1916 in his *Administration Industrielle et Generale,* dealt with what he called the "elements of management."[1] He described them as planning, organizing, commanding, coordinating, and controlling. Together these activities constituted the administrative function. Because Fayol's treatment of the administrative function had a major impact on subsequent formulations of the administrative process, we shall comment further about what he meant by planning, organizing, commanding, coordinating, and controlling. Fayol used the term "planning" to represent the activity involved in foretelling the future and preparing for it. The most important instrument of planning was the *plan of operations* which contained the object in view, the course of actions to be followed, the various stages on the way, and the means to be used. Fayol maintained that the characteristics of a good plan of operations were unity, continuity, flexibility, and precision.

Although he recognized that organizing involved both human and material elements, his chief concern was with the human organization. The principal instrument for achieving an effective human organization was the organization chart which showed "the whole of the staff, the constitution and limits of each department, the man occupying each position, the man whom an employee must obey and the subordinates whom he commands."[2] Even at that time, Fayol recognized the problems posed by a peopled organization and mentioned the need to invest time and energy in the selection of employees, to situate men where they could be of most service, and to adapt organizational requirements in light of available personnel.

For Fayol, commanding meant more than enforcement of obedience, it involved getting the best out of employees in the interest of the concern as a whole. To facilitate command, he suggested that the manager should perform such activities as these: acquire a thorough knowledge of his personnel; eliminate the incompetent; avoid preoccupation with detail; set a good example; and foster *esprit de corps,* initiative, and loyalty among his staff.

Fayol conceived of coordination as being principally concerned with harmonizing all the operations of the organization and with unifying disconnected efforts. He argued that a well-coordinated organization was evidenced by such conditions as an up-to-date program of work for each department and exact instructions about how the various units and subunits were to combine their efforts. Lack of coordination, on the other hand, was signaled when each department made no effort to consider the firm as a whole and willfully ignored the work of other departments. To help staff members coordinate their efforts, Fayol recommended regular meetings of departmental managers.

Controlling, as used by Fayol, signified appraisal and examination of results. The object of control was to uncover weaknesses and errors in order to rectify them and prevent their recurrence. The relationship of

1. See translation by Constance Starrs, *General and Industrial Management* (London: Sir Isaac Pitman and Sons, 1949).

2. See translation by J. A. Coubrough, *Industrial and General Administration* (London: Sir Isaac Pitman and Sons, 1900), p. 58.

control to planning, organizing, commanding, and coordinating was stated clearly by Fayol:

> In an undertaking, control consists in verifying whether everything occurs in conformity with the plan adopted, the instructions issued and principles established. . . . It operates on everything, things, people, actions. From the management standpoint it must be ensured that a plan does exist, that it is put into operation and kept up-to-date, that the human organization is complete, the summarized personnel charts in use, and that command is exercised in line with principles, that co-ordinating conferences are held, etc., etc.[3]

According to Fayol, the administrative function (planning, organizing, commanding, coordinating, and controlling) was present in all business undertakings—simple or complex, large or small. Furthermore, the administrative function was carried out by all members of the organization; however, the relative importance of the ability to perform this function increased as one ascended the organizational hierarchy. For Fayol the administrative function was the essential condition for a successful operation; if the function was effectively exercised in all parts of the organization, the running of the concern would be satisfactory.

Fayol's "elements" of the administrative function were derived chiefly from his experience with industrial enterprises. Soon, however, others were to apply these principles to the public realm. For instance, Gulick[4] suggested how the office of the President of the United States might be organized. He asked the question, "What is the work of the chief executive?" His answer was "POSDCoRB," which sounds a little confusing until one learns that the letters stand for activities necessary to the proper functioning of the office. Gulick himself explains these activities as follows:

> Planning, that is working out in broad outline the things that need to be done and the methods for doing them to accomplish the purpose set for the enterprise;
>
> Organizing, that is the establishment of the formal structure of authority through which work subdivisions are arranged, defined and co-ordinated for the defined objective;
>
> Staffing, that is the whole personnel function of bringing and training the staff and maintaining favorable conditions of work;
>
> Directing, that is the continuous task of making decisions and embodying them in specific and general orders and instructions and serving as the leader of the enterprise;

3. Starrs, *General and Industrial Management,* p. 107.

4. Luther Gulick and L. Urwick, eds., *Papers on the Science of Administration* (New York: Institute of Public Administration, 1937).

> Co-ordinating, that is the all-important duty of interrelating the various parts of the work;
>
> Reporting, that is keeping those to whom the chief executive is responsible informed as to what is going on, which thus includes keeping himself and his subordinates informed through records, research and inspection;
>
> Budgeting, with all that goes with budgeting in the form of fiscal planning, accounting and control.[5]

Gulick acknowledged that the above formulation was an adaptation of the functional analysis previously elaborated by Fayol. Although Gulick was speaking specifically of the office of the President of the United States, he contended that this analysis would be a helpful pattern into which to place the major activities of any chief executive.

Eight years later, Simon extended the work of Gulick and Fayol by treating administrative functions and activities within a decision making framework. Simon[6] maintained that administrative processes were decisional ones and that their purpose was to facilitate the application of organized effort to the group task. To accomplish this purpose, the organization deprives the individual of some of his decisional autonomy and substitutes an organizational decision-making process.

> The decisions which the organization makes for the individual ordinarily (1) specify his function, that is, the general scope and nature of his duties; (2) allocate authority, that is, determine who in the organization is to have power to make further decisions for the individual; and (3) set such other limits to his choice as are needed to co-ordinate the activities of several individuals in the organization.[7]

Although Simon acknowledged the importance of allocating the decision making functions, the central problem he addressed was how the decisions and behavior of employees are influenced within and by the organization.

In his analysis of organizational decision processes, Simon, like Gulick and Fayol before him, was also concerned with such issues as planning, budgeting, controlling, and coordinating. Simon's approach differed from his predecessors, however, in that he examined each of these problems in decisional terms. For example, the functions of review[8] (Fayol's word was *controlling* while Gulick used *reporting*) were to diagnose the quality of decisions, to correct erroneous decisions already made, and to enforce sanctions against subordinates so that they would make decisions consistent with those expected by organizational authority. Simon's em-

5. Ibid., p. 13.
6. Herbert A. Simon, *Administrative Behavior,* 2nd ed. (New York: The Macmillan Co., 1957).
7. Ibid., p. 9.
8. Ibid., pp. 232–234.

phasis on decision making gave his analysis of the administrative process a unity and coherence which earlier formulations lacked.

More recently, Litchfield drew upon the work of Fayol, Gulick, and Simon to formulate a conception of the administrative process which stressed its cyclical nature. Litchfield saw the process as being "at once a large cycle which constitutes the administrative process as a totality and a series of small cycles which provide the means for the performance of specific functions and subfunctions and even for individual technical activities."[9] In the administrative process he included these activities: decision making, programming, communicating, controlling and reappraising. According to Litchfield, the duty of reappraisal makes the group of activities cyclical by bringing the sequence substantially back to the point at which it began.

In his statement on the administrative process, Litchfield set forth the following propositions concerning the process[10]:

1. Decision making may be rational, deliberative, discretionary, purposive, or it may be irrational, habitual, obligatory, random, or any combination thereof. In its rational, deliberative, discretionary, and purposive form, it is performed by means of the following subactivities:
   a. Definition of the issue
   b. Analysis of the existing situation
   c. Calculation and delineation of alternatives
   d. Deliberation
   e. Choice
2. Decisions become guides to action after they have been interpreted in the form of specific programs.
3. The effectiveness of a programmed decision will vary with the extent to which it is communicated to those of whom action is required.
4. Action required by a programmed and communicated decision is more nearly assured if standards of performance are established and enforced.
5. Decisions are based on facts, assumptions, and values which are subject to change. To retain their validity, decisions must therefore be reviewed and revised as rapidly as change occurs.

Litchfield made a number of contributions to the thinking about the nature of the administrative process. He articulated the interdependent nature of the activities in the administrative process and introduced the notion that

9. Edward H. Litchfield, "Notes on a General Theory of Administration," *Administrative Science Quarterly* (June 1956), pp. 3–29.
10. Ibid., pp. 3–29.

the process applied to the way in which an individual or group handles a particular problem as well as to the activities of the organization as a whole. Furthermore, he formulated a number of theoretical propositions about the process and urged their testing.

APPLICATIONS TO EDUCATIONAL ADMINISTRATION

Conceptualization of the administrative process in the field of educational administration has been heavily influenced by the theoretical developments in business and public administration. Sears,[11] the first writer to apply the administrative process to educational administration in a comprehensive fashion, acknowledged indebtedness to other students of administration, including Fayol and Gulick, for their work in the field. According to Sears, the process includes the following activities: planning, organizing, directing, coordinating, and controlling. With only two minor changes, Fayol's five elements emerge in Sears' formulation. The staffing, reporting, and budgeting functions, as presented by Gulick, are subsumed in the other activities which Sears enumerates. For example, much of what Gulick places under budgeting is treated by Sears under the heading of control. Each of the five elements of the administrative process is examined by Sears in considerable detail.

A yearbook of the American Association of School Administrators took cognizance of the administrative process.[12] After noting that administration is essentially a way of working with people to accomplish the purpose of an enterprise, it enumerates some crucial activities in this relationship. An excerpt from the section in which five crucial activities are described follows:

> 1. *Planning* or the attempt to control the future in the direction of the desired goals through decisions made on the basis of careful estimates of the probable consequences of possible courses of action.
> 2. *Allocation* or the procurement and allotment of human and material resources in accordance with the operating plan.
> 3. *Stimulation* or motivation of behavior in terms of the desired outcomes.
> 4. *Coordination* or the process of fitting together the various groups and operations into an integrated pattern of purpose-achieving work.

11. Jesse B. Sears, *The Nature of the Administrative Process* (New York: McGraw-Hill, 1950).

12. American Association of School Administrators, *Staff Relations in School Administration* (Washington: AASA, 1955), chap. 1.

5. *Evaluation* or the continuous examination of the effects produced by the ways in which the other functions listed here are performed.

The above formulation of the administrative process seems to contain one new point of emphasis. For "commanding" (Fayol's term) or "directing" (the term used by Gulick and Sears), the word "stimulation" has been suggested. In view of what is known about motivating group action toward a common enterprise, this may be a significant addition.

A careful examination of the administrative process as it applies in education has been made by Gregg.[13] To him the process has seven components as follows: decision making, planning, organizing, communicating, influencing, coordinating, and evaluating. While Gregg uses many of the components with which we are now familiar, he introduces a number of interesting distinctions and ideas. Decision making is viewed as being different from and perhaps previous to planning. Both communicating and influencing stress the necessity for mobilizing all members of the work group if the organization is to achieve its purpose. In fact, Gregg's treatment stresses time and time again the necessity for involvement of staff if the administrative process is to be effective.

Following the earlier work of Simon, Griffiths asserted that the decision making process is the central process of administration and that the central function of administration is directing and controlling the decision-making process.[14] His version includes the following steps:

1. Recognize, define, and limit the problem.
2. Analyze and evaluate the problem.
3. Establish criteria and standards by which the solution will be evaluated or judged as acceptable and adequate to the need.
4. Collect data.
5. Formulate and select the preferred solution or solutions.
6. Put into effect the preferred solution.
   a. Program the solution.
   b. Control the activities in the program.
   c. Evaluate the results and the process.[15]

In his later empirical work, more particularly the study of the performance of elementary school principals in a simulated situation, Griffiths uncovered a factor similar to his theoretical conception of the process of decision

13. Russell T. Gregg, "The Administrative Process." In Roald F. Campbell and Russell T. Gregg, eds., *Administrative Behavior in Education* (New York: Harper & Brothers, 1957), chap. 8.

14. Daniel E. Griffiths, "Administration as Decision-Making." In Andrew W. Halpin, ed., *Administrative Theory in Education* (Chicago: Midwest Administration Center, the University of Chicago, 1958), chap. 6.

15. Daniel E. Griffiths, *Administrative Theory* (New York: Appleton-Century-Crofts, 1959), p. 94.

making. He named this factor Preparation for Decision v. Taking Final Action. His subsequent attempt to use this re-formulation of the decision-making process in categorizing the performance of executives at work in actual, as opposed to simulated, organizational settings, revealed that the categories were unequal to the task.[16] He found that much of the observed administrative behavior was unrelated to decision making. As a consequence, he developed a new classification system which included 142 characteristics arranged in an ordered relationship described by the following diagram[17]:

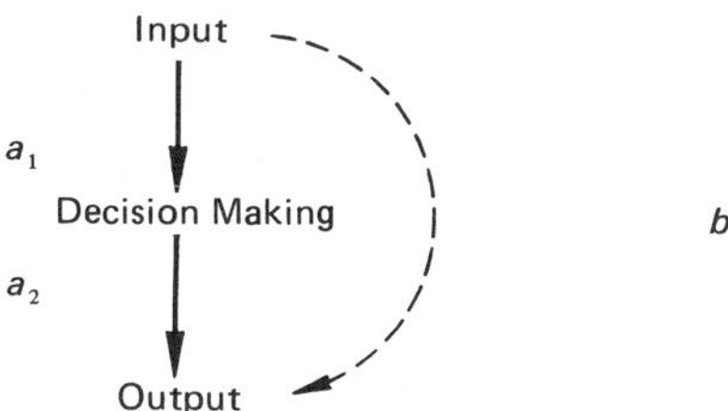

According to Griffiths, outputs may occur either along path a_1, a_2 (involves making a decision), or along path *b* (without a decision being made). He maintains that the behavior of administrators at work in an actual organizational setting is accounted for by this general schema.

THE ADMINISTRATIVE PROCESS AND THE EDUCATIONAL ADMINISTRATOR

For our purpose, we shall define the administrative process as *the way in which an organization makes decisions and takes action to achieve its goals.* We propose that the process is cyclical and contains the following components:

Decision making
Programming
Stimulating
Coordinating
Appraising

Lest this formulation seem too pat and its application too obvious, we refer to a warning given by Halpin:

16. Daniel E. Griffiths, "A Taxonomy Based on Decision-Making." In Daniel E. Griffiths, ed., *Developing Taxonomies of Organizational Behavior in Educational Administration* (Chicago: Rand McNally, 1969), chap. 3.

17. Daniel E. Griffiths and Frank W. Lutz, "Synthesis and Conclusions," in Daniel E. Griffiths, ed., *Developing Taxonomies,* chap. 7.

> Unless one is extremely careful he can be tempted into talking about "process" as if it were a free-floating affair, detached from the behavior of individuals. . . . An outside observer can never observe "process" *qua* "process"; he can observe only a sequence of behavior or behavior-products from which he may infer "process."[18]

These words bring us to emphasize the point that the administrative process is a conceptualization—not an observed phenomenon. The conceptualization is intended as a useful guide to the practicing administrator and suggests how the educational administrator would behave if he wished his activity to result in the greatest attainment of objectives with available resources. Each of the five components of the administrative process suggested above now will be discussed.

Decision making. Decision making can be irrational or rational. In the first instance the decision maker acts on the basis of whim or caprice whereas in the second he deliberates and acts in terms of a careful diagnosis of the situation and a thorough consideration of the means used to achieve a given end. Our concern is with the latter.

Rational choice has two major phases: problem analysis and decision.[19] Problem analysis is aimed at finding the cause of a difficulty while the task of decision is to select a course of action which will eliminate the problem or reduce its negative effects. At the problem-analysis stage the first step is to describe precisely what is wrong; this description is both a matter of what the problem is and what the problem is not.[20] The second step in problem analysis is to locate what is producing the difficulty; the cause often is *a change*[21]—a change in people, technology, or situational circumstances.

When the cause of the difficulty has been identified, the decision maker's consideration shifts to the possible alternative courses of action. For each alternative there are multiple consequences. Some are intended; others are unintended. The unintended side effects may be either positive or negative. A major task of the decision maker during this second principal phase of rational choice is to select the course of action which yields the most favorable consequences and carries with it a minimum of negative ones.

Let us illustrate the decision-making component in the administrative process. Suppose there is a public outcry that the foreign language program in the local high school is failing to prepare students adequately

18. Andrew W. Halpin, "A Paradigm for Research on Administrative Behavior," in Roald F. Campbell and Russell T. Gregg, eds., *Administrative Behavior in Education,* p. 195.

19. See Charles H. Kepner and Benjamin B. Tregoe, *The Rational Manager* (New York: McGraw-Hill, 1965).

20. Ibid., p. 45.

21. Ibid., pp. 45–46.

for college level course work in this curriculum area. In analyzing the problem and precisely pinpointing the difficulty, the administrator needs to ask questions such as: *Who* are the students having the difficulty? Which students do not seem to be having the difficulty? *What* is the nature of the difficulty which the students are having? *Where* are the students who are having the difficulties? *When* did the difficulties begin to appear? *To what extent* do the difficulties apply to all the foreign languages offered in the school? In other words, in what foreign languages do students subsequently have difficulty, and in what languages do they apparently have no problems? Information gathered to answer these questions will enable the administrator to state what the problem is with a reasonable degree of precision.

Suppose that the answers to these questions disclose that not all students who take advanced college level work in a foreign language begun in high school are having difficulties. Rather, only students in modern foreign languages (French, German, and Spanish) are experiencing problems at the college level. Furthermore, not all of the students enrolled in a modern foreign language are having such problems—only those attending *X, Y,* and *Z* colleges. Finally, only local graduates of the last two years have been doing below average work when they continued their foreign language study in college.

Having located more exactly what the difficulty is, the administrator is confronted with this question: Is there any change which took place two years ago in the foreign language programs offered at colleges *X, Y,* and *Z*? Suppose that the administrator discovers that the approach has shifted in these three colleges from an emphasis on reading and writing to an emphasis on speaking.

With the cause of the difficulty now clearly identified, the administrator is ready to consider alternative courses of action and their consequences. For instance, the administrator can choose to ignore the information, use the information as the basis for his arriving at a solution to the problem, or report the information to his staff. With respect to the first alternative, he envisions only negative consequences. Students at colleges *X, Y,* and *Z* will continue to perform poorly, and the public is likely to increase its pressure for some kind of resolution. The second alternative, on the other hand, might have either negative or positive consequences. By acting alone to solve the problem, the administrator sees a speedy resolution possible but subsequent resistance from the staff to an administrator-conceived solution. The third alternative also poses potential costs as well as benefits. In reviewing the information, the staff may feel that the situation is not really a problem because too few students are involved, or the staff may spend an inordinate amount of time reaching a satisfactory solution. However, since the decision is the staff's own, it is likely to be highly committed to its implementation. What the administrator finally does is a function of the consequences he foresees and the value he assigns to each of these consequences.

Although the choice may finally be made by the chief administrator, in all probability other administrative staff members, counselors, and teachers were involved in framing the questions which would guide the attempts to specify the problem. A whole research department may have been involved in gathering the information to answer the questions. The alternative courses of action may have been discussed at length in a meeting attended by the school principal, the language teachers, the department chairman, and the central office staff. Only after analyzing all of the cues supplied by the involvement of these various people in the organization, does the chief administrator make the decision. In a real sense, the decision is an organization one.

Programming. Once a major decision is made, there are a number of implementing decisions to be made. This aspect of the administrative process is often called organizing, but the word "programming" seems to describe it somewhat more accurately. In programming, arrangements for the selection and organization of staff for housing, equipment, and budget must be made. The nature of these tasks has been described in some detail in chapter 5. At this point, it is necessary to point out that the material treated in chapter 5 is but a part of the larger framework of the administrative process.

Let us refer once again to our example of unsatisfactory progress by local high school graduates in modern foreign languages at colleges *X*, *Y*, and *Z*. Suppose the basic decision made in that situation calls for the provision of experiences to develop students' conversational skills. Such a decision requires considerable programming. For instance, what equipment and materials are needed for such a program? What will be the program cost, and how is it to be budgeted? Does the present staff have the requisite abilities to provide such experiences? If not, how will the staff develop these abilities? How will the conversational experiences be introduced into the foreign language course of study? Only after such questions as the above are considered, answered, and acted upon can the decision to offer conversational experiences in Spanish, French, and German be said to be programmed.

Programming, like decision making, tends to be an organizational action rather than a one-man performance. Therefore, several types of organizational personnel may be involved in the programming phase. The superintendent may set budgetary limits for the deliberations but allow complete freedom in deciding how the money is to be spent. Teachers, department chairmen, the principal, and a technical consultant may be constituted as a committee to review the available equipment and materials and specify the limitations, strengths, and costs of each object that is examined. Other staff members may focus singly or in combination on the intended student behaviors, the range of appropriate conversational experiences to be offered, and the way in which these experiences will be ordered and incorporated into the modern foreign language curriculum.

A particular supervisor in the central office may be asked to take over the detailed organization and direction of the curriculum. In all of these activities, the organization is concerned with programming its decision.

Stimulating. The third step in the administrative process, it will be recalled, has at times been called *command* and, at other times, *direction.* While any administrator may on occasion need to command and at other times to direct, we feel the better term for what is involved here is *stimulating.* The objective of stimulating is to elicit individual efforts and contributions in implementing organizational decisions.

To be sure, there are several kinds of stimulation. At one level the organization or the administrator acting for the organization can exercise considerable pressure upon an individual in that organization. Seldom, if ever, can a formal status leader in an organization free himself completely from exercising such influence. At another level, the administrator stimulates by creating a set of conditions which inherently motivate people to act in the situation. In this case, members of the organization are involved in identifying the information they will take as evidence of an existing problem, examining the information which is gathered, judging whether a problem exists, and deciding upon the course of action to be taken.[22] It is our belief that the latter mode of stimulation is more effective than the former one, which rests on pressure.

We do not wish to oversimplify the problem, however. Involvement as a means of stimulating organizational members is most effective when the decision is outside their zone of indifference. Decisions that clearly fall outside members' zone of indifference are those which have consequences for them. Therefore, when the members' personal stakes in the decision are high, their interest in participation should be high.[23] Members should also be interested in considering matters which are within their scope of experience and sphere of competence.[24] To involve organizational participants in decisions they are not qualified to make is to subject them to frustration. As a result, involvement will be most effective on those occasions when the decision is one in which members have a stake in the outcome and expertise in deciding the matter at issue.

Communication has also been found to be of great importance to the stimulation of organization members. Communication needs to be of three kinds: down, up, and across. The Hawthorne studies[25] and other

22. For a discussion of the problems involved in using a fact-minded approach, see Alfred J. Marrow and John R. P. French, Jr., "Changing a Stereotype in Industry," *Journal of Social Issues,* 2, 1 (1945): 33–37.

23. Edwin M. Bridges, "A Model for Shared Decision-Making in the School Principalship," *Educational Administration Quarterly,* 3, 1 (Winter 1967): 49–61.

24. Ibid.

25. See F. J. Roethlisberger and W. J. Dickson, *Management and the Worker* (Cambridge, Mass.: Harvard University Press, 1939).

research have demonstrated that when members of an organization are "in on the know," when they understand clearly what is being attempted by the organization, they tend to be more productive. Face-to-face communication appears to be very important if organization members are to be motivated to do their best.

Let us use our foreign language example above to illustrate *stimulating* as a part of the administrative process. Even after the decision has been made to offer conversational experiences as a means of developing students' skills in speaking, there is still the question of stimulating the teachers to provide such experiences. Some teachers may lack the necessary conversational skills to implement the change. They may be required to take additional training to upgrade their own skill level; even so, the question remains as to how they can be stimulated to do something about modifying their instructional techniques. This is clearly a problem of building attitudes, as well as a problem of acquiring new skills.

However, if teachers have been involved in the decision to initiate a particular programmatic change, their attitudes toward it are likely to be different from what they might have been had the decision been imposed upon them. Moreover, if the information about the foreign language situation at the college level has been shared with the teachers, the need for modifying the modern foreign language program will be as evident to teachers as to administrators. If staff members fail to define the situation as a problem, then the administrator may find no substitute for a frank face-to-face conference with them concerning the possible internal and external consequences of inaction.

As with the other aspects of the administrative process, stimulating is not merely personal behavior on the part of the administrator. Ideally, stimulation should be directed toward the achievement of the purposes of the organization, not merely toward the personal satisfaction of a status leader. Moreover, the work group itself may often provide or contribute to the stimulation needed to get individual members of an organization to increase their contributions to the organization.

Coordinating. A further aspect of the administrative process is that of coordinating. This activity involves bringing into appropriate relationship the people and things necessary for the organization to achieve its purposes. Often, in coordinating, the goals of the organization must be reviewed and made explicit. At times, standards of performance necessary to the achievement of such goals need to be noted. Members of the organization may need to be held to meeting such standards.

The place of coordination may also be illustrated in our foreign language example. As the modern foreign language program seeks to develop student conversational skills, there are at least three kinds of coordination problems which, if not anticipated and solved, will jeopardize the success of the curriculum change.[26] One such problem stems from the interdependent nature of the classroom content. For instance, what a teacher in French II hopes to teach his pupils is contingent upon their having learned something in French I. If this content-sequencing problem is not solved, then students will experience difficulty in making the transition from French I to French II. The difficulty is similar in certain respects to the one faced by the local high school graduates who have been continuing their language study at colleges *X*, *Y*, and *Z*.

A second type of problem may originate from differences in instructional techniques used by teachers. The way in which one teacher offers conversational experiences may create severe difficulties for students when they move to the next higher level in the sequence. For example, a teacher in Spanish I may interpret the notion of conversational experiences as meaning oral reading and brief responses to questions framed by the teacher. The teacher in Spanish II, however, may interpret conversational experiences as meaning student discussions conducted in a small group setting around issues formulated either by the students themselves or by the teacher. Such inconsistencies in the approaches at the two levels can generate problems for both students and teachers. The possibility of this type of problem occurring foreshadows the need for some form of preventive action.

A third possible coordination problem may arise because there is a scarcity of instructional resources. If the new component of the instructional program requires special equipment and it is in limited supply, action must be taken to prevent staff members from making simultaneous demands on the equipment. Anticipation of this coordination problem should reduce the likelihood that equipment will be duplicated unnecessarily and that teachers and students will be frustrated by not having equipment available when it is needed.

The administrator is the key person in helping all members of an organization understand the need for coordination and the role each person is to play. When he becomes lax in his coordinating role, confusion, ineffectiveness, and job dissatisfaction nearly always follow.

Appraising. The last step in the administrative process, as we see it, is that of appraising. Some writers in the field use the term evaluation; and, to be sure, the two terms have many of the same connotations. Because we have used evaluation in a somewhat broader sense in chapter 5, we have chosen the word "appraising" as more suitable to describe one aspect of the administrative process.

---

26. For an insightful discussion of coordination problems, their location and resolution, see W. W. Charters, Jr., "An Approach to the Formal Organization of the School." In *Behavioral Science and Educational Administration,* Sixty-Third Yearbook of the National Society for the Study of Education, Part II (Chicago: University of Chicago Press, 1964), chap. 11.

It seems clear that administrative decisions and subsequent actions, if they are rational, are based upon certain facts, values, and assumptions. In time, any or all of these bases may change, and such change may make both the decision and the implementing action obsolete. The need for continuous appraisal, or reappraisal as Litchfield calls it,[27] is apparent.

There appear to be four purposes or concerns in appraisal. They may be stated as follows:

1. Are the objectives and the procedures chosen to achieve them consistent with one another?
2. Are the procedures operating as intended?
3. To what extent and how well have the organizational objectives been met?
4. To what extent and how well has the organization been maintained?

These points emphasize the fact that organizations exist to achieve some purpose. In the case of the public school, the purpose includes the teaching of literacy and critical thinking. In appraisal, then, key questions would have to do with how well literacy and critical thinking are being taught and learned.

But an organization must also take the long view. In addition to looking at the degree to which its objectives are being met at the moment, it must also be aware of how well the organization is being maintained so that it may continue to achieve its ends. Excessive teacher turnover, for instance, implies that the organization is not being maintained. Moreover, unless the members of an organization continue to grow in competence, the organization cannot be well maintained. It follows that, in public education, teachers and administrators are continually confronted with new challenges and opportunities to meet those challenges.

Let us see how appraising can be applied to our foreign language example. The shift to a greater emphasis on conversational skills has taken place. The change now needs to be assessed. Questions such as the following must be asked: Is there a consistency among the objectives as stated and the recommended course content, instructional techniques, and student examination procedures?[28] Do the actual content of the courses, the instructional techniques being used, and the means for examining students' performance match the stated intent? Have the changes in practices produced the desired conversational skills in students? Do the students with these skills subsequently perform satisfactorily in colleges *X, Y,* and *Z?* Do the students who continue their language study at colleges which

27. Litchfield, *Notes on a General Theory of Administration.*

28. See Michael Scriven, "The Methodology of Evaluation." In *Perspectives of Curriculum and Evaluation* (Chicago: Rand McNally, 1967), pp. 39–83.

stress skills in reading and writing perform as well as they did before the changes in the local program were introduced?

The last three questions are key ones. If practices have shifted in the desired direction, one kind of evidence concerning the effectiveness of the program has been obtained. However, this evidence is intermediate in nature. A more important test comes in determining whether or not the students are actually able to converse in the foreign language as intended. Perhaps in this case the ultimate test is how the students perform in college. Of interest to the organization is the performance of students who attend colleges which emphasize the reading and writing approach to language instruction as well as those students who are enrolled at colleges which stress the conversational approach. The improved performance of the one type of student must not be at the expense of the other.

An appraisal of the performance of students in college may indicate the extent to which the organization is achieving its purpose so far as foreign language is concerned. But what about the maintenance of the organization? Now another set of questions such as the following must be asked: Have the teachers who participated in the program changes identified more fully with the organization? In case the school needs to tackle another problem, are the teachers disposed to help with it? Did the experience result in an increased feeling of professional competence and status? If these questions can be answered in the affirmative, there has been organizational maintenance as well as organizational achievement.

A DESCRIPTIVE VIEW OF MANAGERIAL WORK: THE WORK ACTIVITY SCHOOL

In recent years, researchers have undertaken systematic studies of the work of managers, usually by having them keep diaries or by actually observing them while they work. These studies have focused on administrators at all levels of the hierarchy and in every type of organization: presidents, middle managers, and foremen in large corporations; hospital administrators; and school principals and superintendents. The picture of the executive's job that emerges from these studies provides considerable insight into the content and the characteristics of managerial work.[29]

THE CHARACTERISTICS OF MANAGERIAL WORK

Managers perform a great deal of work at an unrelenting pace. Their work week is long and requires them to work nights and weekends. Senior high

29. Much of this discussion is based on Henry Mintzberg, *The Nature of Managerial Work* (New York: Harper & Row, Publishers, 1973).

school principals, for example, report that they spend more than fifty hours per week on activities related to their jobs; nearly 30 percent work more than sixty hours per week.[30] The work week for the superintendent is even longer; nearly half of the superintendents report that they work more than sixty hours each week. Furthermore, the majority of them work at least two nights a week and devote at least two weekends a month to their work responsibilities.[31] Because administrators work such long hours, there is little opportunity for them to be with their family and friends. Furthermore, the job is sufficiently openended that administrators have real difficulty in telling when their work is finished.

In addition to working long hours at a job with few tangible mileposts, the administrator engages in work activities that are characterized by brevity, variety, and fragmentation.[32] Half of the administrators' activities are completed in less than nine minutes; many are terminated in less than two minutes; few consume as much as an hour. Seldom is the administrator able to spend thirty uninterrupted minutes on a single task regardless of its importance to him or his organization. In short, the administrator is pressured to be superficial in dealing with the bulk of his activities.

Most of the administrator's time is spent in scheduled and unscheduled meetings. As a result, his principal modes of communication are oral and nonverbal rather than written. Administrators seem to show a marked preference for live, current communications and to dislike written correspondence as a medium of communication.

When administrators meet with others to discuss organizationally relevant matters, these "others" are more likely to be subordinates, peers, and outsiders than superiors. Less than 10 percent of the manager's time is spent with his superiors while approximately half of his work day involves interactions with subordinates. The rest of his time is distributed equally between peers and outsiders. The vast majority of these personal encounters are not initiated by the administrators; rather, they are initiated by others. In some respects, the administrator is "a puppet in a puppetshow with hundreds of people pulling the strings and forcing him to act in one way or another." Some administrators decide who will pull the strings and how, and they then take advantage of the moves they are forced to make. Others are unable to exploit the demands of their work environment and are swallowed by the initiatives of others.

---

30. John K. Hemphill, James M. Richards, and Richard E. Peterson, *Report of the Senior High-School Principalship* (Washington, D.C.: The National Association of Secondary-School Principals, 1965), p. 80 and B-39.

31. Stephen Knezevich, *The American School Superintendent* (Washington, D.C.: American Association of School Administrators, 1971), pp. 55–56.

32. According to one study, principals were involved in 50 to 100 different incidents each day. See Ray Cross, "The Principal as a Counterpuncher," *The National Elementary Principal*, 2, 2 (October 1971): 26–29.

The administrator's unique access to information and his special status and authority within the organization make him a central figure in the system by which decisions are made.

THE CONTENT OF MANAGERIAL WORK

Members of the work-activity school have examined the content, as well as the characteristics, of managerial work. In addition to studying such features of managerial work as the length of the manager's work week, the types of individuals with whom managers interact, and the modes of communication they rely on, researchers have sought to categorize the activities which administrators carry out and why. These efforts to categorize the functions of administrators suggest that an administrator enacts three major groups of roles: (1) interpersonal (figurehead, leader, and liaison); (2) informational (monitor, disseminator, and spokesman); and (3) decisional (entrepreneur, disturbance handler, resource allocator, and negotiator). Let us now examine each of these roles in some detail in order to understand what administrators actually do as they attempt to accomplish the goals of the organization for which they are responsible.

Interpersonal roles. According to the adherents of the work activity school, the formal authority and the special status of the administrator lead to three distinct kinds of interpersonal roles. The first of these is the *figurehead* role. This is perhaps the most basic and simplest role which the administrator is obliged to perform as the symbolic head of the organization. In this role, the administrator may lend the dignity and status of his position to a public event deemed significant by some segment of the community. His presence, however, does little more than officially attest to the importance of the occasion. As the organization's figurehead, the administrator is frequently called upon to sign documents on behalf of the institution though his signature represents nothing more than an act of compliance with the law. The most time consuming aspect of the figurehead role, however, is apt to be the need to meet with those individuals who feel that the only way to get something done is to get to the top.

The interpersonal role that has received the most attention in the literature is the *leader* role. As the leader of the organization, the administrator guides and motivates subordinates. He attempts to harness the energies of subordinates by effecting an integration between the purposes of the organization and the motives of the individual. Leadership permeates a great many of the administrator's activities. It is evident in what appear to be casual encounters, for example, when the manager greets a subordinate, asks about his work, and compliments him on achievements. Leadership also manifests itself on those occasions which the organization recognizes as crucial to its well-being, namely, hiring, promoting, or dismissing subordinates.

The third type of interpersonal role is the *liaison* role. In this capacity, the administrator builds and maintains a network of relationships with individuals and groups outside the organization he heads. He builds this network in a variety of ways—by joining important organizations within the community, by attending conferences and social events, and by answering requests promptly. The array of contacts he makes enables him to gain special favors and information at crucial times for him and his organization.

Informational roles. The informational roles of an administrator relate to the receiving and transmitting of information. They derive in large part from the centrality of his position in the organization and the interpersonal roles that he plays. The latter place him in a unique position to get information and to relay it to those who desire or require it.

In his *monitor* role, the administrator seeks and is bombarded with information. This information seems to be of four types: (1) information about what is happening within the organization; (2) information about external events, that is, developments in either the immediate environment of the organization or the profession; (3) information pertinent to pending decisions; and (4) information that represents pressure on the administrator to do something or not to do something. These four types of information are used by the administrator to locate problems and targets of opportunities, to develop a mental image of how the organization and its environment are behaving, and to develop plans or future directions for the organization to pursue.

Access to information shapes the second type of informational role played by the administrator. This access uniquely qualifies him to function as a *disseminator.* In this role, the administrator sends information gathered from external sources into the organization and relays internally generated information from one subordinate to another. The disseminator role creates a significant dilemma for the manager. If the administrator wants a task completed according to his standards, he must spend time on disseminating the information. If he chooses to complete the task himself, he spends time on tasks that could be easily handled by others if they possessed an adequate information base. In either case, the administrator is apt to be overworked. To escape the role overload the administrator may need to accept an imperfect performance. The uniqueness of the administrator's information system, therefore, has the potential to become a major source of frustration for him.

In the third type of informational role, the administrator acts as the organization's *spokesperson.* This role, like that of the disseminator, involves the transmission of information; however, the information is directed toward the environment of the organization rather than to the organization. As the disseminator, the administrator communicates with individuals employed by the organization; as the organization's spokesperson, the administrator keeps two groups informed about the organization's plans, policies, and results. The first is the school board while the second is the organization's various publics—parents, taxpayers, government agencies, sales people, and the like. In this spokesperson role, the administrator is expected to have up-to-the-minute knowledge of the organization and its environment. Additionally, the administrator is expected to have special knowledge about the field of education and to give advice on educational issues that may be relatively unrelated to his own school or district.

Decisional roles. The administrator's unique access to information and his special status and authority within the organization make him a central figure in the system by which decisions are made. When the activities of the administrator are analyzed, four distinct decisional roles are apparent: entrepreneur, disturbance handler, resource allocator, and negotiator. There is some evidence to suggest that the decision-making behavior of administrators does not correspond to the normative view of the decision-making process discussed earlier in this chapter. In enacting their decisional roles, administrators seem to satisfice rather than to maximize.[33] In other words, administrators apparently do not engage in an elaborate consideration of means and ends. Instead, their analysis is quite limited with the test of a good decision typically being agreement by the significant actors in the situation.

---

33. Charles E. Lindblom, "The Science of 'Muddling Through'," *Public Administration Review* 14, 2 (1959): 78–88.

In the entrepreneurial decisional role, the administrator initiates and designs much of the controlled change in his organization. He introduces changes of his own free will, exploiting opportunities and solving nonpressing problems. These changes usually occur through an "improvement project," a sequence of activities designed to ameliorate an undesirable situation or to achieve a higher level of performance in what is already considered to be a satisfactory situation. The more ambitious the improvement project, the more likely the administrator is to experience major difficulties. The creation of new settings is a formidable intellectual undertaking, and there is little evidence that administrators have mastered the complexities inherent in these ventures.[34] Historically, administrators and social scientists have emphasized the importance of overcoming resistance to change and underestimated the cruciality of implementation. As a result, the entrepreneurial role has proved to be a perilous one in educational institutions. The discussion of the administrator as the initiator of action in chapter 10 provides two concrete examples of the difficulties which may arise.

The decisional role which the administrator most frequently fills is that of *disturbance handler.* In this role, the administrator acts because he must. Perhaps the most dramatic instance occurs when the administrator acts in response to a crisis. For example, the administrator due to a decline in enrollment issues a number of termination notices. An irate staff rallies around the dismissed teachers and demands that they be reinstated. If the administrator does not comply with the demands, the staff threatens to strike. The bulk of the disturbances which the administrator handles are not of a crisis character, however. Disturbances generally flow from conflicts between subordinates because of resource demands or personality clashes.

Perhaps the administrator's most important decisional role is that of *resource allocator.* There are three essential elements inherent in this role. The first has to do with the scheduling of time. By allocating how much time he chooses to spend on various organizational issues, he announces to his subordinates that certain matters are important while others are inconsequential. As the organization's chief resource allocator, he establishes the work system of the organization; this system encompasses decisions about what is to be done, who will do it, and what structure will be operative. These decisions are most evident at the beginning and end of the school year and in the context of improvement projects. The resource allocator role also obviously involves budgetary decisions; these

---

34. See Neal Gross, Joseph B. Giacquinta, and Marilyn Bernstein, *Implementing Organizational Innovations: A Sociological Analysis of Planned Educational Change* (New York: Basic Books, Inc., 1971); W. W. Charters, Jr. and Roland J. Pellegrin, "Barriers to the Innovation Process: Four Case Studies of Differentiated Staffing," *Educational Administration Quarterly,* 9, 1 (Winter 1973): 3–14; Smith and Keith, *Anatomy of Educational Innovation;* and Seymour B. Sarason, *The Creation of Settings.*

decisions are both cyclical and ad hoc. The cyclical decisions tend to come in batches. Claims on specific resources are made at one time in light of anticipated needs, available funds, and organizational priorities. Ad hoc decisions, however, involve commitments at various times during the year. Unlike the cyclical decisions, ad hoc requests are presented individually; decisions must be reached without full knowledge of the requests that might subsequently surface. Administrators apparently cope with this ambiguity by approving the requests of those subordinates who are perceived to be the most able and by funding proposals that seem to move the organization in the direction they desire.

The fourth type of decisional role performed by the administrator is the *negotiator* role. Until the decade of the '60s, negotiations played a relatively minor part in the work of the educational administrator. Now negotiations are a vital component of the superintendent's job. As teachers have won the right to engage in collective bargaining, administrators have found themselves in an adversary relationship with their staffs. Initially, bargaining focused on such "bread and butter" issues as salaries and fringe benefits. The scope of bargaining has expanded to include matters of educational policy and practice. In some districts, the strength of teachers' unions has reached the point where parents have formed unions of their own and initiated lawsuits to restore the rights which boards of education have given up at the bargaining table.[35] The educational administrator, unlike his counterpart in private industry, is caught in a crossfire between employees and consumers. Each of these groups has different goals. Thus far, districts have encountered extraordinary difficulties in satisfying the legitimate and conflicting needs of teachers and parents.[36]

VARIATIONS IN THE WORK OF ADMINISTRATORS

The preceding discussion has emphasized the similarities in the work of administrators. This emphasis is consistent with the empirical studies to date which have produced more evidence of similarities than of differences in administrative work. Few of these studies have been done in an educational context, therefore, comments about differences in the job of educational administrators are highly speculative. With this caveat in mind, let us examine some of the variables that seem to be associated with differences in the role requirements and characteristics of managerial work.

---

35. Parents Union for Public Schools in Philadelphia and Jacquelyn Gayle Viale and John Ritter Fernandez v. Board of Education of the School District of Philadelphia in the Court of Common Pleas of Philadelphia County, January Term, 1975.

36. Seymour Sarason et al., *The Community at the Bargaining Table* (Boston, Mass.: Institute for Responsive Education, January 1975).

Size of the organization is a variable that appears to influence the content and characteristics of the manager's work. Administrators of small organizations seem to experience more brevity and fragmentation in their work activities than do the administrators of larger organizations. The former spend less time in scheduled meetings than the latter and conduct their business with much less formality. The chief executives of smaller organizations stress the leader and informational roles and place much less emphasis on the figurehead and liaison roles than is the case for the heads of large organizations.

Level in the hierarchy also has an impact on the work performed by administrators. Brevity and fragmentation are more pronounced at lower levels in the management hierarchy and the figurehead role, as one might suspect, is much less significant. The disturbance handler role increases in importance for lower-level administrators.

The location of the organization in the change-stability cycle is another factor that seems to produce differences in the content of managerial work. During periods of change and expansion, administrators apparently emphasize the entrepreneur and negotiator roles. In periods of stability, the leader and disturbance handler roles assume greater importance.

Experience in the role also shapes the roles which administrators emphasize. If the administrator is newly appointed and relatively unfamiliar with the organization he heads, he concentrates on the liaison and monitor roles. As he acquires an understanding of the organization and its environment, he tends to stress the entrepreneur role. Later the spokesperson, disseminator, negotiator, disturbance handler, and leader roles gain in importance.

CONCLUDING COMMENTS

The normative and descriptive views of administrator's work suggest a number of problems that must be solved if the administrator is to make productive use of himself in his organizational role. One crucial problem indicated by the contrasting views of managerial work has to do with the management of time.[37] If the administrator uses the administrative process as a guide to maximizing the outcomes of his actions, he will need to devote long periods of time to planning activities. The descriptive view, on the other hand, suggests that the administrator faces an enormous agenda of activities to be completed each day and that he rarely has thirty minutes of uninterrupted "alone" time to allocate to a single task or project. Unless the administrator is able to establish priorities and to set aside the time

37. A discussion of how this problem can be handled is in Alan Lakein, *How to Get Control of Your Time and Your Life* (New York: P. H. Wyden, 1973).

that the high priority tasks require, he is apt to be swallowed up by the routine of his job. The results may be even more consequential for the organization. With the administrator continually confronted with the need to respond to the demands, appeals, and requests of others, the organization becomes vulnerable to goal displacement and organizational drift. Those administrators who are able to maintain a long-term planning perspective in a work environment that encourages a short-term orientation and who are able to match the importance of the immediate task with the appropriate level of analysis and planning may well have mastered the essence of managerial work.

SUGGESTED ACTIVITIES

1. Interview a principal or superintendent concerning steps taken in the solution of one of his administrative problems. Write up the case and analyze the extent to which the administrative process as described in this chapter was followed.
2. How do the views of Dill (see below) with respect to the administrative process compare with those presented in this chapter?
3. Use a structured observation patterned after one of the studies reported in Mintzberg (see below) to analyze the characteristics and content of work performed by a principal or a superintendent. How do your results compare with the discussion on managerial work presented in this chapter?
4. Select one of three major role categories (interpersonal, informational, and decisional) described in this chapter and interview several administrators to determine how they handle these roles.

SELECTED READINGS

Barnard, Chester I. *The Functions of the Executive.* Cambridge, Mass.: Harvard University Press, 1938.

Dill, William R. "Decision-Making." In National Society for the Study of Education, *Behavioral Science and Educational Administration,* Sixty-Third Yearbook, Part II. Chicago: University of Chicago Press, 1964, chap. 9.

Gregg, Russell T. "The Administrative Process." In Roald F. Campbell and Russell T. Gregg, eds., *Administrative Behavior in Education.* New York: Harper & Brothers, 1957, chap. 8.

Griffiths, Daniel E. "A Taxonomy Based on Decision-Making." In Daniel E. Griffiths, ed., *Developing Taxonomies of Organizational Behavior in Educational Administration.* Chicago: Rand McNally, 1969, chap. 3.

Kepner, Charles H., and Tregoe, Benjamin B. *The Rational Manager.* New York: McGraw-Hill, 1965.

Lakein, Alan. *How to Get Control of Your Time and Your Life.* New York: P. H. Wyden, 1973.

Litchfield, Edward H. "Notes on a General Theory of Administration," *Administrative Science Quarterly* 1 (June 1956): 3–29.

Mintzberg, Henry. *The Nature of Managerial Work.* New York: Harper and Row Publishers, 1973.

Sears, Jesse B. *The Nature of the Administrative Process.* New York: McGraw-Hill, 1950.

Wolcott, Harry F. *The Man in the Principal's Office.* New York: Holt, Rinehart, and Winston, Inc., 1973.

7

THE SCHOOL AS A SOCIAL SYSTEM

We have viewed administration from the standpoint of its purpose, its tasks, its process, and in terms of administrative behavior. We shall now look at administration in the setting of the school as a social system. This is perhaps our most theoretically oriented approach to administration. While much of the conceptual and empirical work related to this formulation was done in the 1950s and 1960s, it is included here for the reason that it is still useful to both researchers and practitioners. We shall present the theoretical framework of administration as a social process, examine some of the studies which such a framework has generated, note the limitations and extensions of this formulation, and then suggest some implications for practice growing out of such an approach.

THE CONCEPTUAL WORK

The formulation of the concept of administration as a social process was essentially the work of Getzels and Guba.[1] Our description of this concept follows closely part of a paper given by Getzels at a seminar on administrative theory sponsored by the University Council for Educational Admin-

1. Jacob W. Getzels and Egon G. Guba, "Social Behavior and the Administrative Process," *School Review* 65 (Winter 1957), pp. 423–441.

istration and the Midwest Administration Center.[2] The theory has been extended and amplified in a more recent publication.[3]

To comprehend the model described in the next few pages requires some knowledge of concepts found in sociology and psychology. For many students, however, careful reading of these pages and some of the material mentioned in the footnotes will be found rewarding.

Getzels suggests that administration may be conceived structurally as the hierarchy of subordinate-superordinate relationships within a social system. Functionally, this hierarchy of relationships is the locus for allocating and integrating roles and facilities in order to achieve the goals of the social system. It is in these relationships that the assignment of positions, the provision of facilities, the organization of procedures, the regulation of activity, and the evaluation of performance take place.

While the functions named above are the responsibility of the superordinate member of the hierarchy, each function becomes effective only as it "takes" with the subordinate members. This interpersonal or social relationship is the crucial factor in administration as a social process.

The model or concept begins with a consideration of the most general context of interpersonal or social behavior, i.e., a given social system. The term "social system" is of course conceptual rather than descriptive and must not be confused with society or state, or thought of as applicable only to large aggregates of human interaction. Within this framework, for one purpose, a community may be considered a social system, with the school a particular organization within the more general social system. For another purpose, the school itself or even a single class within the school may be considered a social system in its own right. The model proposed here is applicable regardless of the level or size of the unit under consideration.

The social system is conceived as involving two classes of phenomena that may be thought of as independent but, in an actual situation, are interactive. There are, first, the institutions characterized by certain roles and expectations in keeping with the goals of the system. And there are, second, the individuals with certain personalities and dispositions inhabiting the system. The social behavior found in this system may be understood as a function of two major elements: institution, role, and expectation, which together constitute the nomothetic or *normative* dimension of activity in a scial system; and individual, personality, and need disposition, which together constitute the idiographic or *personal* dimension of activity in a social system.

---

2. Jacob W. Getzels, "Administration as a Social Process." In A. W. Halpin, ed., *Administrative Theory in Education* (Chicago: Midwest Administration Center, University of Chicago, 1958), pp. 150–165.

3. Jacob W. Getzels, James M. Lipham, and Roald F. Campbell, *Educational Administration as a Social Process* (New York: Harper & Row, 1968).

THE NORMATIVE DIMENSION

To understand the nature of observed behavior—and to be able to predict and control it—the nature and relationships of these elements must be understood. Certain key terms need further elaboration.

The term "institution" has received a variety of definitions which cannot be reviewed here. It is sufficient to point out that all social systems have certain imperative functions that come in time to be carried out in certain routinized ways. These functions—such as governing, educating, policing within the state—may be said to have become "institutionalized," and the agencies established to carry out these institutionalized functions for the social system as a whole may be termed "institutions." Thus, the school is the institution devoted to educating.

An important part of the institution is the role. Roles are, to use Linton's terminology, the "dynamic aspects" of the positions, offices, and statuses within an institution, and they define the behavior of the role incumbents or actors.[4] In the school these incumbents are superintendents, principals, teachers, and other workers.

Roles are defined in terms of role expectations. A role has certain obligations and responsibilities, which may be termed "role expectations," and when the role incumbent puts these obligations and responsibilities into effect, he is said to be performing his role. For instance, the role expectations for the third grade teacher, the guidance counselor, and the principal are quite different. The expectations define for the actor, whoever he may be, what he should or should not do as long as he is the incumbent of the particular role.

Roles are complementary—interdependent in that each role derives its meaning from other related roles in the organization. In a sense, a role is a prescription not only for the given role incumbent but also for the incumbents of other roles within the organization, so that in a hierarchical setting the expectations of one role may to some extent also form the sanctions for a second interlocking role. Thus, for example, the role of sergeant and the role of private in the army, or of principal and teacher in a school, cannot really be defined or implemented except in relation to each other. It is this quality of complementarity which fuses two or more roles into a coherent, interactive unit and which makes it possible for us to conceive of an organization as having a characteristic structure.

The elements constituting the normative aspects of social behavior have been examined. At this level of analysis, it was sufficient to conceive of the role incumbents as "actors," devoid of personalistic or other individualizing characteristics—as if all incumbents were exactly alike and as if they implemented a given role in exactly the same way. This

4. Ralph Linton, *The Study of Man* (New York: Appleton-Century-Crofts, 1936), p. 14.

permits certain gross understandings and prediction of behavior in an organization. For example, if the roles in a given educational institution are known, some rather accurate predictions of what the people in these organizations do without ever observing the actual people involved can be made.

THE PERSONAL DIMENSION

Roles are of course occupied by real individuals, and no two individuals are alike. Each individual stamps the particular role he occupies with the unique style of his own characteristic pattern of behavior. Even in the case of the relatively inflexible roles of sergeant and private, no two individual sergeants and no two individual privates fulfill their roles in exactly the same way. To understand the observed behavior of specific sergeants and specific privates, it is not enough to know the nature of the roles and expectations—although, to be sure, their behavior cannot be understood apart from these—but the nature of the individuals inhabiting the roles and reacting to the expectations must also be known. That is, in addition to the normative aspects, the personal aspects of social behavior must also be considered. Both the sociological level of analysis and the psychological level of analysis must be included.

Just as it was possible to analyze the normative dimension into the component elements of role and expectation, so it is possible, in a parallel manner, to analyze the individual dimension into the component elements of personality and need disposition. We may turn to a brief consideration of these two terms.

The concept "personality," like that of role or institution, has been given a variety of meanings. Personality is defined by Getzels as the dynamic organization within the individual of those need dispositions that govern his unique reactions to the environment. The central analytic elements of personality are the need dispositions, which we can define with Parsons and Shils as "individual tendencies to orient and act with respect to objects in certain manners and to expect certain consequences from these actions."[5]

Returning to the example of the sergeant and the private, an essential distinction can now be made between two sergeants, one of whom has a high need disposition for "submission" and the other a high need disposition for "ascendance," and a similar distinction between two privates, one with a high need disposition for "submission" and the other for "ascendance," in the fulfillment of their respective roles, and for the sergeant-private interaction. In short, to understand the behavior of specific role incumbents in an institution, we must know both the role expecta-

5. Talcott Parsons and Edward A. Shils, *Toward a General Theory of Action* (Cambridge, Mass.: Harvard University Press, 1951), p. 114.

tions and the need dispositions. Indeed, both needs and expectations may be thought of as motives for behavior, the one deriving from organizational obligations and requirements, the other from personalistic sets and propensities.

One troublesome facet of the model, to which insufficient attention has been given, is the problem of the dynamics of the interaction between these organizationally defined expectations and the personally determined needs. To put the problem concretely, one may ask: How is it, for example, that some sergeants and privates—or to generalize the case, some complementary role-incumbents—understand and agree at once on their mutual obligations and responsibilities, while others take a long time in reaching such agreement and quite frequently do not come to terms either with their roles or with each other?

The essential relevant concept Getzels proposes here is selective interpersonal perception; people see what their own backgrounds permit them to see. In a sense, the prescribed organizational or normative relationships of two complementary role-incumbents may be conceived as being very different. On the one hand, there is the prescribed relationship as perceived by the first organization member in terms of *his* needs, dispositions, and goals. On the other hand, there is the same prescribed relationship as perceived by the second organization member in terms of *his* needs, dispositions, and goals. These private perceptions are related through those aspects of public objects, symbols, values, and expectations which have to some extent a counterpart in the perceptions of both individuals.[6]

When it is said that two role incumbents—for example, a subordinate and a superordinate—understand each other, it means that their perceptions and their own organization of the prescribed complementary expectations are congruent; when it is said that they misunderstand each other, it means that their perceptions and their own organization of the prescribed complementary expectations are incongruent. The functioning of the social system depends not only on a clear statement of the public expectations, but on the degree of overlap in the perception and individual organization of the expectations by the specific role incumbents. As will be shown, the relevant research suggests that when participants evaluate an interaction, the congruence of the perception of expectations often takes priority over actual observed behavior or even accomplishment.

THE MODEL

By way of summarizing the argument so far, the general model is pictured in Figure 7–1.

6. Jacob W. Getzels, James M. Lipham, and Roald F. Campbell, *Educational Administration as a Social Process*, pp. 86–89.

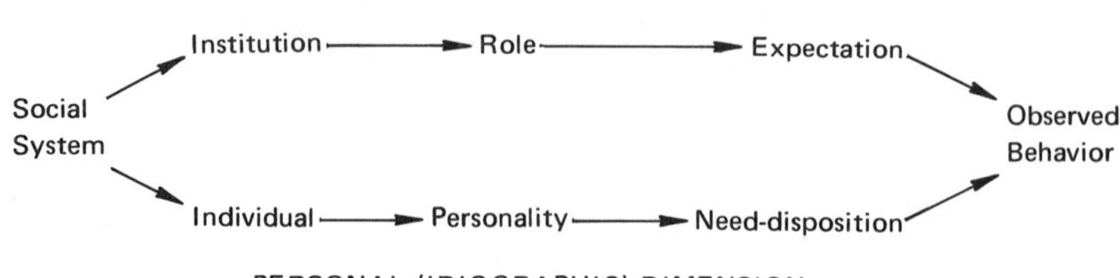

Figure 7–1 General model showing the organizational and personal dimensions of social behavior (from Getzels and Guba).

The normative axis, shown at the top of the diagram, consists of institution, role, and expectation, each term being the analytic unit for the term preceding it. Thus the social system is defined by its institutions, each institution by its constituent roles, each role by the expectations attaching to it .Similarly, the personal axis is shown at the lower portion of the diagram and consists of individual, personality, and need disposition, each term again serving as the analytic unit for the term preceding it.

A given act is conceived as deriving simultaneously from both the normative and personal dimensions. That is to say, social behavior results as the individual attempts to cope with an environment composed of patterns of expectations for his behavior in ways consistent with his own independent pattern of needs. Thus, one may say that behavior in an organization is a function of a given institutional role defined by the expectations attaching to it, and the personality of the particular role incumbent defined by his need dispositions.

The proportion of role and personality factors determining behavior will of course vary with the specific act, the specific role, and the specific personality involved. The nature of the interaction can be understood from another graphic representation, as indicated in Figure 7–2.

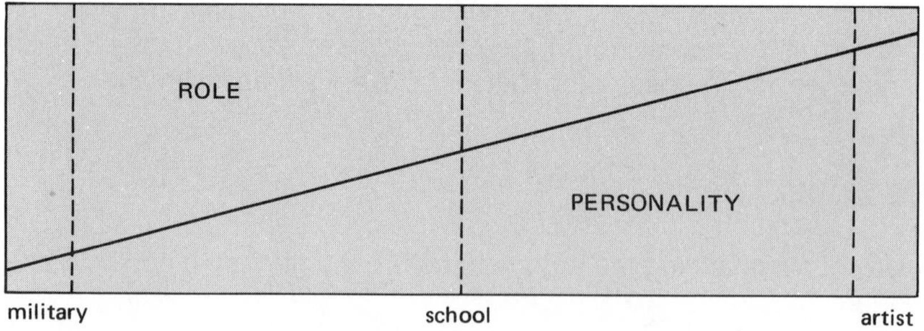

Figure 7–2 The interplay between role and personality in a behavioral act (from Getzels and Guba).

A given behavioral act may be conceived as occurring at a position represented by the dotted line through the role and personality possibilities represented by the rectangle. At the left, the proportion of the act dictated by considerations of role-expectations is relatively large, while the proportion of the act dictated by considerations of personality is relatively small. At the right, the proportions are reversed, and considerations of personality become greater than those of role-expectation. In these terms one may, for example, have on the one hand the behavior of an army private conforming almost entirely to role demands and on the other the behavior of a freelance artist deriving almost entirely from personality dispositions. Most schools are probably somewhere between these extremes. In a given setting, administration always deals with proportions of both these components.

In any case, whether the proportion tends toward one end or the other, behavior insofar as it is social remains a function of both role and personality, although in different degree. When role is maximized, behavior still retains some personal aspect, because no role is ever so closely defined as to eliminate all individual latitude. When personality is maximized, social behavior still cannot be free from some role prescription. Indeed, the individual who divorces himself from such prescription is said to be autistic, and he ceases to communicate with his fellows.

Some criticis of the social process model have maintained that it lacks a dynamic quality. Abbott[7] suggested some intervening variables between the normative and personal dimensions and some feedback mechanisms which may help answer this criticism. He summarizes his argument as follows:

> . . . a formal organization may be viewed as a specific social system in which role expectations become formalized and institutionalized. Such expectations constitute a codified behavior system, which is more or less explicit but which is generally understood by all employees. As specific individuals, with their own patterns or organizationally relevant needs, are socialized in respect to the organization's codified behavior system, they achieve a cognitive orientation to roles and they respond affectively to this orientation. Thus, behavior in a formal organization is conceived as deriving simultaneously from an individual's cognitive orientation to roles and his affective responses to roles.
>
> Both the cognitive orientation to roles and affective responses to roles are modified over time, largely as a function of the operation of two feedback mechanisms within the organization: the reward system and the reference-group norms. Feedback, in this sense, is a perceptual process in which the cognitive

7. Max G. Abbott, "Intervening Variables in Variables in Organizational Behavior," *Educational Administration Quarterly* 1 (Winter 1965): 1–14.

> orientation is monitored in terms of its congruence with the "real" situation.[8]

The relevance of the general model for administrative theory and practice becomes apparent when it is seen that administration inevitably deals with fulfillment of both organizational and personal requirements within the context of a particular social system, and that these requirements may be modified over time.

SOME EMPIRICAL STUDIES

A theory, as we suggested in chapter 4, should, among other things, generate hypotheses that can be tested. The theory described above has been the source of a number of hypotheses which have become the bases for empirical studies, some of which will not be reported. These reports should be read not only for their findings, but also to illustrate the way by which studies may be derived from a theoretical framework.

SELECTIVE PERCEPTION

One of the early studies dealt with selective interpersonal perception. To Ferneau the theory suggested that when two or more persons come in contact with each other over a sufficient length of time, each begins to have certain expectations as to how the other will act or behave.[9] He wished to examine the expectations of superintendents of schools and consultants from state departments of education as they worked together on curriculum problems.

He reasoned that expectations become generalized. For example, while the contact may have been with only two or three consultants, the school administrator begins to expect much the same behavior from all consultants. In turn, the consultant working with a few administrators begins to have certain expectations as to how all administrators will behave. Expectations on the part of either the administrator or the consultant are not completely rigid. There is what is termed a "range of permissiveness." Either may exhibit a variety of behavior within certain limits and still stay within the expectations of the other. However, when the actions of one fall outside this range, the other rejects such behavior. This situation results in a lack of rapport, in one or both becoming defensive or aggressive, or in some other attitude which makes their contacts useless.

Ferneau was able to describe three possible roles for consul-

8. Ibid., pp. 12–13.
9. Elmer F. Ferneau, "Which Consultant?" *Administrator's Notebook* 2, 8 (April 1954).

tants: the expert, the resource person, and the process person. He then developed a check list of sixty items which required respondents to choose for each item the preferred behavior of the consultant. One hundred thirty-two superintendents in the states of Kansas, Michigan, Nebraska, and Wisconsin who had recently used consultants from their respective state departments of education responded to the instrument. These same superintendents, in another study, had previously given an evaluation of these consultant services. In these same states forty-three consultants who had given these services to the superintendents also completed the check list and evaluated the effectiveness of the services as they viewed them.

With these data available, it was possible to match the replies of the consultants with those of the administrators whom they had attempted to help. It was possible also to determine the behavior the administrators had expected the consultants to exhibit and what the consultants had expected of the administrators. Then it was possible to compare the administrator's evaluations of the consultations in which both administrator and consultant behaved as the other expected him to behave and when the behavior of one differed from that which the other expected.

In responding to the various statements used in the questionnaire, the respondents rated each behavior on a six-point scale with regard to its appropriateness. When a consultant and an administrator disagreed by as much as an average of two points in evaluating each statement, nineteen out of twenty times the consultation in which they were involved was rated as of low value by one or both. This finding was tested in three ways; each test gave the same result. Consultants and administrators must perceive each other as functioning in the manner expected if the consultation is to be effective.

Within each of the four states included in the study there was much greater agreement between consultants and administrators as to the behavior that they expected of each other than there was among the consultants and administrators in the states as a group. For example, in one state both administrators and consultants ranked first among the four states in the number of times they expressed preference for behavior classified as the "expert" approach. In another state, both groups ranked last in the number of times they expressed such a preference.

This study seems to support the idea that expectations have more to do with the judged effectiveness of consultant services than the nature of the service itself. There is at least the suggestion that in any interaction between two people the congruence of expectation of behavior may be most important.

ROLE-PERSONALITY CONFLICT

One of the most definitive studies on the model was done by Merton Campbell, who examined the degree of self-role conflict (the amount of spread between the two dimensions of the model) existing among teachers and the relationships between such conflict and satisfaction, effectiveness, and confidence in leadership.[10] Included in the study were fifteen schools and 284 teachers. Appropriate instruments were developed to test the variables being studied.

Four of the hypotheses developed by Campbell were from the standpoint of an outside observer, as suggested by *A* in Figure 7–3.

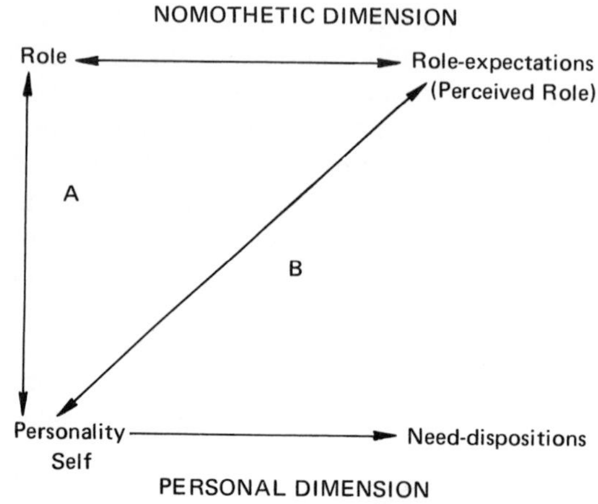

Figure 7–3 Partial social process model showing variables tested.

It was hypothesized that teachers identified as having a low degree of self-role conflict in the teaching situation will (1) rate themselves higher in teaching satisfaction, (2) rate themselves higher in teaching effectiveness, (3) be rated by the principal as more effective teachers, and (4) express greater confidence in the leadership of the principal than will those teachers with a high degree of conflict.

Hypotheses 1, 3, and 4 were confirmed. Teachers with a low degree of self-role conflict expressed greater satisfaction in teaching than did high-conflict teachers. Low-conflict teachers were rated as more effective by their principals than were high-conflict teachers. Low-conflict teachers expressed greater confidence in the leadership of their principal than did high-conflict teachers. Hypothesis 2 did not hold: low-conflict and high-conflict teachers were not differentiated on the basis of their own ratings of effectiveness.

Another set of four hypotheses was developed from the standpoint of the teacher (the actor), suggested by *B* in Figure 7–3. It was hypothesized that teachers with a low degree of conflict between self and

10. Merton V. Campbell, "Self-Role Conflict Among Teachers and Its Relationship to Satisfaction, Effectiveness, and Confidence in Leadership." (Ph.D. diss., Dept. of Education, University of Chicago, 1958).

perceived role will (1) rate themselves higher in teaching satisfaction, (2) rate themselves higher in teaching effectiveness, (3) be rated by the principal as more effective teachers, and (4) express greater confidence in the leadership of the principal than will those teachers with a high degree of conflict.

Again, hypotheses 1, 3, and 4 held. With respect to the conflict between self and perceived role, the low-conflict teachers expressed greater satisfaction than high-conflict teachers. Principals rated the low-conflict teachers as more effective than the high-conflict teachers. Low-conflict teachers expressed greater confidence in the leadership of their principals than did high-conflict teachers. As before, however, low-conflict and high-conflict teachers did not differ significantly on the basis of their self-ratings of effectiveness.

These findings led the investigator to conclude:

> Teachers do differ from each other in respect to the degree of self-role conflict and the degree of conflict between self and perceived-role. It is possible to order the teachers on each of these two indexes. This tends to substantiate the theoretical framework of this study, that role and personality (self) are two important constructs to be considered when studying the administration of a social system such as the school. This study provides an empirical link with the conceptual creation of a social system, by using an on-going real life setting to test the theoretically contrived hypotheses.[11]

ROLE CONFLICT

Moyer[12] did a study of the principal's leadership role, the attitudes of teachers and principals toward the role, and the relationship between these attitudes and teacher satisfaction. His hypothesis was as follows: close correspondence between teachers' and principals' attitudes toward leadership will be associated with a high degree of teacher satisfaction.

Two styles of leadership—leader-centered and group-centered—were defined, and *Q*-sort statements were developed to permit teachers and principals to choose items which would describe their ideal principal. A rating scale for teacher satisfaction was also developed. These instruments were administered to the principals and teachers of seven schools—four elementary and three secondary. In the analysis, the responses from the principal and teachers of each school, from 12 to 15 in number, were treated separately.

Some of the major findings follow: (1) the closer the correspon-

11. Ibid., pp. 140–141.

12. Donald C. Moyer, "Teachers' Attitudes Toward Leadership as They Relate to Teacher Satisfaction." (Ph.D. diss., Department of Education, University of Chicago, 1954).

dence of attitudes and needs toward leadership within a teaching group (group solidarity), the higher the overall satisfaction of the teachers in the group; (2) the closer the members of a teaching group correspond in group-centered attitudes toward leadership, the higher the level of teacher satisfaction in the group; (3) the extent to which a principal defines his ideal principal as one who encourages teachers to be less dependent on him and more interdependent, the higher the overall satisfaction of the teachers in his group.

While Moyer may have been more preoccupied with teacher satisfaction than with role definition and role conflict, his findings do suggest the importance of role perception on the part of both teachers and principals. Moreover, conflict in how the principal's role is perceived does affect the satisfaction and presumably the productivity of members of the organization.

PERSONALITY CONFLICT

The third type of conflict suggested by the model lies within the idiographic or personal dimension. Getzels and Guba did some work at Maxwell Air Force Base in which this aspect of the theory, among other things, was tested.[13] The setting was Air University, an advanced training center for higher echelon officers in the Air Force. At the time the research was undertaken, the university consisted of what they called nine "courses" but which we may call "schools." The institution was staffed by officers, chiefly of field rank, and the study was initiated because of certain strains in the institution and dissatisfaction among the personnel. An analysis of the existing social system in the terms of the model revealed that each officer-instructor occupied two roles which were in fundamental conflict along a number of dimensions. On the one hand, there was the officer role with certain military expectations, and, on the other hand, the instructor role with certain opposing educational expectations. In addition to stimulating the overall study, the model suggested hypotheses for testing both role conflict and personality conflict.

We shall report here only the part of the study relating to personality conflict. With respect to individual differences among the faculty in felt conflict, it was hypothesized that the intensity of such conflict would vary as a function of certain emotional characteristics. For example, officer-instructors who were "rigid," "defensive," "extrapunitive," and so on, would be more conflicting than other officer-instructors. Personality data were obtained by three standard instruments: the Guilford-Martin Inventory GAMIN and STDCR, the California E and F Scales, and the Rosenzweig Picture—Frustration Study.

13. Jacob W. Getzels and Egon G. Guba, "Role, Role Conflict, and Effectiveness: An Empirical Study," *American Sociological Review* 14 (April 1954), pp. 164–175; "Role Conflict and Personality," *Journal of Personality* 24 (September 1955), pp. 74–85.

To test the hypothesis having to do with differences in personality conflict among instructors, the quarter of officer-instructors scoring highest in felt conflict was compared with the quarter scoring lowest in felt conflict on each of the personality variables provided by the three experimental instruments. Significant differences were found on seven of the ten factors of the Guilford-Martin, on both the E and F sections of the California Scale, and on five of the six variables of the Rosenzweig; and in each case, the results were in the direction predicted by the model. For example, those high in felt conflict were found on the Guilford-Martin to have a greater "feeling of inferiority," to be more "nervous," "introverted," "depressive," and "cyclical in temperament"; on the California E-F Scale to be more "rigid" and "stereotyped"; and on the Rosenzweig to be more "extrapunitive" and "defensive."

LEADERSHIP STYLE

The model suggests that some leaders may be more nomothetic or normative in their behavior and some more idiographic or personal in their behavior. Moser was able to use these ideas and define three styles of leadership as follows[14]:

1. The nomothetic style is characterized by behavior which stresses goal accomplishment, rules and regulations, and centralized authority at the expense of the individual. Effectiveness is rated in terms of behavior toward accomplishing the school's objectives.
2. The idiographic style is characterized by behavior which stresses the individuality of people, minimum rules and regulations, decentralized authority, and highly individualistic relationships with subordinates. The primary objective is to keep subordinates happy and contented.
3. The transactional style is characterized by behavior which stresses goal accomplishment, but which also makes provision for individual need fulfillment. The transactional leader balances nomothetic and idiographic behavior and thus judiciously utilizes each style as the occasion demands.

Moser undertook to examine the relationships between the behavior of superintendents and principals in the performance of their different, yet complementary, roles. He also undertook to assess the relationship between the leader-follower leadership styles of superintendents and principals and their effectiveness ratings, confidence in leadership, and job satisfaction.

14. Robert F. Moser, "The Leadership Patterns of School Superintendents and School Principals," *Administrator's Notebook* 6, 1 (September 1957). The *Administrator's Notebook* is published by the Midwest Administration Center at the University of Chicago.

Twelve superintendents and twenty-four principals in twelve school systems participated as subjects in the study. The superintendents and principals answered interview questions designed to stimulate subjective responses concerning perceptions of their own and the others' leadership style, their major problems as leaders, and their relationships to each other. In addition, each participant responded to a series of instruments designed to permit analysis which would produce indices related to the following variables: leadership style, agreement or disagreement on role definition, ratings of effectiveness, confidence in leadership, and satisfaction.

In relating the perceived and professed leadership styles of principals and superintendents to the relationships that exist among them, Moser found the following points significant:

1. Superintendents express highest confidence in and give the highest effectiveness ratings to those principals whom they perceive as exhibiting transactional behavior. Superintendents express less confidence in and give the lowest effectiveness ratings to principals whom they perceive as exhibiting idiographic behavior.
2. Superintendents express the highest confidence in and give the highest effectiveness ratings to principals who profess to be nomothetic.
3. Superintendents who profess nomothetic behavior are given the highest effectiveness ratings by principals and enjoy the confidence of principals.
4. Superintendents expect principals to be transactional, with emphasis upon the nomothetic. Likewise, principals expect superintendents to be transactional-nomothetic. Principals want positive leadership from superintendents, and superintendents want principals who are positive leaders.
5. Principals tend to emphasize idiographic behavior in dealing with teachers and nomothetic behavior in their relations with the superintendent. This indicates that the principal is subjected to different expectations from his superintendent than from his teachers and that the principal behaves differently with his superiors than with his subordinates.
6. The principal's rating of the superintendent's effectiveness is a function of the agreement between the superintendent and the principal on the expectations held for the principal role. On the other hand, the superintendent's rating of principal effectiveness depends upon the superintendent's and principal's agreement on the definition of both roles.
7. High mutual ratings of effectiveness and confidence by superintendents and principals are accompanied by similarities in leadership style, feelings of security, general satisfaction with the relationships, desire to consult with one another on important matters, and clear delineation of duties and authority of decision making.

This short review of some of the studies generated by the social-process model should demonstrate that the model has been useful in suggesting research. The findings of a single study, however, should be accepted with considerable caution. One should recognize that the population included, the nature of the instruments used, the limited variables being tested, and other factors will often limit the generalizations that may be drawn from a single study. We shall have more to say about the implications of these and related studies later.

LIMITATIONS AND EXTENSIONS OF THE THEORY

Initially, the social process view of administration appeared to be a most useful way of looking at the in-organization relationships of a school or school system. It seemed to serve less well as a way of viewing the out-organization relationships of a school or school system. As we shall show later, implications for personnel selection and supervision, for instance, were readily apparent. On the other hand, implications for the relationships between the school organization and the larger society of which the school is a part were not so readily apparent. The theory did little, for instance, to explain operating-levy elections in a community.

Every administrator is aware that he has many out-organization relationships as well as in-organization relationships. One of us participated in a study in which the interactions of four superintendents over an extended period of time were observed and described.[15] In this study 515 of the interactions of the four superintendents, observed a half-day each week over a six-month period, were with organizational members, but 256 of the interactions were with the board of education, community groups, and professional groups. Community groups included governmental agencies at local, state, and national levels, and nongovernmental organizations and individuals of many kinds. The reality of these out-organization relationships is illustrated in the following description of one incident from the study:

> The newspaper reporter pulled a chair up to the front of the superintendent's desk, moved the name plate and calendar to one side, and started taking notes. After several questions the reporter said, "Now about that budget hearing this week, I think I ought to tell you that the industrial group is going to be down at County Seat to fight the budget you have proposed, along with the Tax Committee of the industrial group, though I don't know why."

15. Midwest Administration Center, "Observation of Administrator Behavior" (Chicago: The Center, University of Chicago, 1959), p. 188.

> The superintendent replied, "Well, I'm a little surprised at that, as I thought they were on our side."
>
> The reporter then asked who all would represent the schools at the hearing, and he added, "I suppose it will be a knock-down, drag-out affair."
>
> The superintendent told him that the director of finance, the attorney, the principals, the PTA president, the representatives of the teachers' union, the representatives of the labor organization in industry, the voters' organizations, the legal organizations, and certain civic groups would represent the schools. In addition, he said, "It may be that the president of one of the big industries will be there, also, to say that they do not go along with the members of the opposition group." Then the superintendent laughed and said, "Now don't go list all of this, or you will really stir up the opposition." The reporter added that he would not, but he said, "We'll have someone down covering the hearing by telephone, and I'll be writing the story at the *Herald,* so all of this background helps. Hell, I wouldn't have told you about who was planning to oppose this unless I had a little judgment, although this bit about their industry people jumping the traces is really 'hot' and would break the opposition right into two camps."
>
> "That's exactly what we hope to do," replied the superintendent.
>
> "That's fine for now; we'll see you tonight at the meeting," the reporter concluded.[16]

Getzels and Thelen, recognizing the limitations of the initial social process model, developed a new dimension designed to picture more adequately the reality of the school in the larger society.[17] Just as one is able to think of organizations in sociological terms, one may also think of them in cultural terms, for the organization is embedded in a culture with certain mores and values. The expectations of the roles must in some way be related to the ethos or cultural values. This relationship, however, is by no means clear. Parsons and Shils, for example, view cultural elements as a highly complex constellation of elements that tend to become organized into systems.[18] Yet this system is not viewed as a motivated system, but as patterned symbols and value orientations which may become embodied either in institutionalized role expectations or in the superego structure of the personality.

Perhaps just as one can analyze the sociological dimension utilizing the central analytic elements of role expectations, one can also focus

16. Ibid., p. 85.

17. Jacob W. Getzels and Herbert A. Thelen, "The Classroom Group as a Unique Social System." In National Society for the Study of Education, *The Dynamics of Instructional Groups* (Chicago: The University of Chicago Press, 1960), chap. 4.

18. Parsons and Shils, *Toward a General Theory of Action,* p. 21.

on values as analytic elements of the cultural or anthropological dimension. The term value, like that of role, has been used in many different ways and in many different contexts.

An entirely new concept of values was suggested by Spindler when he said, "Conflicts between groups centering on issues of educational relevance, and confusions within the rank and file of educators, can be understood best, I believe, in the perspective of the transformation of American culture that proceeds without regard for personal fortune or institutional survival."[19] Spindler defines values as objects of possession, conditions of existence, personality or characterological features, and states of mind that are conceived as desirable and act as motivating determinants of behavior. He has characterized values as traditional or emergent.

The rationale of Spindler has been elaborated by Getzels to distinguish between *sacred* and *secular* values.[20] The sacred values—which we all tend to accept—were seen as democracy, individualism, equality, and human perfectability. The traditional secular values—the operating, down-to-earth beliefs—were seen as the work-success ethic, future-time orientation, independence or the autonomous self, and puritan morality. Getzels suggested that the sacred values have remained stable, but that the secular values are liable to the strains and cleavages of regionalism, rural-urban differences, social class, and social change. Encroaching upon the traditional secular values are the emergent values of sociability, conformity, relativism and present-time orientation.

In analyzing the relationship between the anthropological and the sociological dimensions, one must recognize that the two dimensions are not necessarily parallel to each other. However, the relationship may be represented schematically according to the diagram shown in Figure 7–4. The model with three rather than two dimensions is shown in Figure 7–5. This model permits one to posit some relationships between cultural values and institutional expectations, a possibility which stimulated Abbott to undertake a study of the influence of values upon the superintendent—school

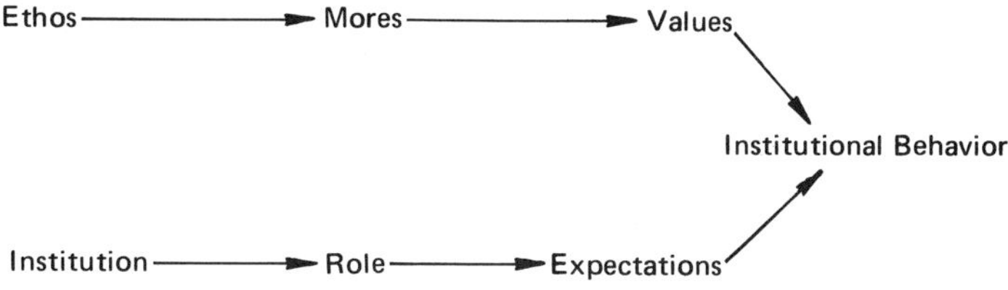

Figure 7–4 The relationship of the anthropological and social dimensions of social behavior (from Getzels and Thelen).

19. George Spindler, "Education in a Transforming American Culture," *Harvard Educational Review* 25, 3 (Summer 1955): 156.

20. Jacob W. Getzels, "Changing Values Challenge the Schools," *The School Review* 65 (Spring 1957): 92–102.

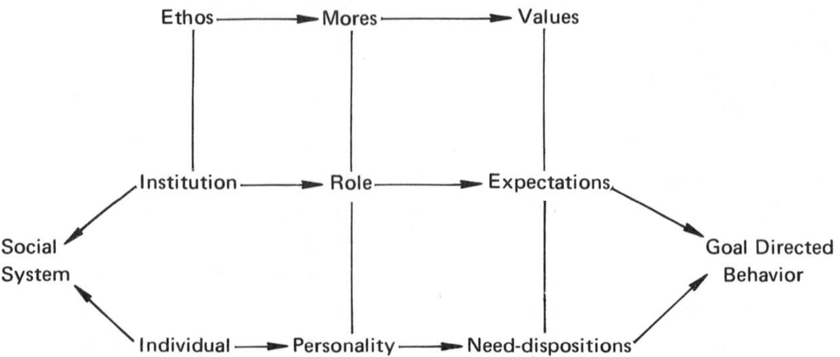

Figure 7–5 Extended model showing a third or cultural dimension of social behavior (from Getzels and Thelen).

board relationships.[21] The central thesis of the investigation was that difficulties in interpersonal relationships may be expected to arise, not so much from complexities and differences in values that are in the open and understood, as from complexities and differences that are underground and misunderstood.

Two hypotheses were formulated, based on prior theoretical and empirical work in the general area of values: first, an individual's own values were expected to influence his perceptions of the values held by others; second, both an individual's values and his value-perceptions were expected to influence his relationships with others.

The following questions provided the focus for the investigation:

1. What is the relationship between superintendents' value-orientations and their perceptions of the values held by individual board members? Conversely, what is the relationship between board members' perceptions of superintendents' values and their own value-orientations?
2. What is the relationship between the confidence that board members evince in their superintendents' leadership and (a) congruence in value-orientations, (b) accuracy of perception of value-orientations, and (c) perceived similarity in value-orientations?

A values inventory was used to obtain from board members and superintendents responses to a series of items that represented a traditional—emergent value dichotomy. From the responses that were obtained, both self-scores of respondents and their perceptual scores of others were derived. A confidence-in-leadership scale was used to ascertain board members' confidence in their superintendents.

21. Max G. Abbott, "Values and Value-Perceptions in Superintendent-School Board Relationships," *Administrator's Notebook* 9, 4 (December 1960).

Thirty-seven superintendents and 213 board members from twenty-seven elementary districts, five high school districts, and eight unit districts, all located in the Midwest, made up the sample.

Interpersonal relationships were indeed influenced by the values people held and by the way in which those values were perceived. An individual's own values had an important influence upon his perceptions of the values held by others. Persons who held emergent values tended to view others as being emergent, while those who held traditional values tended to view others as being traditional. Moreover, these patterns of perception were unrelated to the actual values of those whose values were being perceived.

The values held by individuals had an important influence upon kinds of perceptual errors made. When the values of the perceiver and the perceived were similar, errors tended to be random. When the values of the perceiver and the perceived were dissimilar, errors followed a systematic pattern and tended to move in the direction of the perceiver's own value position with a frequency that was significantly greater than would have been expected to occur by chance.

The hypothesis concerning the relationship between confidence-in-leadership and agreement on values was substantiated. Board members whose values were most similar to those of their superintendents expressed slightly higher confidence to those superintendents than did board members whose values were least similar.

There was a relationship also between confidence-in-leadership and the accurate perception of values. Board members who were most accurate in perceiving their superintendents' values expressed significantly higher confidence in their superintendents than did board members who were least accurate.

A strong relationship was found between confidence-in-leadership and perceived similarity in values. Board members who perceived their superintendents to be most similar to themselves in values, regardless of actual similarity, expressed significantly higher confidence in their superintendents than did board members who perceived their superintendents to be least similar to themselves.

In general, it may be said that confidence was related positively to the accuracy with which board members understood their superintendents' value positions. Confidence was also related positively to the extent that board members assumed that they themselves were in agreement with their superintendents on basic issues. Whether or not this presumed agreement actually existed appeared to be relatively unimportant.

The concept of selective interpersonal perception is, therefore, important in understanding administrative relationships. In a sense, each person may be said to function in a world of his own making. His attitudes and values serve as a perceptual screen; he interprets his environment according to the way he perceives it; and he reacts to that environment in accordance with his interpretations. Thus, in analyzing the superintendent-school board relationship, it is not sufficient merely to determine whether or not superintendents and board members are in agreement on basic issues. It is necessary also to know how each member of the relationship perceives the positions of other members, since it is these perceptions which influence largely the action that will be taken. The findings of this investigation suggest that harmonious interpersonal relationships can be maintained despite differences in basic value positions, provided the differences are assessed accurately.

The extension of the social process model is dealt with more fully in recent work by Getzels and others.[22] This extension illustrates another characteristic of theory: it has within it the seeds of its own destruction and reconstruction. In other words, if the theory does not depict reality accurately, the testing of the hypotheses generated by the theory will reveal the shortage and will call for revision of the original formulation. With its new dimension the social process model describes a larger segment of administrative behavior—whether large enough remains to be seen.

IMPLICATIONS FOR PRACTICE

While, as Griffiths[23] suggests, the study of theory may be more useful to researchers than to practitioners, we believe that a theory of administration should suggest implications for practice as surely as it does hypotheses for research. Let us see if the social-process theory can meet such a demand.

IN-ORGANIZATION MEDIATOR

Within the organization it seems clear that the theory we have been discussing makes the administrator a mediator between the normative and the personal dimensions. At one point as organizational spokesman he will find it essential to explain, to reinforce, to emphasize the school's objectives and procedures. At another point he will find it desirable to listen to members of the organization, to ascertain their feelings about certain school practices, and to diagnose as best he can why they take the positions they do. When and under what circumstances he does either is part of the art of administration. Clearly, there are no recipes as to when the administrator behaves normatively or personally, but his judgment regarding such matters may be sharpened if he knows that both kinds of behavior

22. Jacob W. Getzels, James M. Lipham, and Roald F. Campbell, *Educational Administration as a Social Force,* pp. 89–102. For a treatment of the environment and organizational behavior, see also Paul R. Lawrence and Jay W. Lorsch, *Organization and Environment* (Homewood, Ill.: Richard D. Irwin, Inc., 1969).

23. Daniel E. Griffiths, "Some Thoughts about Theory in Educational Administration—1975." *UCEA Review* 17, 1 (October 1975): 17.

are appropriate for the administrator. Some examples may help clarify this point.

The capacity of the administrator to be aware of both normative and personal roles is illustrated in the employment of personnel. Such a process is critical both for the school and the person, and thus the interests of both should be thoroughly explored in the employment process. The administrator should do his best to make clear the goals, program, and characteristics of the school and the expectations held for the prospective staff member. At the same time, every effort should be made to understand the aspirations, the values, the motivations, and the strengths of the person being considered. Such a process can do much to insure some congruence between organizational expectations and personal dispositions should the candidate become a staff member, a condition necessary for best school operation.

A similar demand pertains in terms of the assignment of personnel. If the administrator emphasizes only his normative role, he will tend to look upon staff members as cogs in the organizational machine, each somewhat alike and replaceable by the other. On the other hand, if the administrator becomes completely personal he will strive to make assignments conform to individual whim with little or no regard for the total program of the organization. Clearly, neither extreme is acceptable; few administrators act completely one way or the other. It may help, however, to recognize that at times even unpopular assignments have to be made if the total program is to be served. At the same time, it should be clear that people tend to be more productive if at least part of the time they are doing those things they enjoy and for which they have competence.

Perhaps in the supervision of personnel the two dimensions of the model are even more suggestive. The aim of supervision is the improved performance of personnel, which in a school system means enhancement of the teaching-learning process. Both in the diagnosis of any difficulties a teacher may be having and in developing ways for overcoming such difficulties, the two dimensions of the model seem pertinent. The difficulty may lie, for instance, in a misunderstanding of what the school expects, or it may lie in unrealistic aspirations on the part of a teacher. Such diagnosis suggests the remedial measures: clarification of school goals in one instance, and modification of individual standards in the other.

Guba has extended the model by way of suggesting the actuating force or power of an administrator in an organization. His concept is shown in Figure 7–6. The administrator is seen as having two kinds of power: status and authority, which reside at the role or normative dimension; and prestige and influence, which reside at the person or idiographic dimension. The first kind of power resides in the office and is vested in the administrator. The second kind of power must be earned and is entrusted to the administrator. Clearly, an effective administrator has and exercises both kinds of power.

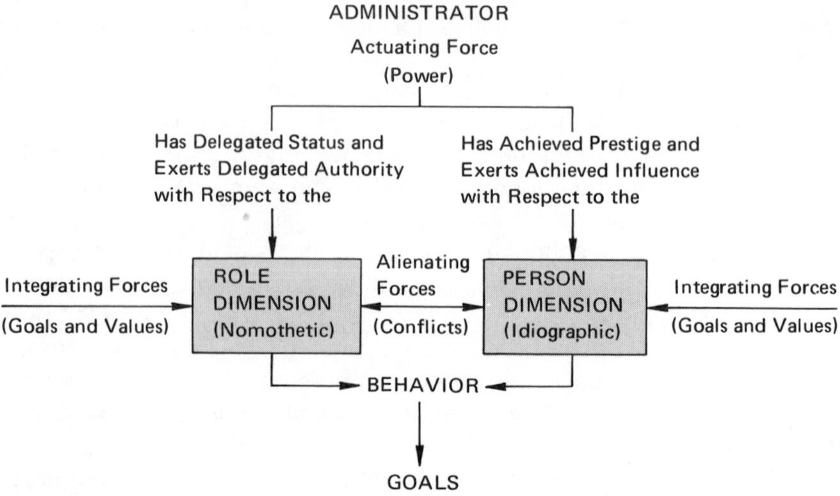

Figure 7–6 The power relationships of the administrator.[24]

Conflict between institutional expectations and personal dispositions is seen as alienating forces in an organization. For instance, a school may establish ability groups in mathematics or English. Some of these groups will be composed of slow learners but, even so, they must have teachers. If assigned to teach one of these groups, a teacher who has no patience with slow learners will probably resent the task and may actually sabotage the program. In any case, the lack of congruence between institutional expectations and personal dispositions is clear.

The alienating force of this conflict may be reduced by employing goals and values as integrating forces. Thus, in our illustration the forming of ability groups may be seen as one way of differentiating instruction for pupils who have a wide range of capacity. Moreover, the desirability of giving even slow learners an opportunity to do their best may be seen as consonant with the values of schools within a democratic society. This kind of exploration may make teaching a group of slow learners more rational and possibly more palatable. If at the same time such an assignment can be coupled with teaching a fast-learning group, more in keeping with the personal dispositions of the teacher, the total assignment may become quite acceptable.

THE ADMINISTRATOR IN THE MIDDLE

Another implication of the model, particularly when the cultural dimension is included, places the administrator squarely in the middle of a number

24. Egon G. Guba, "Research in Internal Administration—Is It Relevant?" In R. F. Campbell and J. M. Lipham, eds., *Administrative Theory as a Guide to Action* (Chicago: Midwest Administration Center, University of Chicago, 1960), chap. 7.

of reference groups. There is the community with its many publics, the board of education with some lay and some professional understandings and convictions, the school system itself with its own set of social arrangements, and the impingement of the larger world at both lay and professional levels. Within this welter of forces there are many conflicting expectations and demands.

Conflicts within some of the reference groups have been very well documented. Ordinarily, the people of a community are not of one mind. One public, for instance, may wish the school to provide a program of released time for religious education, while another public opposes any such idea. One public may advocate extensive provisions for vocational education, while another public would leave all such efforts to industry. One public may place great stress upon the intellectual purposes of the school, while another public would give almost equal emphasis to social purposes.[25] These conflicts may become so sharp that they furnish the battleground for conflicts between competing leadership groups in the community.

Within the school itself there may also be sharp conflicts. In recent years labor-management issues tend to divide teachers and teacher organizations from administrators and school board members. This division apparently receives reinforcement from state-level attempts of teacher organizations and other actors to influence policy making for schools. In the twelve states studied by the Educational Governance Project, teacher organizations were nearly always seen by governors, legislators, and other actors as the strongest education lobby, stronger than either administrator or school board organizations.[26]

In many school systems a number of other conflicts may be observed. Elementary and secondary school teachers differ in their viewpoints on many questions. Elementary school principals are seldom accorded the same status as secondary school principals. Some secondary school teachers believe that the high school should be a selective institution, whereas others think it should serve all youth. Although some teachers want almost complete freedom in their work, others have great need for direction from administrative and supervisory personnel.

Boards of education ordinarily talk out their conflicts until they reach agreement, but this should not obscure the fact that board members too have different expectations of administrators. One board member may think that the superintendent should be a "strong" leader, while another may believe he should consult freely with his staff. Still another may value above all else careful financial management and be opposed to all expansions of program regardless of need. Or current issues, such as changes

---

25. Lawrence W. Downey, *The Task of Public Education* (Chicago: Midwest Administration Center, University of Chicago, 1960).

26. Roald F. Campbell and Tim L. Mazzoni, Jr., *State Policy Making for the Public Schools* (Berkeley, Calif.: McCutchan Publishing Corp., 1975), chap. 5.

in attendance area boundaries to further integrate schools or the need to close schools due to enrollment declines, may divide board members just as they do citizens at large.

Even the influences of the larger world upon the administration of a school district are not of one voice. School practices in other communities may be quite diverse. Programs at the state or federal level may actually seem unacceptable to the people of a local school district. Witness, for instance, state programs of school district reorganization which are seen as undue meddling with local operation. Or note the number of school districts that have difficulty with the implementation of some of the federal programs.

Alas, even the professional voices heard by the administrator are not in complete unity. Within his own faculty and administrative staff some may be encouraging the adoption of innovative practices and others cautioning against change. He may find in his professional magazines descriptions of opposing school practices, each of which is reputed to be professionally sanctioned.

Each of the reference groups to which we have alluded—the community, the board of education, the school system itself, and the larger environment—may have in a particular school community some common expectations for school administrators, but within each group there appear to be many real or potential conflicts. The administrator must chart a program despite these conflicts.

Perhaps even more significant to school administration than the differences within the various reference groups, as noted above, are the differences among these groups. Halpin found, for instance, that school staff members and board members usually agreed within their respective groups in describing the leadership behavior of superintendents, but that the two groups did not agree with each other.[27] Many principals have found that teachers and parents hold quite different expectations for the behavior of the principal. Parents often see the principal's first duty as that of developing relationships with parents and other groups in the community. Teachers, on the other hand, often see the principal's first duty as that of being available to teachers and frequently in supporting teachers in face of parental criticism.

In a sense these conflicting expectations among reference groups place the school administrator squarely in the middle. In order for the principal to meet the expectations of the parents, he may not be able to meet the expectations of the teachers, or vice versa. In like manner a superintendent may find his board of education holds one set of expectations for him, while his staff holds another. This is not merely a theoretical matter; it is one which has been documented time and again in practice. Consider the expectations each group holds for the superintendent on the question of

27. Andrew W. Halpin, *Theory and Research in Administration* (New York: The Macmillan Co., 1966), chap. 3.

salary negotiations. Or reflect upon the superintendent's dilemma when a board of education is anxious to improve the physical plant of the district and the teachers are in great need of an improved salary scale. Or think of the school administrator who gets caught in a school district reorganization hassle, with his local community resisting any change and the state department of education and other professionals urging a larger district and combination of high schools.

The dilemma of the administrator as the man in the middle is shown in Figure 7–7. Each major group holds expectations for the admin-

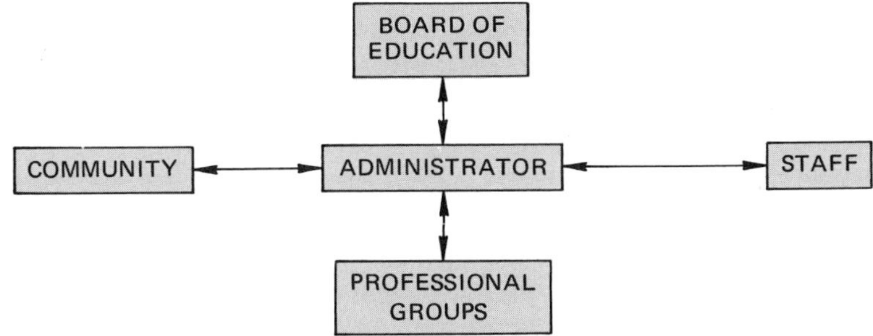

Figure 7–7 The administrator and some of his major reference groups.

istrator, and there is often conflict among these expectations. Within each of these groups there may also be conflict in terms of what is expected of the administrator. We might conclude, after noting the conflicting expectations facing administrators both within and among the various reference groups, that the only alternative is to do nothing. Actually, it is not that simple; to do nothing is in a sense a program and some groups will, after a time, object even to that program. The administrator is thus faced with the development of the best program that can be devised within the limits of the situation.

Despite the many limitations which characterize most situations, there is on most questions some flexibility, or an "area of tolerance." Although the board of education, for instance, may not believe in citizens' advisory committees in general, it may be willing to try out a citizens' advisory committee organized around a particular task, such as a bond campaign. Or teachers may be dead set against a merit factor in a salary schedule, but they may be willing that a program designed to evaluate teaching be developed for instructional improvement purposes only. It is within these areas of tolerance that a school administrator may be able to resolve at least some of the conflicts which seem to exist both within and among major reference groups.

The limits discussed above also suggest the real challenge to educational administration; most of the limits have a time dimension. A position taken by a community, a board, or a faculty today need not hold forever. We have only to look at a few of the positions taken by such groups a decade or two ago to find how true this is.

But the administrator cannot be content merely to wait in hopes that time will alter the situation. He needs some way of getting at the dynamics of the situation. The questions become: Under what circumstances do people have a chance of changing their minds? How and to what extent may I bring these circumstances about?

While the answers to these questions are by no means complete, one prerequisite to bringing some harmony out of disagreement seems to be face-to-face communication. School boards and faculties usually find more in common when they have many opportunities to talk together. In like manner teachers and parents find the grounds of agreement broader when they confer frequently with each other. The administrator can facilitate the kinds of communication alluded to above.

Another element in the process of change appears to be complete information. To be sure, some people are like the chap who said, "My mind is made up; don't confuse me with the facts," but most people are willing to give some attention to the facts that are relevant to a problem. Often these facts include a description of what is being done elsewhere. While this proves nothing, the example of others is a powerful argument to many people. Again an administrator can facilitate the processes of fact-gathering and presentation.

Complete integrity on the part of the administrator is also necessary if people are to be willing to make compromises or arrive at new positions. This situation may mean that no group comes to love the administrator, but all groups come to respect him. Seldom can the educational leader take a position completely to the liking of a particular reference group, but his reasons for not doing so should be clear, and he should be seen as serving a larger constituency. Difficult as this role may appear, it is only leadership of this kind which will help the school fill its unique place in our society.

In the great dilemma about which we have been speaking lies the real challenge to administrative leadership. If areas of tolerance are to be extended, if members of reference groups are to understand how the school must stand above the welfare of a particular group in order to serve all groups, if change is to be seen as a way of life, the leadership of the administrator must help all groups understand the viewpoints of other groups and the administrator's position as a competent adjudicator.

SUGGESTED ACTIVITIES

1. Describe the similarities and differences between the initial Getzels-Guba model and the major concept of Argyris or the two dimensions suggested by Cartwright and Zander.

2. Formulate a few simple questions pertaining to some issues affecting the public schools of your community, and use these questions to interview a number of citizens. Note the similarity and diversity of their opinions.
3. As one of your questions above, ask each citizen to name the three most influential people in the community. To what extent do you get a duplication of names? Determine to what extent incumbent school board members are numbered among the community leaders named by citizens.
4. Interview a number of teachers, a number of pupils, and a number of parents in a particular school or school system, and ask them what they consider the important duties of the school principal to be. Note similarities and differences in the responses.

SELECTED READINGS

Argyris, Chris. *Integrating the Individual and the Organization.* New York: Wiley, 1964.

Campbell, Roald F., and Gregg, Russell T., eds. *Administrative Behavior in Education.* New York: Harper & Brothers, 1957, chap. 7.

Cartwright, Dorwin, and Zander, Alvin. *Group Dynamics: Research and Theory,* 3rd ed. New York: Harper & Row, 1968.

Downey, Lawrence W. *The Task of Public Education.* Chicago: Midwest Administration Center, University of Chicago, 1960.

Getzels, J. W.; Lipham, J. M.; and Campbell, R. F. *Educational Administration as a Social Process.* New York: Harper & Row, 1968.

Griffiths, Daniel E., ed. *Behavioral Science and Educational Administration,* Sixty-third Yearbook, N.S.S.E. Part II. Chicago: University of Chicago Press, 1964.

Gross, Neal; Mason, Ward S.; and McEachern, Alexander W. *Explorations in Role Analysis: Studies of the School Superintendent Role.* New York: Wiley, 1958.

Guba, Egon G. "Research in Internal Administration—What Do We Know?" In R. F. Campbell and J. M. Lipham, eds., *Administrative Theory as a Guide to Action.* Chicago: Midwest Administration Center, University of Chicago, 1960, chap. 7.

Halpin, Andrew W. *Theory and Research in Administration.* New York: The Macmillan Co., 1966.

Katz, Daniel, and Kahn, Robert L. *The Social Psychology of Organizations.* New York: Wiley, 1966.

Lawrence, Paul R., and Lorsch, Jay W. *Organization and Environment.* Homewood, Ill.: Richard D. Irwin, Inc., 1969.

Monahan, William G. *Theoretical Dimensions of Educational Administration.* New York: Macmillan Publishing Co., 1975.

8

SYSTEMS PERSPECTIVES AND THE EDUCATIONAL ADMINISTRATOR

For our final approach to educational administration, we will review some of the important ways to view management in systemic terms. Each of the analytical tools that will be examined in this chapter is rooted in two commonly shared beliefs: (1) It is better to have some idea where one is going than to fly blind, and (2) It is better to be orderly than haphazard when one defines problems and makes decisions.[1] Consistent with these beliefs, each mode of thought provides a way of viewing a problem, breaking it down into its component parts, and showing the linkage among these parts. In introducing the reader to these various analytical tools we will briefly describe the key ideas embodied in each mode of thought, provide illustrations of the tool's applicability to the educational administrator, and point out difficulties which may be encountered in attempting to use the conceptual tool. The five modes of thought to be considered in this chapter include: Systems Analysis, Input-Output Analysis, Planning-Programing-Budgeting-System (PPBS), Organizational Development (O.D.), and Network Analysis.

1. Alice M. Rivlin, *Systematic Thinking for Social Action* (Washington, D.C.: The Brookings Institution, 1971), p. 2.

SYSTEMS ANALYSIS: A GENERAL FRAMEWORK

Perhaps the simplest definition of system is the one by A. D. Hall and R. E. Fagen because it contains the basic elements embraced by most definitions of the term. According to Hall and Fagen, "a system is a set of objects together with relationships between the objects and between their attributes."[2] The word system can refer to a set of objects from the smallest 'whole' to the entire universe. There are basically two types of systems—an open system and a closed system. The characteristic state of the system depends on the presence or absence of exchanges with the environment. If no material enters or leaves the system, it is a closed system; if there is import and export, and, therefore, change of the components, the system is an open system.[3]

We share with Emery and Trist[4] and Katz and Kahn[5] the belief that organizations are not closed systems, i.e., they are not sufficiently independent to allow most of their problems to be analyzed with reference to their internal structures and without regard to their external environment. Educational organizations in particular require a perspective that reflects the mutual permeation of the organization and its environment. Consequently, our treatment of systems analysis will reflect open system conceptions.

Systems analysis is a process which involves breaking a whole into its component parts (objects and attributes) and relating these parts to each other and the whole. The objective of systems analysis is to enable the analyst or the administrator to acquire a better understanding of the behavior of the whole system by studying the behavior and interactions of its parts. The systems analyst believes that a person should keep five basic considerations in mind when he sets out to describe a system:

1. What are the total system objectives and the performance measures of the whole system?
2. What is the system's environment?
3. What are the system's resources?
4. What are the components of the system, their activities, goals and measures of performance?
5. What is the management of the system?[6]

---

2. A. D. Hall and R. E. Fagen, "Definition of System," in *General Systems,* Yearbooks of the Society for General Systems Research, vol. 1 (1956), p. 18.

3. L. von Bertalanffy, "The Theory of Open Systems in Physics and Biology," *Science,* vol. 3 (1950), pp. 23–9.

4. F. E. Emery and E. L. Trist, "Sociotechnical Systems," in C. West Churchman and M. Verhulst, eds., *Management Sciences, Models and Techniques,* vol. 2 (London: Pergamon Press, 1960).

5. Daniel Katz and Robert L. Kahn, *The Social Psychology of Organizations* (New York: John Wiley and Sons, Inc., 1966).

6. This section draws upon C. West Churchman, *The Systems Approach* (New York: Dell Publishing Co., Inc., 1968), pp. 28–47.

In seeking to identify the objectives of the system, the systems analyst does not limit his search to the public pronouncements and the official documents of the organization. He recognizes that the chief executive of an organization may portray its mission in lofty terms even though there is little or no correspondence between the stated and the actual goals of the organization. Such misrepresentation of reality can occur when the administrator inadvertently confuses what should be happening in the organization with what is actually happening,[7] as well as when the administrator withholds information in the interest of personal or organizational goals.

This dysjunction between stated and real goals is not limited to the superordinate levels in organizations; it also can be discerned at the lower levels of the hierarchy. Teachers, for example, may maintain that they want students to develop critical capacities, to express opinions, to evaluate the soundness of arguments, and to be creative.[8] Students, on the other hand, may accurately perceive that these qualities of mind are not assessed on the tests constructed by the teacher; rather, the teacher evaluates students' performance in terms of their ability to recall facts, concepts, and generalizations. Recognizing the disparity between the stated and the actual outcomes which are valued by the teacher, the student may neglect the development of higher level mental processes and concentrate on memorizing the bits of knowledge to be covered on the test.

If the student is willing to forego a thorough understanding of the course content in order to receive a high grade, the systems analyst would conclude that the stated purpose of the student is to learn but the real measure of the performance is the grade. This conclusion rests on the notion of sacrifice, for the ultimate test of the objective of a system is to determine what goals the system will knowingly sacrifice in order to attain a particular objective. Although we have identified the crucial test for determining a system's objectives, we must also point out that it is no easy task to determine the real objectives of a system. At the present time, the search strategies for locating the objectives of a system are not fully developed.

The systems analyst also faces similar difficulties in describing the environment of an open system. Environmental identification problems arise because the environment is typically described as everything outside the boundary of a system. The boundary of a system is a more or less arbitrary demarcation of that which is included and excluded from the system.[9] Such statements supply little guidance to the individual intent on defining a system's environment.

Aware of the difficulties involved in describing the environment

7. See Seymour B. Sarason, *The Culture of the School and the Problem of Change* (Boston: Allyn and Bacon, Inc., 1971), pp. 62–87.

8. Benson R. Snyder, *The Hidden Curriculum* (New York: Alfred A. Knopf, 1971).

9. Glenn L. Immegart, "Systems Theory and Taxonomic Inquiry into Organizational Behavior in Education," in Daniel E. Griffiths, ed., *Developing Taxonomies of Organizational Behavior in Educational Administration* (Chicago: Rand McNally and Company, 1969), pp. 165–238.

of a system, Churchman has set forth two additional criteria which reduce to some extent the problems of defining a system's environment. If things or persons affect the performance of a system in some way and are not subject to the administrator's control, these objects constitute the environment of the system. In other words, the environment of a system consists of those "givens" which influence the attainment of objectives. For example, substantial inequalities in the capacities (a "given") of school districts to tax and spend are presumed to imply differentials in educational quality.[10]

Systems may have objective and subjective environments. The objective environment refers to those system-relevant constraints which have an existence independent of the perceiver while the subjective environment represents those system-relevant factors which the administrator mistakenly regards as being beyond his control or influence. A conventional school building with its "egg crate" architecture is an aspect of the objective environment as the features of the structure are fixed and affect the kinds of activities which can occur within it. One's perceptions of the expectations which his superiors hold for his role may be incongruent with the objective reality of the situation, however. If, for example, as is sometimes the case in urban settings, the principal believes that his superiors' role expectations are immutable when in fact they are not, we consider the expectations to be located in the subjective environment.[11]

Systems may fail to operate properly because the administrator erroneously believes that some relevant aspect of the world is outside the system and not subject to his control. Since such errors may unwittingly occur, the administrator may with profit scrutinize each factor in the environment to determine if it belongs to the objective or subjective environment of the system. If the factor lies in the subjective environment, the administrator may be able to improve the system's performance by considering the factor as a part of the system rather than the environment. By way of illustration, a newly appointed principal was led to believe that one of his foreign language teachers was steadfastly opposed to trying any new instructional strategies. Refusing to accept someone else's judgment of the teacher's opposition to change, the principal probed the teacher's interest in switching to an approach which emphasized oral rather than written language. The teacher revealed that she had been considering such a possibility and sought the help of the principal in exploring the alternative. Within a year, the teacher had broadened her language competence through summer study overseas and was teaching without a text, something she had not attempted in her previous fourteen years of teaching.

One of the most important aspects of the environment is the requirement schedule, i.e., the demands for the system's products or ser-

10. For an analysis of the complexities inherent in this presumption, see Kenneth L. Karst, "Serrano v. Priest's Inputs and Outputs," *Law and Contemporary Problems* 38, 3 (Winter-Spring 1974), pp. 333–349.

11. Sarason, *The Culture of the School,* pp. 133–150.

vices. The significance of demands has been quite evident in the field of education. Declining enrollments at all levels in the educational system have exerted enormous pressures on educational institutions to reduce staff, to institute new offerings, and to curtail the activities of certain departments. Shifts in the demands for the products and services of various components of the educational system will in all likelihood continue to affect the performance and character of the system as the demands represent a substantial constraint on what the system may undertake and accomplish.[12]

A third consideration of the systems analyst centers on the resources of the system, i.e., the means which the system has at its disposal to perform its jobs. The resources are located inside the system and, unlike the factors in the environment, are subject to control by the managers of the system. Some of a system's major resources are money, man hours, and equipment. When examining these resources, the systems analyst, as we will detail in later sections of this chapter, is interested in knowing more than what resources are available and how they are allocated. He is also interested in estimating the lost opportunities, those benefits which might have been realized if the resources had been allocated in other ways. To estimate these benefits, the administrator needs extensive information; without an adequate data base the administrator will discover that determining the wisdom of resource allocations within a system is of no less difficulty than determining the objectives and the environment of the system.

Similarly, the user of systems thinking may confront problems in adequately describing the components, parts, or subsystems of a system. The problems he faces are apt to be of a political, as well as an intellectual, nature. Members of a system are inclined to view it as consisting of departments or divisions while the analyst tends to conceive of the system's components as the basic missions, activities, or jobs of the system. Thus, as the administrator begins to ignore traditional organizational labels in his search for missions, he may encounter resistance from individuals in the system who strongly identify with their own work units, however they may be designated. For example, the administrator may consider reading to be a basic mission of the system and decide that the activities of social studies and science teachers, along with the English instructors, contribute to the reading skills of students. Ultimately he hopes to determine the magnitude of the contributions which the social studies and science teachers make to the students' reading skills. The teachers in these two subject matter fields may not share the administrator's goals, however. Instead, they may oppose any actions that blur the distinction between the activities of their work unit and those of other departments. Without the cooperation of organizational participants, the administrator may be unable to bring his analysis of the system parts to a fruitful conclusion.

12. Mark Rodekohr, "Adjustments of Colorado School Districts to Declining Enrollments" (Ph.D. diss., University of Colorado, 1974). Rodekohr's research suggests that the larger the district undergoing decline the better its chances for making a successful adjustment.

The intellectual problems associated with adequately specifying the missions of the systems are probably no less complex. There is little to guide the administrator's quest for missions beyond such simple admonitions as: ignore the traditional lines of division, persist in talking about missions rather than departments, and look for those components which have measures of performance related to the measure of the overall system. The design of valid measures for describing the performance of components is another type of intellectual problem that must be solved if the ultimate aim of component specification is to be achieved, namely, determining how the performance of each component is related to the performance of the total system.

The last element in systems thinking which we will consider is management as it is vitally concerned with the other four aspects we have discussed—objectives, environment, resources, and components. Management has responsibility for generating the plans of the system and seeing that the plans are being implemented. In light of the difficulties involved in correctly defining objectives, characterizing the environment, allocating resources, and identifying the system's components, any plan must necessarily include provisions for changing the plans after they have been put into effect. Despite the importance of monitoring a system's performance and of modifying the plans in accordance with the unanticipated circumstances, there is evidence that school administrators often fail to perform these management functions, especially at times when major changes are introduced into the system.[13]

INPUT-OUTPUT ANALYSIS

One of the simplest applications of systems thinking to educational decision making is input-output analysis. In its most elementary form, input-output analysis ignores the inner workings of a system and concentrates on identifying those resources which affect a system's output. This form of analysis has been used within educational settings to determine the extent to which differences in student achievement can be explained by variations in the kinds and amounts of school resources. Such input-output analyses often rely on multiple-regression statistical techniques to estimate the magnitude of the relationships between school district characteristics (e.g., starting salary for teachers, number of books, and age of school building) and pupil scores of school achievement.

Thomas, for example, examined the relationships between thirty-

13. See Neal Gross, Joseph B. Giacquinta, and Marilyn Bernstein, *Implementing Organizational Innovations: A Sociological Analysis of Planned Educational Change* (New York: Basic Books, Inc., 1971), and W. W. Charters, Jr., and Roland Pellegrin, "Barriers to the Innovation Process: Four Case Studies of Differentiated Staffing," *Educational Administration Quarterly* 9, 1 (Winter 1973), pp. 3–14.

two independent variables and mean school scores on eighteen subtests of the Project TALENT achievement test battery.[14] Included among the thirty-two independent variables were financial inputs, organizational arrangements, and community socioeconomic characteristics. The eighteen subtests assessed intellectual performance in such areas as math, physical science, English, and reading. Both the level of resources and the manner in which they were allocated seemed to possess high explanatory power for student achievement on the various subtests. The salary level of beginning teachers was uniformly the single best predictor of test scores; the potency of starting salaries was evident even after the socioeconomic characteristics of the community were taken into account. Age of the school building and experience of the teaching staff also were associated with student performance on most of the subtests. Since the study used a nationwide sample of 206 schools drawn at random from all public high schools in communities with populations of 2,500 to 25,000, it is possible to generalize the results to other high schools in communities of this population range.

Although input-output studies like Thomas's represent an important advance over approaches which blindly equate variations in input levels with variations in levels of quality, the user of input-output analyses faces a number of difficulties. Several unstated assumptions may be built into the input-output analysis; if these assumptions are invalid, the user may unwittingly base his actions on erroneous conclusions. Even if the conclusions are correct, the user still must decide how the input-output analysis will be incorporated into the process for reaching allocation decisions. Let us now briefly examine each of these potential difficulties.

There are at least three implicit assumptions which the input-output analyst may make that pose potential problems for the user. The first of these assumptions involves the concept of input. There are *two concepts of input* rather than one—*inputs as disbursed* by the system and *inputs as received* by the pupil.[15] These two types of input may differ as is the case when there is a loss between the disbursement of an input and its reception. For example, textbooks may be more subject to loss or destruction in lower class schools than in middle class schools. If the central office expects books to be used for four years, children in the lower class sections of the city will receive less actual use of texts during that period even though the disbursed input of textbooks for lower and middle class schools is identical. Similarly, there may be a discrepancy between disbursed and received inputs in the form of time on instruction. A school district may allocate thirty hours per week for instruction; however, the amount of time devoted to instructional purposes may differ systematically from one school

14. J. Alan Thomas, "Efficiency in Education: An Empirical Study," *Administrator's Notebook* 11, 2 (October 1962).

15. James S. Coleman, "Evaluating Educational Programs," *Urban Review* 3, 4 (February 1969): 6–8.

to another. If the rate of discipline problems is high, teachers may spend more time on managing the students than instructing them. One estimate is that time devoted to teaching ranges from 10 to 90 percent in different classrooms. Since the inputs as received may be a more important determinant of output than the inputs as disbursed, the user of input-output analyses should determine which type of input was analyzed.

A second assumption which warrants scrutiny is that the *output variable* is *not influenced by any factors outside the system.* Since our knowledge of educational systems is incomplete, the systems analyst may inadvertently overlook factors which are relevant to the systems' performance. The realism of this possibility is underscored by the recent work of David Wiley and Annegret Harnischfeger.[16]

Drawing on the theoretical work of Carroll,[17] Wiley and Harnischfeger reasoned that exposure to schooling represented an important input which previous researchers[18] had neglected in their analyses of school effects. To measure exposure to schooling, they considered average daily attendance (ADA), length of the school day, and the length of the school year. Using this simple indicator of exposure to schooling, Wiley and Harnischfeger found substantial variation in the total number of hours of schooling per year. For example, exposure to schooling ranged from 710 to 1150 hours in the Detroit Equality of Educational Opportunity Survey (EEOS) data. More importantly, variations in the quantity of schooling were significantly related to the verbal ability, reading comprehension, and mathematics achievement of sixth grade students. Furthermore, exposure to schooling was associated with achievement after three background characteristics of students were taken into account: race, number of possessions in the child's home (from a list of nine) and number of children living in the child's home. In terms of typical gains in achievement over a one year period, Wiley and Harnischfeger estimated that in schools where students receive *24 percent more schooling,* they will *increase their average gain in reading comprehension by two-thirds* and their *average gains in mathematics and verbal ability by one-third.* By redefining the system to include exposure to schooling, Wiley and Harnischfeger found that schooling does affect student performance. Previous researchers using the same output data, but a more limited set of input data, had reached the opposite conclusion.

Faulty assumptions also may arise when an input-output analyst

---

16. David E. Wiley and Annegret Harnischfeger, "Explosion of a Myth: Quantity of Schooling and Exposure to Instruction, Major Educational Vehicles," *Educational Researcher* 3, 4 (April 1974), 7–12. A critique of this work appears in Nancy Karweit, "Quantity of Schooling: A Major Educational Factor?" *Educational Researcher* 5, 2 (February 1976): 15–17.

17. J. B. Carroll, "A Model for School Learning," *Teachers College Record,* 1963, 64, 723–33.

18. For example J. S. Coleman et al., *Equality of Educational Opportunity* (Washington, D.C.: U.S. Government Printing Office, 1966), and F. Mosteller and D. P. Moynihan, eds., *On Equality of Educational Opportunity* (New York: Random House, 1972).

studies the outputs of a system one output at a time. By studying each output in isolation of all other outputs, the analyst assumes that variations in the input variables do not affect any other objectives to which he or others may attach importance. Stated more simply, the analyst assumes that the input variables do not produce any significant, unintended side-effects. The questionable validity of this assumption is readily apparent in the field of medicine, less so in education. In the case of medicine, there is the well-known example of Thalidomide, a drug designed to provide relief for nauseous pregnant women. Thalidomide achieved its objective, however, the users of the drug frequently bore deformed children. The drug manufacturers erroneously presumed that the babies of Thalidomide takers would be unaffected by the drug. Unfortunately, the physical well-being of the baby was impaired at the time the mother's well-being was improved.

As for education, the examples are less dramatic and more difficult to document because the educational community has not traditionally examined the relationships between inputs and outputs. Even on those infrequent occasions when such relationships have been examined, educational researchers have not generally studied the simultaneous impact of input variables on two different types of output variables. A noteworthy exception to this typical pattern is the work conducted by Block on mastery learning. Block investigated how the performance standard which a student is required to attain on each segment of his instruction influences cognitive and affective outcomes. He found that the maintenance of performance levels throughout the instruction did have a positive impact on the cognitive performance and affective states of the learner.[19] Furthermore, the particular performance level which yielded the best outcome was not the same for both the cognitive and affective criteria. Cognitive outcomes were greatest when learners were required to master 95 percent of the material covered before they proceeded to the next unit of instruction, while affective outcomes were maximal when the mastery level was set at 85 percent. These results point to the fruitfulness of an input-output approach that considers two or more outputs simultaneously; the attainment of one valued objective is not necessarily independent of the achievements on other objectives as some input-output analysts in education are inclined to assume.

A final set of difficulties which input-output analysis potentially poses for the user centers around the role of such analyses in the decision-making process. Input-output analysis strives to foster rationality and efficiency in the allocation of resources; yet, decision-making processes in education at times involve strategies that rely on power rather than reason to settle disputes. How should the administrator behave when teachers' organizations press for greater fringe benefits when the input-output studies

19. James H. Block, "Student Evaluation: Toward the Setting of Mastery Performance Standards" (Paper delivered before the American Educational Research Association, Chicago, April 9, 1972).

show reduced class size to be more effective in promoting pupil outcomes? Input-output analysis may assist the administrator in anticipating future effects of resource allocation decisions; however, the administrator must decide which effects should be pursued in the face of intense conflict and opposition.

PLANNING-PROGRAMING-BUDGETING SYSTEM (PPBS)

The Planning-Programing-Budgeting System (PPBS) is an approach to decision making designed to make as explicit as possible the costs and consequences of choices and to encourage the use of this information in allocating resources.[20] Proponents of PPBS for schools generally agree that a program budget system requires clear statements of goals, sound measures of how well the goals are being met, practicable alternative programs for reaching the goals, and reliable estimates of program costs. Adherents of PPBS also agree on the characteristics which distinguish it from conventional approaches to budget making. Costs and benefits are considered simultaneously, therefore, considerations of efficiency and effectiveness are meant to be highly prominent during the budget-making process.

PPBS advocates do not concur, however, on the specific applications of their philosophy to the schools. Some urge total implementation of PPBS by school districts.[21] Sweeping proposals of this type are based largely on the need to justify continuing increases in educational costs. Others feel that performance budgets are appropriate in a much more restricted sense. One or two programs are selected annually for budgeting on a performance basis; different programs are selected each year so that every program eventually is subjected to a PPBS analysis.[22] Another approach to program selection is to consider only those programs in which major modifications are being contemplated. This approach is in line with the view that PPBS is oriented toward change and is designed to serve the purposes of rethinking existing programs and planning new ones.[23] Still another approach is proposed on the grounds of feasibility; PPBS should

20. Jack W. Carlson, "The Status and Next Steps for Planning, Programing, and Budgeting," in Robert H. Haveman and Julius Magolis, eds., *Public Expenditures and Policy Analysis* (Chicago: Markham Publishing Company, 1970), pp. 367–412.

21. K. George Pedersen, "Program Budgeting: Bane or Boon?" (Presentation made to the Ontario Institute for Studies in Education Residential Workshop for Superintendents, Trent University, June 15–28, 1969).

22. J. Alan Thomas, "Educational Decision Making and the School Budget," *Administrator's Notebook* 12, 4.

23. Tyll van Geel, "PPBS and District Resource Allocation," *Administrator's Notebook* 12, 1.

be introduced in those areas of school operation which are already supported by detailed performance data and some cost accounting.[24] According to Burkhead, food services, attendance services, and library services are such areas.

Regardless of the approach he uses to install a PPB System, the administrator will probably need to retain the traditional line-item budget. Two reasons dictate the retention of the line-item budget. First, there are usually legal statutes which stipulate the categories districts must use when reporting their actual and anticipated expenditures. Second, the program budget is often designed to supplement and improve existing budgeting systems. To establish connections between the line-item budget and the program budget, the administrator must create a budget-crosswalk, a document which relates figures in the program budget format to the line-item format and vice versa. Translated into actual practice, the budget-crosswalk enables the reader to determine how much of the total money budgeted for salaries, equipment, transportation, maintenance, and the like is allocated to such program areas as twelfth grade mathematics or ninth grade English.[25] For some districts, the budget-crosswalk document represents their total attempt to implement a PPB System. In these case, PPBS is little more than a euphemism for cost accounting.

In addition to constructing a more complex budget document, the administrator of the ideal-type PPB System must also arrange for the development and maintenance of an information system. Stored in this information system are data on program costs, including expenditures for teachers' salaries, retirement, textbooks, and instructional equipment; data on student cognitive and affective outcomes; and data on the socioeconomic background of students. Advocates of PPBS maintain that such an information system will initially enable the administrator to gauge the relative efficiency and effectiveness of the various programs. As the district accumulates detailed knowledge of the relationships between the input and output variables, the administrator then will be able to use this information system to anticipate with reasonable accuracy the effects of budget cuts or increases on programs incorporated into the PPB System. Ultimately, the information system in combination with the program budget presumably will make it possible for the administrator to identify where expenditures can be curtailed with the least sacrifice and to determine where additional investments can be made in order to yield the greatest returns. The validity of such expectations has not been substantiated, how-

---

24. Jesse Burkhead, "The Theory and Application of Program Budgeting to Education," in *Trends in Financing Public Education* (Washington, D.C.: National Education Association, 1965), pp. 180–190.

25. In seeking to identify the programs in a PPB System, the administrator probably faces the same kind of intellectual and political problems that the management scientist confronts in describing the components, parts, or subsystems of a system. Refer to the earlier discussion under the section on "Systems Analysis: A General Framework." Even when the administrator can readily identify the programs in his district, he is likely to encounter difficulties in deciding what costs should actually be charged against each program.

ever.[26] Moreover, the results of recent attempts to field test PPBS reveal a number of difficulties which must be overcome if it is ever to be implemented to the point where the benefits attributed to the approach can be assessed.

Paradoxically, one of the major deterrents to wide-scale trial and adoption of PPBS is its installation and maintenance costs. Much of PPBS's appeal stems from its potential to curtail expenditures and to optimize the returns and benefits from investments in education. An intensive effort to operationalize a program budgeting system in fourteen districts[27] within the state of California suggests that the costs of such a program may have been underestimated by its supporters.[28] Expected costs for the program budgeting, reporting, and accounting structure were one dollar per unit of average daily attendance during the first year of implementation with a continuing cost of seventy-five cents per unit of ADA for each subsequent year. Based on the field trial experience, cost estimates for the first year of operation were revised upwards with anticipated costs highest in Unified Districts followed in descending order by High School and Elementary Districts. Within each of these three types of districts, costs decreased as the size of the district increased. In no case was the cost less than $2.58 per unit of ADA, a figure which was more than two and one-half times the initial estimate.

Research conducted in twenty-one California school districts implementing PPBS indicates that the administrator who wishes to adopt this approach to educational decision making may face opposition from teachers and subordinate administrators.[29] "Massive hostility," a term used to describe a situation in which 25 percent of the respondents perceived the majority of their teacher colleagues to express open hostility toward PPBS, existed in fourteen of the twenty-one districts surveyed. Most teachers felt that morale declined rather than improved as their district shifted to PPBS. Although administrators seemed to be less opposed to PPBS than their teaching staffs, there was open hostility expressed by administrators in twenty percent of the districts surveyed.

Professional opposition to PPBS in education seemingly derives from conditions which are incompatible with a resource allocation philosophy rooted in concerns for effectiveness and efficiency. Equity is often a

26. Henry M. Levin, "A Conceptual Framework for Accountability in Education," *School Review* 82, 3 (May 1974), pp. 363–391.

27. For a detailed description of California's attempt to operationalize PPBS, see *An Educational Planning and Evaluation Guide for California School Districts: A Program Planning and Budgeting System* (Sacramento: California State Department of Education, 3rd Preliminary Edition).

28. A. Alan Post, "Status of the Development of a Program Budgeting System for California School Districts" (Sacramento: California State Department of Education, August 1972). Mimeographed.

29. *Summary of Responses of Teachers and Site Administrators on PPBS Survey,* Research Department, Special Report H-72 (Burlingame, Calif.: California Teachers Association, May 1972).

ruling norm in educational institutions; such a norm dictates that financial resources will be distributed among schools so that each unit receives its fair share.[30] A fair share is represented by some criterion like x-dollars per student in average daily attendance rather than by the effectiveness or the efficiency of the school's services.

Collective bargaining also may be an impediment to implementation of PPBS. Negotiations typically focus on input, not output, standards. For example, a teachers' bargaining unit may demand that "there shall be one teacher for every twenty-six pupils" or that "there shall be one teacher aide for every one hundred pupils." Once a board of education agrees to meet demands of this type, the administrator's latitude for action has been diminished and the thrust of PPBS for efficiency and effectiveness has been blunted. Finally, there is evidence which suggests that some school personnel do not view their responsibilities in terms of changing pupils, an implicit assumption of the PPBS approach. Rather, such teachers and lower-level administrators seem to regard their role as providing students with "an opportunity to learn."[31] Whenever school personnel view their professional responsibilities in ways which are incompatible with the philosophy of PPBS, the administrator will need to bring the philosophy and the role conceptions in line with one another if the anticipated benefits of PPBS are to be realized.[32]

ORGANIZATIONAL DEVELOPMENT (O.D.)

Organizational Development provides an interesting contrast with input-output analysis and PPBS. All three underscore the importance of establishing clear goals, selecting the most appropriate means for achieving the goals, and evaluating the extent to which the goals have been achieved. O.D., PPBS, and input-output analysis differ, however, in the substantive disciplines which inform their efforts and in the central problems which they address. PPBS and input-output analysis rely heavily on economics and quantitative methods in dealing with their major concern, namely, how to allocate resources in order to maximize efficiency and effectiveness. Organizational Development, on the other hand, is principally influenced by social psychology and is mainly concerned with improving the ability of subsystems of a school district to change themselves. Finally, O.D. seems to have more empirical evidence available to demonstrate the effec-

30. van Geel, "PPBS and District Resource Allocation."

31. Ibid.

32. For another approach to PPBS, see Ralph A. Dusseldorp, Duane E. Richardson, and Walter J. Foley, *Educational Decision Making Through Operations Research* (Boston: Allyn and Bacon, Inc., 1971), pp. 134–152.

tiveness of its efforts than either PPBS or input-output analysis, at least in the field of education.[33]

For the Organizational Development specialist the environment plays a key role in his thinking. He assumes at the outset that the environment of schools is dynamic rather than static and that no particular form of organizational structure will enable a school or a school district to survive for an extended period of time in a turbulent environment. According to the O.D. specialist, schools will have a greater chance of adapting successfully to a changing environment if they can effectively bring their resources to bear on the problems created by changes in the environment. Effective resource utilization is achieved by focusing on the process of using resources, especially the interpersonal processes within and between the various subsystems of a school district (such as teachers' groups, administrators, advisory committees, and central-office departments).

To improve the interpersonal processes within the organization and the way in which the various subsystems relate to one another, organizational training is used. This type of training seeks to develop skills in interpersonal communication and organizational problem solving and to foster a restructuring of roles and norms in the relevant subsystems. Organizational training is explicitly geared to the effectiveness of groups as task-oriented entities; personal development is not the targeted objective.[34] Any improvement in the intrapersonal functioning of individuals is quite incidental.

Since the subsystem and not the individual is the target of change, organizational development takes place with intact work groups. An entire work force of a school may be involved in organizational training as was the case in an Oregon junior high school where secretaries, cooks, and custodians were included along with teachers, counselors, and administrators.[35] Because this particular organizational training project exemplifies some of O.D.'s basic characteristics and possible outcomes, we will describe it in detail.

Prior to the opening of school the entire training staff was involved in a six-day training laboratory. The first two days were spent in group exercises designed to increase awareness of interpersonal processes and organizational processes. Although the exercises resembled games, they vividly showed the importance of communication in effectively dealing with tasks which required collaboration. Following each exercise, participants explored ways in which the processes observed during the exercise were dif-

---

33. For a brief, but informative description of O.D.'s historic lineage and contemporary theory and practice, see Carl R. Steinhoff and Robert C. Owens, "Techniques for Assessing Organizational Environment and Their Implications for Intervention Style," *Journal of Educational Administration* (in press).

34. Richard A. Schmuck et al., *Handbook of Organization Development in Schools* (Palo Alto, Calif.: National Press Books, 1972), p. 6.

35. Richard A. Schmuck and Philip J. Runkel, *Organizational Training for a School Faculty* (Eugene, Oregon: The Center for the Advanced Study of Educational Administration, 1970).

ferent from or similar to what usually happened in their school. Specific training in interpersonal communications stressed skills of paraphrasing, describing behavior, describing feelings, and perception checking.

During the final four days the group worked on real issues that were interfering with the organization's functioning. A standard problem-solving sequence consisting of five phases was used to deal with the identified problems. The sequence involved: (1) specifying the problem in behavioral terms, (2) using force-field analysis to identify the driving and restraining forces,[36] (3) brainstorming to generate actions aimed at reducing the restraining forces, (4) designing a specific course of action, and (5) trying out the plan behaviorally through a simulated activity involving the entire school staff. This problem-solving sequence was followed in working through three problems—insufficient clarity in the roles of administrators and counselors, failure to draw upon staff resources, and low staff participation and involvement.

Two additional interventions occurred during the school year. One was held for one and a half days in December. This intervention also emphasized communication skills and problem-solving capabilities, first in the context of exercises and later in connection with actual problems of the organization. Some of the problems addressed were how to increase the effectiveness of area coordinators as communication links between teachers and administrators and how to help the faculty reduce its role overload. The last training intervention took place in February. Its main objective was to evaluate the staff's progress in solving the problems of role clarity, resource utilization, and staff participation. During this final one and a half day training session, the various groups identified the incompleted tasks and prepared plans of action for completing the work before the end of the school year.

The changes which could be attributed to the organizational training were both numerous and far-reaching. A large majority of the teachers reported improvements in their classroom group processes. The Principal's Advisory Committee, composed of administrators and area coordinators, increased its power. Administrator-teacher and teacher-teacher relationships showed marked improvement. New norms developed which resulted in greater openness in interpersonal communications, greater willingness to talk about feelings, and greater readiness to seek and offer help. Faculty turnover was only 3 percent contrasted with 10 to 16 percent in comparable neighboring schools. New methods of solving problems and new organizational structures were developed; innovations of this nature were more frequent than in other faculties used for comparison purposes. Finally, the staff created a new role, vice-principal for curriculum, to provide assistance

36. See David H. Jenkins, "Social Engineering in Educational Change: An Outline of Method," *Progressive Education* 26, 7 (May 1949): 193–197, for a detailed discussion of force-field analysis, a model of change that views the present level of behavior or organizational functioning in terms of its total field of social and technological forces. To change behavior, one alters the forces which are maintaining the behavior in a state of equilibrium.

on interpersonal relationships within task groups and to act as a connecting link between the school and other elements in the district.

Despite the apparent success of this O.D. effort and others such as the one conceived, implemented, and evaluated by Coughlan,[37] Organizational Development may pose a number of potential problems for the school administrator.[38] If the administrator is to benefit fully from O.D., he needs to be sensitive to what these potential difficulties are.[39] Since O.D. practitioners are deeply concerned about the quality of work life in organizations, some of them may promote authenticity and openness in human encounters even when these patterns do not enhance effectiveness. If the O.D. specialist happens to be a social reformer intent on transplanting humanistic practices, he may or may not be aware of how much this social concern has dimmed his concern for increasing organizational effectiveness.

Another potential difficulty may arise from conflicts of interest. O.D. personnel are frequently employed by universities; if their major base of operation is an institution of higher education, there is the possibility that the consultant may be conducting research and engaging in O.D. in the same organization simultaneously. In such cases, a consultant may be tempted to subordinate the O.D. work to the research activity. To guard against this possibility, the administrator will need to determine how the consultant intends to keep the research and consulting roles separate. By clarifying the relationship between the research and the O.D. efforts, the administrator may minimize the risk of having the O.D. goals neglected or distorted.

The school administrator also may encounter the type of difficulty which any client may be exposed to when he hires a consultant, namely, a preference for a small set of solutions. O.D. specialists may recommend a solution such as team-building interventions or intergroup confrontation, regardless of the problem. If the administrator is impatient and eager to bypass the diagnostic stage, he may be stuck with a simple, patent remedy of the consultant even if it is inappropriate.

Finally, the unwary administrator may employ an O.D. practitioner whose specialty is sensitivity training as opposed to organizational training. The sensitivity trainer, unlike the organizational trainer, may be inclined to stress "personal growth" and concentrate on freeing the individual from his fears about expressing emotions publicly. Negative feelings and deep revelations of self are encouraged in the name of "trust" and "authen-

---

37. Robert J. Coughlan, Robert A. Cooke, and L. Arthur Safer, Jr., *An Assessment of a Survey Feedback-Problem Solving-Collective Decision Intervention in Schools,* Final Report Project No. O-E-105 (U.S. Office of Education, Bureau of Research, 1972).

38. For an informative description of the difficulties involved in implementing O.D., see Stephen Weiner and Dan Weiler, *A Public School Voucher Demonstration: The First Year at Alum Rock* (Santa Monica, Calif.: The Rand Corporation, 1974).

39. Suggested by Richard E. Walton and Donald P. Warwick, "The Ethics of Organizational Development," *The Journal of Applied Behavioral Science* 9, 6 (1973): 681–698.

ticity." The use of *T*-grouping or sensitivity training with intact work groups, particularly those with little previous history, could have the consequences observed by Smith and Keith at the Kensington School.[40] In that setting self-revelation led to year long feelings of vulnerability, frustration, and anxiety. The intense experience also sharpened the dichotomy between processual and substantive concerns and led to permanent schisms within the faculty. Some teachers became so capitivated with group processes that they *T*-grouped their classes all year long. O.D. obviously means different things to different people; the administrator who looks to O.D. for a solution to his organization's problems needs to know what it means to the O.D. specialists he hires either on a temporary or a permanent basis.

NETWORK ANALYSIS

The Critical Path Method (CPM) and Program Evaluation Review Technique (PERT) are two of the best known examples of network analysis,[41] a tool for planning and controlling projects. CPM and PERT are especially applicable to the problems of managing and allocating time. These two techniques originated outside the field of education. The Department of Defense devised PERT to plan, schedule, control, and coordinate its Polaris missile program; it is estimated that the use of PERT enabled the government to complete the Polaris program two years ahead of schedule. CPM, on the other hand, was developed in the business sector by DuPont to schedule and control its construction programs. Although both techniques were conceived around 1958, neither of them received much use in education until the mid-1960s. Desmond Cook was instrumental in generating applications of network analysis, particularly PERT, to problems of an educational nature.[42]

CPM and PERT, as we have noted, are most useful in allocating and managing time. Both techniques require the user to do the following:

1. Identify the activities involved in the project.
2. Determine the sequence in which the activities must be completed. Draw a network showing the sequence.
3. Estimate the time needed to complete each activity. Any unit of time (e.g., hours, days, weeks) may be used; however, the same unit must be used throughout a given network.

---

40. Louis M. Smith and Pat M. Keith, *Anatomy of Educational Innovation* (New York: John Wiley and Sons, Inc., 1971), pp. 89–99.

41. For a simple introduction to PERT and CPM, see van Dusseldorp et al., *Educational Decision Making,* pp. 114–133. A more detailed discussion of these techniques is to be found in H. W. Handy and K. M. Hussain, *Network Analysis for Educational Management* (Englewood Cliffs, New Jersey: Prentice-Hall, Inc., 1969).

42. Desmond A. Cook, *PERT: Applications to Education* (Office of Education Monograph no. 17, U.S. Government Printing Office, 1966).

4. Compute the time required to complete the project.
5. Determine the times at which each activity must be completed in order for the entire project to be completed on time.

The critical path is that path in the network containing activities which if not completed on time will cause the entire project to be completed behind schedule.

To illustrate the PERT and CPM concepts described in the preceding paragraph, let us consider an example involving an improvement project that centers on team teaching. Suppose a high school principal is interested in introducing team teaching into his school. He elects not to make the decision unilaterally; rather, he is prepared to live with whatever decision his staff reaches after exploring the matter of team teaching in depth. Since only two and a half months remain in the school year and the principal wants a decision before the end of school, he decides to employ network analysis to insure that the staff reaches its decision by the close of the school year. He proceeds as follows:

Identifies the activities.

Arrange for the staff to select those teachers who will consider the issue of team teaching.

Gather printed materials which deal with team teaching.

Identify schools that have adopted team teaching.

Arrange for visits to demonstration sites.

Identify specialists in team teaching who can serve as resources to the teacher group.

Arrange for specialists to meet with teacher representatives.

Meet with teacher representatives to acquaint them with task, resources, and time deadlines.

Have teacher representatives make their report and conduct a vote.

Determines the sequence in which the activities must be completed.

Arrange for staff to select teacher representatives.

Gather printed materials.

Identify schools.

Identify specialists.

Arrange for site visits to schools.

Arrange for meeting with specialists.

Meet with teacher representatives.

Have teacher representatives weigh information and prepare their report.

Hold staff meeting to consider report and to conduct a vote.

Draws the network. (Two types of elements, activities and events, are depicted in a network. An event is the beginning of an activity, the termination of an activity, or both; events are represented in the network as circles. Activities are the jobs to be performed; the sequence of activities, as well as the activities which can take place concurrently, are shown by the arrows in the network.)

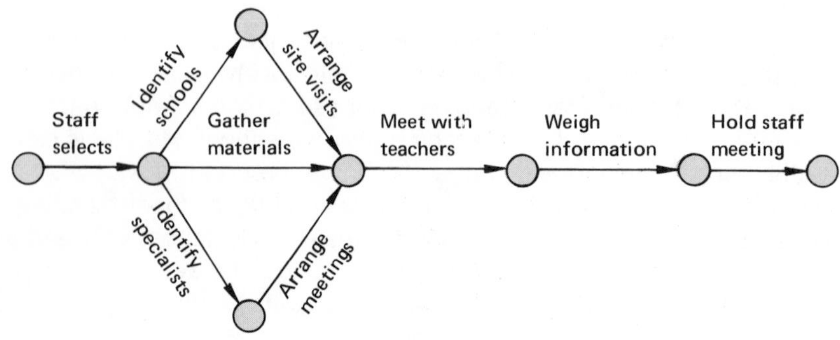

Figure 8–1 Events and activities in the network analysis of the team teaching improvement project.

After the network is drawn, the events are numbered (see Figure 8–2) so that both events and activities can be referred to by numbers. Several examples of events and activities follow Figure 8–2.

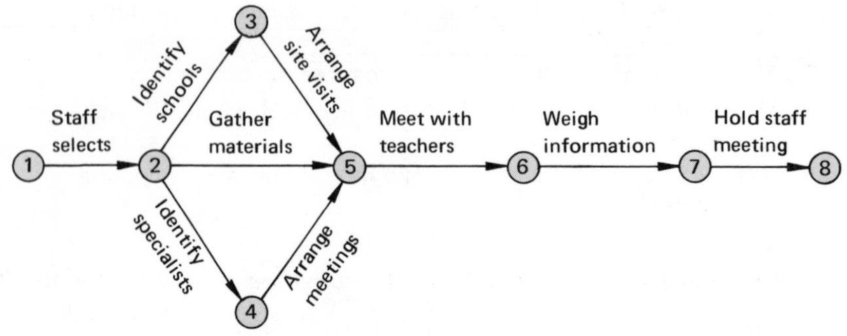

Figure 8–2 Numbered events in the network analysis.

Activities

1–2 Arrange for staff to select its teacher representatives.

5–6 Meet with teacher representatives for orientation to tasks, resources, and time deadlines.

7–8 Hold staff meeting to hear report of teacher representatives and to conduct vote.

Events

3 Begin the job of arranging site visits.

5 Termination of activities 3–5, 2–5, and 4–5. (Note that activities 2–3, 3–5, 2–4, and 4–5 run concurrently with activity 2–5.)

Estimates of the time needed to complete each activity.

Activity	*Time in Days*
1–2	4
2–3	10
2–4	10
2–5	15
3–5	3
4–5	4
5–6	1
6–7	20
7–8	1

Computes the time required to complete the project. To compute the total amount of time required to complete the project, the administrator redraws the network and inserts the time estimated to complete each activity. When time estimates are included in the network, the administrator identifies the path of activities requiring the most time to complete the project. Referring to Figure 8–3, we see that there are three paths: 1–2–5–6–7–8; 1–2–3–5–6–7–8; and 1–2–4–5–6–7–8. The first path named requires 41 days for completion while the other two require 39 and 40 respectively. Since the project can be completed within 41 working days if it stays on schedule, the project will be finished before the end of school. Approximately 60 working days remain in the school year. The heavy arrows of path 1–2–5–6–7–8 signify that this is the critical path since a delay on any activity in this path will result in the project being completed behind schedule.

Determines the times at which each activity must be completed in order for the project to finish on time. These times are determined simply by translating the events and activities in the network into dates on the calendar. *(See page 230)*

Before leaving this illustration of how CPM and PERT can assist the administrator in managing time, we would like to emphasize that our example has obscured a number of complexities involved in using these techniques of network analysis. For example, PERT employs three time estimates (optimistic, pessimistic, and most likely) in determining the time required for job completion, while CPM uses just one time estimate. Furthermore, in PERT it is necessary to calculate the probability of completing the project

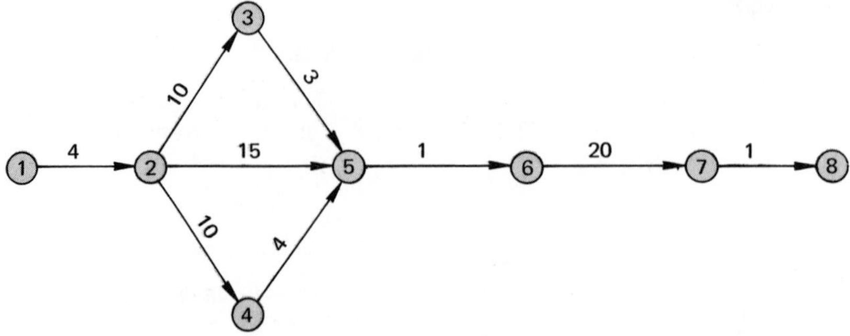

Figure 8–3 Time estimates of the activities included in the network analysis.

in a specified time. Also, network analysis in its more sophisticated forms involves the use of computers and elaborate detailing procedures.

Regardless of the level of complexity which the use of PERT or CPM entails, the administrator may confront several difficulties when using these techniques. The network analysts assume that the individual who constructs the network has sufficient experience and knowledge of the particular situation to be able to identify what the relevant activities are and how much time is required to complete each of these activities. As a result, the utility of the network analysis will be limited by the administrator's judgments of the relevant activities and the time needed to complete them. Furthermore, if the administrator recognizes that his judgments or estimates are in error after the project is underway, he will have to rely on the ingenuity of himself or others in selecting the course of action most likely to place the project back on schedule.

SUMMARY

Throughout this chapter we have examined some of the basic perspectives in systems thinking. The intent underlying our discussions of Systems Analysis, Input-Output Analysis, Planning-Programing-Budgeting System (PPBS), Organizational Development (O.D.), and Network Analysis (CPM and PERT) was to broaden the reader's understanding of how systems thinking may be used to deal with educational problems. Our comments have focused on some of the key concepts underlying each approach and some of the difficulties which may be encountered in applying the conceptual tool in the real world of the practicing administrator. Since our discussion has been somewhat abbreviated, the reader who desires to master one or more of these approaches might begin by consulting the appropriate references listed under *Selected Readings* at the end of this chapter. Hopefully, our introduction to each of these approaches will enable the reader to choose those most relevant to his professional problems.[43]

SUGGESTED ACTIVITIES

1. In this chapter, Input-Output Analysis, PPBS, O.D., and Network Analysis were treated independently of one another. How might one integrate all four approaches in attacking a major problem?
2. Identify a school district which has tried to use one of the approaches described in this chapter. While interviewing the participants, try to determine how the approach was implemented and how their experiences were consistent or inconsistent with the discussion in this chapter.
3. Select one of the approaches, study it in depth and identify those concepts and issues which we neglected to discuss. In what respects do these concepts and issues affect your judgment of the potential utility of the approach?

SELECTED READINGS

Churchman, C. West. *The Systems Approach.* New York: Dell Publishing Co., Inc., 1968.

Dusseldorp, Ralph A.; Richardson, Duane E.; and Foley, Walter J. *Educational Decision-Making Through Operations Research.* Boston: Allyn and Bacon, Inc., 1971.

Handy, H. W., and Hussain, K. M. *Network Analysis for Educational Management.* Englewood Cliffs, N.J.: Prentice-Hall, Inc., 1969.

Hartley, Harry J. *Educational Planning, Programming, Budgeting: A Systems Approach.* Englewood Cliffs, N.J.: Prentice-Hall, 1968.

Immegart, Glenn L. *An Introduction to Systems for the Educational Administrator.* Reading, Mass.: Addison-Wesley Publishing Co., 1973.

Kaufman, Roger A. *Educational System Planning.* Englewood Cliffs, N.J.: Prentice-Hall, Inc., 1972.

Schmuck, Richard A., and Runkel, Philip J. *Handbook of Organization Development in Schools.* Palo Alto, Calif.: National Press Books, 1972.

---

43. The authors wish to acknowledge the assistance of Berthold Killait in preparing this chapter.

9

ROLES OF SCHOOL PERSONNEL IN ADMINISTRATION

If, indeed, the school administrator is a leader among the various reference groups with which he works, and if the school operates as a social system in the manner previously described, many people participate in the educational enterprise, with the administrative head giving direction to and coordinating their involvement. This chapter deals with the implications of theory and experience for a cooperative working relationship among school employees. For the most part, this discussion will be confined to the internal operation of the school. We shall not attempt to give a comprehensive list here of all the duties of all school personnel. Rather, our purpose in this chapter is to highlight those roles of superintendents, members of the central office staff, principals, teachers, and other school employees which are synchronized to provide a coordinated organizational effort.

THE ROLE OF THE SUPERINTENDENT

The superintendent of schools accepts final responsibility for the operation of the schools. The accountability of the total staff to the public is usually marked by pressure upon the superintendent. While in many school systems the superintendent delegates authority and some degree of responsibility to assistant superintendents, business managers, directors, coordinators and supervisors, principals, teachers, and other personnel, he cannot delegate final accountability for the tasks which they perform.

This dilemma in delegation may govern the degree of the superintendent's direct involvement in the activity assigned to other persons, and his understanding and perception of his and others' roles in the performances of administrative tasks. Delegation is also dependent upon the understanding which other staff members have of their roles and their readiness to accept the roles.

Various leader behavior styles or patterns are observable in the working relationships between the superintendent and his staff members. One superintendent may delegate so completely that he participates very little in the proposing, planning, conducting, and evaluating of programs. Another superintendent may work with members of his staff in such a way as to enhance the leadership performance of those individuals directly responsible to him. Still another superintendent might keep a tight rein on all activities conducted by his associates.

While, conceivably, in the variety of situations that exist, superintendents may operate successfully at any point within the range of practices just described, the latter practice of "being in on everything" becomes less and less tenable as the size of school districts becomes larger. One fact is clearly established: the course of action that the superintendent chooses to take must be generally acceptable to the board of education and to his staff. The wise superintendent makes clear his perception of his role and seeks general agreement from these two important reference groups to operate in accordance with this perception.

A GENERALIST

As the number of school districts is reduced and the size of many is increased, it seems reasonable to expect that the superintendent will, more and more, assume the role of a generalist rather than that of a specialist in a particular phase of school operation. That is, the trend is in the direction of establishing an administrative team, including a number of specialists whose work he must coordinate. It is the superintendent whose responsibility it is to view the entire enterprise in broad perspective.

Miller describes the superintendent as a perceptive generalist:

> The perceptive generalist must know enough of the general field and enough of the nature and problems of the specialists so that he can communicate with them with understanding, comprehensible among the specialists as a collective group and meaningful between specialists and the general public. He will miss the detail of many of the specialists but he sees all of them in wider configuration than do the specialists.[1]

1. Van Miller, "The Superintendent of Schools." In D. J. Leu and H. C. Rudman, eds., *Preparation for School Administrators* (East Lansing, Mich.: Michigan State University, 1963), chap. 5. For a more recent discussion of the superintendent-specialist relationship, see *The Administrator* vol. 4, no. 4 (Summer 1974).

The superintendent's expertness lies in his conceptualization of the tasks to be performed, in his inventiveness and genius in organization, and in his ability to work with people. His is an overall or *general* perspective, which he utilizes in charting the course that the school is to take. Although his staff assists him in achieving this perspective, he must articulate it, and he must have the power to use it as a guide for action.

A STAFF LEADER

It is often said that the strength of a superintendent can be measured by the competence of his staff—a statement which does not mean that a strong staff has no need of a strong superintendent. We hope that we have made it clear that staff strength is dependent upon leadership strength. The leader and his staff are dependent upon one another; the strength of one enhances the strength of the other.

As a consequence of the acceptance of this point of view, much is done to build up staff strength. Assessment and appraisal are common activities used to find the most competent teachers. Recruitment, selection, and orientation of new teachers have been seen as important administrative functions in recent years. In-service education and individualized help in instruction have become increasingly important as the rate of staff turnover has declined.

An important aspect of staff leadership is selection. Except in very small school districts where he may participate directly in the selection of all employees, the superintendent is generally involved in this process at two levels. He or she will participate directly in selecting his or her staff and will also help establish criteria and procedures for selecting other district employees. The latter can have a very important impact upon the character of the school district. For example, it is possible to place varying degrees of emphasis upon hiring teachers who did or did not grow up in the local district, who did or did not attend nearby colleges and universities, and who may or may not practice particular teaching strategies. It would appear that opportunities to make such choices will increase in the future. The problem of coping with a teacher shortage has been replaced in large measure by the opportunity to make selections from a larger pool of candidates. With this opportunity, however, has come the problem of being more explicit about the qualities to be sought in personnel and devising more sophisticated means of assessing these qualities.

Not only are the better superintendents of schools alert to the sources of competent personnel; they devise ways of improving the competence of the personnel already on the job. They find ways of deploying the services of their staff members to accomplish the tasks of the school as effectively and efficiently as possible. If necessary, they separate the incompetents from the school system. The tasks involved in personnel development have become so important and so complicated that specialists in personnel and instruction have been employed with assignments in their particular fields.[2]

A SYMBOL

In spite of much talk in our society about equalizing the status of the leader and the members of his group, it is still a fact that in schools the status of the superintendent permits him to establish, in marked degree, the behavior pattern of the staff. "Businesslike procedures," "good communication," "courage to act," "kindness with firmness," "vision and foresight," "a good organizer" are typical of terms used by staff members to denote the tone set by superintendents whom they respect. On the other hand, lack of respect for superintendents is shown by such terms as "careless business practices," "lack of integrity," "favoritism among staff members," "failure to communicate," "poor organization," and "lack of vision."

Reference has been made to the fact that students of leadership and of administrative behavior agree that staff morale is as much a function of staff accomplishment as of warm human relationships. Whether the superintendent wishes it or not, he or she becomes the symbol of his school; in turn, perhaps to a somewhat lesser degree, the school tends to be described in the same terms as those applied to the superintendent. Therefore, regardless of the number of helpers he or she has or their disposition toward the tasks to which they have been assigned, the superintendent is the head of the school system and cannot escape the role of setting the stage for staff participation.

The superintendent may also be a symbol in the eyes of the community. It has not been uncommon for groups of citizens who were unhappy about the schools to view the superintendent as the cause and, in a way, the symbol of all school problems and demand his ouster as a first step to school improvement. Conversely, a number of outstanding educators have achieved local and national prominence as the symbols of fine school systems. Much of the superintendent's image in the community depends upon the ways he interacts with the public. As in matters of staff participation, people look to the behavior of the superintendent as a model to follow in school-community relationships.

THE ROLES OF CENTRAL OFFICE PERSONNEL

With the growth in the complexity of school systems, we witness a corresponding growth in the number and complexity of the functions of the cen-

2. For a discussion of the personnel function, see William B. Castetter, *The Personnel Function in Educational Administration,* 2nd ed. (New York: The Macmillan Co., 1976).

tral administrative office. These new demands upon the central office have created a need for the development of new and more efficient ways of conceptualizing school district organization and structure. Systems analysis and research as it is applied to educational institutions seems to offer an important means by which educational leaders can analyze, and adapt to, the changing role which the central office must play.[3] Hencley uses a form of systems analysis when he writes:

> The need for developing goal-centered and implementation-centered policies, and the parallel need for integrating, formalizing, and unifying workflow patterns in organizations requires members of administrative performance systems to be sophisticated in various administrative processes. Functional order in organization, adjustments in organizational workflow patterns, and maintenance and improvement of the organizational environment exchange system are achieved through administrative processes such as communication, decision-making, change, and morale maintenance. The need for competence in such processes is not restricted to intraorganizational settings. As figure 10 indicates, the administrative performance system is an

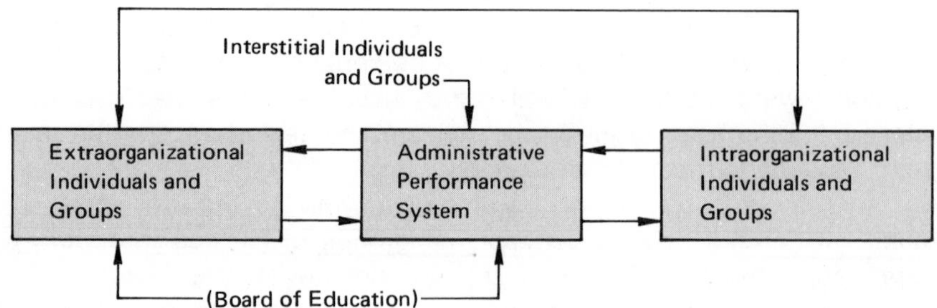

Figure 10 The administrative performance system as an open system (from Leu and Rudman).[4]

> open system which interacts and exchanges information with its environment. Thus sophistication in the use of administrative processes is necessary in several kinds of settings: intraorganizational, extraorganizational and interstitial.
>
> . . . . Perhaps the most important point brought out by study of figure 10 is that all members of the administrative performance system require some sophistication in the process area

3. See D. E. Griffiths, "The Nature and Meaning of Theory." In National Society for the Study of Education, *Behavioral Science and Educational Administration,* 63rd Yearbook, Part II (1964), pp. 116–118.

4. S. P. Hencley, "Functional Interrelationships Within Administrative Performance Systems." In D. J. Leu and H. C. Rudman, eds., *Preparation Programs for School Administrators* (East Lansing, Mich.: Michigan State University, 1963), p. 82.

> of administration. However, the degree of sophistication required is determined by the level and function of the various positions and by the number, type, and complexity of social and organizational variables confronting administrators in those positions.[5]

While it is not our purpose here to elaborate on all of these functions and processes, we call attention to the fact that the growth of the central office staff of a school system comes about, in general, in response to the need for greater specialization in various aspects of school administration, better coordination of the separate but related phases of the school program, and increased services to the several operating units of the systems. We shall discuss the roles of central office personnel in terms of these functions.

SPECIALIZATION

The role of some persons on the central office staff is that of providing special expertness in certain phases of school operation.[6] Assistant superintendents are examples of people who assume such a role. They may be placed in charge of instruction, staff personnel, pupil personnel, business or other functions. While each assistant superintendent is responsible to the superintendent, he has been employed because of his expertness in his particular field of specialization. The employment of an assistant superintendent of schools is based upon the assumption that his special expertness will be directed to that limited sphere of school operation designated by his assignment.

Other specialists are often needed in the school. They may have various titles depending upon where they work and the manner in which their specialty is used. The title of administrative assistant or assistant to another administrator connotes a *staff* rather than a *line* responsibility. *Staff* personnel carry out specific assignments for their superior officer, while *line* officers are responsible for a subunit of the organization such as a school and direct the work of a number of other people. The superintendent may employ a *general* administrative assistant who performs a variety of tasks assigned to him. In contrast to this, a research assistant or an assistant in communications may have a *specific* function.

Specialists may be assigned to work at almost any level of the administrative hierarchy and with either staff or line responsibilities. To bring special expertness to the instructional program, for example, an assistant superintendent in this area may decide that he needs *directors* of elementary and secondary education, each of whom can center attention

5. Ibid., p. 89.
6. For a discussion of such roles, see American Association of School Administrators, *Profiles of the Administrative Team* (Washington, D.C.: AASA, 1971).

upon that part of the program for which he is responsible. In turn, the director of elementary education may assign a specialist in reading to serve as a supervisor, consultant, advisor, or teacher helper in the several elementary schools of the system.

Griffiths has made an interesting distinction between various kinds of staff officers. He writes that:

> Staff officers may be classified as either coordinative or advisory. Coordinative staff officers assist the chief administrator in the discharge of many detailed functions of his position and aid him in the general coordination of school affairs. Any authority they may exercise is derived from the chief school administrator and exercised in a specific situation. For example, staff officers are not assigned authority to handle an area of school operation or given responsibility for that area. This type of staff officer must, however, be a generalist skilled in working with people.
>
> Advisory staff officers are specialists who supply expert assistance upon request. They have no authority except that which comes from their specialized knowledge in an area. An example of such a position in the public schools would be the subject-matter consultant or helping teacher. On a higher authority level, an assistant superintendent for business affairs or instruction might be placed in such a position. He would have hierarchical authority over those persons connected directly with his central office staff, but none over building principals or teachers.[7]

There is a growing trend in larger school systems toward a decentralized organizational structure. Decentralization in a school system requires, in most cases, the assumption of greater line authority by building heads, or principals, or area administrators, and the increased specialization of staff personnel at the central office. Under a decentralized arrangement most of the central office personnel will be either coordinative or advisory staff officers.

The increased size and complexity of many modern school systems have created a need for the central office to make proper use of innovations such as data processing systems, computer information systems, and centralized purchasing-accounting systems. These developments have created the need for a different breed of specialization. For example, a school system utilizing computer-based data processing will need both technicians to operate and program the machines, and research-oriented analysts to provide questions and research frameworks for the machines.

The reader should recognize that the practice of discussing organization in terms of line and staff positions has some limitations. A clear

---

7. Daniel E. Griffiths et al., *Organizing Schools for Effective Education* (Danville, Ill.: Interstate Printers & Publishers, 1962), pp. 23–24.

dichotomy between *line* (denoting authority) and *staff* (denoting a consultive or coordinating role) should not be made. Experience has shown that such a dichotomy is inadequate for describing precisely how people function in a school system and how jobs get done.

Thus, the function of providing greater expertness through specialization can be accomplished through the services of a number of different kinds of personnel working at different levels and in various ways throughout the school system. Their competence supplements and complements that of other specialists—the superintendent, the principal, and the teacher. Increased specialization in the central office should make it possible both to intensify and diversify the educational effort of the school system.

COORDINATION

The assistant superintendent of instruction must give his attention to planning and coordinating instruction throughout the school system. Thus, while he serves as a specialist in instruction, in contrast to specialists in staff personnel and business, he also serves the school in the capacity of a coordinator. Assistant superintendents must view their coordinating role in at least two ways. One of these we have just mentioned, namely the system-wide coordination within his sphere of school operation. Another essential view, however, concerns the coordination of efforts among the several task areas of administration. That is, business, staff personnel, instruction, and other functions must be worked out together.

There are other levels at which coordination plays an important part in the operation of the school. Coordinators of elementary education, of pupil personnel, and of audio-visual education all have responsibilities for system-wide coordination within their functional areas as well as for seeing that pupil personnel services and the facilities of the audio-visual instructional department are used to facilitate instruction in the various elementary schools of the system. This example clearly illustrates our point that personnel in the central office do have a coordinating role and that coordination is important both within and among divisions of school operation.

SERVICE

Many schools employ a number of persons whose primary function is that of service to the several building units.

Resource people. Supervisors, consultants, and resource persons may be classed primarily as service personnel. Their function is to help teachers or other school workers carry out their specific assignments. True, they are specialists who may have particular competence in diagnosing difficulties and improving upon the means generally used to overcome them. However, their usefulness to the school system is demonstrated by their acceptance as helpers rather than by the authority of the status position that they hold.

In a certain sense all central office personnel perform a service role. They are employed to carry out those functions that facilitate teaching and learning. The effectiveness of the central office operation depends, in large measure, upon the acceptance and utilization of its services in the several school units in the system.

Other service personnel. In additional to the members of the professional staff, there are other employees whose work contributes to the system-wide effort. Many of them are associated in some way with school management. Among such employees are the school clerk who keeps the official records of the board of education; various clerical workers, such as secretaries, filing clerks, typists and stenographers, and bookkeepers; custodians, bus drivers, cafeteria managers and cooks.

Although most of these people do not expect to take an active part in making the professional decisions with which our previous discussion has been concerned, they are an integral part of the school system. Their effectiveness is dependent both upon how well they understand the roles they play and the degree to which they feel that they truly belong to the school system.

Job descriptions are often useful in clarifying assignments. In-service education meetings to discuss improvements in procedures and the improvement of skills can also be very helpful. Often, training programs are provided at the state, regional, or university level for up-grading the services of such personnel. The advantage of the utilization of such means to the improvement of services cannot be overstressed.

THE ROLE OF THE PRINCIPAL

The individual school is the center for all teaching and learning. In any given neighborhood the effectiveness of the local school may be the criterion by which people judge the effectiveness of the entire school system. Hence the principal is a key person in the administrative organization.[8] He performs administrative tasks similar to those of a superintendent of schools, but he does so within the policy limits of the system. Instructional leadership, community relationships, staff personnel, pupil personnel, facilities, finance and business management, and organization are all areas in which tasks must be performed at the school-building level as well as

8. For a discussion of this role, see James M. Lipham and James A. Hoegh, Jr., *The Principalship: Foundations and Functions* (New York: Harper and Row, 1974).

the level of central-office administration. Public pressure for community control has accentuated the importance of the principal in many areas.

The nature of the responsibilities differs somewhat among elementary schools and junior and senior high schools. High schools, for example, tend to recognize more managerial responsibilities than do elementary schools. The size and complexity of the schools are factors that affect the nature of these responsibilities also. Ordinarily we transport high school youth greater distances than we do elementary school children. Enrollments in high schools are usually larger than in elementary schools. The curriculum of the comprehensive high school is extensive and complex. The role of the middle school or junior high school in the American school system is not as clear as that of the elementary and high schools. Thus, not only are the functions of administration at the building level as varied as those for the entire system, but in addition they are complicated by circumstances that require treatment unique to each school.

AN ORGANIZER

While principals in smaller school systems are expected to perform all of the tasks associated with the office, this expectation results from a lack of appreciation for the scope and comprehension of the job. In larger school systems, where the complexity of the work of the principal is more apparent, specialized personnel often are assigned as regular assistants to the principal or are supplied by the central office.

Whether or not the principal himself performs all of the tasks associated with his office, he must organize his school in such a way that the tasks are accomplished. True, the basic administrative unit of which the principal's school is a part determines the financial structure for the system and it provides the building and furnishings. The financial resources of the total school system provide for the operating expenses of the school, including the teachers' salaries. As indicated previously, the central office provides for many resources. But these provisions do not make a school. The principal must understand how to weld these resources—those of his teachers, of the neighborhood which his school serves, of special personnel, and of the students—into a school community that has a character of its own.

A COMMUNICATOR

Another reason why the principal holds such a key position in the organizational structure of a school system is that he stands in an intermediate position between the central office and his teachers, and between the people of his local school neighborhood and the citizens of the entire attendance unit. It is not enough that his school take on a unique character indigenous to the particular circumstances immediately surrounding it. The individual school is also a part of a system. The principal is the chief interpreter of official policy of the system for his staff and for the school community. It is also largely through him that certain special contributions of the individual school become incorporated as integral parts of the total system. Thus, his understanding of the decision-making process and his ability to communicate to staff and community and to central administrative officers are one measure of his competence.

AN INSTRUCTIONAL LEADER

Important as it is for the principal to play the roles of organizer and communicator well, they are inadequate to explain the common reference to him as a *key* administrator. Like the superintendent of schools, he holds a position of high visibility in his community. He must not only be articulate about the purposes which his school is to serve, but he must demonstrate that under his leadership the school is achieving them in reasonable degree. He is at once a diagnostician of the problems that this school needs to solve and a synthesizer of the forces that must be brought together to solve them. If he fulfills this expectation, he develops a congenial working relationship among his staff members; he encourages their creativity by seeking out the special talents of individual members and encouraging their innovation and experimentation.

It should be noted that the contemporary role of instructional leader is not that of a "super-teacher"[9] who directs teachers in the specifics of teaching. Given the complexity and variety of the school curriculum as well as the increasing preparation and sophistication of teachers, such a role is no longer realistic. However the principal can assist teachers by sharing his impressions of their work and encouraging them to do the same for each other. Working with his staff, he assesses the need for the use of resource personnel and deploys them to spots where they may be effective. He also works with them to appraise the effectiveness of the instructional program and to take the steps necessary to improve it.

A LINE OFFICER

The principal is in most forms of administrative organization, the line authority in his building. His authority evolves from the laws of the state and, through the superintendent, from the board of education and the people of the community. This vested authority is the principal's legal traditional source of power. However, to operate successfully within his school, the

9. For a review of research which notes this perspective, see Donald A. Erickson, "The School Administrator," *Review of Educational Research* 37 (October 1967): 417–431.

principal must possess the entrusted authority—authority based on *competence,* as noted in chapter 7.

The range of matters about which a principal must possess competence was indicated in a survey conducted by the Consortium for Educational Leadership and the Industrial Relations Center, The University of Chicago.[10] The purpose of this survey was to determine the way in which principals define their jobs. Responses from 619 principals in ten states indicated that major responsibilities of principals could be categorized as relations with people and groups, curriculum, personnel administration, and general administration. Major functions in the first category include personal handling of student adjustment problems, organizations and extracurricular activities, individualized student development, utilization of specialized staff, evaluation of teacher performance, collegial contacts, racial and ethnic problems, trouble shooting and problem solving, community involvement and support, and dealing with gangs. Major functional areas in the second category include curriculum development and instructional materials. Those in the last two categories are staffing, working with unions, working with the central office, safety regulations, and fiscal control. The responses also indicated that the relative importance of these factors for particular principals varied in relation to several characteristics including those related to the type and size of the school and the composition of the student body and teaching staff.

The pivotal nature of the position occupied by the principal is illustrated by the tendency of citizens as well as central office officials to hold him responsible for what occurs in the school building. Citizens in recent years have often pressed for the removal, resignation, or transfer of principals from a building where dissatisfaction was present. Such community pressure focuses questions in any particular situation about what constitutes responsiveness to the community, reasonable expectations for principals, and fair treatment for principals who come under fire.[11]

THE TEACHER'S PLACE IN THE ORGANIZATION

The teacher derives considerable satisfaction from the recognition of the importance of his task. The satisfactions resulting from a successful experience in the classroom are among the enduring benefits of the teaching

10. "A National Occupational Analysis of the School Principalship" (Chicago: Consortium for Educational Leadership and Industrial Relations Center, The University of Chicago, June 1975).

11. See Mark M. Krug, "Chicago: The Principal's Predicament," *Phi Delta Kappan,* 56, no. 1 (September 1974), pp. 43–45.

profession. Lortie[12] has shown that the job rewards which teachers consider most meaningful are those achieved through interaction with students. However, as schools have become larger and an organizational effort is required to do the total job of the school, the need for identification with the total organization has increased. The teacher of the one-room school knew how he fared in the school enterprise, because there were no intermediaries between him and the school board on the one hand, and the children and the parents on the other. Furthermore, this teacher taught all of the children in all grades. He determined the standard of achievement at all grade levels.

INTERDEPENDENCE OF TEACHERS

In the school of today each teacher is a contributor to the total educational endeavor; he cannot carry out his assignment alone. He works in a cooperative enterprise in which the educational process is a team affair. This interdependence among contributors to the educational process is a phenomenon of the multiple-teacher school. The larger and more complex the school or school system, the more important this phenomenon becomes as a factor in organization and administration.

It is now common to speak of the ungraded primary divisions of the elementary school, team teaching, the utilization of master teachers either within the school system or by television, and various forms of grouping of pupils; and of teaching machines, the teacher's helper, and other novel ways of organizing the school and combining various forms of instruction to meet differentiated learning needs of pupils. In addition to distinguishing various faculty roles, differentiated staffing proposals call for enlarged faculty responsibility in planning and coordinating the instructional program.[13] Implementation of such plans will increase faculty interdependence.

The modern school system is an intricate network of varied activities and services carried on by personnel who assume a variety of responsibilities for the teaching-learning process. Teachers are aware that the organizational achievement is more than the sum of their individual efforts. Their satisfaction must be derived from the knowledge that their individual and collective efforts have contributed both to the formulation and to the achievement of the school's goals. Teachers who gain these satisfactions feel an identification with the organization, its purposes, and its methods of achieving these purposes.

---

12. Dan C. Lortie, *Schoolteacher: A Sociological Study* (Chicago: University of Chicago Press, 1975).

13. For an example and discussion of such a plan, see M. John Rand and Fenwick English, "Towards a Differentiated Teaching Staff," *Phi Delta Kappan* 44 (January 1968): 264–268.

THE TEACHER'S POSITION IN THE HIERARCHY

Teachers and administrators should strive to understand the working relationship among those who have responsibility for the day-by-day operation of the school. One method of accomplishing this purpose is to supply school personnel with a handbook of policies, regulations, job specifications, and diagrams showing working relationships thought to be instrumental in achieving the goals of the school. Organization charts shown in such handbooks describe line and staff organizations which illustrate the functional relationship between citizens of the community, the board of education, the superintendent of schools and the central office staff, the principals, the teachers, and the pupils.

A very careful explanation of such a chart should contribute to the teachers' understanding of their places in the total organization. The diagram shows that the teachers are members of the organization. It suggests, too, that the teachers are responsible *to* the principal and *for* the pupils. It identifies a line of authority. It indicates that there is a functional relationship between certain staff and line personnel. All of the variations in the understandings and the misunderstandings of the faculty concerning the administration of a school cannot be diagrammed, however. Administrative organization will actually be understood only when it becomes a legitimate subject for study by the faculty.

An administrative problem of particular concern to teachers involes the hierarchical levels on which personnel are classified. Some administrators fear that teacher participation in decision making jeopardizes the exercise of their authority. Teachers, on the other hand, accuse administrators of being too authoritarian. Is there a master-servant relationship that must be maintained? Does the administrator have more or less authority than the teacher? What is the source of authority? Does authority flow down from the top through the administrative line? Or could it flow in the opposite direction also?

These are difficult questions to answer, and the administrator who attempts to be democratic by including the faculty and other reference groups in decision making often becomes discouraged when he finds that he must accept responsibility for a decision with which he does not agree. The obvious consequence is that, losing faith in broad participation in the making of decisions, he resorts to the more comfortable autocratic procedure which he previously abandoned. With this reversal of action the teachers see the administrator becoming more dictatorial and their own importance in the organization diminishing. They, in turn, may counter by seeking to expand their decision-making prerogatives and limit those of the principal through collective negotiations.

The administrator of a school system has a responsibility to see that the decisions which are made contribute to the accomplishment of the overall purpose of the organization. He may feel that teachers or any other single group of people associated with the school are not in a position to see this total purpose. He may think that their participation in decision making reflects the bias that results from the limited perspective with which they view the problem.

On the other hand, teachers who would like to participate in making important decisions about school practices must find a way to gain the perspective of other groups which have a stake in the decisions that are made. The opportunity to make decisions also carries with it the responsibility for them. Neither teachers nor administrators have found a satisfactory means for sharing the responsibility for many decisions which they have made together. It must be remembered that even though an administrative procedure has been developed from faculty thinking, it is often the administrator whom the board of education and the people of the community hold responsible for the decision.

While we would not argue that the administrator's judgment and wisdom are necessarily any better than the judgment and wisdom of his teachers, the administrator does occupy a position that requires him to look at problems in terms of the interests of all groups affected by the school—the pupils, the citizens of the local community, the teachers and other school employees, the board of education, the state, the schools and education at large, and the total profession. This is what makes the participation of special-interest groups so very difficult. If administrators have been wary of teacher participation in the past, it may have been largely because they have not yet found a satisfactory means by which teachers could perceive the total problem without spending so much of their time on it that their effectiveness in the classroom was jeopardized.

The problem with which we are faced is one of reducing the master-servant feeling while at the same time maintaining an organizational arrangement that permits an efficient system of decision making, respected by all for its fair treatment of everyone's interests. The method of solving the problem has been to increase the amount of participation of those groups concerned. The solution has not been easy and has often required substantial time investment by teachers and administrators. Continued efforts in this direction are called for nevertheless. As schools and teaching have become more complex, the competence to deal with particular matters has been distributed more widely among school staff members.[14]

The modern concept of administration rejects the idea that the administrator is "the boss" who makes decisions for the group, and it will not condone the paternalistic attitude of the administrator who, through his kindly and fatherly wisdom and maturity, makes decisions for the welfare of the group. But this modern viewpoint rejects also the notion that the

14. For a proposal to increase collegial authority in schools, see Thomas J. Sergiovanni and Fred D. Carver, *The New School Executive* (New York: Dodd, Mead, and Co., 1973), chap. 8.

administrator simply leaves decisions up to the group. It espouses a participative structure that recognizes the administrator as the person who, through his leadership or by the authority granted him by the group, leads his teachers toward the achievement of a goal that has come to be accepted as desirable. The realization of such a concept will be achieved neither by teacher demand nor by administrative compromise. Both teachers and administrators need to work at the problem together. A little success from small beginnings will open the door to new ventures in cooperative decision making.

THE TEACHER AND ADMINISTRATIVE AUTHORITY

A second factor that has in many instances served as a serious deterrent to good working relationships among teachers and administrators has been confusion concerning the nature and the extent of the authority of the administrator. Here again, although there is considerable precedent upon which we may draw in arriving at a satisfactory understanding, teachers and administrators within a given school system need to arrive at their own understandings of how and where authority is to operate in the organization that has been built to accomplish their purposes.

Actually, there may be a number of sources of authority. Certainly the state, charged with the reponsibility for the public school system, has powers that are vested in it by the authority of law. The community has certain authority which it exercises through local option. The teachers have authority in their own classrooms. Much of this kind of authority is legal in character. It can be tested in the courts. It can be described by a chain of relationships leading from the state, through the local school organization, to the pupil.

The state has delegated certain of its powers to the board of education of the local school district. This delegation of powers gives the board the authority to exercise these powers. The citizens of the school district by vote and moral support add to the authority of the local school board. In turn, an administrative organization is developed to execute those functions of the board which deal with school operation. The administrator of the school is charged with responsibility for the effective operation of this organization to accomplish the purposes for which the school exists. Administrators differ in the manner in which they carry out this responsibility. Those who abuse their authority in discharging their responsibilities are misusing the powers of their office.

There is another kind of authority that must be recognized if the school is to accomplish its purposes. This is the authority derived from the philosophy and science of education. It emanates from the theory of how children learn and from the values that people hold for education. This source of authority, while alluded to in the professional literature and in our professional associations, has not been given consideration equal to that of legal authority in designing administrative organization. In reality, this source of authority cannot be used effectively in determining organizational structure unless the teachers play an active role both in the accumulation of new knowledge about education and in the assessment of values which people hold for education. The teachers have very real responsibility for the interpretation of the implications of this knowledge and these values for organizational structure. By virtue of their knowledge and competency, teachers have a right to some degree of authority in the administration of schools. However, the teaching profession seems to have encountered a major problem in getting its right to authority recognized and legitimatized in the legal-traditional channels of the American educational system. The existence of this "problem" may explain, in part, the trend toward increased formal professional organization of teachers into teachers' unions or associations.[15]

Many attempts have been made to picture a type of organization built out of a consideration of these two kinds of authority. The object of such a representation is to show that important considerations flow in both directions along the line—from the bottom to the top as well as from the top down. As one administrator has so aptly stated, "Authority bubbles up as well as trickles down." The two-way flow of authority in the line concept of administration may be pictured as follows:

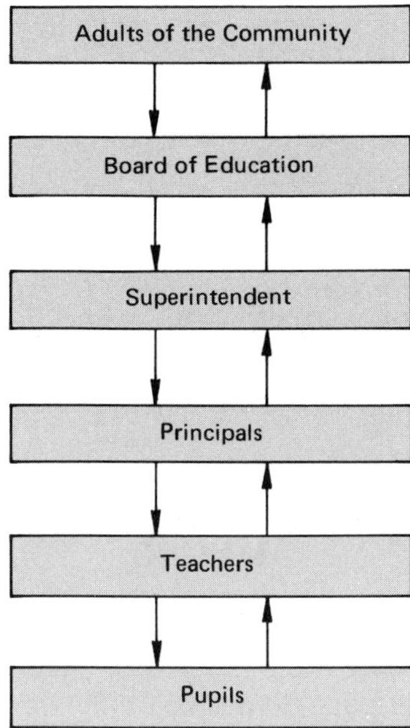

Figure 9–1 A flow chart on authority relationships in education.

15. See Ronald G. Corwin, "Professional Persons in Public Organizations," *Educational Administration Quarterly* 1 (Autumn 1965): 1–22.

In deciding matters of some consequence to the school, the administrator, before exercising the authority vested in him by the board of education, usually seeks the counsel of those who are most directly affected by the decision. Often he asks that a study be made by professional people whose competence in such matters can be respected. The administrator's recommendation to the board of education is based upon this study. Most school systems, for example, accept the judgment of teachers as the most authoritative source of information on the selection of textbooks and other instructional materials. For all practical purposes the teachers make the decision, even though their decision must be formalized by the board of education.

This means, then, that the functions of the participants in the organization are established on a rational basis, giving due consideration to the kinds of influences that have a bearing on these functions. The effective educational administrator knows that the organization succeeds insofar as there is mutual acceptance of these functions and the relationships that are established and maintained between the participants who must carry out these functions. This mutual understanding and acceptance of the working arrangement that is to exist is what we have chosen to call *organizational* or *normative authority.* It is that type of authority which Dubin says is "based on rational grounds."[16]

According to this concept, it is conceivable that an administrator may make decisions for the organization because it makes sense for him to do so, rather than because he has traditionally been given the power to do so, or because he possesses an unusual or superior wisdom. He simply occupies a position where, if he is competent, the purposes of the organization are best achieved this way. The rules established for the operation of the organization determine the authority structure. The administrator derives his authority from them. It is from this same set of rules that the teacher, too, obtains organizational authority, and thus group approval, to carry on those functions assigned to him. We hope, of course, that a process of interaction can be established whereby the mutuality of understanding of the organizational structure is maintained among the administrators and the other groups who have a stake in the educational enterprise.

THE TEACHER'S PART IN DECISION MAKING

Teachers do not want to participate in all decisions that administrators need to make; in fact, they chafe at some of the decision making in which they are asked to take part. Sometimes their reluctance is justified, because the decisions are of so little consequence to teachers that the time

16. Robert Dubin, ed., *Human Relations in Administration* (Englewood Cliffs, N.J.: Prentice-Hall, 1951), pp. 196–197.

used on them is a waste of human resources. Faculty meetings often deal with routine matters that were previously settled and are being announced in a group meeting. Such administrative behavior is not conducive to further staff participation. On the other hand, administrators have a justifiable criticism of teachers who are unwilling to spend the time or accept the responsibility for shared decisions. Since in the great majority of our schools both administrators and teachers have to learn how to share in decision making, it seems appropriate at this time to discuss those areas in which teacher participation has the most promise of success.

DETERMINING GOALS AND OBJECTIVES

While cultural values and the community's interpretation of the implications of these values have much to do with the determination of goals and objectives to be achieved by the schools, the teacher feels that he has a stake in this important decision-making process. Certainly there is no group in the school community that has had more opportunity than the professional staff to study the role of the school in American society. If we accept the proposition that the professional knowledge of the staff is essential to intelligent decision making in this area, we have established a very important responsibility for the teachers in the school. According to this proposition, the teachers of the school, because of their insight into the educational alternatives open and the implications of each alternative for society, should take positions of leadership in helping the citizens determine the kind of educational program which they can actively support.

It is a mistake for the administrator, either superintendent or principal, to assume that he can obtain an effective community understanding of the purposes of the schools by "going it alone." Citizens with widely varying backgrounds are interested in helping to shape school policies and programs. *How* decisions are made seems to be just as important as a determiner of group action as *what* decisions are made. For purposes of this discussion, then, the people involved in determining goals and the way goals are set are crucial factors in bringing about their achievement. A mutual understanding of goals derived by faculty and citizen cooperation is urged as the really effective means by which community support for the school is derived and maintained.

POLICY MAKING

As suggested above, another kind of decision making in which teachers can participate effectively is in the area of policy making at both the school building and the system levels. Teacher organizations have worked hard in recent years to legitimatize this kind of participation through collective negotiations agreements. Such agreements are policy statements in themselves and often specify conditions for involving teachers in certain other policy decisions (the selection of textbooks or acceptance of curriculum guides). There is considerable evidence that teacher organizations are expanding their previously dominant concern with "bread and butter issues" to curriculum and other policy matters of educational substance.

Teachers are interested not only in those policies which affect teacher personnel practices, but they have much to do—and, hence, to say—about daily school procedures relating to marks, promotion, reporting to parents, attendance, the punctuality of pupils, discipline, grade placement of pupils, use and distribution of resources, selection of textbooks, standards of achievement, and many other school operations. However, some administrators and teachers act as if they must actively participate in each of the myriad operating decisions that must be made about matters of every kind in the course of a school year even if the matters do not directly concern them. How much better it is to arrive at *policy* agreements, which give to the individuals most directly concerned the *authority of the organization* to act without having to get a decision from an entire staff each time an action becomes necessary.

APPRAISING THE EDUCATIONAL PROGRAM

Much of the responsibility for achieving the objectives of the school rests with the teachers. Both their individual efforts as classroom teachers and the total organizational effort to which they contribute are important factors in the school's achievement. Hence the school cannot really take stock of its efforts without involving its teachers. But what are the measures of a good school program? How should these measures be applied and by whom?

The critics who decry the ineffectiveness of our schools on the basis that our young people have not mastered the 3 *R*'s suggest one criterion for appraisal. Those who think that the schools should prepare youth to meet successfully the highly competitive challenges of industrialized society suggest more emphasis on a program designed to meet the needs of the gifted child. Some people are concerned about the youth who leave school earlier than is normal. Does a high drop-out rate in a school suggest that the program is not meeting the needs of students? What is the meaning of low test scores on a school-wide basis? What are the students' needs, and what are the needs of society that the schools must try to meet? These and other questions that could be raised relate to the objectives of the school. Even these are difficult to answer. A school has established some basis for an appraisal program when it has answered for itself these and similar questions that have been at issue in the district in which it operates. The cooperation of the teachers is essential in creating such understanding in the community.

Measurement of the effectiveness of the school in achieving these objectives is still a problem. Available measuring instruments are crude. If their limitations are recognized, however, they can serve a useful purpose. It is not the measure of the pupils' achievement that causes the great difficulty. Crude as the instruments may be, they do provide us with meaningful information concerning the pupils' growth. However, once we know that pupils are or are not achieving, how do we establish the positive and negative influences of the school? Can these be traced to the influences of poor, average, or superior teachers?

PROVIDING FOR IN-SERVICE EDUCATION

The need for the professional improvement of school personnel is practically taken for granted as an essential part of a staff personnel program. The new knowledge that is accumulating concerning the learning process, human relations, and administrative behavior, and the rapidly changing character of our society amply show that acquiring the knowledge necessary to become and continue to be a good teacher or educational leader is a lifetime endeavor. Four- and five-year teacher education programs do not adequately prepare prospective teachers for their careers. All that can be claimed for them is that they provide the prospective teacher with the basic knowledge and skill which he must use to continue to develop his competence throughout his career. Part of the continuance takes place in graduate programs of education. Much of it is done through in-service education.

In those schools where in-service education programs are proving to be successful, teachers participate in planning, organizing, and evaluating them. Programs planned for the teachers solely by the administrators are doomed to failure before they begin. Teachers as well as administrators must be in on the process of growing. An adequate program provides growth opportunities for both.[17]

CHANGING THE CURRICULUM

The dynamics of curriculum change have been suggested in the previous discussion of teacher responsibility in decision making. If teachers participate in the determination of goals and objectives, policy making, the appraisal of effectiveness, and in-service growth activities, they have gone a long way toward curriculum planning and change. The important principle to keep in mind here is that curriculum change is dependent upon the

17. For suggestions regarding in-service education programs see Louis J. Rubin, ed., *Improving In-Service Education: Proposals and Procedures for Change* (Boston: Allyn and Bacon, Inc., 1971).

changes that take place in people. Thus curriculum change must eventually be implemented at the local level even if it is stimulated by national programs of training and/or materials development. For purposes of this discussion the changes in teachers' beliefs about the role of education in our society, their understandings about how learning takes place, their interpretations of the needs of children and youth, their interpretation of the impact which the demands of society should make upon the program, their increased knowledge about the world in which we live, and their development of skills in working with pupils, parents, and others who have an effect upon learning are some of the factors that change the learning activities provided and the way teachers relate themselves to the teaching-learning process.

Change, however, must be of two kinds—change in individual staff members and institutional change. The teachers' changing conceptions of what and how to teach must add up to orderly program changes. Some program decisions must be made for the school, the school district of which each school is a part, and for the state. The suggestion made here is that program changes for the total institution emanate from changes in individuals, largely changes in the understandings of teachers; but some effort needs to be made to group these changes in meaningful and related learning experiences for pupils. Leadership and coordination on the part of administrators should provide not only the climate for change to occur, but the procedures by which changes in individuals can add up to system-wide or institutional changes.

PLANNED STAFF PARTICIPATION

Effective staff participation does not just happen. It must be nurtured. The assumption that there is a democratic working relationship when each employee is permitted to go his own way has led not only to individual stagnation but to lack of organizational achievement as well. Fortunately, studies of teacher participation indicate that both teachers and administrators desire an organizational pattern in which there is some structure to guide their behavior. The most effective teacher-administrator relationship, from the standpoint of both morale and productivity, is a participative one. That is, a condition must exist whereby both administrators and teachers call upon each other to define the structure that increases their productivity in achieving the ends desired by their organization, the school. Teachers need to know that, with the help of their administrative leaders, they are working on vital educational matters. They need to know that when they give time, energy, and interest to the consideration of crucial matters, their ideas or proposals for action make a difference to those who have the power to make final decisions.

In developing an organizational structure which optimizes staff participation in decision making, the administrator must remember that his purpose is not one of concession to others. The school is operated to educate effectively its children and youth. The wise administrator knows that he must capitalize on the creativity of all his staff members in building a structure that places a premium upon the cooperative effort required to do this job. In other words, the cooperative method is better than any other yet devised.

BUILDING SOUND PERSONNEL POLICY

The interests of staff members in personnel policy are broad and varied. Sometimes they are criticized because their interests in what appear to be matters of their personal welfare overshadow their concern for the solution of other professional problems. Those who are active in programs for the welfare improvement of staff personnel take the position, however, that this is an integral part of a broad program of professional improvement. In other words, sound personnel policies form a foundation upon which to build sound programs for professional advancement.

Personnel policy statements with which we are familiar include such topics as these:

1. Absence
2. Affirmative action
3. Assignments and transfers
4. Benefits and services
5. Contractual status
6. Discharge
7. Suspension
8. Employee-group relationship
9. Ethics
10. Evaluation
11. Exchange teaching
12. Extra duties and compensation
13. Grievances
14. Health and safety
15. In-service growth
16. Leave of absence
17. Official communications
18. Orientation
19. Outside employment
20. Overtime
21. Pay procedures
22. Probation
23. Professional meetings
24. Promotions and demotions
25. Re-employment
26. Resignations
27. Responsibilities
28. Definition of positions
29. Retirement
30. Salary schedules
31. Selection
32. Seniority
33. Sick leave
34. Substitute teachers
35. Vacations
36. Workmen's compensation
37. Work schedules, daily and yearly

Any complete textbook on staff personnel gives an even more comprehensive list of personnel concerns with which the school administrator must deal. His problem is to provide leadership in determining who should make what decisions. It is generally agreed that to develop satisfactory personnel policies for a school system, it is necessary to involve those who are affected by such policies. We know, also, that all school employees respect the fact that their welfare is conditioned by organizational agreements other than their own personal interests. Studies of teacher participation have shown that teachers differ widely in their opinions about the degree to which they should participate in decisions concerning themselves and those who are soon to join their ranks. For example, not all of them are agreed that they should participate in the actual selection of new teachers, in promotions, or in the evaluation of the effectiveness of their colleagues. On the other hand, a great many teachers do have definite opinions concerning the criteria to be used for their selection, promotion, and evaluation.

In some schools, teachers are ready to assist in the formulation of procedures to be applied in carrying out a given policy. In most school systems teachers insist on having some voice in the determination of salary schedules, teaching assignments, work schedules, and benefits to be derived in the form of compensation for extra duties and extra preparation for teaching.

Bridges[18] has discussed the conditions under which principals can share decision making most effectively. He noted that teachers do not want to participate in all decisions but have greatest interest in those which bear directly upon classroom affairs. The first task for the principal who wishes to extend participation is to determine which matters fall within the range of teacher interests and expertise. A second step is to decide exactly what teachers should help do (define the problem, suggest alternative courses of action, or select one of the alternatives). It is important that these decision-making boundaries be made absolutely clear.

Bridges[19] noted that the third step is to determine the mode in which the decision-making group will operate. One mode is participant-determining, in which it is agreed that a decision is reached only when all members of the group achieve consensus. A second is the parliamentarian mode where a decision is achieved when a majority of the group agree. The third mode is the democratic-centralist, in which one member retains the authority to decide after considering the views of others in the group. The role of the administrator will vary in each instance. In the first, he must help to build consensus. In the second, his task is to encourage the full expression of minority views and to maintain group strength in the face of divided opinion. As the person who probably reserves the right to decide in the third instance, he must help the group explore all relevant aspects of the problem and encourage the discussions of varying alternatives and their consequences.

---

18. Edwin M. Bridges, "A Model for Shared Decision-Making in the Principalship," *Educational Administration Quarterly* 3 (Winter 1967): 49–61.

19. Ibid. This part of Bridges' discussion is based upon Guy E. Swanson, "The Effectiveness of Decision-Making Groups," *Adult Leadership* 8 (June 1959): 48–52.

While Bridges' article focused upon the role of the principal in facilitating group decisions, it applies to other administrators as well. The following section describes some patterns of staff participation in which these suggestions for administrators can be applied.

PATTERNS OF STAFF PARTICIPATION

Various attempts have been made to involve the staff of the school in decision making. Not all of them are successful; examples of unsuccessful faculty meetings are legion. Yet we suspect that the faculty meeting called by the superintendent of the district or by the principal of the building is the only formal means by which many teachers have an opportunity to participate, even passively, in matters pertaining to the entire school. Often these meetings are nonparticipative; their agenda are not planned with the purpose of engaging the faculty in a consideration of matters that make a difference in the operation of the school. The following organizational patterns, which have been tried for the purpose of improving instruction, show promise for improvement in other aspects of the school also.[20]

Central office planned participation. Some school systems, in an effort to improve the education of children and youth, have enlarged their central office staff to include personnel to plan teacher involvement, particularly in the area of improvement of instruction. Conferences and workshops are planned to assist in instructional improvement. Orientation programs are planned to acquaint new teachers with the local school program. Committees of teachers assist in selecting textbooks, in planning courses of study for each of the several grade levels, and in solving a number of problems which are defined by the central office personnel.

This pattern of organization is based on the belief that improvement programs should be determined, planned, initiated, and carried out by central office personnel who call upon the teachers for assistance and advice. Often it is a program organized *for* the teachers rather than *by* the teachers.

It has the advantage of being easily controlled. Originating in the central office, it can be as narrow or as broad in scope as the central staff wishes. Plans can be put into operation quickly. New techniques or methods to be employed can be defined by relatively few people and brought to the attention of teachers by direct communication from the central office. There can be little question about the fact that recommendations have the support of the administration and therefore carry the weight of administrative authority. Its greatest advantage is that it focuses upon the problems of the entire school system rather than upon those

20. These patterns have historical roots. For discussion, see Ronald C. Doll et al., *Organizing for Curriculum Improvement* (New York: Teachers College, Columbia University, 1953).

which seem important in a particular school only or to a few individuals.

In recent years, schools that operate in this pattern of organization have greatly broadened their opportunity for teacher participation. Many teachers become involved in getting the work done. Often a wide range of resources is used in meaningful ways to solve school problems. Curriculum leaders, special supervisors, and special service personnel have been added to the central office staff to assist teachers in improving learning.

In some situations, however, participation planned and conducted by central office people does not accomplish its purpose. Teachers participate, but fail to identify themselves with the problems on which they are working. There is no real involvement, because teachers are called upon to work on problems that were originally identified not by them but by their superiors. No matter how sincere administrators may be in wanting to serve the school's purpose through such an organizational pattern, those who fail in its application do so largely because they have not succeeded in imbuing the entire staff with their own faith in the cooperative process.

School-building autonomy in planning. In contrast to this highly centralized system, some school administrators, community leaders, and educational theorists have advocated decentralization in programs for school improvement. Under such a system, the building principal becomes the administrator who is charged with the responsibility of giving leadership to the improvement of the educational program in his building.

The effectiveness of this plan depends to a great extent upon the ability of the individual principals to work with their teachers. Some principals are prepared neither to institute an improvement program of their own design nor to involve their teachers in building a cooperative plan for improvement. But where principals are capable of good leadership, effective results may be obtained from improvement programs in individual buildings.

It is obvious that one of the purposes to be achieved by the decision to use a decentralized plan of attack on the problems of the school system is to obtain greater involvement of school personnel. Hence, the principal who is autocratic in his dealings with faculty, or who is inept in teacher involvement, defeats the plan at its inception.

An advantage of the decentralized system is that the focus is upon the work to be done at the place where the need is. If the teachers are given an opportunity to define the problems of the school, and if the principal is authorized to take action upon the recommendations that they make for solving these problems, much can be accomplished. Thus, school programs can be adjusted to the particular needs of the residential area which the school serves. Often such an adjustment causes no system-wide problem. On the other hand, where the instructional problem is complex, where services in the several schools of the district differ, or where practices in dealing with the public vary from school to school, questions may be raised concerning the equality of the educational opportunity afforded by the several schools.

The flexibility of decentralized planning lends itself to adaptation to the needs of particular schools. The planning and the program for improvement, however, may be as different as the several staffs who engage in it. Without some leadership from the central office, there is no guarantee that individual schools within a school district will continue to improve simply upon the initiative of the local staff. It is important to raise the questions of how much and what kind of flexibility or uniformity is necessary in a school system to provide equal educational opportunity.

Central office coordinated planning. This plan incorporates certain features of both the centralized and decentralized plans described above. Both the faculty of each building and the personnel of the central office are involved in the planning. Ideas for improvement originate with the teachers, the principals, and the central office personnel. (Sometimes this includes pupils, parents, and other community representatives, also. It is not implied that these groups are unimportant; since this chapter deals with teacher participation, these groups are omitted.) By a system of representation from each of the several groups involved, a coordinating council is organized. This body receives ideas, sorts them in terms of urgency or need, establishes its best judgment concerning the wishes of the people whom it represents, and finally emerges with recommendations for administrative action.

After receiving administrative approval, the plan of action is generally executed through the usual line and staff organization. To the extent that the plan involves individual buildings, the principals are called upon for leadership. Teacher representatives who have been active on the coordinating council furnish excellent assistance. However, the major interest of teachers is that their ideas get to the administration and that they have some voice in determining what should be done about them. They are not vitally concerned that they have an active role in executing these ideas. If, on the other hand, the administration fails to take any action, the coordinating council reports this matter to its group members, who may decide to use the force of their numbers to apply pressure on the administration. The employment of the centrally coordinated plan of participation implies that the chief administrator believes in action and that this action is most effective when it grows out of the intelligent thinking of the groups who are affected by it.

One school system that has used central office coordination with real success began by asking the teachers, the officers of the Parent-Teachers Association, and the members of the board of education to list the major needs of the school. The superintendent of schools enlisted the cooperation of each of the building principals in securing the initial list of these needs which, incidentally, contained more than 500 items. A temporary committee consisting of three teachers, a principal, a P.T.A. officer, and a representative of the central office staff sorted the items and ranked them according to the frequency with which each was mentioned. The committee also suggested a classification of items which made possible the grouping of related problems.

The next step taken by the committee was to check this classification and ranking of items with all of the groups that had participated in preparing the original list. With this portion of the work approved, the committee then suggested immediate action for certain improvements which the responses to the checklist showed to be the most urgent. This suggestion was accepted by the superintendent of schools. From his study of the list of needs, the superintendent discovered several problems that he believed could be solved almost immediately with a minimum of study, time, materials, and expense. He informed the members of the committee that he was ready to act on these matters. He further instructed them to devise a plan for studying some of the more intricate problems to which the teachers, parents, and board members had given a high priority.

This administrative act proved to be a great morale builder for the teachers. In fact, a number of teachers who had expressed a lack of enthusiasm for the project originally were pleasantly surprised to find that the administrator meant business. This was not a "talking game," an expression they used to describe previous in-service and improvement projects.

In the course of the two years during which this project was observed, it was not possible to make changes as rapidly as some people would have liked. What was evident, however, was that during this brief period there was a growing confidence in the leadership of the superintendent of schools; the coordinating council (an outgrowth of the temporary committee that acted in this capacity) had gained in status; and the morale and productivity of the teachers had steadily improved. Many of the little annoyances—such as leaking faucets in the rest rooms, failure of janitors to sweep adequately, and torn window shades—were quickly corrected. Program changes came more slowly. Differences in points of view among teachers concerning standards of achievement at the several grade levels were still apparent, but one observable accomplishment was agreement that there was no simple answer to this problem. Teachers found that they could discuss the matter calmly as a problem to be solved rather than in terms of emotionally charged biases. Furthermore, after two years of cooperative effort, the staff showed a readiness to agree that many of the most important problems which they listed required intensive study before action should be taken. Many of these problems became subjects for study by faculty and community groups, to whom resource persons from neighboring schools and universities were found to be of great assistance.

In a discussion with the members of the coordinating council, at least two principles of action emerged as being of real importance for administration. They are (1) that teachers (and representatives of all participating groups) must believe that their ideas are wanted by the administrator and that their ideas will have an effect upon the actions that the administrator recommends, sanctions, or makes himself; and (2) that some action on matters of prime importance to teachers should be initiated by the administrator and vigorously supported on the basis of the evidence available. The members of this particular coordinating council did not feel that the administrator needed to be always in agreement with his teachers. It was their judgment, however, that if an administrator fails to approve a group decision or if he recommends an action contrary to that approved by the group, he should report the same and give his reasons.

No generalizations concerning the relative merits of these three patterns of organization can be drawn from one incident. It merely illustrates that teacher participation can be meaningful or not according to the insight and skill of the administrator. There is no gainsaying the fact that teachers need to grow, that they learn by doing just as surely as do the pupils, and that helping to solve the problems of the school is probably more meaningful to them than many simulated growing experiences that are created for them.

COLLECTIVE NEGOTIATIONS

Teacher participation in policy development has, in the past, resulted from the board of education's voluntary cooperation with the teachers involved. Behind this action has been the belief that those who would be affected by changes of policy should, after all, have some voice in these changes. However, since boards of education have had the legal right to control their relationships with teachers, it cannot be said that these relationships were fully bilateral.

Now as the result of many complicated, frequently misunderstood, and interrelated forces, American teachers are demanding the right to play a stronger role in the formulation of educational policy. The emergence of teacher militancy was discussed in chapter 3. A comprehensive discussion of collective negotiations is not appropriate here, but it is important to note certain aspects of the phenomenon as they relate to teacher and administrator participation in decision making.

The initial step in collective negotiations is the recognition of a bargaining agent. To some extent, this is a matter of statute. Most states have enacted laws which permit or in some instances require boards of education to negotiate with teacher organizations.[21] These statutes typically specify conditions for selecting a bargaining agent and the general condi-

21. For a review of such legislation, see Appendix E, and Lawrence Pierce, "Teachers Organizations and Bargaining: Power Imbalance in the Public Sphere," pp. 122–159. National Committee for Citizens in Education, *Public Testimony on Public Schools* (Berkeley, Calif.: McCutchan Publishing Corp., 1975).

tions which may be negotiated. They often contain a formula for resolving impasses which develop in bargaining and frequently contain a section which prohibits work stoppages. In the absence of statutes in several other states, bargaining agents have been selected and negotiations taken place in numerous instances.

Both the AFT and NEA seek exclusive bargaining rights for teachers at the local level. The logic of such a position is that it enables the teachers to speak with one voice and also encourages the development of organizational strength. Common methods for selecting a bargaining agent are examination of organizational membership rolls and employee elections. NEA and AFT locals have waged some strongly contested campaigns in such elections.

The selection of bargaining agents can pose a problem for middle-echelon administrators, whether they are or are not included in the same bargaining unit with teachers. In the first instance, they may find it difficult as outnumbered representatives of "management" to have their views about some items given the emphasis they desire in negotiations. In the second case, they may find themselves entirely without representation in dealing with the board of education. Two courses of action have been taken to achieve greater role clarity for principals and other middle-management personnel. The first has been to identify them as part of the management team and incorporate their views with those of the board of education in negotiations. The second has been the organization of independent administrator groups which also seek to negotiate with the board of education. While such groups have often been relatively weak in negotiations, their entry to the arena has added to the complexities of the process.

The principal parties in collective negotiations are the board of education which has the legal authority to make policy decisions and the teachers' association which seeks to influence those decisions. In some school districts, members of the board conduct face-to-face negotiations with officers of the teachers' organization. As the process of negotiations has become more time-consuming and complex, both of these bodies have shown a tendency to delegate this responsibility. The board often delegates it to the superintendent and/or a committee of administrators. Some school districts following the pattern established by industry have employed specialists to work full time on negotiations and related matters. Others employ such persons on a part-time, consulting basis to negotiate for them or to advise their own local team. Teacher organizations have acted similarly; local affiliates often receive assistance from negotiations experts employed by state or national parent organizations. When the representatives of the two bodies reach an agreement, they present it to the board and often the membership of the teacher organization for their approval. Of course, the board and at least the officers of the teachers' group generally consult with their negotiators about respective offers and counteroffers as the process goes on.

The objective of negotiations is to reach agreement, usually in the form of a written contract, about matters of interest to one party or the other. In the early stages of collective negotiations in education, the process was generally one in which the teachers submitted a set of demands to which the board responded. Now it is common for both parties to submit a set of demands, and for negotiations to involve board expectations for teachers as well as matters introduced by the teachers.

The actual negotiations process is the culmination of much research and discussion by all who are involved. It requires parties on both sides to identify problems from their own perspective, to determine the amount of resources available, and to establish priorities for the allocation of these resources. From this perspective, bargaining is a rational process which forces attention to organizational problems and priorities. It provides an opportunity for both sides to agree and act upon priority items and to bring items of disagreement to public attention.

However, the process is also based upon an adversary concept. Resources are limited and each side has a constituency to which it feels responsible. Their priorities may differ. This is perhaps most clearcut when the issue is one of salaries or other benefits, but it is applicable in other areas as well. Considering the matter of salaries, negotiators for the teachers will clearly win more support from their constituents as they win larger salary increments at the bargaining table. Board members, on the other hand, while perhaps desirous of raising salaries somewhat, may also be mindful of citizen pressures to keep taxes down. Thus, negotiators for each side feel a need to "win."

The adversary nature of the process gives rise to some informal rules which often govern the bargaining process. For example, neither party is likely to yield to the other at the outset lest their constituents accuse them of "giving in without a fight." Both sides are likely to present an inflated set of demands at the beginning. This has the dual effect of providing interested outside parties with an image that emphasizes willingness to seek the maximum while simultaneously providing some "throwaway items" which can be surrendered in return for concessions on matters considered more important. The resulting agreement can then be termed a "compromise"—a very acceptable word in American ideology, in which both parties come to agreement upon what is best for the total school program.

Agreement is not always reached easily, however. Sometimes, the respective parties are unable to persuade each other of the accuracy of their facts or the validity of their claims. This condition is termed an impasse.[22] There are several ways to resolve an impasse. One is to rely upon

---

22. The dynamics of negotiations and impasse procedures are discussed by Myron Lieberman and Michael H. Moskow. *Collective Negotiations for Teachers* (Chicago: Rand McNally, 1966), pp. 248–324. Also see Myron Lieberman, "Negotiations: Past, Present and Future," *School Management* (May 1973), and Patrick W. Carlton and Harold I. Goodwin, eds., *The Collective Dilemma: Negotiations in Education* (Worthington, Ohio: Charles A. Jones Publishing Co., 1969).

the power of one side or another to force a settlement. This means is most common in industrial settings, and strikes and lockouts are the principal techniques associated with it. A second method is fact finding, in which both sides agree upon a reputable outside party to study the situation and make a public declaration of the facts inherent in it. The theory here is that public disclosure of the facts as determined by such a party will encourage both sides to reach agreement. A third process is mediation, in which an outside party is invited to work with both sides, privately and together, in an effort to find basis for agreement. A fourth means of resolving impasse is submission of issues to binding arbitration. Under this procedure, both parties agree upon an arbitrator and consent to abide by the decision he renders after examining the case presented by each of them. All of these means have been employed at one time or another to resolve differences between school boards and teacher organizations.

One other aspect of collective negotiations which has particular relevance to administrators is that of administering the resulting contract. As noted earlier, there is a tendency for contracts to include provisions which deal with many aspects of the teachers' working day besides salaries and fringe benefits. The administrator must be knowledgeable about these provisions and how they affect his formal role vis-à-vis his staff. It is also important that he understand the leadership role of the teacher organization representative in his building or unit. Progress in many instances may depend upon the ability of these two persons to cooperate in their relations with each other and the total staff. From time to time, instances will arise in which a teacher or administrator will feel that the other has violated some provision of the contract. Such matters can often be settled through discussion by the parties involved. Sometimes the teacher-organization representative at the building level can serve as an informal mediator. In the event that such disputes cannot be resolved informally, many school systems with negotiated teacher contracts have formal grievance procedures included in them. These procedures vary, but generally include a number of levels of appeal including the board of education and, in some cases, an outside source if the grievant is not satisfied by the board.

NO PLAN IS A PANACEA

In developing the teamwork approach to the solution of problems in the school, the administrator must remember that no plan is a panacea. Possible approaches have been explained very briefly to provide the administrator with suggestions upon which he may build a program suited to the needs of the school in which he has such a responsibility.

None of the approaches discussed in the first part of this section included suggestions on handling the changes brought about by the introduction of formal negotiation procedures into the school's organizational structure. Certainly the introduction of such procedures will create different conditions in the internal organization of school districts, but they need not obviate the possibility of cooperative planning. The administrator should recognize that most of the policies and practices that serve to increase staff participation in planning and administration are viable in school districts with formal provisions for staff representation as well as in those which do not have such provisions.

The implication is clear that the administrator of the modern school should be more a leader of people than a manipulator of things. The accomplishment of the school's task requires a teamwork approach. Teachers and other school employees are a significant part of this team. It is essential, therefore, that an administrator be able to understand and work with his staff. The plan he will use must be built upon a profound insight into human relations and a sound set of principles of cooperative action.

SUGGESTED ACTIVITIES

1. Study the organizational structure of the school in which you work. Describe the role of teachers in this organizational pattern.
2. Visit a neighboring school system and, by observation and interview, determine the organizational structure. Draw a diagram of the administrative organization, and describe briefly how it works in making curriculum changes. Check your description with the superintendent, the principal, and a group of teachers.
3. Obtain a copy of a formal agreement between a board of education and a teachers' organization. Apply the agreement to your school system, or to a system with which you are familiar. Acting under the terms of this agreement, how would the role of teachers differ from that which they now play in decision making? What are the potential advantages and disadvantages of operating under the terms of a formal agreement with the board of education?
4. Attend a state meeting of a professional organization. Prior to your attendance set up criteria for effectiveness. After attendance write your evaluation of the meeting based on your established criteria.
5. Examine the minutes of the board of education in your school district. List the personnel policies which you find recorded there or in other school documents. Add to this list the areas in which you think there is further need for policy.

SELECTED READINGS

American Association of School Administrators. *Profiles of the Administrative Team.* Washington, D.C.: The Association, 1971.

Carlton, Patrick W., and Goodwin, Harold I. *The Collective Dilemma: Negotiations in Education.* Worthington, Ohio: Charles A. Jones Publishing Co., 1969.

Castetter, Wm. B. *The Personnel Function in Educational Administration,* 2nd ed. New York: The Macmillan Co., 1976.

Griffiths, Daniel E. *The School Superintendent.* New York: The Center for Applied Research in Education, 1966.

Lieberman, Myron, and Moskow, Michael H. *Collective Negotiations for Teachers: An Approach to School Administration.* Chicago: Rand McNally, 1966.

Lipham, James, and Hoegh, James A., Jr. *The Principalship: Foundations and Functions.* New York: Harper and Row, 1974.

Miller, Van; Madden, G. R.; and Kincheloe, J. B. *The Public Administration of American School Systems,* 2nd ed. New York: The Macmillan Co., 1972.

Rubin, Louis J., ed. *Improving In-Service Education: Proposals and Procedures for Change.* Boston: Allyn and Bacon, Inc., 1971.

Sergiovanni, Thomas J., and Carver, Fred D. *The New School Executive: A Theory of Administration.* New York: Dodd, Mead, and Co., 1973.

10

ADMINISTRATIVE BEHAVIOR AND EDUCATIONAL ADMINISTRATION

Having viewed educational administration in terms of its meaning and purpose, its tasks, and its process, we will now look at the administration of the school from the standpoint of the behavior of those who occupy administrative positions. In this chapter we will examine the administrator's behavior from two vantage points: the administrator as an initiator of action and the administrator as a recipient of action. Our intent is to sensitize the prospective administrator to the possibility that he will both influence and be influenced, and to increase his knowledge and understanding of both processes.

THE ADMINISTRATOR AS AN INITIATOR OF ACTION

Since the turn of this century, much has been written about the administrator as an initiator of action. Some of it has been prescriptive; some descriptive. Regardless of its character, this work generally uses the term *leadership* to denote the behavior of administrators who originate action for others. To be considered a leader, the administrator must act as a causal agent for someone else's behavior. The administrator is leading only when he is guiding and influencing what others in the organization are thinking, feeling, valuing, believing, or doing. If the administrator is unable to exert such influence, then he is not a leader.

Consistent with this general usage of the term *leader,* we define a leader as an administrator who has a mission or a special sense of direction for the organization and who is able to secure the commitments and efforts of subordinates in service of this mission. According to this definition, the educational administrator must possess two essential characteristics if he is to be regarded as a leader. First, he must have a special sense of where the organization is going, a vision which excites the imagination and challenges the best in people. This noble purpose gives people something to work for, something which they do not yet know how to do, and something which they will be proud of when they achieve it.[1] Such a vision gives calm perspective to the hot issues of the day and affects the significance of everything the administrator does.[2] The essence of leadership, therefore, is "choice, a singularly individualistic act in which a man [administrator] assumes responsibility for a commitment to direct an organization along a particular path."[3] This commitment stimulates and guides action.

The second essential characteristic which the educational administrator must have if he is to be considered a leader is the ability to influence people, to bind their wills in the accomplishment of purposes beyond their own ends.[4] If the administrator has a worthy organizational objective and a sense of direction which is designed to give continuity to individual actions over time but is unable to elicit the requisite energies and commitments of others, then he is not a leader according to our definition. To be a leader, the administrator must be able to realize his intent in the attitudes, values, and behavior of his subordinates. Functioning as a leader means that the administrator is guiding and shaping what individuals do in service of the organization and its mission.[5]

THE LEADER AND HIS ORGANIZATIONAL MISSION

Given the current state of our society, man reaches out for something to believe in, something that will give meaning to his job. He searches for this

1. Charles H. Granger, "The Hierarchy of Objectives," *Harvard Business Review* 42, 3 (May-June 1964): 63–74.

2. O. A. Ohmann, "Skyhooks," *Harvard Business Review* 48, 1 (January-February 1970): 4–22 and 166.

3. Abraham Zaleznik, "The Management of Disappointment," *Harvard Business Review* 45, 6 (November-December 1967): 59–70.

4. Chester I. Barnard, *The Functions of the Executive* (Cambridge, Mass.: Harvard University Press, 1962), p. 283.

5. For a discussion of how this conception of leadership may be dysfunctional for the formal leader, see Seymour B. Sarason, *The Creation of Settings and the Future Societies* (San Francisco: Jossey-Bass, 1972), pp. 181–215.

meaning because his former psychological anchors are rapidly disappearing.[6] People are on the move; geographical mobility is the rule rather than the exception. A mobile society brings with it several disruptive effects. People are now reluctant to establish enduring friendships and ties with others because they wish to avoid the pain of separation. People are unlikely to be living in the same neighborhood for any extended period of time; space is, therefore, no longer the source of psychological support and identity it once was. Nor is the extended family unit likely to be found living in close proximity; people cannot turn to fathers, mothers, sisters, brothers, uncles, and aunts for help and comfort in time of need. With these three traditional threads of continuity and sources of identity disappearing, the individual looks to the organization in which he works to furnish the psychological anchor outside himself which will give meaning to his life. People want and need a leader who believes in something and in whom they can believe. Let us now turn to two concrete examples of such a leader in two quite different educational settings.

A suburban example. Smith and Keith,[7] in describing and analyzing a highly innovative elementary school, highlight an administrator who inspired his staff to pursue a bold new conception of education—a conception free of the myriad ills which characterize the traditional American elementary school. The central thrust of this "School of Tomorrow" was to help students become "fully functioning mature human beings." The objectives of this school were fivefold:

1. to develop each child to the limits of his potentialities
2. to help each child achieve complete living in all phases of his life
3. to assist each child in becoming the architect of his own character
4. to foster self-actualization and self-realization
5. to develop the child intellectually, socially, emotionally, and physically

The administrator proposed to achieve these objectives through individualized instruction—i.e., differentiation in the rate of presentation and content according to the needs of each child.

To create a sense of special significance for this school, the administrator continually contrasted the School of Tomorrow with the schools of today and yesterday. He bestowed the School of Tomorrow with heroic qualities and the traditional schools with villainous ones. The traditional school was characterized as an "egg crate" whereas the School of Tomorrow reflected an open-space concept. The architecture of the

6. Harry Levinson, *The Exceptional Executive: A Psychological Conception* (Cambridge, Mass.: Harvard University Press, 1968), p. 28.

7. Louis M. Smith and Pat M. Keith, *Anatomy of an Educational Innovation* (New York: John Wiley and Sons, 1971).

school was distinctive and was used to reinforce the image of a school destined to be distinctive in functioning and having effects on children. The school was going to replace the "lock-step" curriculum with one based on continuous progress for each individual. Goals were to be set by the students rather than by the teachers. Students worked individually and in groups of varying sizes as opposed to the conventional classroom with thirty students. Daily schedules for students were arranged according to the needs and interests of each pupil and not according to a prearranged schedule that was the same for each day. Responsibility for what went on in the school was shifted from the teacher to the pupil. Textbooks were abandoned because they were viewed as a deterrent to instruction and to learning. Divergent thinking rather than rote memorization was stressed.

The overall organization of the school was changed from six grade levels to three divisions—the Basic Skills Division, the Transition Division, and the Independent Study Division. The function of the Basic Skills Division was to provide the competencies in communication and computation which are essential for acquiring knowledge, as well as the social skills which are necessary for the development of mature human beings. As the student moved to the Transition Division, he was taught to pursue knowledge independently but within the structure of the school. In the Independent Study Division, teachers assisted the pupils in discovering knowledge about the world in which they lived. In all three divisions the intent was to provide a flexible program of study based on the individual needs, interests, and abilities of students and to guide them into the repeated experiencing of success rather than failure.

Staff members were totally committed to this conception of education and were convinced of the worthiness of the principal's mission. They labored unceasingly, many to the point of exhaustion, in trying to achieve this grand goal. Smith and Keith report that they had never witnessed such total absorption in the work of an organization. The enthusiasm and the commitment were short-lived, however, and the results deviated dramatically from the ideal. At the beginning of the third year, the school board had been voted out of office, the superintendent had resigned, the principal had departed, the curriculum director had taken a position in another district, and only two of the original teaching staff remained. The program of the school reverted to the traditional pattern, and the wall-less building was transformed into one with self-contained classrooms. Why this undertaking proved so disastrous will be treated in a later section of this chapter.

An inner-city example. McPherson,[8] in a case study of two inner-city elementary schools with radically different teacher turnover patterns dur-

8. R. Bruce McPherson, "A Study of Teacher Turnover in Two Inner-City Elementary Schools" (Ph.D. diss., Department of Education, University of Chicago, 1970).

ing the same five-year period, found a sense of mission evident in the low turnover school. At this school's inception, the principal communicated to prospective staff members his desire to create an intellectual oasis in the inner city—a school where lower class black children would learn to read effectively and succeed academically. The principal was convinced that such an oasis could be created and was instrumental in getting his staff to believe that if it could accomplish this objective, then others would look at the school and say, "How come we can't do it if the Vesey Elementary School can?" Vesey's success would demand more oases. The sense of special significance was the commitment to establishing an exemplary inner-city elementary school which would become the model for inner-city education in the future. By solving the educational problems at the Vesey Elementary School, the staff would be leading the way toward solving the problems in inner-city education everywhere, a noble purpose indeed.

In recruiting teachers for his staff, the principal of Vesey Elementary School looked for experienced, well-educated, and highly competent individuals who had a Peace Corps sense of mission and who shared his conviction that an intellectual oasis was possible in the inner city. He sought teachers who desired to help black students succeed academically and experience joy and happiness while in school. He searched relentlessly for teachers with interests and abilities in more than one area, for teachers who understood and enjoyed working with inner-city black youngsters, and for teachers who regarded their jobs as more than just a way to occupy time between 9 and 3 o'clock. As the result of his efforts, the principal and his staff shared a common understanding of what the school was about, and were convinced that the objective was attainable. There were unusually high expectations for success—a feature missing in most schools in this setting.

At the end of a five-year period, the school was successful by many different criteria. There was virtually no vandalism in the school; windows were not broken, and the washrooms and corridors were free of the usual graffiti. The students enjoyed coming to school and a potentially militant community was supportive of the school's efforts to educate the students in its charge. On the single salient measure of success of teachers, however, the school was a failure. Despite the best efforts of a dedicated, determined group of competent educators fully expecting to be successful in fostering the intellectual development of their students, the academic performance of students was apparently no different than in other inner-city schools. Most of the students who had spent their first four years in Vesey School were reading below grade level, and a number of them actually regressed. As one teacher phrased it, "Some of these kids started out right, but somewhere we lost them." How this school and the one in the suburban setting happened to fail to achieve their mission is the subject of the next section.

MISSION FAILURE AND ITS IMPLICATIONS FOR ADMINISTRATIVE BEHAVIOR

In neither of the two examples which we have cited was the mission achieved. The answer to why the ventures failed may be a simple one. Given the circumstances, both visions may have been unrealistic and unattainable. The educators may have plunged headlong into these undertakings with an extravagant conception of the potentialities of the future and were totally ignorant of the difficulties involved.[9] If so, then the implications for the administrator who wishes to be a leader are rather clear. Before committing the organization to a particular direction, he should seriously ponder this question: "Can this be done?" In this case the peculiar genius of leadership is the ability to distinguish between the possible and the impossible, but with the willingness to get dangerously close to the latter.[10]

We believe that the preceding answer as to why the undertakings failed is inadequate. Another explanation seems more plausible. In neither school did the principals intellectualize the mission fully. There was no deliberate effort to break up the mission into immediate, visible targets; rather, the principals amplified the remote targets and underplayed the close ones.[11] No one seemed to be asking and seeking answers to this question: "What is it that we should be doing if we are to achieve our mission?" There were general goals but no clear and carefully thought out plan for mission attainment. For example, in the inner-city school both the principal and his staff believed that if a school has an able, dedicated principal and staff who have a high expectancy of success, then high academic achievement will be the result. It was not clear then, nor is it clear now, how these admittedly desirable qualities of principal and staff necessarily lead to high student achievement, particularly in reading. The problem of student reading was never attacked head on; no plan or program for improving the reading performance of students in that school was ever developed. In short, the sentiment of expectancy for student success in reading was never transformed into a plan for action. Important as enthusiasm and commitment are, they are insufficient by themselves for producing the desired results. These sentiments must be accompanied by a reasoned plan of action directly aimed at the problem which the organization is committed to solving.[12]

---

9. Eric Hoffer, *The True Believer* (New York: Harper & Row, 1951), p. 21.

10. Granger, "The Hierarchy of Objectives," p. 70.

11. For an interesting statement on a gradualist approach to change, see Amitai Etzioni, *Studies in Social Change* (New York: Holt, Rinehart & Winston, 1966), chap. 3.

12. See Neal Gross, Joseph B. Giacquinta, and Marilyn Bernstein, *Implementing Organizational Innovations: A Sociological Analysis of Planned Educational Change* (New York: Basic Books, Inc., 1971).

THE LEADER AND HIS PROBLEM OF INFLUENCE

As we mentioned earlier, in order to be considered a leader an administrator must be able to influence people in addition to having a mission which gives continuity to actions over time. Influencing others in the context of an organization, particularly one which is staffed by people who regard themselves as professionals, will inevitably be problematic for the administrator. In our two earlier examples, the principals were able to minimize the influence problem to a considerable extent because they opened new schools and consciously recruited staff members who found the principals' missions appealing. Most administrators will confront settings and situations with personnel who have life histories in the organization and who have developed vested interests and commitments which are incompatible with the would-be leader's mission. Such people may not readily adopt an organizational objective no matter how worthy it is and may resist attempts by the administrator to influence them in minor, as well as in major, organizational matters. Even those who wholeheartedly embrace the administrator's mission may oppose either covertly or overtly efforts to influence them.[13] Since we believe that the administrator cannot take his capacity to influence others for granted, we will examine this problem in greater detail.

In dealing with the problem of influencing others within the context of a formal organization, we shall consider that influence has occurred when the administrator attempts to modify another person's attitudes, values, beliefs, thoughts, or ways of behaving,[14] and succeeds in his attempt. For example, a principal recognizes that one of his staff members believes that inner-city children simply cannot learn, and the principal seeks to influence the teacher *to adopt the belief that these children can learn.* If the principal succeeds in altering the teacher's belief in the manner desired, we regard him as being a leader in that situation. We assume that such a belief does contribute either directly or indirectly to achieving the organization's mission as envisioned by the principal.

Our treatment of influence will focus on the various ways in which the administrator may seek to influence others and some of the conditions under which each mode of influence may be most effective. No single method is universally applicable since the effectiveness of any given mode is dependent upon the exact nature of the administrator, the person who is the object of the influence attempt, the change desired, and their interrelationships. Therefore, each administrator who aspires to be a leader will have to assess these various factors before he selects the particular

13. Seymour B. Sarason, *The Culture of the School and the Problem of Change* (Boston: Allyn and Bacon, 1971).

14. H. D. Lasswell and A. Kaplan, *Power and Society* (New Haven: Yale University Press, 1950).

mode of influence which he will use. The discussion that follows is aimed at helping the administrator make this selection.

Training. As a mode of influence, training is particularly applicable when a person is willing to change but lacks the requisite skills which may be developed through some type of training program. Furthermore, the person agrees with the administrator that the new belief, value, or way of behaving is a desirable one. For example, a foreign language teacher may be willing to switch her emphasis from teaching students to read and write in the foreign language to teaching them to converse in the language. The major obstacle to be overcome is arranging opportunities for the teacher to acquire the requisite conversational skills before undertaking the new approach. In such a case, the administrator might seize the initiative in identifying the opportunities which are available, and in helping the teacher take advantage of these opportunities. The latter might even include payment of the costs associated with the training and compensation for time spent in securing the necessary training.

Informing. There is a different type of situation, one which is conducive to influence by informing. In this situation the individual who is the object of influence is both willing and able to change in accordance with the views of the administrator. The major obstacle to change is the person's lack of knowledge about his present behavior and how it departs from some ideal. Therefore, the way in which the administrator influences others is to provide the information which vividly describes the state of the present situation.

For example, let us assume that the teachers in a given school are committed to the idea that a major function of formal education is to develop the powers of critical thinking in students. An important question to be answered is: "Are teachers structuring experiences which demand and foster critical thinking? If so, how frequent are these occasions?" The administrator, with the cooperation of his staff and outside consultant help, may create a plan and a set of procedures for answering this question. The plan may involve a systematic examination of the classroom tests which teachers use, the types of questions posed by teachers to students during question-answer periods, and the nature of the homework which is assigned. The leadership role of the administrator is twofold: to take the initiative in establishing a system which will yield information about the present practices in the school and to feed back the information to the members of his staff.

Supporting. Supporting, as a mode of influence, is appropriate when an individual is predisposed to change his behavior and is capable of making the change, but is fearful and anxious about being able to behave effectively in the new way. As in the preceding two modes of influence, the interpersonal relationship between the individual and the administrator is a positive one. In this type of situation, the major obstacle to change is the individual's anxiety and uncertainty about the future. Consequently, the administrator is likely to be successful in his influence attempt if he can be supportive and understanding while the individual works through his decision about changing and seeks to implement it.

By way of illustration, suppose a principal wishes to embark on a program designed to improve school-community relationships. What he has in mind is a two-year program. In the first year, he intends to meet in the homes of parents with groups ranging in size from eight to fifteen people. The length of these meetings will be one hour and a half, and they will center on topics of interest to the people present. He plans to open each meeting by presenting some ideas for changes which are being contemplated for the following year and indicating that he would be eager to discuss these ideas or to react to specific questions which parents might wish to raise at that time. In the second year, he plans to have parents visit the school, again in small groups of eight to fifteen people, and to witness first-hand the innovations which are being tried in the school program. The principal himself is somewhat uncertain about this course of action, however, and has asked the superintendent for a conference to discuss the matter.

Early in the conference, the superintendent senses that the principal doubts his own ability to handle the program successfully. The superintendent suppresses his tendency to respond in the usual ways. He does not give the principal bland assurances that he will be able to function well in these meetings with parents, nor does the superintendent give bits of wisdom about what to do to make these meetings successful. Rather, he listens and acts as a sounding board[15]; he helps the principal to recognize and to deal with his misgivings about being able to function effectively in these admittedly unpredictable meetings with parents. The superintendent also explores ways in which his office might be of help by asking if the principal has thought about assistance which the superintendent might be able to provide. By acting in this manner, the superintendent is being supportive and is influencing the principal with respect to some future activity.

Advising. Influence by advising is likely to be most effective when a person is dissatisfied with the existing set of circumstances but is unable to determine the particular condition or state which will yield more satisfying outcomes. At the same time, the administrator is perceived to have the knowledge and expertise necessary to extricate the individual from his current problematic situation. The major obstacle to change is the person's inability to identify the state or condition which represents a solution to his problem; therefore, the individual is susceptible to influence by

15. Harry Levinson, *Emotional Health: In the World of Work* (New York: Harper and Row, 1964), pp. 223–227.

the administrator if the latter has the intellectual resources to solve the problem.

There is evidence[16] which suggests that, in fulfilling their supervisory functions, principals are quite sensitive to this type of situation. Principals report that *unsolicited* advice or suggestions to teachers on matters related to the teaching process has crucially different implications from *requested* advice. The former carries with it a questioning of professional competence, and the professional receiving it is apt to react with considerable affect. A major factor which governs the person's reaction to unsolicited advice is the degree of respect which the person has for the supervisor. Principals who recognize this fact of organizational life consider their qualifications and those of the advisee and adapt the content of their suggestions and advice accordingly.

Involving. On occasion, the administrator will confront a situation in which a person is willing and able to change, but will oppose it if the administrator makes the decision unilaterally. The resistance develops because the person feels that the administrator does not have the legitimate right to make a decision about the change without first consulting the people who have a stake in the outcome. In this situation, the major obstacle to change is one of legitimation; consequently, the administrator can influence the person to behave in a new way by involving him in the decision about whether the change should be made.

For example, let us assume that a principal wishes to change the length of class periods and the number of days a given class meets each week and to drop study halls. The three changes are interrelated. The majority of discipline problems have occurred during study hall periods. As one might expect, students who have been in trouble have not used the study time to do their homework even though homework was assigned. Furthermore, the students report that they do not use the study time to do their homework because they do not understand how to do it. The standardized test results indicate that these students probably are experiencing the difficulties which they report. As a solution to this problem, the principal proposes to lengthen the class periods from forty to seventy minutes, with approximately thirty minutes to be allowed for supervised study by the teacher who has assigned the homework. Classes would meet four days rather than five days each week, and all study halls would be dropped from the schedule.

The principal carefully documents the discipline referrals and when they occur. He notes the reasons for these referrals and indicates the ability levels of those who are referred for some sort of disciplinary action. Armed with this information and his proposed solution, the principal meets with his staff. He presents the findings of his study and what

16. Anne E. Trask, "Principals, Teachers and Supervision: Dilemmas and Solutions," *Administrator's Notebook* 13, 4 (December 1964).

he thinks is a viable means of dealing with the problem. He encourages teachers to find fault with the proposal, to foreshadow the problems which might develop if the plan were implemented, and to express their own personal fears and concerns with respect to what he has proposed. Following a discussion of the plan, the principal might decide the issue in one of three ways: (1) by making the decision himself (sensing that there is no clear opposition to the proposal), (2) reaching the decision by majority vote, or (3) seeking to resolve the matter by reaching consensus.[17]

Rewarding. As a mode of influence, rewarding is appropriate when the individual believes that the benefits associated with the change do not exceed the perceived costs and when the administrator has control over resources which the other person values. In this situation, the major obstacle to change is that the person sees no net gain for himself by altering his behavior. If the administrator is to influence the other person, the administrator must make rewards available which are sufficient to induce the person to change his way of thinking or behaving.

Almost every school system has its own reward system. People quickly come to recognize what kind of behavior counts. Praise, promotions, salary increases, access to scarce organizational resources, and preferential treatment can be important incentives for behavior. The anticipation of these rewards, as well as the actual offering and receipt of them, can motivate people to act in ways which are congruent with the administrator's expectations. In some cases, it must be evident that a positive response to the administrator's influence attempt will lead to certain tangible rewards for compliance.

Commanding. There will be times when the administrator must resort to commanding as the mode for influencing an individual to modify his behavior. When the person has shown himself unwilling but able to change his way of behaving and the administrator has the organizational authority to demand compliance, the administrator will need to bring the power of his office to bear on the other person. The major obstacle to change is the person's refusal to behave in accordance with organizational norms; the administrator influences in such cases by insisting that the change be made and by applying the prescribed sanctions if necessary.

By way of illustration, a principal had been working with the chairman of the Physical Education Department in a concerted effort to develop a program of study. The principal had tried to build upon the ideas of the chairman but he had none. Contrary to the opinions of the members of his department, the chairman indicated that no additional equipment was necessary and that the existing program was more than adequate. He steadfastly refused to consider the changes which his colleagues proposed, and ignored the problems inherent in the present practices. An out-

---

17. This is discussed more fully in chapter 9.

side study team with expertise in this area visited the school, examined what was being done, and recommended massive reform in the present program. When the chairman opposed the recommendations, the principal ordered the chairman to implement the recommendations as soon as possible or else he would be replaced.

Designing. Up to this point in our discussion of modes of influence, we have dealt only with methods which are directed specifically at another person by the administrator and which result in awareness by the individual that he is being influenced by the administrator. There is an influence mode called designing, or *ecological control,*[18] in which the administrator takes some action that modifies the other person's social or physical environment on the assumption that the new environment will subsequently bring about the desired change in him. In this mode, the person is unaware that he is being influenced by the administrator. This mode of influence is apt to be used when the other person is committed to the status quo and/or when he would resist more direct influence attempts by the administrator.

For example, a principal during his first year as high school principal noted that the English department was oriented toward the use of anthologies; and, there were no attempts made to use reading materials which appealed to a range of abilities and interests. Most of the teachers appeared to be highly committed to the continued use of these materials primarily because they made the teachers' job a relatively easy and undemanding one. The principal felt that one teacher in particular was anxious to try a more differentiated approach because she recognized that many students were bored by the current materials. Also, a number of students were incapable of reading what was available. The principal approached the teacher and asked if she would be interested in having a paperback book library for her room. Together with a consultant secured by the principal, the English teacher put together four separate lists of paperback books; each list contained a variety of books geared to a range of interests and abilities. Within a month after the new materials were put into use, other teachers who were pressured by their own students came to the principal and requested that the same materials be made available for use in their classes.

A CONCLUDING COMMENT ABOUT MODES OF INFLUENCE

Throughout our discussion of influence, we have for ease of presentation showed only one influence mode being used in connection with each in-

18. M. Rosenberg and L. Pearlin, "Power-Orientations in the Mental Hospital," *Human Relations* (1962): 335–350.

fluence attempt. For any given situation, the administrator may need to employ several different modes if the person is to be influenced to accept or to adopt a change. By way of illustration, an individual may be confronted with the knowledge that there is a discrepancy between his present state of behavior and some future state (*informing*) but be unable to adjust his behavior because he lacks the requisite skills. To move the person from his present way of behaving, the administrator may need to couple the training, rewarding, and supporting modes with informing. In the final analysis, the particular mode of influence or combination of various modes which the administrator chooses will depend upon his perception of the personal and situational conditions that exist in each concrete case. Hopefully, our discussion of influence modes will improve the administrator's perceptiveness and facilitate his choices.

THE ADMINISTRATOR AS A RECIPIENT OF ACTION

Administrators are recipients, as well as initiators, of action.[19] As a recipient of action, the administrator's behavior is best understood as being guided, shaped, and even controlled by the intent and actions of others. Influence flows to the administrator, as well as from him. Since our knowledge and understanding of this side of administrative man is quite limited, our discussion of the administrator as a recipient of action will lack the extensive empirical and theoretical base which supported our treatment of administrative man as an initiator of action. Our comments will focus on three different ways in which the behavior of the administrator is guided, shaped, and influenced by others and will be organized around the following rubrics:

1. *Recipient of action by choice.* The administrator, willingly and knowingly, uses the goals of others as the principal basis for choosing the course of action he will take.
2. *Recipient of action against his will.* The administrator is most certainly not acting on his own and is aware that the goals underlying his behavior are primarily those of others and not his own.
3. *Recipient of action without his knowledge.* The administrator clearly is not acting on his own, but he is unaware that his behavior matches the intent of others and is caused by their purposes, desires, and aims.

---

19. This section is based primarily on an article by Edwin M. Bridges, "Administrative Man: Origin or Pawn in Decision Making?" *Educational Administration Quarterly* 6, 1 (Winter 1970): 7–25.

RECIPIENT OF ACTION BY CHOICE

The administrator governs by consent. This is true because in the final analysis the administrator's authority is determined by the willingness of others to accept his directives, orders, and suggestions as the basis for their behavior.[20] To maintain his authority, the administrator must maintain a balance between the contributions he expects of others and the inducements which they receive for their contributions. In other words, he gives in order to get. The administrator attempts to satisfy the goals of others in the immediate situation in order to elicit their compliance or cooperation with decisions he makes in some future situation.

As the administrator tries to satisfy the goals and needs of others, he confronts a number of problems; these problems are either an intentional or an unintentional consequence of their efforts to originate action for the administrator. One unintended problem stems from the ambiguous way in which people articulate their needs. Their stated goals are ambiguous because their goals or needs are obscure even to themselves. As a result, the person is able to communicate only that he has a strongly felt sense of need. He is aware that something is wrong, but has no clear understanding of what is wrong. The person recognizes that he is in a state of deprivation or in a state of needing, but has no firm notion of what actions, conditions, or objects will eliminate the state of deprivation or will satisfy the need.[21] For example, students in high schools, colleges, and universities are seeking in varying degrees of intensity to become involved in organizational decision-making processes. In some undefined number of cases, administrators are genuinely interested in satisfying students' needs for involvement. The administrator's decisions in these situations are complicated perhaps less by the willingness of faculty members to forego some of their prerogatives than by the students' lack of a clear grasp of what is required to satisfy their need for involvement. The administrator is unable to take action until he can identify or help the students clarify what modes of involvement they deem "good enough"—i.e., capable of meeting their need for involvement. Unfortunately, we know very little about how administrators perform this clarifying role and how they behave when confronted with this type of ambiguity.

Unintended problems also may arise even if the person is aware of his state of deprivation and the conditions which will rectify the deprivation. These difficulties occur when individuals incompletely communicate what their needs are. For example, a subordinate communicates his need in terms of the actions which will eliminate the deprivation, but inadvertently neglects to articulate what the basic need-as-felt is. If the subordinate has

---

20. Barnard, *The Functions of the Executive,* pp. 161–165.

21. This distinction between need as a state of deprivation and need as a material thing or set of conditions which fills a lack is drawn from Joseph J. Schwab, *College Curriculum and Student Protest* (Chicago: The University of Chicago Press, 1969), p. 152.

erred in judging the capability of the action for achieving his desired state, and the administrator makes his decision consistent with the subordinate's explicit definition of the situation, then the administrator will believe that his decision is "good enough" when in fact it is not.

This is not the major problem posed by the incomplete communication of others, however. If the administrator accepts the need-as-stated as the basic need-as-felt, then he is severely limited in the range of alternatives he can consider as being potentially "good enough." To return to the issue of student involvement, college students may express the desire to have a vote equal to that of the faculty in matters relating to the hiring, firing, and promotion of faculty members. Underlying this stated goal is a firm conviction that faculty members are not adequately fulfilling their responsibilities to students; as a result, students are not performing at the level to which they aspire. The administrator, acting in terms of the expressed desire, will fail to locate a satisfactory alternative if the faculty opposes student involvement, or if the institution's bylaws prohibit this form of student participation. Alternative courses of action which are "good enough" are much more likely to be found, however, if the basic need is identified—i.e., "We are not performing at the level to which we aspire." The need, thus redefined, allows a range of other possible solutions to be considered. Conversion of the need-as-stated into the basic need-as-felt is an important facet of administrative man which has been overlooked.

Difficulties which hamper the administrator's efforts to find a solution that is "good enough" to others also are posed by the intentionally misleading way in which they represent their needs. Under certain conditions, people communicate that they require one thing when they actually require another. Gouldner, for example, in his study of worker-management relationships, describes how complaints stemming from changes in management practices were channeled into a demand for more money.[22] Several factors contributed to this misrepresentation, including the workers' belief that their real complaints were not legitimate in the eyes of management and the workers' desire to have an issue on which unity of action was possible.

Confusing or misleading statements of needs by others, regardless of their intentionality, are not the only sources of problems for the administrator who is a recipient of action by choice. Problems also arise from the administrator's own attribution processes. Prior to reaching unilateral decisions, administrators frequently rehearse in their mind's eye the consequences of the alternatives under consideration. One important source of consequences is the anticipated reactions of others. The goals which administrators attribute to other persons in such cases influence the selection of alternatives. Incorrect inferences are both a persistent fear and a bane of the administrator.

---

22. Alvin W. Gouldner, *The Wildcat Strike* (New York: Harper & Row, 1954).

RECIPIENT OF ACTION AGAINST HIS WILL

In a collective bargaining setting, the administrator's behavior is frequently guided by the goals and demands of others. The flow of influence is not unilateral, however. Each side uses a range of tactics to advance its purposes and to achieve its goals within an institutionalized mechanism for handling intergroup conflict. The tactics used by both sides in this setting—deception, bluff, threats, and threat fulfillment—conform to a power strategy.[23] The process involves a series of demands and counter-demands, offers and counter-offers. There is an expectation by both parties that not all of their goals will be realized and that goal attainment by one party probably means a commitment which satisfies the goals of the other party. For the most part, neither side agrees with alacrity to accept the goals of the other. On those few occasions when one party is willing to satisfy the other's needs or goals, this willingness is concealed; and the object of attraction is used to extract concessions from the other side.

Influence of the administrator against his will is not limited to the collective bargaining setting, however. In his daily organizational routine, the administrator on occasion comes to act contrary to his own wishes and preferences as a consequence of the efforts of others. These occasions are occurring with increased frequency; teachers, students, and citizens are demanding that the school administrator become more sensitive to their goals.[24] There appear to be two approaches which they are using in an effort to realize this end. One approach focuses on the administrator prior to his reaching a decision; the other concentrates on him after he has made a decision which is inconsistent with the wishes and goals of others.

In using the latter approach, the intent may be to obtain a reversal of the administrator's decision. For example, students and parents may want an administrator to rehire a particular teacher whom he has just fired. The demand may be accompanied by a disruption of the school's activities. Parents picket the school and the district's administrative offices. Students go on strike and refuse to re-enter the school until the teacher is rehired. Violence and damage to the school building may also result unless the administrator changes his decision. Convinced of the rightness of their demands, such groups may resort to any tactic, legal or otherwise, to achieve their ends.

---

23. Richard E. Walton, "Two Strategies of Social Change and Their Dilemmas," *The Journal of Applied Behavioral Science* 1, 2 (1965): 167–179.

24. For a discussion of these occasions and how the administrator might deal with them, see Edwin M. Bridges, "Subjective and Objective Aspects of Demands for Involvement," *Administrator's Notebook* 17, 6 (February 1969).

Some decisions, however, are irreversible in that there is no way of undoing the damage which people perceive has been inflicted on them. In such cases, persons may use tactics which are designed to establish a clear cause-effect relationship in the mind of the administrator. The latter, in one sense, is led to expect negative consequences if he behaves in ways which thwart the goals of the group in question. If the relationship between the group and the administrator is affectively neutral or positive at the time, then the group in all likelihood will limit its tactics to the communication of intensely strong negative affect by means of nonverbal cues. However, if the relationship is such that the group believes the expression of negative sentiments will not make the administrator more responsive to its goals, the group may resort to tactics like sabotage, ritual insubordination, or strict bureaucratic interpretations of its obligations to the administrator. Such tactics frequently are accompanied by a variety of verbal and muted cues to establish an unmistakable relationship between these events and the administrator's action.

Individuals or groups also attempt to influence the administrator before he reaches a decision. This happens when they know that the administrator is considering a particular issue and they want to affect the outcome, or when they want the administrator to take action that they perceive he is unwilling to initiate on his own. In trying to exert influence on the administrator, people find ingenious ways of letting the administrator know how they feel about a situation and what action they consider appropriate. If their stake in the outcome is high and they attribute obduracy to the administrator, then they, in addition, may subtly foreshadow certain difficulties and link them to the administrator's decisions. For example, work groups may let it be known that they have been preparing a list of grievances which they plan to present to the union representative or to the administrator's superior. There may be hints that the group will no longer help out in crisis situations by doing work that is not stipulated in the contract. There may even be threats of a walkout or some other form of harassment, inconvenience, or embarrassment. Regardless of the tactic, the objective is the same. The group hopes to create a decision situation for the administrator which offers only negative choices. The administrator yields to the preferences of others because he dislikes the other alternatives open to him even more.

We suspect that yielding to the preferences of others against his will is likely to be an unusually stressful event for the administrator. The stress is produced in no small measure by the image of administrative man as the initiator of action (leader), which is consistently portrayed in the literature on educational administration. Because of this image, being the influencee rather than the influencer poses far more difficulties for him than for others—particularly his subordinates. How the administrator copes with this role reversal and what the consequences are for his subsequent behavior represent an interesting area for future inquiry.

RECIPIENT OF ACTION WITHOUT HIS KNOWLEDGE

In both of the preceding discussions of the administrator as a recipient of action, the administrator has been portrayed as *knowingly* being guided or governed in his actions by the efforts and goals of others. As recipient of action by choice, he willingly permits the influence to occur. As the recipient of action against his will, the administrator yields to the preferences of others because he wishes to avoid the real or imagined costs of noncompliance. In the third and final recipient-of-action-state to be discussed, stress will be placed on the more subtle tactics people use to influence the behavior of the administrator. Contrary to the popular conception of administrative man as the one who influences, he will be treated as the one who is being influenced without his knowledge.[25]

People seek to influence the administrator without his awareness for a variety of reasons. They wish to elude the unpleasantness and the risks of a direct confrontation with an administrator who might retaliate when he is challenged. They derive a sense of satisfaction from outwitting the bearers of formal authority. They have purposes which, if public, either could not be realized or perhaps would have a lower probability of being achieved. The objective sought determines in part which tactics are considered, for one objective is attained more efficiently and more effectively by one type of maneuver than by another. The choice of tactics is further limited by the availability of the conditions and the resources that the tactic demands. For example, if the tactic requires knowledge of persons on whom the administrator relies for advice and counsel and this knowledge is lacking, then the individual must look for a tactic which can be employed with existing means, knowledge, and circumstances.

Research and theoretical work are relatively silent on the ways in which an administrator's behavior is influenced by others without his knowledge. However, from our own informal observations of organizations at work and from discussions with occupants of subordinate positions within the organizational hierarchy, two types of tactics have emerged. One type depends upon the cooperation of a second party, whereas the other type may be implemented by the would-be influencer alone. Examples of the first type include resorting to disguised flattery and exerting influence through a significant other. Examples of the second type include creating an illusion of influence and biasing the information on which the administrator is apt to base his actions.

---

25. See Aaron Lowin and James R. Craig, "The Influence of Level of Performance on Managerial Style: An Experimental Object Lesson in the Ambiguity of Correlational Data," *Organizational Behavior and Human Performance,* vol. 3 (1968), pp. 440–58, and Bruce J. Crowe, Stephen Bochner, and Alfred W. Clark, "The Effects of Subordinate Behavior on Managerial Style," *Human Relations,* vol. 25, no. 3, pp. 215–237.

Creating an illusion of influence. In one sense, the image of administrative man as a leader provides a potential Achilles' heel for the unwary administrator. As we mentioned earlier in this section, the administrator encounters an idealized conception of his role in the literature which he reads during his preparatory program. This conception is apt to be reinforced by his employer when the administrator assumes his first managerial position. As a consequence, the administrator who believes that he is acting as a leader should derive a strong feeling of satisfaction and a sense of accomplishment. A resourceful person may take advantage of this situation in ways limited only by the extent of his own imagination. Regardless of the method selected to achieve his goal, the person has but one major intent. He is striving to develop a definition of the situation in which the administrator sees himself as trying to persuade or to influence the individual to behave in a particular way. The social reality of the situation, however, is that the individual is both willing and able to act in this fashion but has led the administrator to believe otherwise. The administrator perceives that he has succeeded in influencing the person, and experiences satisfaction from performing this leadership act. One party has been influenced—but the influencee is the administrator, not the other person as the administrator believes.

A classic illustration of this form of influence was discovered in a manual which had been prepared by a creative group of high school students intent on helping their peers to succeed in their academic work. The students were advised to perform poorly on the first examination or two in the class and to seek help and guidance from the teacher. As the teacher provided this assistance, the students were advised to show gradual but steady improvement on subsequent tests and to express their appreciation to the teacher for having helped them to increase their understanding of the course content. Through this technique, the teacher, according to the students, would come to regard herself as the principal cause for the students' improvement, feel good about having reached the students, and reward the students with a higher mark than they might have attained otherwise. (Students reported using this tactic with highly satisfactory results.)

Biasing the information on which the administrator is apt to base his actions. Because other people are often the source of information on which administrators in large part base their decisions, these people have ample opportunity to influence these decisions without the administrator's knowledge. Subordinates, for example, employ a variety of techniques to influence the decisions of their superior as they perform their relay function in the organization's communication network. The tactics that we have identified have one aspect in common. The information that is presented contains no recommendations or advice; the burden of inference is placed on the administrator. The situation is arranged, however, so that the latter arrives at conclusions which are favored by or are favorable to subordinates. Such slanting occurs when the subordinates plant clues which, if detected by the administrator, lead him to expect certain positive outcomes from one course of action and certain negative consequences from other alternatives. Subordinates also affect their superior's decisions by supplying information which points to one particular definition of the problem. By biasing the information to suggest that the cause of the difficulty lies one place rather than another, the subordinate increases the probability that the administrator will restrict the alternatives he considers to those aspects of the situation which the subordinate wants handled. Subordinates also strive to influence administrative decisions by staging their presentation. The subordinate reports in considerable detail how he went about gathering the information, the sources he tapped, the ingenuity he exercised in obtaining the information from uncooperative sources, and the data he has assembled. The subordinate not only slants the information on which the decision is to be made, but seeks to heighten the credibility of the evidence by dramatizing the care and thought which "obviously" went into it.

Exerting influence through a significant other. When people believe that they have a greater likelihood of influencing the administrator's decisions by persuading a second party to initiate the influence attempt, there are at least two basic types of significant others from whom willful or unwitting cooperation is sought. These two types are differentiated by the nature of the party's affiliation with the organization. One member type is the confidant of the administrator (such as his secretary) who functions as an adviser, a sounding board, and a wailing wall. A second member type is one who occupies a position bearing more formal authority than the administrator who is the primary target of influence. Two nonmember types used by individuals, especially subordinates, in an attempt to sway the administrator are clients and the organization's public-in-contact or some segment of it. Accessibility and ease of eliciting cooperation are major determinants of which type people will choose to use. Regardless of the type selected, people hope that the administrator will believe that the source of influence is the significant other and not themselves. So long as this fiction is maintained, the legitimacy of the influence attempt never becomes a salient issue.

Resorting to disguised flattery. A subordinate may wish to obtain preferential treatment from his superior and to enhance his own potential for advancement within the organization. One way subordinates endeavor to accomplish this is to make themselves more personally attractive to their chief administrator through the use of compliments. However, since the administrator controls resources important to subordinates, he expects to be the target of ingratiation attempts[26]; consequently, he is suspicious of compliments from his subordinates. Under these conditions, the major task confronting the subordinate is to create the impression that the compliments are "honest" ones. In order to increase the chances that the compliments will be taken at face value, the subordinate enlists the cooperation of an individual who has no apparent reason to make the compliment. This individual then communicates to the administrator a prearranged compliment, and attributes the opinion to the administrator's subordinate. For example, a teacher subordinate may have a friend who works in another school within the district and whose civic responsibilities bring him into occasional contact with the teacher's building principal. The friend is prompted to ask the principal, when the opportunity arises, if he anticipates a vacancy in the near future. When, as expected, the principal proves curious and seeks a reason for the inquiry, the friend is to respond "spontaneously" that he has heard so many fine comments from Teacher *X* about the way the school was being run that he was considering a possible transfer. Credibility of the compliment is increased on several grounds—its apparent spontaneity, its source, and its subtle nature.

SUMMARY

In this chapter we have tried to present a balanced view of administrative behavior which is congruent with the realities of organizational life. We have noted that the educational administrator is both an initiator and a recipient of action. As the initiator of action, the administrator (if he is to be considered a leader) must have a sense of organizational mission and be able to elicit the requisite energies and commitments of others in service of the organization and its mission. Our discussion of administrative man as the initiator of action centered on eight modes of influence which the administrator might use to elicit the desired contributions from others and the conditions under which each mode was likely to be most effective. In dealing with the administrator as the recipient of action, we stressed three sets of conditions under which the administrator is guided, shaped, and influenced by others. We noted that the administrator can be a recipient of action by choice, against his will, and without his knowledge.[27]

In one sense, however, the discussion was imbalanced. We emphasized the ways in which the administrator influences others in service of organizational goals and the ways in which organization members seek

26. See Edward E. Jones and Keith E. Davis, "From Acts to Dispositions." In Leonard Berkowitz, ed., *Advances in Experimental Social Psychology,* vol. 2 (New York: Academic Press, 1965), pp. 220–266.

27. For a provocative discussion of how the administrator can deal with a condition of powerlessness, see Michael D. Cohen and James G. March, *Leadership and Ambiguity: The American College President* (New York: McGraw-Hill Book Co., 1974), pp. 205–215.

to influence the administrator in an effort to achieve their own individual goals. We recognize also that the administrator may attempt to influence others in order to achieve his own goals and that subordinates may attempt to influence the administrator in ways which are consistent with organizational purposes. Only as more research is done which takes these various possibilities into account will we be able to present a description of administrative behavior that is even more congruent with the realities of organizations in action.

SUGGESTED ACTIVITIES

1. Interview a number of principals and superintendents to determine the ways in which they try to influence members of their staffs. Focus your discussion with these administrators on concrete examples, and seek to identify what conditions prompted the administrator to use one particular influence mode in preference to another. How do these influence modes and conditions correspond to the discussion in this chapter?
2. Observe several administrators at work. Does their behavior appear to be more usefully understood in terms of the administrator as an initiator of action or as a recipient of action? Support your conclusion.
3. Talk with several teachers and try to discover the ways in which they attempt to influence the administrators with whom they work. See if you can determine why the teachers choose to use one tactic rather than another. What insights does this information provide you into understanding administrative behavior?

SELECTED READINGS

Bridges, Edwin M. "Instructional Leadership: A Concept Re-examined," *The Journal of Educational Administration,* 5, 2 (October 1967): 136–147.

Cartwright, Dorwin. "Influence, Leadership, Control." In James G. March, ed., *Handbook of Organizations.* Chicago: Rand McNally, 1965, pp. 1–47.

Cohen, Michael D., and March, James G. *Leadership and Ambiguity: The American College President.* New York: McGraw-Hill Book Co., 1974.

Fiedler, Fred E. *A Theory of Leadership Effectiveness.* New York: McGraw-Hill, 1967.

Gibb, Cecil A. "Leadership." In Gardner Lindzey and Elliott Aronson, eds., *The Handbook of Social Psychology.* Reading, Mass.: Addison-Wesley, 1969, vol. 4, pp. 205–282.

Gross, Neal, and Herriott, Robert E. *Staff Leadership in Public Schools: A Sociological Inquiry.* New York: Wiley, 1965.

Halpin, Andrew W. *Theory and Research in Administration.* New York: The Macmillan Co., 1966.

Katz, Daniel, and Kahn, Robert L. *The Social Psychology of Organizations.* New York: Wiley, 1966.

Levinson, Harry. *The Exceptional Executive: A Psychological Conception.* Cambridge, Mass.: Harvard University Press, 1968.

National Society for the Study of Education. *Behavioral Science and Educational Administration,* Sixty-Third Yearbook, Part II. Chicago: The Society, 1964.

Sarason, Seymour B. *The Creation of Settings and the Future Societies.* San Francisco: Jossey-Bass, 1972.

Stogdill, R. M. *Handbook of Leadership: A Survey of Theory and Research.* New York: Free Press, 1974.

Vroom, Victor H., and Yetton, Philip. *Leadership and Decision Making.* Pittsburgh: University of Pittsburgh Press, 1973.

Zaleznik, Abraham. *Human Dilemmas of Leadership.* New York: Harper & Row, 1966.

11

PERSONAL MOTIVATIONS FOR ADMINISTRATOR BEHAVIOR

Administrators, like all human beings, act in an environment in which the conditions are never completely known. Psychologists tell us that even the physical conditions which surround us have an effect on behavior. The comfort of working conditions, the color of the room, the adequacy of the lighting, and the relative humidity of the atmosphere all have their effect upon what people do. When the environment contains people who react differently to these and other existing conditions, and to each other, the problem of explaining behavior becomes exceedingly difficult. Indeed, when we consider the fact that one's reaction to one's surroundings is a function of conditions within the person as well as those outside him, the intricacy of the science of human behavior is obvious.

FACTORS AFFECTING BEHAVIOR

In this chapter we shall not attempt to assume the role of psychologists or psychiatrists in explaining or dealing with the problems of human behavior. Nevertheless, since the administrator's stock in trade is human relationships, his or her behavior should have a sound psychological base. A guide to understanding the basis for the administrator's actions is that *behavior is dependent upon the interaction of the conditions within the person and those which surround him.* Allport describes a field theory of personality in much the same way that the physical scientist speaks of the "field" in the atomic theory of matter. As he says, "Roughly speaking, the field theory of personality regards the total environmental setting as well as the inner structure of the person as decisive in the shaping of conduct."[1]

Allport's field theory is similar to what many psychologists refer to as an "open system" in which one's own fund of understandings forms the basis for his understanding of the world around him. In turn, what he perceives in the outside world affects his inner self. A transaction between his inner and outer worlds is constantly changing both of them.[2]

Thus, psychologists provide us with a clue for thinking about human behavior. To understand it we must know something about the nature of the "field" in which behavior is exhibited. Yet the characteristics of the field are not directly observable. They must be inferred from the observations of people who, themselves, are a part of this field. To illustrate this in educational administration, let us take the case of two administrators who at different times held the same administrative position. For one of them, the position presented the challenge through which he successfully developed his leadership potential. The other found the position uninteresting and exceedingly limited in the opportunity it gave him to do those things that he felt compelled to do as an administrator.

Apparently *the person in the situation* made the difference. Conditions in the situation elicited different responses in each of them. In turn, each of them had different effects upon the situation. Forces, reactions, circumstances, and relationships among things and people were altered by the exchange of the two administrators. Observing these two administrators, one would find it difficult to attribute differences in their behavior merely to the observable conditions in the school district in question. Part of the cause must be attributed to what Allport has referred to as "the inner structure" of the persons involved.

Careful observers of human behavior find it difficult to attribute a specific behavior to a particular cause. Rather, they agree that the behavior of individuals is due to a combination of causes difficult to unscramble. There is, therefore, a reluctance among these observers to establish a cause and effect relationship between specific behaviors and the elements of the situation merely on the basis of observational evidence. At the present stage in the development of the science of human behavior, it is probably more meaningful to speak not of causes of behavior but of factors that may affect behavior. We shall deal primarily with those factors which may

---

1. Gordon W. Allport, *Personality: A Psychological Interpretation* (New York: Holt, Rinehart & Winston, 1937), p. 364.

2. For a brief review of pertinent literature, see Daniel E. Griffiths, Lawrence Iannaccone, and James Ramey, *Perception: Its Relation to Administration* (New York: University Council for Educational Administration, 1961), p. 11.

be altered by educational processes—namely, one's assumptions, beliefs, values, concepts, motivations, perceptions, and skills.

The major purpose of this chapter is to help the prospective administrator begin his assessment of the internal conditions that prompt him to act as he does. Our chief concern will be with those personal factors that may be changed by the individual as he comes to develop an understanding of the ways in which these factors may affect how he behaves. One ever-present danger of such self-examination is that introspection may block desirable action and result in indecision. The reader should keep this caveat in mind as he examines his own behavior in light of the factors that we discuss in the remainder of this chapter.

The four factors that we will consider include: (1) the administrator's perception of others; (2) his perception of himself; (3) his values and beliefs; and (4) his concepts of success. In our discussion of these factors we will illustrate how they may affect the administrator's behavior.

PERCEPTION OF OTHERS

How an administrator works with people is partially dependent upon the assumptions which he makes about them.[3] Two such key assumptions center around what people *will* do and what they *can* do. These assumptions about people's motives and abilities form a set that influences how the administrator assesses individuals and how he behaves toward them.

An administrator can, for example, be predisposed to attribute negative motives to his subordinates. He may view them as working only to maintain a decent standard of living for themselves and their family, as wishing to avoid responsibility, as having little or no ambition, as wanting security above all else, as being indifferent, and as having a "take-it-easy; don't burn yourself out" attitude.[4] On the other hand, the administrator may be inclined to attribute positive motives to subordinates. He may believe that work is their central life interest, that they are self-directed and industrious, that they derive a sense of accomplishment from doing a job well, and that they are challenge-seeking rather than challenge-avoiding.

Similarly, an administrator can ascribe either positive or negative abilities to his subordinates. He may assume that they are creative, that they know what to do when discretion must be exercised, that they have the capacity to induce and deduce, and that they are capable of doing a variety of things. On the other hand, the administrator may be pessimistic about his subordinates' abilities and operate on the assumption that they

3. For a thorough discussion of the assumptions which people make about the nature of man and of the role which these assumptions play in affecting behavior, see Lawrence S. Wrightsman, *Social Psychology in the Seventies* (Monterey, Calif.: Brooks-Cole Publishing Co., 1972), pp. 69–96.

4. Douglas McGregor, *The Human Side of Enterprise* (New York: McGraw-Hill, 1960).

are unimaginative, unable to work jointly with others on a common task, possess limited intellectual resources and competencies, lack ingenuity, and are incapable of consistently exercising good judgment.

The nature of the abilities and motives which the administrator attributes to the people with whom he works can influence his actions and reactions in a variety of ways. His assumptions can affect how he defines his role as a supervisor, how he deals with people who break organizational rules, and how he approaches the task of introducing organizational change. Let us now look at the manner in which the administrator's assumptions may guide his behavior in each of these areas.

SUPERVISION

A major responsibility of administrators is the supervision of subordinates' performance. How the administrator elects to carry out this function is determined in part by his assessment of his subordinates' motives and abilities.[5]

If he assigns negative motives and abilities to them, he is apt to regard close supervision as an organizational imperative. A subordinate who is viewed as being an unwilling contributor to the achievement of the organization's goals and as having little concern for the quality of his performance is one who certainly bears watching. The administrator who suspects his subordinates' motives and abilities will no doubt feel the need to hold frequent inspections to assure himself that their behavior conforms to the organization's expectations. He will frequently check to see that people are reporting to work on time, that they are not leaving the building before the prescribed time of departure, that they are at their work stations, that they are adhering to the course of study, and that they are exercising good judgment in using it. In short, the suspicious administrator is driven by the constant need to verify that rules and regulations are being followed and that performance meets acceptable standards.

If, on the other hand, the administrator believes that his subordinates are highly motivated and are capable of superior role performance, then his approach to his supervisory responsibilities may be quite different. The administrator who trusts his subordinates will monitor their work efforts less frequently.[6] In consequence, his chief concern as a supervisor may shift from an identification of individual departures from organizationally prescribed role expectations to a search for the barriers that hamper the performance of his subordinates. The administrator not only locates such obstacles; he also removes them. Furthermore, he is confident that his

5. See R. Christie and F. L. Geis, eds., *Studies in Machiavellianism* (New York: Academic Press, 1970) for studies relating Machiavellian attitudes to interpersonal behavior.

6. Lloyd H. Strickland, "Surveillance and Trust," *Journal of Personality* 26, 2 (June 1958): 200–215.

subordinates are capable of and interested in identifying the resources which will facilitate their performance; and, he actively seeks to secure these resources for them.

RULE ENFORCEMENT

The motives and abilities which an administrator attributes to organizational participants also influence how he attempts to explain their behavior. In seeking to find a sufficient reason for people's actions, the administrator may look for an explanation based on either some *inner* qualities of the individuals involved or some *external* environmental factors acting upon them at the time. The capabilities and the intentions which the administrator ascribes to people affect whether he is likely to establish an internal or an external locus of causation for their behavior. Where the administrator locates the cause for individuals' actions determines how he evaluates them and subsequently behaves toward them.[7]

Let us consider an example of how these attribution processes may influence the way in which an administrator handles behavior that violates certain rules of organization. A high school principal reported having received the following note from one of his English teachers:

> Mr. Jones, Bernie Miller has been a persistent problem in my class. During study periods he wastes time and makes it difficult for his neighbors to do their homework. He seldom has his assignments ready to hand in and shows no interest in school. I've kept him after school and punished him in other ways, but NOTHING SEEMS TO WORK! My class would be better off without him so why don't you transfer him or assign him to a study hall?

In this episode the principal, Mr. Jones, has several possible ways of coping with this situation; the options he considers are determined in part by the assumptions which he makes about students' motives and abilities. If the administrator believes that most high school students are in attendance against their will and will do only what is demanded of them, then he is apt to think about the various sanctions that he might use or threaten to use in getting the boy to do his homework. The principal might insist that the student remain in school each day until he completes his homework. The principal might threaten to call in the boy's parents if he continues to ignore his teacher's assignments. Or, the principal might threaten the student with dismissal or suspension from the basketball squad.

If, on the other hand, the principal is inclined to attribute a full measure of interest in school to students, then he is likely to look elsewhere for the cause of the student's failure to hand in his homework. In

7. F. Heider, *The Psychology of Interpersonal Relations* (New York: Wiley, 1958).

this particular case Mr. Jones doubted that motivation was the problem and sought to locate other possible causes for the boy's behavior. The principal's first step was to ask the English teacher, Mrs. Pollock, if there were other students in the class who were not handing in their homework. Mrs. Pollock identified nine other students—five boys and four girls—who frequently did not complete their assignments; however, these students, unlike Bernie Miller, behaved themselves in class.

With this additional information, Mr. Jones set out to discover what distinguished these ten students from the seventeen other pupils who seemed to do their work consistently in Mrs. Pollock's class. The search was a brief one. The ten nonhomework students were at least three full years below grade level in reading while the text from which the homework assignments were made was written at grade level. Mr. Jones made these findings available to the teacher; she requested and received materials that were within the reading comprehension of the students and which appealed to a broader range of interests than the single text.

The problem had nothing to do with motives; rather it stemmed from a combination of internal (low reading ability of students) and external (available reading materials) factors. The student was not punished, nor was the organization's homework requirement set aside. However, the subsequent assignment of homework took into account the varied abilities and interests of students in the class.

MANAGEMENT OF CHANGE

A third area in which the administrator's basic assumptions about people's motives and abilities are partial determinants of his behavior is that of organizational change. How he approaches the problem of effecting change in organizational goals, structure, practices, and procedures is influenced by his conceptions of his subordinates. The administrator may assume that people have a preference for predictability; that people when confronted with a choice between stability and change will opt for stability; that people by their very nature will resist any tinkering with the status quo; that people develop vested interests in organizational arrangements which accentuate their fundamental orientation to resist changes; and that people are security-conscious, always favoring the old and established ways of doing things to the new, untried, and unproven ways.

Or, the administrator may assume that human beings are novelty-seeking; that they are eager to experiment because such occasions offer opportunities to develop competence and to demonstrate mastery of the environment; and that they derive satisfaction from such activities as exploring, investigating, and manipulating an unknown environment.[8] These two conceptions of how man orients himself to change, coupled with as-

8. Robert W. White, "Motivation Reconsidered: The Concept of Competence," *Psychological Review* 66, 5 (1959), pp. 297–333.

sumptions about the individual's abilities, can heavily influence the manner in which the administrator approaches change as shown in the example that follows.

In recounting a recent experience he had with his math department, a high school principal in his first year on the job told about the way he had handled a decision concerning whether the school should adopt new programmed texts in algebra and geometry. Shortly after the opening of school the principal received a memo from his superintendent about these programmed texts. The superintendent stated that he was impressed by the idea of individualized materials which enabled students to proceed at their own pace and that he hoped the high school math staff would use these materials, at least on a trial basis, with several classes. As the principal re-read the note from his superior, he recalled a sarcastic comment made by his predecessor, "Those old-guard math teachers are really in a rut. They are the arch enemies of institutional change."

Faced with a superior who was obviously interested in new curriculum ideas and practices, and a staff who had been labeled as being opposed to innovation, the principal pondered several possibilities. He could accept the previous principal's view of the teachers in the math department. If he did this, he recognized that his strategy would be aimed at minimizing staff resistance to an administrator-initiated change. To cut down the opposition and perhaps even avoid intentional efforts to sabotage the new practice, the principal considered that he would need to give the staff full information about the necessity for the change. At the same time, he thought that he might share control in putting the change into effect by having the math department decide how many algebra and geometry classes would use the new programmed materials. Through such tactics the principal did not expect to eliminate the resistance; however, he did anticipate that the staff would be less likely to torpedo his efforts.

Another possibility which the principal considered was that these teachers would be willing to try a promising idea and would welcome the chance to experiment with a challenging practice. The principal seriously entertained this more positive view of his staff's motives and eventually decided to have his staff scrutinize the texts and decide whether they should be used.

The staff ordered the programmed materials, wrote the publisher for the names of schools in the area who were using the new texts, requested and received permission to visit these schools, and set out to locate penetrating analyses of this approach to math instruction. After five months of intensive study, the math department unanimously recommended the use of the texts only as supplementary materials for students who were experiencing difficulties in mastering specific math concepts.

Accompanying the recommendation was a thoughtful, detailed commentary on the shortcomings of the approach and on the conditions under which the new materials showed some promise of being useful and effective. The report which the staff prepared was sufficiently convincing that the superintendent realized how even a limited, full-scale trial in but a few math classes could have led to serious problems. To his surprise, the report reflected the staff's willingness to innovate and showed its ability to gather evidence and use it wisely.

PERCEPTION OF SELF

How an administrator perceives himself influences his thoughts and actions in several important ways. First, the administrator uses himself as a norm for judging others; what he looks for in people is influenced by his own traits. The more he understands himself and the kind of person he is, the fewer errors he is likely to commit when making inferences about other people. Second, the administrator makes certain assumptions about what controls his behavior. Some administrators tend to see their behavior in the organization as being largely self-determined; others believe that events external to themselves and beyond their control govern their behavior. The administrator's perceptions of the primary locus of causation for his own behavior shapes his organizational conduct. Third, administrators make certain assumptions about their ability to act as a causal agent for the behavior of others. Some administrators expect that certain anticipated consequences will follow from their actions while other administrators lack this sense of efficacy. What the administrator chooses to undertake is partially determined by how efficacious he views himself in generating the outcomes he seeks.

AWARENESS OF SELF

People use themselves as the standard by which they perceive or judge others; administrators are no exception. One way in which the administrator's traits influence what he looks for in someone else is that they help to furnish the categories he uses in perceiving others.[9] His characteristics, needs, and values both expand and limit his vision as they sensitize him to certain aspects of other people and blind him to other aspects. For example, an administrator who is a nonauthoritarian person is more likely to view other individuals in terms of their psychological and personal characteristics and be less concerned about their orientation to power than is an authoritarian administrator. An administrator who is warm and friendly

9. Sheldon S. Zalkind and Timothy W. Costello, "Perception: Implications for Administration," *Administrative Science Quarterly,* 7 (September 1962), pp. 218–235. For a discussion of how we form our impressions of other people, how accurate these impressions are, and whether our perceptions of the world and people about us are influenced by social or cultural factors, see Stuart Oskamp, "Social Perception," in Lawrence S. Wrightsman, *Social Psychology in the Seventies,* pp. 431–458.

is apt to look for these qualities when he forms impressions of others. An administrator who is blunt and straightforward may tend to use these characteristics in describing other people.

Whether the administrator rejects or accepts his own characteristics also determines in part how he perceives and evaluates others. What the individual *does not accept* about himself he is set to recognize in other individuals. For instance, the administrator may be assertive and inclined to impose his will on those who work with him. At the same time, he may be extremely sensitive to this characteristic in others—even to the point of seeing an autocratic intention behind people's actions when there is none. Since the administrator regards the trait as being undesirable in himself, he negatively evaluates those people in whom he sees a similar trait.

An administrator who is *accepting* of a particular characteristic in himself is also set to look for this same quality in others. How he responds depends upon whether he views his trait as a deficiency or as a virtue. If the administrator has a deficiency (not meeting deadlines for periodic reports or being late for appointments) which does not disturb him, then he may make undue allowances in others who have near-identical deficiencies. On the other hand, if the administrator prizes the quality in himself, then he is likely to be attracted to others who have the trait and to be repelled by those who lack it. For example, the administrator who is obeisant to his superiors and assigns substantial significance to this characteristic will judge his own subordinates in terms of their obeisance to him; submissive subordinates will be accepted and non-submissive subordinates will be rejected.

However, the administrator's own personal characteristics are not the only inner factors which may color his perceptions of other people. The current emotions which the administrator is experiencing also can shape what he sees in others.[10] An administrator who becomes insecure when an organizational change is announced will look for signs of insecurity in those with whom he works. As he interprets the behavior of others as revealing "unmistakable" signs of insecurity, his own feelings of security will be correspondingly diminished. Similarly, an administrator who is anxious about how others are perceiving him during an important meeting may discern meanings in people's actions which were never intended.

The administrator who has insight into his own personality is less likely to have his perceptions of others distorted by his own personal characteristics.[11] Admittedly his perceptual processes, like those of other individuals, are intricate and complex. However, as the administrator comes to know the categories he uses in perceiving others, the amount of weight he attaches to these categories, and how the categories and their signifi-

10. S. Feshback and S. D. Singer, "The Effects of Fear Arousal upon Social Perception," *Journal of Abnormal and Social Psychology,* 55 (1957): 283–288.

11. Zalkind and Costello, "Perception: Implications for Administration."

cance to him are related to his own characteristics, he can have somewhat greater confidence in his judgments. In the meantime, the administrator is advised to guard against making snap judgments and to seek reliable evidence as a firm basis for his evaluations of others.

PERCEIVED CONTROL OF SELF

Some persons believe that they are, in a sense, masters of their fate. They approach life as though they can do what they will to do. Such individuals are inclined to view their actions as products of their own choosing; they initiate rather than follow. Other persons consider that their behavior is determined by external forces beyond their control.[12] These people link what they do to outer factors rather than to inner ones. This type of person tends to see few options for himself and to act only when he has a clear, unambiguous mandate to do so. Where the administrator locates the control of his own behavior will partially determine how he enacts his organizational role.

In the mid-1960s, a number of big city school systems sought to decentralize their operations. The trend toward decentralization was prompted by several conditions. There was a growing recognition by chief school officers that a six- or seven-layered bureaucratic cake was inefficient. So many decisions were being referred to the top that long delays resulted; patient and impatient citizens alike charged officials with being evasive and unresponsive. Simultaneously, school administrators were becoming convinced that the right to make final decisions should be vested closer to the scene of action where knowledge of local problems and circumstances was greatest. By increasing the amount of discretion which could be exercised by administrators at lower levels, the men at the top hoped to cut down their own occasions for decision; to reduce the time lag between the occurrence of a problem and its attempted resolution; and to effect more intelligent, informed choices throughout the organization. What frequently happened was more of a change in rhetoric than a change in actual practices, however.[13]

A sizable number of lower level administrators failed to exercise the newly granted discretionary powers. Administrators did not adopt the new view of themselves and continued to behave as though they lacked the ability to control their own actions. In the face of unclear boundaries around their choices, administrators would not make decisions independently; they continued to seek approval to make decisions or to pass the problems to higher levels for a resolution. Some of these administrators

12. For an application of these concepts to the principalship, see Seymour B. Sarason, *The Culture of the School and the Problem of Change* (Boston: Allyn and Bacon, Inc., 1971), pp. 133–149.

13. See Thomas R. Williams, "An Exemplary Design for the Administrative Organization of an Urban Public School System" (Ph.D. diss., University of Michigan, 1968).

undoubtedly were unsettled by the responsibility which accompanied the redistribution of decision-making authority. Others, however, because of their innate or organizationally acquired predispositions to ascribe an external locus of control for their own behavior, could not act as though they were self-governing. They did not test the limits of their powers because they perceived they had none.

PERCEIVED CONTROL OF OTHERS

A pervasive but frequently unstated assumption in the myriad discussions of leadership is that a leader views himself as being a causal agent of other people's actions.[14] By implication the administrator who does not believe that the behavior of others is contingent upon his own actions is not apt to engage in leadership acts. Unfortunately, we lack much systematic research into the conditions under which an administrator is likely to connect the behavior of others with his own deliberate management of the environment. Also, we do not know a great deal about how an administrator behaves when he does and when he does not regard himself as being a significant factor in what others do, think, and feel. Although our knowledge in this area is limited, what we have learned is enlightening.

At least two conditions can affect whether an administrator perceives himself as being a causal agent for another's actions. If the administrator ascribes the quality of immutability to other people's behavior, then he is apt to persuade himself that no one can have an impact on the person and he acts accordingly. For example, in a recent study,[15] elementary principals expressed the belief that the expressive (personal-social) characteristics of beginning teachers were not amenable to change. At the same time, the principals seemingly were convinced that the instrument (task performance) characteristics of teachers could be modified. Since the principals ascribed stable and enduring properties to the expressive characteristics, they were significantly less inclined to invite a teacher with somewhat weak expressive qualities for a job interview than a teacher with weak instrumental characteristics.

How an administrator perceives his own skills, resources, and characteristics can also color his inferences about his potential for acting as a causal agent for others. By way of illustration, former President Lyndon B. Johnson decided not to seek reelection to his country's highest executive office; he gave as a major reason his conviction that he could not unify the nation. Johnson evidently believed that unification was possible; however, he felt that he was not the man who could help the country achieve a unified

14. Edwin M. Bridges, "Administrative Man: Origin or Pawn in Decision Making?" *Educational Administration Quarterly* 6, 1 (Winter 1970): 7–25.

15. Edwin M. Bridges, "Preferences of Principals for Instrumental and Expressive Characteristics of Teachers," *School Review* 76, 3 (September 1968), pp. 324–338.

perspective. He cited several of his own qualities (being from the South at that period in American history and lacking the personal characteristics which appeal to fairly large segments of the American public) as representing significant obstacles to his being able to develop the sense of national unity which the country sorely needed. If Johnson had perceived himself differently, he might have sought reelection and, perhaps, even won it.

Important as perceptions are in determining behavior, they are subject to error. Administrators can misjudge their own available resources for affecting the actions of others and can err in their judgments of the immutability of certain human characteristics. We suspect that administrators are more likely to underestimate than to overestimate their potential for influence. As a consequence, we believe that the prospective administrator can profitably examine the assumptions which he brings to the causal agent facet of his organizational role. If he is to function as a leader, he must necessarily view other people's actions as contingent upon his own behavior. Some of the conditions which may affect his perceptions about his capacity to influence others are discussed in chapter 10.

VALUES AND BELIEFS

Values and beliefs also partially determine a person's behavior as they constitute important premises which guide and direct action. These two types of decisional premises[16] differ in several respects. A belief is an expectation held by an individual that a given cause leads to one or more results. The results may be either positive or negative, wanted or unwanted; what is significant is that the person connects the results with a particular cause. For example, an administrator may have a belief about how certain teacher characteristics affect what students learn or fail to learn. Specifically, the administrator may have formed the expectation that students will learn more when taught by warm, friendly, and understanding teachers. With this belief, the administrator is apt to rate teachers with these characteristics much higher than teachers who are businesslike, cold, and aloof. Not infrequently, the connective link between the expected cause and result is unclear to the individual with the belief. He does not know, nor has he thought about, how the cause produces the result. Nevertheless, he acts as though the belief were a valid one.

A value, on the other hand, is an expectation by the individual about what ought to be. Unlike a belief, a value is concerned with what should be the case rather than with what is the case. An individual acting consistently with his values does what he does because he feels that it is

16. Manley Howe Jones, *Executive Decision Making* (Homewood, Ill.: Richard D. Irwin, 1962), pp. 56–96.

legitimate, good, or right. If a person believes that by acting in a particular way he can effect a given result, he may be unable to take the action because it is inconsistent with his values. By way of illustration, an administrator was being urged by his subordinates to take action with which he was not in basic agreement. He was convinced that he could successfully avoid giving in to their demands and escape a charge of dereliction by using the technique of "negative timing."[17] Use of this power tactic would involve his initiating action on the demand but delaying final action until it was either too late or the plan "died on the vine." The administrator, however, elected to take a riskier action because the negative timing technique ran counter to his moral code. Let us now look at three areas in which the administrator's values and beliefs can make a difference in his behavior.

ROLE OF AUTHORITY

Most organizations are hierarchically structured with superordinates having authority over their subordinates. Although superordinates possess organizational authority or the right to command subordinates, the superordinate still faces the task of influencing subordinates to act in ways consistent with his directives.[18] What distinguishes a leader from an administrator, as we noted in Chapter 10, is that the leader is successful in his attempts to influence others. Therefore, for the administrator to function as a leader he must be able to convert his organizational authority into compliance by his subordinates. How the administrator chooses to exercise authority over his subordinates is affected by his beliefs and values about the nature of authority and the way in which an authority relationship is established.

Some administrators believe that their subordinates will do simply as they are told. When faced with the necessity to guide and direct the choices of subordinates, these administrators use straightforward and uncomplicated tactics to effect an authority relationship. They may say on an individual basis to a subordinate, "I wonder if you would have time to . . . ," "Would you please . . . ," or "From now on we will need to. . . ." Or, they may issue a memorandum to the work group stating, "In the past we have. . . . Henceforth, we will. . . ."

Other administrators believe that their subordinates will obey instructions out of a sense of duty to the organization or because they fear sanctions for non-compliance. An administrator with these beliefs is likely to sandwich an order between an emphasis on the subordinates' organizational obligations and some sort of veiled threat. The announcement might read something like the following: "In the best interests of the orga-

17. Norman H. Martin and John Howard Sims, "Power Tactics," *Harvard Business Review* (November-December 1956), pp. 25–29.

18. Jones, *Executive Decision Making,* pp. 125–126.

nization and everyone involved, the staff will be expected to . . . beginning next week. Regrettably some individuals were penalized in the past for ignoring instructions; I'm sure such action won't be necessary this time."

Still other administrators believe that subordinates will follow commands which are accompanied by proof[19]—proof of the wisdom of the administrator's proposal for action. To elicit support for his recommended course of action, the administrator may take one or more of the following steps:

1. He elaborates on the problem which gave rise to the need for such action.
2. He specifies in detail the various other alternatives which were considered.
3. He shows how the orders he has issued will eliminate the problem completely or will check the unwanted consequences in the problem situation.
4. He comments about the possible effects of the administrator's instructions on the individual as well as the organization.

The administrator fully expects such steps to result in willing compliance.

Values also figure in how an administrator responds to the authority inherent in his organizational role. An administrator may feel that his orders should never be questioned by subordinates. He views arguments which are raised against his proposals as challenges to his authority and as assaults on the authority structure of the organization. His reactions are swift. He reprimands his subordinates. He lets them know how inappropriate their actions are. He even threatens them with dismissal if the behavior is repeated.

Another administrator may feel that it is quite proper for subordinates to raise questions about the instructions he gives. He regards such behavior as their legitimate right. Consequently, when subordinates oppose his attempts to exercise authority over them, the administrator seeks reasons for their opposition. He listens attentively to what they say. He probes for unwanted consequences which they may see but to which he may be blinded. He searches for what and how they feel about the matter. Even if the administrator chooses not to reverse his earlier decision, he does not censor his subordinates for their actions unless they subsequently refuse to follow his directions.

ROLE OF THE SCHOOL

The concepts that people have of education's role in our society differ greatly. For some, the major function of education should be to bring every-

19. Ibid., pp. 173–182.

one to a given standard of performance in reading, writing, and arithmetic. Those people who place heavy emphasis on the 3 *R*'s maintain that no one who possesses the necessary intellectual prerequisites should fail to reach a certain minimum level of performance in the basic subjects. Other people insist that the essential function of public education should be to enable each person to attain his full potential. The individuals holding this view of education stress above everything else that the schools should help a person achieve optimum expression and realization of his talents and interests. Neither of these views necessarily excludes the other; however, an emphasis on one as opposed to the other will result in different patterns of behavior. Consequently, the way an administrator defines what the role of the school should be makes a difference in the kind of leadership which he gives in developing the school program.

The administrator with an educational philosophy which attaches considerable significance to a universal standard of performance in the basic skill subjects is likely to behave in certain ways. He scrutinizes the results of standardized achievement tests. He looks for individual as well as group departures from the criterion of mastery which has been set. He stimulates teachers and other members of the professional staff to define precisely the nature of the substandard performance, to identify its causes, and to institute both corrective and preventive measures. He searches for and eliminates institutional obstacles and barriers to students' productivity. He holds tenaciously to the view that environment, rather than heredity, is a principal determinant of the student's in-school performance. In short, this type of administrator believes that the school can effect certain minimal results in the basic subjects for almost everyone and, furthermore, that it should. Activities which are less relevant to his notion of the school's central mission are regarded as frills and potential time-burners.

An administrator who assigns an individual self-actualizing function to the schools is apt to reflect a different emphasis in the leadership he gives to the school's program. He looks for evidence that teachers and other professional staff members are conscientiously searching for the special genius, talent, or strengths which each student has. He urges school personnel to structure numerous opportunities for students to explore a variety of interests, to determine whether they have the competencies required for successful performance in a number of fields, and to assess whether there is a fit between themselves and the modes of thought peculiar to a given field of study. He works for the removal of institutional requirements that prevent students from exploring their interests and talents in a range of future work roles.

Being concerned with creating an institution which is responsive to the needs and goals of students, the administrator also develops mechanisms for receiving and acting upon student-initiated ideas. He strives to nurture these ideas, and he does this in a variety of ways. He arranges for students to receive help in sharpening and clarifying their thoughts. He acts quickly and responsibly upon their requests. He seizes upon opportunities in the extracurriculum, as well as in the curriculum, for students to discover, to test, and to develop their abilities and their interests. The administrator consistently behaves in ways that mirror his beliefs and values concerning the feasibility and desirability of the schools' fulfilling a self-actualizing role.

ROLE OF THE EDUCATIONAL ADMINISTRATOR

School districts vary in the expectations which they hold for the occupants of administrative roles. One district might expect its administrators to give priority to the definition and determination of ultimate, intermediate, and proximate goals. Another district might feel that its administrators should spend the bulk of their time on matters relating to instruction. Still another district might expect its administrators to determine what educational services should be offered to the students and residents of the community, and to secure the resources which are needed to provide these services. No doubt, such organizationally prescribed duties and priorities influence an administrator's leadership style; however, the administrator's own personal values and beliefs concerning the role of the educational executive also shape the behavior he exhibits in the organization.

Some administrators feel that administrative roles should be geared to achieve specific organizational results. Although these administrators may share a similar set of values about what the role of the educational administrator should be, they may have dissimilar beliefs about how the desired results are achieved. One administrator may believe that satisfactory results are obtained by constantly letting people in the organization know what the actual results are and how they deviate from established standards. He, therefore, sets up procedures for gathering information about system performance, monitors what is happening, and sees that people are acting intelligently upon the information at their disposal. Another administrator may believe that he contributes to a realization of the intended outcomes by checking upon people to see that their behavior matches the expectations for their role. He sees that courses of study are being followed, that available instructional materials and resources are being used, and that recommended procedures are in effect.

A quite different role for the educational administrator is one that stresses his obligation to foster high staff morale. An administrator who feels that he should create a high level of *esprit de corps* within the organization may have any one of several beliefs about how morale is built and maintained. He may believe that people are most satisfied when they have a clear notion of what the organization's goals are and what procedures they are to follow in achieving these goals. The administrator seeks to build morale by delineating the relationship between himself and members of the work group, and by establishing well-defined patterns of organization, channels of communication, and methods of procedure.[20]

On the other hand, an administrator who values a role definition which stresses the morale of subordinates might believe that they develop *esprit de corps* when the administrator shows them consideration.[21] He does personal favors for his staff members and looks out for their welfare. He makes staff members feel at ease when talking with them. He spends time listening to his subordinates' problems and difficulties; he both empathizes and sympathizes.

There are countless other ways in which the educational administrator can define the role he should play in the organization, just as there are numerous beliefs about how the role can be effectively fulfilled. Our examples have merely served to illustrate the impact that personal values and beliefs can have on administrative behavior. Most administrators never bother to reflect on the values and beliefs which guide their behavior. However, a few examine them and agonize over the issues which an intensive examination inevitably raises. When not done in excess, the soul-searching activity can inform administrative action and can provide a significant basis for altering how the individual behaves in his role as an educational administrator.

CONCEPT OF SUCCESS

In understanding the emotional status of a person, his goals, and his social relations the importance of success and its stablemate, failure, has been universally recognized.[22] The expectation of success and the fear of failure orient an individual's behavior and outlook. People usually thrive on success—the sense of accomplishment and well-being which derives from the knowledge that a goal has been achieved. At the same time, they are inclined to wither when they experience failure—the sense of inadequacy which stems from the knowledge that a goal has not been attained. Consequently, how an administrator defines what constitutes success and failure and how he reacts to these two conditions should play a significant role in how he behaves. However, before examining these issues, let us look briefly at the more general phenomenon of success and failure.

Objective achievement does not necessarily correlate with the

20. Andrew W. Halpin, *Theory and Research in Administration* (New York: The Macmillan Co., 1966), pp. 81–130.

21. Ibid.

22. Kurt Lewin, "The Psychology of Success and Failure." In Harold J. Leavitt and Louis R. Pondy, eds., *Readings in Managerial Psychology* (Chicago: University of Chicago Press, 1964), pp. 25–31.

feeling of success or failure. "The same achievement can result once in the feeling of great success, another time in the feeling of complete failure."[23] Furthermore, the same achievement can be a success for one person and a failure for the other. For example, a high jumper may leap 6′4″. He may experience success for this feat at the beginning of the track season and experience failure if the performance is repeated near the end of the season. On the other hand, another high jumper may deem himself successful if he can jump consistently at this height. What determines whether an achievement is regarded as a success or as a failure depends upon the relationship between the achievement and the person's level of aspiration.

An individual's aspiration level is not fixed. Generally, the level is set quite low when an activity is done for the first time.[24] How the person performs in this situation affects his subsequent level of aspiration. If he succeeds, he is likely to raise his expectations. Similarly, if he fails, he is apt to reduce his level of aspiration. Although these responses to success and failure are typical ones, they by no means exhaust the various ways in which people react to either the congruence or the incongruence between their level of aspiration and their actual performance.

THE NEED FOR KNOWLEDGE OF RESULTS

People differ in their capacity to work without knowledge of results.[25] Some individuals can exercise discretion for long periods of time and be unaffected by a lack of information about the consequences of their actions. They are content to act with little or no knowledge of how well they are doing, and experience minimal discomfort when they have no idea of the quality of their performance. These people can function effectively for a lengthy time span without any evidence of success or failure. Other people function best when they have full knowledge of the wisdom of their actions. They bog down if they have no feedback about the consequences of what they have been doing. These people become unsettled unless there is some immediate knowledge of results. They are unable to sustain effective performance without fairly regular evidence that they are succeeding or failing.

Just as people vary in their capacities to work without knowledge of results, work roles vary in their potential for yielding information about success and failure. For instance, a researcher may decide to inquire into the antecedents and consequences of executive succession and wait three

23. Ibid., p. 26.

24. Ibid.

25. Elliott Jaques, *Measurement of Responsibility* (Cambridge, Mass.: Harvard University Press, 1956).

to five years before he learns whether he succeeded or failed in his undertaking. A personnel director may know inside a week or two whether he made a wise choice in the secretary he hired. A TV repairman who specializes in trouble-shooting may be called in to repair a perennially troublesome TV and locate the difficulty within an hour.

The myriad activities associated with the same work role also may differ in the opportunities which they afford for knowledge of results. For example, an administrator may know in less than an hour how well he has handled an irate parent. He may wait three to four months before he learns about the outcome of his negotiations with his teaching staff. He may even go a year or two without any really clear picture of how his Board of Education feels about the leadership he has been giving the school district.

When we combine the differences in the feedback potential of various roles and activities, with the differences among people in their desire for feedback, we can begin to get some idea of how these differences can influence what an administrator chooses to do in his organizational role. The administrator who wants to know in a relatively short period of time the results of his actions may occupy himself with routine activities which provide immediate tangible results. He may spend a great deal of time on clerical matters and attack personnel problems with gusto. He burdens himself with day-to-day matters that generate a quick payoff and neglects the intermediate and general planning activities which may give continuity to his actions over time. He does not labor over long-range goals which can offer no clear-cut evidence of attainment, nor does he set goals which entail long periods of uncertainty before success or failure can be assessed. The organization may suffer because this type of administrator is unwilling to introduce changes that involve a lengthy time span during which it is difficult to ascertain the extent of success or failure.

DEFINITION OF SUCCESS AND FAILURE

What results people regard as significant and the yardsticks they use to measure success and failure are as diverse as the line and staff roles pictured on an organizational chart. Some persons may judge the extent of their success by the speed with which they move up the district's administrative ladder and the rung they finally reach. This type of individual engages in GASing (Getting the Attention of his Superiors)[26] behavior and is extremely responsive to the criteria which he perceives that his superiors use in evaluating performance. These criteria guide the choices he makes about how to allocate his time and efforts. The GASer is likely to make heavy investments in what he deems to be high payoff activities and to slight responsibilities which his superiors regard as being less important.

26. Daniel E. Griffiths et al., "Teacher Mobility in New York City," *Educational Administration Quarterly,* 1, 1 (Winter 1965), pp. 15–31.

Other persons may view their success in terms of their progress through the profession; these people, unlike the GASers, are career-bound rather than place-bound.[27] To facilitate his mobility to more and more prestigious roles within the profession, the career-bound individual may behave in one of several ways. For example, a career-bound superintendent may strive to earn a reputation for doing some task very well; therefore, he specializes in such areas as public relations, buildings, curriculum, or finance. He concentrates his energies and efforts on his specialties and is both prepared and eager to move to a more prestigious superintendency which needs the unique strengths and competencies which he has.

Another career-bound superintendent may take pride in moving all phases of the educational program. This type usually stays in the same position for five or ten years before moving to a more highly regarded school district. He is concerned with upgrading the quality of all aspects of the district's operations and with maintaining a similar standard of quality for each and every aspect.

A third possible yardstick of success which an administrator might use is the opinions of subordinates. An administrator who records his success in these terms looks carefully at the satisfaction exhibited by his subordinates. He wants people to feel good about the organization as a place to work, and he attaches great importance to the feelings of success which they experience in doing their work. He, unlike the GASer, is willing to act as their advocate and does not hesitate to confront his superiors if he believes that the welfare of his subordinates is at stake. He is sensitive to the personal goals of his subordinates and is anxious to please them. Because of the priority he assigns to their feelings, he may even set aside the interests of the organization when these come into conflict with individual goals and concerns.

There are other administrators who measure their success by how smoothly the organization runs. These "efficiency experts" pride themselves on having a predictable, well-organized, and synchronized organizational environment. They carefully attend to details and derive immense satisfaction from bureaucratizing the organization's operations. They develop rules, systematize procedures, and elaborate policies. They experience a profound sense of accomplishment when people conform to regulations, when people know what is expected of them, and when things happen as planned and scheduled. Success for these administrators is the attainment of order and predictability in organizational life.

RESPONSE TO SUCCESS AND FAILURE

When administrators receive knowledge of the results they have achieved or failed to achieve, there are a number of possible responses they can

27. Richard O. Carlson, *Executive Succession and Organizational Change* (Chicago: Midwest Administration Center, The University of Chicago, 1962).

make. With the knowledge that aspiration has exceeded performance, one administrator might rid himself of the feeling of failure by rejecting his responsibility for the outcome. He might try to do this by attributing the disappointing result to bad luck or to someone having a grudge against him. If he arrives at the latter conclusion and firmly believes that he has been denied success as represented by his being bypassed for promotion, he may adapt by developing an "I don't care" attitude. He reduces his commitment to the organization and is content to do no more than is necessary to retain his present position in the organization.

Acceptance of personal responsibility for the failure is another possible response. An individual who blames himself for his failure may lower his self-confidence and self-esteem. If he comes to doubt his ability to achieve the results he desires, he may re-set his goals and become satisfied with a much lower level of performance. A fairly extreme reaction might be for the person to withdraw completely from situations where he risks experiencing success or failure.

Diminished self-confidence is not the necessary outcome of assuming personal responsibility for one's own failures, however. An individual might fail but continue to hold a positive view of himself. Consequently, he is able to react by studying the situation carefully in an effort to identify how his behavior contributed to the unsatisfactory outcome. He uses occasions of failure to develop self-awareness; the insight which he achieves may even add to the confidence that he shows when he approaches his next task.

People's responses to success are also varied. One person might be inclined to set an unrealistic and unattainable goal for himself subsequently. His sense of accomplishment may prompt him to overestimate his capacities. His aspiration level soars in consequence and destines him to failure. Another individual might attribute his success to good fortune and, as a result, act conservatively in the goals he sets because the law of averages will be against him in the future. Still another person might be spurred to analyze what led to his success in the expectation that he might be able to repeat the performance or to reach a slightly higher goal if he thoroughly understands the ingredients of his present success.

SUMMARY

In essence, we have said that there are many factors, both within and without the person, which affect behavior. Our primary concern has been with the inner factors which may be altered by the individual as he becomes aware of the personal bases for his actions. We intended for this chapter to stimulate the reader to think about himself and to consider how his perceptions of others, his perception of self, his values and beliefs, and his concept of success guide and shape his behavior. The conscientious student of administration will continue his personal assessment while on the job, and will strive to develop the self-awareness necessary to perform effectively in his administrative role.

SUGGESTED ACTIVITIES

1. Interview several administrators and try to determine how they judge their success, whom they regard as the people who are in the best position to judge their success, and the reasons for these perceptions.
2. Read one of the cases in the series prepared by the University Council for Educational Administration[28] and analyze the administrator's behavior in terms of some of the ideas contained in this chapter.
3. Go with an administrator (principal, supervisor, or superintendent), and observe his behavior in all the activities in which he is engaged in fulfilling his professional responsibilities for the day. Try to analyze his behavior in terms of the assumptions, values, and beliefs that seem to underlie his behavior.
4. Observe an administrator in a staff meeting, a meeting of the board of education, or a meeting of his administrative advisory council. From what he does, interpret his view of the role of authority and the role of the educational administrator. Give reasons for your interpretation.
5. Think of an instance in which you have disagreed with the action of the administrator of your school. Describe the situation briefly, tell what the administrator did, tell what you would have done, and try to indicate the nature of the inner factors which you believe lie behind the two different kinds of behavior.

SELECTED READINGS

Allport, Gordon W. *Pattern and Growth in Personality.* New York: Holt, Rinehart & Winston, 1961.

Argyris, Chris. *Personality and Organization.* New York: Harper & Row, 1957.

Blake, Robert R., and Mouton, Jane S. *The Managerial Grid.* Houston, Texas: Gulf Publishing Co., 1964.

Bridges, Edwin M. "Personal Success as a Determinant of Managerial Style." In Kenneth E. McIntyre, ed. *The Principalship in the 1970's.* Austin: University of Texas Press, 1971, pp. 13–24.

Cartwright, Dorwin, ed. *Field Theory in Social Science.* New York: Harper & Row, 1951.

28. Available through the University Council for Educational Administration, 22 Woodruff Ave., Columbus, Ohio 43210.

Christie, R., and Geis, F. L., eds. *Studies in Machiavellianism.* New York: Academic Press, 1970.

Heider, Fritz. *The Psychology of Interpersonal Relations.* New York: Wiley, 1958.

Jones, Edward E., and Davis, Keith E. "From Acts to Dispositions." In Leonard Berkowitz, ed. *Advances in Experimental Social Psychology.* New York: Academic Press, 1965, pp. 220–266.

McGregor, Douglas. *The Human Side of Enterprise.* New York: McGraw-Hill, 1960.

Ohmann, O. A. "Skyhooks," *Harvard Business Review* 48, 1 (January-February 1970), pp. 4–22.

Wrightsman, Lawrence S. *Social Psychology in the Seventies.* Monterey, Calif.: Brooks-Cole Publishing Company, 1972.

12

CHOOSING EDUCATIONAL ADMINISTRATION AS A CAREER

In this chapter we shall focus on the decision to become an educational administrator and on some of the issues which are relevant to this career choice. While the ideas we set forth may seem more useful to one who has just begun to consider administration as a possible career, the person who has already given serious thought to what his life work will be, can also benefit from our discussion. The discussion is intended to assist anyone who is deciding whether to commit himself to a career in educational administration, to remain in his current post, or to seek another type of educational position.

Although a person may wish to ponder such decisions indefinitely in order to reduce the risk of making an unwise choice, postponement of commitment can create problems for one who eventually decides to become an educational administrator. In the first place, delay can hinder a person's advancement within the profession. For most administrators the route to a top-level administrative post proceeds through several positions of lesser responsibility. The older a person is before he starts in an administrative position, the fewer opportunities he will receive to realize his full potential.

Secondly, administrative positions currently require more formal education of their incumbents than was once the case. It is not at all unusual today to find vacancy notices for superintendencies and for high school principalships which state that preference will be given to the holders of a doctor's degree. Acquiring formal education takes time. Many universities discourage students from undertaking a doctoral program after they reach the age of forty. Additionally, few men and women who have reached that age can afford the educational costs and the loss of income which are entailed in full-time graduate study. While exceptions could be pointed out, the decision to start a doctoral program in educational administration is probably best made before a person reaches the age of thirty.

A third problem generated by procrastination in the career decision-making process is the delay it causes in making and following a plan to implement the decision. Ordinarily, there are many steps required between making a decision and reaching the point dictated by that choice. These steps need to be planned carefully if the ultimate goal is to be reached. Whether or not a person decides to enter administration, he does have a future ahead of him. The longer a person takes in deciding what he wants this future to be, the less future remains for him to realize his aims.

As a person attempts to make a decision about his future in educational administration, he should not restrict the scope of his choices to one position—for example, the city superintendency. Unfortunately, many writers use the terms *educational administration* and *superintendency* as if the latter were all-inclusive of the former. Such a concept produces an unnecessarily limited view of administration and forces unrealistic choices upon anyone who thinks that he wants to be an administrator but is certain he does not want to be a superintendent.

To illustrate the wide variety of opportunities in the profession of educational administration, we will describe in the next section a number of different types of positions and will highlight their functions. Although our overview will tend to emphasize administrative positions in public school systems, we will pay some attention to opportunities in higher education and other educational agencies. Following our discussion of the available positions, we will examine what research has to say about the requisite competencies and traits for some of these administrative posts, particularly the superintendency and the school principalship. The chapter will close with a portrayal of the intrinsic and extrinsic rewards and the stresses and the strains of headship.

POSITIONS AVAILABLE

Although there is some evidence that the number of administrative positions in this country is declining, there remain thousands of such positions. The largest employer is the public school system. More people are employed in the school principalship than in any other administrative role.

In 1971–72, there were 97,211 principals and assistant principals in public schools.[1] In addition there were 37,495 positions in which the titles consultant or supervisor of instruction were used.[2] As one would expect, there is much less room at the top, with the number of local district superintendents at 14,848 in 1970.[3] Assisting the chief executive in the running of the school system are countless central office administrators functioning between the superintendent and the building principal. Administrative opportunities also exist outside of local public school systems; there are positions in state educational agencies, the United States Office of Education, and institutions of higher education as well as in private schools and the business world. Regrettably, there are no reliable estimates on the number of these positions.

As we begin to describe the administrative positions mentioned in the preceding paragraph, it seems important to indicate that the positions and functions as we picture them are under careful study and review by both educational practitioners and theorists.[4] The prospective administrator finds himself at a point in time where one of his crucial tasks will be the restructuring of the organization and administration of education. His viewpoints, then, should not be "frozen" by a description of what exists.

PRINCIPALSHIPS

Description. The principal is the chief administrative officer of an attendance unit in a school system. Such an attendance unit may be an elementary school, a junior high school, a senior high school, or some combination of these, according to the organization of the school district. In some cases, the administrative head of a junior college is referred to as a principal, but this usage is not common. The common pattern in describing the principalship is to speak of elementary school, middle school, or secondary school principalships. The junior high school is usually considered to be a secondary school, although somewhat inaccurately. In some states, a junior high school principal may hold either a secondary or an elementary school principal's certificate; in others, the required certificate depends upon whether the junior high school is a departmentalized school (secondary school) or consists primarily of self-contained classrooms (elementary school); and in still others, a junior high school principal's certificate is issued.

---

1. National Center for Education Statistics, *Digest of Education Statistics,* 1974. (Washington, D.C.: U.S. Government Printing Office, 1975), p. 46.

2. Ibid.

3. Steven J. Knezevich, ed., *The American School Superintendency* (Arlington, Va.: AASA, 1971).

4. For example, see Donald A. Erickson, "Forces for Change in the Principalship," *Elementary School Journal* 65 (November 1964): 57–64, and "Chautauqua '74, The Remaking of the Principalship," *National Elementary Principal* vol. 53, no. 5 (July-August 1974).

In the larger school systems, the meaning of the term "principal" is quite clear. But in smaller school systems, usage often leads to confusion between principalships and superintendencies. It is often true that the administrator in a small school faces the difficult task of attempting to perform three roles—those of teacher, principal, and superintendent. The great difficulties of such a task are often not fully appreciated. For the purposes of this discussion, a principal is considered to be the executive officer of an attendance unit, but not the executive officer of an administrative unit. He does not, for example, have responsibilities as the professional executive officer of a board of education. In several states, the term "supervising principal" is used to describe what is essentially a superintendent. For our purpose, we would not consider this position a principalship.

Functions. Most educators would agree that the principal's basic responsibility should be directing the educational program of the school he heads. To fulfill this responsibility the principal should engage in a variety of activities. He should work with teachers in the appraisal and improvement of the educational program. He should work with the superintendent of schools to secure staff, material, and facilities for this program. He should work with his community to determine its specific educational needs and the extent to which the school is meeting these needs.

How principals actually spend their time on the job does not match perfectly with the prescribed role priorities, however. For example, elementary school principals typically spend 13 percent of their work week on routine clerical tasks processing records and reports. These same principals devote 30 percent of their time to the supervision and coordination of instruction and another 30 percent to administration—i.e., making management decisions, formulating rules, maintaining communication with other schools and the central office, and coordinating activities of pupils and teachers. Less than 7 percent of the elementary school principals' work week involves activities with parents, laymen, and civic groups. Only about half of the principals report involvement in the selection of instructional materials; one-third have nothing to say in the selection of teachers.[5] Principals of junior and senior high schools describe the distribution of time among these various activities in much the same terms.[6] The one major difference is that secondary school principals report spending considerable time on disciplinary matters.

Principals at all three levels devote a great deal of time to their

5. Department of Elementary School Principals, *The Elementary School Principalship in 1968* (Washington, D.C.: Department of Elementary School Principals, National Education Association, 1968).

6. See Donald A. Rock and John K. Hemphill, *Report of the Junior High-School Principalship* (Washington, D.C.: The National Association of Secondary School Principals, 1966) and John K. Hemphill, James M. Richards, and Richard E. Peterson, *Report of the Senior High-School Principalship* (Washington, D.C.: The National Association of Secondary-School Principals, 1965).

jobs. The typical principal works from fifty to fifty-four hours per week at school and in school-related activities. At the senior high school level, 29 percent of the principals report that they work more than sixty hours per week. The percentage drops to 15 percent for junior high school principals and to 2 percent for elementary school heads. Less than 5 percent of all principals work less than forty hours weekly.[7]

SUPERVISORY POSITIONS

Description. The supervisor in a local school district is usually attached to the central staff of a school system rather than assigned to a single building. Supervisors are also found as staff members in intermediate units serving a number of smaller districts, and, in many states, certain supervisors of specialized types of instruction are members of a state department of education rather than staff members in intermediate or local administrative units. Supervisors are usually classified in one of several ways. It is common to speak of elementary school or secondary school supervisors. Within these classifications are found general supervisors and special supervisors; the latter deal with special subject matter areas, while the former deal with more general questions of methods and materials. It is thus likely that a larger school system will have one or more general elementary supervisors and general secondary supervisors, as well as several special supervisors.

Functions. The supervisor plays a special role in the program for the improvement of instruction. Lucio and McNeil state that supervision is concerned with the determination of ends to be attained, the design of procedures for effecting the ends, and the assessment of results.[8] In meeting this function, supervisors perform a number of activities. Included among these are individual classroom visits and teachers' conferences; evaluating and selecting books and other instructional materials which can subsequently be recommended to individual teachers or to groups of teachers for use; helping individual teachers or groups of teachers develop resource or teaching units; organizing and working with groups in curriculum development or improvement programs; organizing and directing conferences or workshops for teachers; assisting individual teachers or groups of teachers in the administration of tests and the interpretation and use of test data; preparing or assisting in the preparation of manuals and bulletins to aid teachers in instruction; assisting in the development and use of programs

7. Estimate based on data from the three national studies of the principalship. See Department of Elementary School Principals, *School Principalship, 1968;* Rock and Hemphill, *Junior High-School Principalship;* and Hemphill et al., *Senior High-School Principalship.*

8. William H. Lucio and John D. McNeil, *Supervision: A Synthesis of Thought and Action* (New York: McGraw-Hill, 1969), p. 46.

for the general evaluation of a school program or phases of the program; conducting demonstration teaching classes; performing as a consultant for local faculties as they study instructional problems; or assisting in the development of plans for reporting pupil progress to parents.[9] Even though this list is by no means exhaustive, it indicates the scope of the activities that may fall within the duties of the supervisor.

While we would not attempt to discuss in detail here the function of the supervisor, it is important to mention that ability in getting along with people is a vital asset. Often the supervisor must inspire teachers who are self-satisfied to strike for improvement. At times the supervisor must overcome a teacher's opinion that he is a "central office inspector." Not only must the supervisor be knowledgeable in the field of general instruction and perhaps also in special subject matter areas such as art or music, but he must have the ability to work with people so that this knowledge can be put to use in the improvement of instruction. Skills in group processes, individual conferences, and general human relations are important parts of a supervisor's equipment.

CENTRAL OFFICE POSITIONS

Description. In speaking of central office positions, we are referring to those positions in a school system which are concerned more with some phase of the overall operation of the system than with the operation of a single attendance unit within the system. While it is somewhat difficult to generalize on the exact titles or descriptions of these positions as found throughout the country, certain positions are common. Some of the more common positions include administrative assistant to the superintendent, assistant superintendent for instruction, assistant superintendent for business, assistant superintendent for staff personnel, assistant superintendent for pupil personnel services, director of buildings and grounds, and director of planning.[10] Obviously, only the largest system would have all of these positions on a full-time basis. In many cases, for example, an assistant superintendent for instruction would fulfill the functions covered by such additional positions as director of elementary education, director of secondary education, and director of curriculum. It should also be noted that there is usually a hierarchy in central office positions. A number of directors responsible for various phases of the instructional program would be under the immediate direction of the assistant superintendent for instruction.

Functions. The central office administrative staff is necessitated by at least two major facts. In the first place, even a small school system is a

---

9. For a comprehensive list of supervisory activities, see Lucio and McNeil, *Supervision.*

10. See C. Arnold Anderson and Mary Jean Bowman, "Theoretical Considerations in Educational Planning." In Don Adams, *Educational Planning* (Syracuse, N.Y.: Syracuse University Press, 1964).

complex operation. One man cannot be everywhere and do everything involved in the overall administration of such a system. For this reason, he must have the help such a staff provides. Secondly, studies of administration have long shown that the top administrator in an organization cannot deal effectively on a direct and continuous basis with every other member of the organization. We have mentioned earlier the concept of span of control[11] and indicated that many people feel that the chief administrator should have a limited number of people reporting directly to him. The implementation of this concept requires a central staff through which the great number of people in an organization can report indirectly to the chief administrator.

One major function of central office staff members is the direction of various parts of the school organization. In order, however, that the school system as a whole operate as an integrated unit, this same staff must assist in the equally important task of coordinating these various parts of the organization. Often the major administrative assistants in a larger school system form a kind of cabinet which works with the superintendent on problems of coordination as well as on other aspects of administration. In somewhat smaller school systems, this same function is performed by the building principals.

Members of the central office staff also function as advisers to the superintendent on matters relating to their special fields of competency. Because the staff members are dealing only with segments of the total school system, they have opportunities to keep abreast of trends, techniques, skills, needs, and content in their respective areas which are not possible for the superintendent. Effective superintendents must become effective generalists and rely upon central staff members for specialized advice.

SCHOOL DISTRICT SUPERINTENDENT

Description. Probably little needs to be said to define the position of school district superintendent. We find in practice, however, that there are differences in terminology even in listing this position. We define a school district superintendent as the chief administrative officer of an administrative unit that operates public schools. He is directly responsible to a local board of education, although there are some few states where he is elected rather than appointed by the board of education. He is the executive officer of the local board of education.

While the common term for such a person is "superintendent of schools," certain variations are found, particularly in rural school districts. In some cases, and in terms of our definition presented above, people with

11. For a review of the theoretical and empirical work concerned with "span of control," see Robert J. House and John B. Miner, "Merging Management and Behavioral Theory: The Interaction Between Span of Control and Group Size," *Administrative Science Quarterly* 14, 3 (September 1969): 451–465.

the following titles are actually superintendents: supervising principal, local executive, general superintendent, local superintendent, and superintendent of instruction. So long as the title describes a person who meets the criteria implied by our earlier definition, we consider the position to be that of a school district superintendent, now commonly known as the superintendent of schools.

Functions. The major functions of the district school superintendent are to help define and clarify the purpose and direction of the school system, to establish and maintain an organization to work at these purposes, and to secure and allocate resources needed by the organization to achieve these purposes. While the traditional view is that the superintendent is a mere implementor of school board policies, in the real world the superintendent and board of education function more nearly as partners in the establishment of policy. Most boards seek advice from their superintendent on policy questions.[12]

Although the superintendent plays an important role in the definition and clarification of direction, he occupies an even more central role in the establishment and maintenance of the organization. The superintendent has considerable discretion in how school personnel are deployed to get the job done. In maintaining the staff the superintendent stimulates, challenges, rewards, and creates the conviction that the organization has a worthy purpose that is fully capable of being achieved.

To support the school system as it strives to attain its purposes, the superintendent is expected to assume a major role in securing and allocating resources. His efforts to secure funds frequently lead to active involvement at local, state, and federal levels of government. Perennially faced with a shortage of money the superintendent has the heavy burden of allocating the available financial resources to promote the greatest educational benefit for pupils. With increasing frequency the superintendent is called upon to answer questions such as: Should an additional $50 per child be spent in reducing class size, in acquiring more instructional equipment, in providing a mathematics supervisor for each building, or in raising teachers' salaries?

STATE EDUCATIONAL AGENCIES

Description. The state, as we mentioned earlier, is the governmental unit in our country that is responsible for the development and general control of systems of public schools. While states do not usually operate schools, there are a number of administrative positions associated with state edu-

---

12. This section on functions of the superintendent is based on Roald F. Campbell, "The Changing Role of the Superintendent," *Contemporary Education,* 39, 6 (May 1968): 249–254.

cational agencies. State departments of education, as these state agencies are most commonly known, are under the direct administrative control of a professional educator. This officer usually has the title of state superintendent of public instruction and is responsible to a governing board. Under the superintendent are a number of divisions, each of which is headed by a director. Some typical divisions in state departments of education are certification, vocational education, federal programs, research, and school plant. These major divisions are further subdivided into branches, with lower level administrators being responsible for the activities of each branch.

Functions. The broad functions of state departments may be classified under five principal headings: operational, regulatory, service, developmental, and public support and cooperation.[13] Operational functions refer to those activities in which the state department directly administers schools and services. An example is the operation of special schools for the blind, the deaf, and the otherwise handicapped. The administration of such services is largely a twentieth-century addition to the duties of state departments.

According to state and federal statutes, state departments must regulate many aspects of the programs, plants, and administrative procedures of local districts. These regulatory activities involve systematic monitoring of local school districts to determine their conformance to certain minimum standards and imposing penalties and sanctions whenever these standards are not being met.

Service activities of the department, on the other hand, entail the dissemination of expertise to the local schools. The majority of service activities are geared toward the improvement of instruction. Some specific examples of service activities are preparation of curriculum materials, consultation on new instructional approaches and technology, and advice on legal aspects of school system operation.

Developmental functions center around long-range planning and staff improvement. Planning necessitates making an assessment of the long-range needs of local schools, while staff improvement relates both to the recruitment of talent and the extension of the capabilities of existing personnel.

A final set of state department functions is concerned with securing the support and cooperation of the general public and of subsections within the public. Support is needed to maintain the numerous current activities and to launch new projects. Support activities include communication through the mass media, political activities with the legislature and governor, relations with the federal government, and intrastate cooperation and articulation.

---

13. This section on functions of state agencies is drawn from Roald F. Campbell, Gerald E. Sroufe, and Donald H. Layton, *Strengthening State Departments of Education* (Chicago: The Midwest Administration Center, University of Chicago, 1967).

UNITED STATES OFFICE OF EDUCATION

While considering governmental service and educational administration, it is important to devote some attention to educational administration at the federal government level. The United States Office of Education is one of several agencies in the Department of Health, Education and Welfare. It is under the leadership of the United States Commissioner of Education, who serves directly under the Secretary of Health, Education and Welfare. The United States Office of Education is organized in divisions, each one under the direction of an assistant commissioner. The divisions are organized in branches, each of which is headed by a director. Within some branches there are also bureau chiefs. The Commissioner is an appointive officer, while the remaining personnel in the Office are wholly or partially under Civil Service.

The primary function of the Office of Education is to marshal resources on a national scale for the improvement of public education in the nation. In addition, the Office provides valuable consultative service as well as conducting many statistical studies to provide insight into national educational trends. The Office has few regulatory functions, in keeping with the established doctrine that public education is a state matter.

There are, however, a variety of operational responsibilities within the functions of the Office. Beginning with the passage of the National Defense Education Act, the participation of the federal government in education has grown rapidly and extensively, culminating in the passage of the Elementary-Secondary Education Act of 1965 (PL 89–10), which represents the greatest single commitment ever made by the federal government for the support of education. This legislation, coupled with the massive Higher Education Facilities Assistance Act passed in 1964 and the Higher Education Act of 1965, has placed great responsibilities and major operational functions within the U.S. Office of Education.

ADMINISTRATION IN HIGHER EDUCATION

There are many educational administration positions in higher education. It should be noted, however, that administrators in higher education are not drawn only from the ranks of those we have been calling educational administrators. It is unlikely, for example, that the dean of a college of commerce would be selected from the field of educational administration, even though his position would be an administrative position in an educational undertaking. Those to whom this text has been primarily addressed might more logically aspire in higher education to one of the following positions: chairman, department of education; director, school of education; dean, college of education; registrar, college or university; and president, college or university.

In addition, there are many administrative positions in junior colleges which are well within the province of educational administration. Some junior colleges are organized under the control of local boards of education and offer positions somewhat similar to those of a superintendent or of a principal. Other junior colleges are organized more in terms of college or university structure under the direction of a board of trustees. In this case, junior college administrative positions may be similar to college deanships or presidencies.

PROFESSORSHIPS

One final kind of position is available to the person interested in educational administration. This position involves the preparation of educational administrators through service as a professor in an institution conducting such a program of preparation. Although this position is not in itself an administrative position, it is a position for which administrators might aim.

The professor of educational administration has unique opportunities to engage in the three activities commonly considered a part of university teaching: instruction, research, and service.[14] He is, first of all, a teacher who is concerned with developing the prospective administrator's skills, attitudes, and values. He is, secondly, a researcher who is concerned with the advancement of knowledge about the organization and administration of schools. Finally, he provides service to the field. Because of continuing opportunities in research and study which are not ordinarily available to the practicing administrator, the professor can be of assistance to practicing administrators in helping them develop new approaches to the solution of administrative problems.

REQUISITE COMPETENCIES AND TRAITS

As our preceding discussion of available administrative positions suggests, there are numerous opportunities for those who are interested in a career in educational administration. Unfortunately, however, not everyone who aspires to be an administrator is selected to be one; nor is everyone who is chosen to hold an administrative post destined to become a successful administrator. Confronted with these harsh realities, the administrative aspirant undoubtedly wants to know what research has to say about the competencies and traits which are related to appointment as an educational administrator and to success in the job once he is appointed.

For purposes of our discussion, we will distinguish between per-

14. See Roald F. Campbell and L. Jackson Newell, *A Study of Professors of Educational Administration* (Columbus, Ohio: University Council for Educational Administration, 1973).

sonal and prestige traits. Personal traits are those individual attributes, qualities, or characteristics which are innate and not subject to environmental influence—for example, sex and age. Prestige traits, on the other hand, are those qualities or characteristics which an individual acquires through affiliation with an institution or a formal organization. Experience as a teacher, degree held, and field of graduate work are examples of prestige traits.

Competencies, unlike traits, refer to skills and abilities that can be developed. The emphasis is on what an individual can do and accomplish rather than on what personal and prestige traits he possesses. One specialist in administration maintains that effective administration depends upon three basic competencies or skills: technical, human, and conceptual.[15] Technical skill involves specialized knowledge and facility in the use of specific tools and techniques. Human skill is primarily concerned with building cooperative effort within the human organization the administrator leads. Conceptual skill relates to recognizing the interrelationships of the various situational factors and to taking that action which achieves the maximum good for the total organization.

WHO GETS APPOINTED?

Personal traits. There is little doubt that educational administration is a profession dominated by males. Although principals and superintendents are drawn almost exclusively from the teaching ranks and there are more females than males in the teaching force, the percentage of administrators who are female is relatively small (see Table 12–1). Only in the elementary principalship is there any sizable proportion of women; even here the percentage is steadily declining. In 1928, 55 percent of the elementary principals were women; forty years later, the figure was only 22 percent (see Figure 12–1). Regrettably, the data do not allow us to answer this important question: Do the percentages reflect less of an interest in administration by women than men? Or, do the percentages reflect a preference of employing officials for male administrators?

Age is another personal trait which has relevance to appointment as an educational administrator. Individuals are most likely to be appointed to their first principalship between the ages of 30 and 34. Few people become principals before age 25. For example, only 11 percent of the senior high school principals are under 25 years of age at the time of their first appointment.[16] After a person reaches the age of 45, the probability of selection for a principal's post declines. Less than 8 percent of the senior high school principals are older than 45[17] when they are appointed to their

15. Robert L. Katz, "Skills of an Effective Administrator," *Harvard Business Review* 33, 1 (January-February 1955): 33–42.
16. Hemphill, Richards, and Peterson, *Senior High-School Principalship.*
17. Ibid.

TABLE 12–1 Sex of Administrator by Type of Position Including Nature of Sample and Year Reported

POSITION	MALE	FEMALE	NATURE OF SAMPLE	YEAR
Elementary Principal	77.6%	22.4%	National	1968[a]
Junior High Principal	96.0%	4.0%	National	1966[b]
Senior High Principal	98.0%	2.0%	National	1965[c]
Superintendent	100.0%	—	National	1960[d]
	98.0%	2.0%	Statewide (California)	1966[e]
	98.9%	1.1%	National	1970[f]

[a] Department of Elementary School Principals, *School Principalship,* 1968.

[b] Rock and Hemphill, *Junior High-School Principalship.*

[c] Hemphill, Richards, and Peterson, *Senior High-School Principalship.*

[d] American Association of School Administrators, *Professional Administrators for America's Schools* (Washington, D.C.: The Association, a department of the National Education Association, 1960).

[e] William C. Schutz, *Procedures for Identifying Persons with Potential for Public School Administrative Positions* (Berkeley, Calif.: University of California, Cooperative Research Project No. 1076, 1966).

[f] Stephen J. Knezevich, ed., *The American School Superintendent* (Washington, D.C.: American Association of School Administrators, 1971).

first principalship, while the figure is approximately 16 percent for elementary principals.[18] There are some sex differences, however. Men are far more likely than women to be appointed before age 35 (67 percent v. 39 percent).[19] After age 35, a woman has a greater likelihood of being appointed than a man does. Age also is a factor in appointment to the superintendency; when one reaches 50, the probability of becoming a superintendent is quite low.[20]

	1928	1948	1958	1968
Men	45%	59%	62%	78%
Women	55%	41%	38%	22%

Source: Department of Elementary School Principals, *School Principalship,* 1968.

Figure 12–1 Sex of elementary principals for the period 1928–1968.

PRESTIGE TRAITS

Graduate work leading to an advanced degree is an imperative for those who aspire to appointment as educational administrators. More than 90 percent of the principals and superintendents in this country have at least

18. Department of Elementary School Principals, *School Principalship,* 1968.
19. Ibid.
20. Knezevich, *The American School Superintendent.*

a master's degree. Moreover, the trend is toward even higher levels of formal education. For example, in 1928 only 16 percent of the elementary principals had a master's; twenty years later the percentage had climbed to 67 percent; by 1958 the figure was 82 percent; and today it is 90 percent.[21] The doctorate is more apt to be held by superintendents (29 percent) than by principals (approximately 3 percent). As the size of the district increases, there is a correspondingly higher probability that the superintendent will need a doctor's degree. In cities with more than 100,000 population the figure is 86 percent.[22]

The field in which the graduate work is taken is most likely to be educational administration and supervision. Approximately 70 percent of all principals and superintendents have selected educational administration as their major field of concentration. Few administrators, less than 4 percent to be exact, have majored at the graduate level in one of the traditional academic subjects (English, mathematics, science, or social studies).

In addition to possessing an advanced degree with work concentrated in educational administration and supervision, the administrator is likely to have taught either at the elementary or secondary levels. The average junior high and senior high school principal has taught from seven to nine years,[23] while the average elementary principal has six years of classroom teaching experience.[24] Ninety-nine percent of the junior high school principals have taught for at least one year[25]; the percentage for senior high school principals is quite similar (98 percent).[26] The typical woman elementary school principal has had three times as much experience in the classroom as has her male counterpart.

The experience picture is somewhat different for the superintendency, though not markedly so. Nearly 96 percent of the superintendents have had teaching experience. The setting for this experience is far more likely to have been at the secondary rather than at the elementary level. Most superintendents (71 percent) have also served as building principals.[27]

Competencies. Researchers have virtually ignored descriptive data dealing with the relationship between specific administrative competencies and appointment to different types of administrative positions. If some minimal level of performance in any given category of competencies is demanded for appointment to an administrative position, the research literature that we have examined provides no clue as to what the minimal levels might be. The fact that the literature is silent on this issue does not mean, however,

21. Department of Elementary School Principals, *School Principalship,* 1968.
22. Knezevich, *The American School Superintendent.*
23. Rock and Hemphill, *Junior High-School Principalship;* Hemphill, Richards, and Peterson, *Senior High-School Principalship.*
24. Department of Elementary School Principals, *School Principalship,* 1968.
25. Rock and Hemphill, *Junior High-School Principalship.*
26. Hemphill, Richards, and Peterson, *Senior High-School Principalship.*
27. Knezevich, *The American School Superintendent.*

that school districts take no steps to ascertain the kinds and levels of competencies which potential candidates possess.

Some districts may require some minimal level of performance on a test of professional knowledge (the *School Administration and Supervision* section of the National Teacher Examinations). Other districts may arrange for candidates to exhibit certain competencies by reacting to case studies and by indicating how they would handle different kinds of administrative problems posed by an interviewing committee. Still other districts may seek to assess administrative competencies by introducing candidates to a mythical school district through the use of films, filmstrips, printed materials, and recordings. After this introduction, the candidates receive items which are typically found in an administrator's in-basket. The responses of the candidates are judged to determine how well the problems have been handled.

WHO SUCCEEDS?

How to judge success in administration is a persistent problem for both researchers and employing officials. Interest in the problem stems from a desire to help individuals make wise career choices and a wish to increase the number of sound personnel decisions which are made by institutions. Three unresolved issues have made the judging of success problematic:

1. The criteria to be used.
2. The kind of evidence to be gathered to establish the extent to which the criteria have been met.
3. The priority to be assigned to each criterion.

For the most part, success in administration has been determined by using effectiveness ratings provided by the administrator's superiors or subordinates. Seldom are the criteria and the importance which is attached to those criteria made explicit. With these caveats in mind, let us now turn to the results of the studies which have been undertaken to differentiate between successful and unsuccessful administrators.

Personal traits. In our earlier discussion of *appointment* to administrative roles, we noted that sex has utility as a predictive factor; significantly more men than women occupy administrative posts. When sex is related to success in an administrative role, however, it has little value in differentiating between successful and unsuccessful administrators. Studies of the principalship by Hemphill et al.[28]; Lipham[29]; and Schutz[30] show that males

28. John K. Hemphill, Daniel E. Griffiths, and Norman Frederiksen, *Administrative Performance and Personality* (New York: Teachers College, Columbia University, 1962).

29. James M. Lipham, "Personal Variables of Effective Administrators," *Administrator's Notebook* 9, 1 (September 1960).

30. Schutz, *Procedures for Identifying Persons with Potential.*

and females do not differ in how they are rated by either superiors or subordinates. In a major study of the elementary principalship, Gross and Herriott reported that sex was unrelated to Executive Professional Leadership—i.e., efforts by the principal to upgrade the performance of his staff.[31]

The evidence regarding age of the principal is less clear. Hemphill et al., and Lipham found little relationship between age and successful performance of the principal's duties. Gross and Herriott, on the other hand, concluded that older principals provide less Executive Professional Leadership than younger ones do. Gross and Herriott also observed a trend which suggests that the younger a principal is at the time of his first appointment to the principalship, the stronger his subsequent professional leadership is likely to be.

Prestige traits. Most studies show no relationship between amount of educational training and subsequent success as an administrator. Four different measures of educational preparation apparently are unrelated to judged effectiveness: (1) number of years spent in college,[32] (2) number of years devoted to graduate study,[33] (3) number of hours taken in undergraduate education,[34] and (4) number of hours in graduate education courses.[35] A fifth measure, the total number of courses in educational administration, is related to the exercise of Executive Professional Leadership; moreover, the relationship is negative. Principals with less extensive formal preparation in the field of educational administration exhibit greater professional leadership.[36] Unfortunately, none of these studies concentrated on the nature of the training received or considered qualitative differences among training programs.

Teaching experience, much like training, bears no relationship to success as an administrator when simple forms of statistical analysis are used, and no effort is made to control for the effects of other variables. Hemphill et al.; Lipham; and Gross and Herriott found that the amount of teaching experience a principal has is unrelated to his success in the principalship. Using a much more complicated type of statistical analysis, which is designed to detect a relationship masked by the influence of other important variables, Schutz uncovered a negative relationship between teaching experience and success as a principal. In fact, total experience as a classroom teacher was more negatively related to administrative effectiveness than any other variable studied.

31. Neal Gross and Robert E. Herriott, *Staff Leadership in Public Schools* (New York: Wiley, 1965).

32. Hemphill, Griffiths, and Frederiksen, *Administrative Performance and Personality.*

33. Lipham, "Personal Variables of Effective Administrators."

34. Gross and Herriott, *Staff Leadership in Public Schools.*

35. Ibid.

36. Ibid.

Competencies. Measures of technical and professional knowledge generally show little or no relationship to success on the job; when a relationship is reported, it is a very weak one. Schutz found that mastery of the content of educational administration—namely, school law, finance, personnel, and school facilities—was unrelated to administrative success either as a principal or superintendent. On the other hand, the study by Hemphill et al., of elementary principals uncovered a moderate, positive relationship between professional knowledge and ratings by superiors.

SITUATIONAL CORRELATES

Research in the field of educational administration, as well as in the fields of business and public administration, points to success as being in large part a function of situational circumstances.[37] An individual who is successful as an administrator in one type of situation may be a dismal failure in another. Research which has examined the correlates of success by taking into account the possible interaction between characteristics of the individual and the institutional setting has yielded somewhat more informative results than research which has focused solely on the individual. Schutz, for example, using various measures of school district type, was able to increase the predictive power of personal traits and competencies when type of district was introduced into his analyses. Furthermore, the traits and competencies associated with success differed among district types. Unfortunately, studies of success that consider individual and institutional factors simultaneously are rare.

REWARDS

Rational decision making involves a consideration of the costs and benefits that may follow from taking a particular course of action. If the decision to become an educational administrator is to be a rational one, then the individual must balance the costs against the benefits before he makes his final choice. Costs in the form of stresses and strains are the subject of the next section of this chapter. Our current concern is with the benefits—the extrinsic and intrinsic rewards associated with headship. For purposes of our discussion, we will treat extrinsic rewards solely in terms of tangible financial earnings; intrinsic rewards, on the other hand, will be viewed in terms of the gratifications derived from performing administrative tasks and from having chosen educational administration as a career.[38]

37. R. M. Stogdill, "Personal Factors Associated with Leadership: A Survey of the Literature," *Journal of Psychology* 25 (January 1948), p. 64.

38. The definition of intrinsic rewards is drawn from Neal Gross and David A. Napior, *The Job and Career Satisfaction of Men School Principals* (Cambridge, Mass.: Harvard University, Graduate School of Education, Cooperative Research Project No. 2536, 1967).

EXTRINSIC REWARDS

Current salary situation. Not surprisingly, the extrinsic rewards for superintendents and principals exceed the rewards received by classroom teachers. Superintendents of districts with 6,000 or more students have average annual incomes of approximately $29,000[39] while teachers on the average earn approximately $10,500.[40] The discrepancy between administrators and teachers is somewhat lower when the salaries of principals are compared with those of teachers; the salary difference between elementary principals and teachers is the smallest.

There are, however, marked differences within each type of administrative position, and these differences are most pronounced when size of the school district is taken into account. Generally, the larger the number of students enrolled in the school district, the larger is the salary paid on the average to administrators; this pattern holds irrespective of the type of position held.[41]

The salary situation over time. The differences in income for administrators and teachers widened from 1962 until 1971. During this time period, the salaries for administrators climbed at a faster rate than those of teachers. However, in 1972 the pattern was reversed; at this point in time, superintendents and principals at all levels received less of a salary increase percentagewise than teachers did.[42] Whether this trend reversal is temporary or is evidence of a new pattern brought about by collective bargaining remains unclear.

INTRINSIC REWARDS

Systematic inquiry into the intrinsic rewards experienced by educational administrators is quite limited. Studies which compare the intrinsic rewards of administrators with teachers are even more rare. Investigations that focus on intrinsic rewards for administrators at different time periods and which might show definite trends are nonexistent. However, the data which are available on intrinsic rewards suggest that they are adequate for the majority of people who occupy either a principalship or a superintendency.

One way in which researchers have examined the issue of in-

39. Educational Research Service, Inc., *Salaries Scheduled for Administrative and Supervisory Personnel in Public Schools, 1973–74.*

40. Research Division, National Education Association, *26th Biennial Salary of Public School Professional Personnel, 1973* (Washington, D.C.: National Education Association, 1973).

41. Ibid.

42. These conclusions are based on an analysis of the salary statistics reported in the National Education Association's *24th* and *26th Biennial Salary Surveys* and the Educational Research Service, Inc., *Salaries Scheduled for Administrative Personnel.*

trinsic rewards is by asking administrators some variation of the following question: Would you make the same choice if you had it to do all over again? In one national study, 54.4 percent of the superintendents responded that they certainly would choose educational administration again, while only 6.1 percent indicated that they probably would not or certainly would not.[43] Similarly, 52.9 percent of the elementary school principals reported they certainly would become elementary school principals if they were starting over, while 6.8 percent said that they probably would not or certainly would not.[44] Junior high and senior high school principals, on the other hand, were somewhat more likely to indicate that they would not choose educational administration as a career if they had their life to live over; the exact figures were 12 percent for the former and 17 percent for the latter.[45] Even so, 64 percent of the principals at the junior-high school level and 60 percent at the senior-high school level reported that they would make the same choice; the remaining principals were uncertain.

A second technique used by researchers to examine the intrinsic rewards of administrators is to assess how much satisfaction and enjoyment administrators derive from performing a variety of their activities. Gross and Napior, for example, looked at the degree of enjoyment male elementary, junior high, and senior high school principals experience in twenty separate work activities.[46] In approximately 75 percent of these activities, more than half of the respondents indicated that they experienced either a great deal of or very much enjoyment. There were five work activities in which 80 percent or more of the principals expressed that they enjoyed the activity a great deal or very much; these activities included the following:

1. Working with exceptionally able teachers.
2. Supervising the instructional program.
3. Working with guidance personnel.
4. Talking with parents about a problem concerning their child.
5. Talking with a group of parents about a school problem.

There was no work activity in which a majority of the principals reported very little or no enjoyment.

The degree of gratification experienced by educational administrators apparently is less a function of the characteristics of the individual than of the situation. Gross and Napior found that only four of the myriad individual attributes which they examined were related to job satisfaction. Principals who were disposed to accept authority and who were positively oriented to authority figures were more satisfied than principals with more

---

43. American Association of School Administrators, *Professional Administrators.*

44. Department of Elementary School Principals, *School Principalship,* 1968.

45. Rock and Hemphill, *Junior High-School Principalship;* Hemphill, Richards, and Peterson, *Senior High-School Principalship.*

46. Gross and Napior, *The Job and Career Satisfaction of Men School Principals.*

negative orientations toward authority. Individuals who underplayed rather than emphasized the hierarchical aspects of the teacher-principal relationship were somewhat more satisfied with their work. Blacks were more satisfied than whites, Jews were more satisfied than Catholics who, in turn, enjoyed their work more than Protestants.

According to Gross and Napior, situational characteristics which are related to principal job satisfaction tend to center around the relationships a principal has with his superiors and his subordinates. Particularly crucial in the relationship between the principal and his superior is the amount of autonomy a principal is granted by his superior; the importance a superior attributes to the principal's work; the degree of role ambiguity present; the adequacy of communications from the superordinate; the availability of constructive suggestions, professional encouragement, and socioemotional support from the superior; the effectiveness of the decision-making machinery at higher levels; and the skill with which the superior handles his own routine managerial tasks. With respect to the relationships a principal has with his staff, four factors seem to affect his level of work satisfaction: (1) the amount of personal loyalty and support the staff gives him, (2) the interest it has in innovation and change, (3) the commitment of staff members to their work responsibilities, and (4) the quality of the staff's performance.

A number of properties of the school setting in the Gross and Napior study did not differentiate between highly satisfied and less well-satisfied principals, however. These properties included size of the school, socioeconomic composition of the student body, and grade levels encompassed within the school—namely, elementary, junior high, and senior high.

Unfortunately, little or no attention has been devoted to the intrinsic rewards of the superintendency. We lack information such as the following: the amount of gratification associated with the performance of various work activities, how the degree of work gratification compares with principals and teachers, what personal characteristics are related to work satisfactions, and what situational characteristics affect the superintendent's enjoyment of his work. Perhaps future researchers will inquire into such issues and others that relate to the intrinsic rewards of managerial roles in education.

STRESSES AND STRAINS

OCCUPATIONAL STRESS AND ITS PHYSIOLOGICAL CORRELATES

The significance of occupational stress has been demonstrated by medical researchers in recent years. Work-connected emotional stress has been linked to a range of physical disorders including coronary disease, high blood pressure, and high cholesterol levels which presumably foreshadow strokes and heart attacks. The deleterious effects of occupational stress have been evident when researchers have controlled for previously identified causes such as heredity, dietary fat, tobacco smoking, obesity, and physical activity. Studies which have shown that occupational stress leads to unwanted and undesirable physical consequences for the human organism have essentially been of two types. One type has been concerned with the relationship between the incidence of physical disorders and the stress levels of various occupational groupings.[47] A second type has concentrated on physical changes as a function of cyclic variations in job stress within the same occupation.[48] The findings of both types have been generally consistent; increases in occupational stress are accompanied by a higher incidence of physical ailments and undesirable changes in bodily functions.

OCCUPATIONAL STRESS AMONG BUSINESS EXECUTIVES

When we consider executives or managers as one occupational category, we find an interesting pattern with respect to stress and physiological correlates. In board rooms, hallways, executive suites, and popular novels, there is an emphasis on the strains of executive responsibility. The theme usually runs like this. Promotion which entails an increase in executive load is almost certain to result in psychic and physical disturbances. The verbal imagery is striking. The picture of the executive is one of a man doubled-over clutching his ulcer-ridden stomach with the left hand and reaching frantically for a bottle of tranquilizers with the other hand. Tension, anxiety, high blood pressure, stomach troubles, and chest pain frequent the conversations about administrative man.

Although the folklore abounds, serious systematic study of executive stress is scant. What evidence we do have is not altogether consistent with the personal tales, testimonials, and accounts of what it is like to be an executive. In fact, executives appear to be in better physical condition than non-executives.[49] Moreover, level of responsibility within the administrative group is unrelated to differences in physical health; top executives

47. H. I. Russek, "Emotional Stress and Coronary Heart Disease in American Physicians, Dentists, and Lawyers," *American Journal of Medical Science* 243 (1962): 716–725.

48. M. Friedman, R. H. Rosenman, and V. Carroll, "Changes in the Serum Cholesterol and Blood Clotting Time of Men Subject to Cyclic Variation of Occupational Stress," *Circulation* 17 (1958): 852–861.

49. See Richard E. Lee and Ralph F. Schneider, "Hypertension and Arteriosclerosis in Executive and Non-executive Personnel," *The Journal of the American Medical Association* 167, 12 (July 19, 1958): 1447–1451. See also Robert L. Kahn, Donald M. Wolfe, Robert P. Quinn, and J. Diedrick Snoek, *Organizational Stress* (New York: Wiley, 1964).

do not have higher incidences of arteriosclerotic disease and heart disease than middle management and minor executives.[50]

OCCUPATIONAL STRESS AMONG SCHOOL EXECUTIVES

Role conflict as a source of stress. The empirical work dealing with stress among school executives has primarily been of one type. Researchers have focused on role conflict and have made the assumption that role conflict leads to stress and has adverse consequences for individuals who are exposed to such conflict.[51] Rarely has this assumption been tested, however.

In studying role conflict among school administrators, researchers have almost exclusively been concerned with examining the extent to which administrators are confronted with role conflict. Generally, the presence of conflict has been signaled by the existence of incompatible expectations for performance. By *incompatible expectations,* researchers mean that there are simultaneous demands for behaviors which are mutually exclusive, contradictory, or inconsistent.

The research in this area clearly shows that school administrators, particularly principals and superintendents, are highly vulnerable to role conflict. Incompatible expectations for the administrators' performance seem to arise in three ways. One source of role conflict is the conflict that arises between two roles held by the same person. For example, Gross et al.,[52] found that 48 percent of the superintendents he studied confronted conflicting expectations in their roles as school administrators and as fathers. Superintendents were expected to spend a lot of time working in the evening on school-related matters and also to be with their families attending to their needs. Superintendents also reported conflict stemming from role obligations to personal friends and the school system. Friends sought special consideration and treatment for their children in such matters as assignment to or transfer from a particular school or to a particular teacher; consideration of this sort resulted in conflict when the superintendent was expected by the school board and teachers to follow a set of procedures which were at variance with requests of friends.

A second source of role conflict is the conflict that develops when *two or more groups have incompatible expectations for the same role.* Halpin, in his influential study of the school superintendency, found that school board members expect superintendents to be very strong in initiat-

50. Lee and Schneider, "Hypertension."

51. For a review of the role conflict studies, see Jacob W. Getzels, James M. Lipham, and Roald F. Campbell, *Educational Administration as a Social Process* (New York: Harper & Row, 1968).

52. Neal C. Gross, Ward S. Mason, and Alexander W. McEachern, *Explorations in Role Analysis* (New York: Wiley, 1958).

ing structure while staff members prefer much less structure.[53] In other words, school staffs and boards of education differed significantly in their expectations for leadership behavior, which involved efforts to establish well-defined patterns of organization, channels of communication, and methods of procedure. Hencley[54] also discovered inconsistencies between teacher and school board expectations for the superintendent's behavior in three major administrative task areas: staff personnel, curriculum and program, and finance and business management.

Incompatible expectations held by two or more groups also have been observed for principals. On the basis of a comprehensive study of the school principalship, Moser[55] concluded that principals are subjected to conflicting expectations by teachers and superintendents. Teachers want their principals to keep things on an even keel, to cater to the individual needs of staff members, to advocate the staff's point of view with top management, and to seek suggestions from the staff when action is needed. The superintendents of these same principals, on the other hand, expected the principal to be forceful in his relationships with subordinates, to initiate action, to emphasize the achievement of organizational goals, and to show greater concern for the institution than for the individual.

A third source of conflict for school administrators rises from *contradictory expectations held by members of the same group for the occupant of the same role.* Moyer,[56] for example, in his study of teacher expectations for the leadership behavior of principals, showed that teachers within the same building had opposing conceptions of how their principal should behave. One group of teachers believed that the principal should make the decisions and run the school according to his best judgment while another group expected the principal to rely heavily upon his teachers for help with school problems.[57]

The vulnerability of school administrators to role conflict is also evident in studies concerned with the number of administrators experiencing role conflict in certain areas of decision making. By way of illustration, Gross et al., found that a high percentage of superintendents had been exposed to role conflict in the four decision situations which he examined. More than 90 percent of the superintendents were faced with role conflict when making budget decisions; a similar percentage was exposed to con-

---

53. Andrew W. Halpin, *Theory and Research in Administration* (New York: The Macmillan Co., 1966).

54. Stephen P. Hencley, "A Typology of Conflict between Superintendents and Their Reference Groups" (Ph.D. diss., Department of Education, University of Chicago, 1960).

55. Robert P. Moser, "A Study of the Effects of Superintendent-Principal Interaction and Principal-Teacher Interaction in Selected Middle-Sized School Systems" (Ph.D. diss., Department of Education, University of Chicago, 1957).

56. Donald C. Moyer, "Teachers' Attitudes Toward Leadership as They Relate to Teacher Satisfaction" (Ph.D. diss., Department of Education, University of Chicago, 1954).

57. For a discussion of how principals deal with role conflict, see Donald L. Sayan and W. W. Charters, Jr., "A Replication Among School Principals of the Gross Study of Role Conflict Resolution," *Educational Administration Quarterly* 6, 2 (Spring 1970), pp. 36–45.

flicting expectations when deciding what level of salary increases to recommend for teachers; nearly three-fourths of the superintendents encountered role conflict in hiring and promoting personnel; and slightly more than one-half reported contradictory expectations for how they should spend their time outside their regular office hours.

This study by Gross is one of the few studies which has sought to test the assumption that exposure to role conflict results in adverse consequences for the individual. Superintendents faced with contradictory demands in making budget recommendations were much less satisfied with their jobs and worried more than superintendents who were not exposed to role conflict in this area. Superintendents who encountered role conflict with respect to time allocation also seemed to worry more than those who perceived no role conflict in this area. Many more studies of this type must be conducted, however, before we can conclude that role conflict does lead to occupational stress which in turn generates physical disorders and disturbances for the individual.

OTHER SOURCES OF OCCUPATIONAL STRESS

Role conflict is not the only factor which is presumed to be a contributor to occupational stress among school executives. Stress apparently is engendered by a number of conditions in the administrator's work environment which do not necessarily involve incompatible, contradictory, or inconsistent expectations for performance. Although these conditions have not been studied as systematically as role conflict has been, the available evidence is highly suggestive, nonetheless.

Six conditions which seemingly lead to stress among school executives are pressures of declining enrollments and financial resources, career crises, decisions in the face of uncertainty, decisions in the midst of crisis, obligations to make decisions that affect the fates of others, and occasional periods of role overload.

The shift from an expanding to a declining organizational state has brought new tensions for the school administrator. Financially pressed districts are unable to satisfy the salary demands of teachers; these teachers are venting their wrath against their administrators. The teachers act out their own frustrations by devaluing the contributions of administrators and by insisting that their number should be reduced substantially. The administrator is bluntly told that his services are unwanted and unnecessary. He encounters abuse rather than admiration, rejection rather than acceptance. Financial pressures and enrollment declines further increase the likelihood of personal stress through the demotion, if not the outright dismissal, of the administrator. The incidence of downward mobility has jumped in recent years; although exact figures are not available, demotions probably occur with greater frequency now than at any time since the great depression. We know woefully little about the nature and consequences of "skidding" for the individual and the organization.[58]

The career cycle is also a breeding ground for stress. During middle-age, administrators may face a career crisis.[59] Such individuals recognize that they may have reached their maximum; their hopes for the future are no longer a source of comfort in a time of despair. Rather, they see the future as a source of fresh disappointments, a grim reminder of defeat and unfulfilled hopes and dreams. Retirement is another event within the normal career cycle that may produce an emotional ordeal for the administrator.[60] The period of disengagement signifies the administrator's loss of identity and his primary source of self-justification. How the administrator copes with this separation from the world of work is a subject that has escaped the attention of researchers.

Spalding's[61] comprehensive and analytical treatment of the anxieties inherent in the superintendent's role focuses on uncertainty as a major determinant of executive stress and strain. One area of uncertainty is the impact of administrative action on organizational achievement and functioning. According to Spalding, the effects of an executive's decisions are not always immediately observable. Rather, the degree of success is evident only after a considerable length of time; and, in some instances, the results are never clearly evident. At the same time and in the absence of any knowledge of results, the superintendent must continue to take action which assumes that earlier decisions led to successful outcomes. The exercise of discretion under such circumstances, as Spalding notes, is not conducive to an easy state of mind.

Stress is also engendered by the need to make decisions under crisis conditions. With increasing frequency, school administrators are having to reach decisions in situations which involve a time deadline and threat of injury or harm to both the organization and administrator. Confrontation and crisis-induction are becoming standard tactics for militant community groups, teachers, and students.[62] These power-oriented techniques cause administrators pain and anguish as evidenced by the upsurge of premature retirements and requests for transfer.

A fifth source of felt difficulty for administrators is in the area of personnel decisions. In every organization, someone is assigned the re-

58. See Thomas E. Powers, "Administrative Behavior and Upward-Mobility," *Administrator's Notebook,* vol. 9, no. 1 (1966); Douglas M. More, "Demotion," *Social Problems* 9 (Winter 1962): 213–221; and Fred H. Goldner, "Demotion in Industrial Management," *American Sociological Review* 30 (1965): 714–724.

59. Harry Levinson, "On Being a Middle-Aged Manager," *Harvard Business Review* (July-August 1969), pp. 51–60.

60. Edward Gross, "Work, Organization and Stress," in Sol Levine and Norman A. Scotch, eds., *Social Stress* (Chicago: Aldine Publishing Company, 1970), pp. 57–110.

61. Willard B. Spalding, *The Superintendency of Schools—An Anxious Profession* (Cambridge, Mass.: Harvard University Press, 1954).

62. Edwin M. Bridges, "Student Unrest and Crisis Decision Making," *Administrator's Notebook* 18, 4 (December 1969).

sponsibility for deciding whether individuals are to be re-appointed, promoted, demoted, or discharged. Ordinarily, principals and superintendents are expected to make these choices in educational organizations. Decisions of this type involve a lot of stress and anxiety for the decision maker,[63] as he recognizes that the decision has important, serious, and potentially negative consequences for the future life chances of the individual who is demoted or fired. Frequently, the individual's family is adversely affected by the administrator's judgment as well. More likely than not, such decisions create stress and disturb administrators because few people like to view themselves as precipitating life crises for others.

Role overload[64] is a sixth potential source of stress and strain for the administrator and may take one of two forms. Role overload may represent a condition in which the individual is faced with a set of obligations which requires him to do more than he is able in the time available. When considered separately, each demand is within the capabilities of the administrator; however, time limitations and deadline pressures make it impossible for him to deal with the entire set of obligations. Role overload also may represent a condition in which the individual lacks either the personal or organizational resources to meet his role obligations. In either case, the role overload can have similar consequences—high levels of stress and physical or emotional disturbances.

SUMMARY

Throughout this chapter we have concentrated on factors which individuals may wish to ponder as they consider their choice about a career in educational administration. We have shown that a person interested in administration can serve education in a wide variety of ways; the field, as we noted, offers an exciting array of career possibilities. Furthermore, we have cited evidence which shows clearly, if not dramatically, that the extrinsic rewards are greater for administrators than for teachers. Our discussion of the intrinsic rewards and the stresses and strains inherent in executive roles has provided a glimpse into the affective side of administration, a side which has been somewhat neglected by previous theorists and researchers interested in administration as a field of inquiry. Our review of the research dealing with traits and competencies has furnished some clues as to who gets appointed and as to who succeeds in various types of administrative positions. Hopefully, the knowledge we have brought to bear on the topics in this chapter will enable the individual to arrive at a more rational career choice than otherwise would have been possible.

63. Harry Levinson, "On Being a Middle-Aged Manager," *Harvard Business Review* 47, 4 (July-August 1969): 51–60.

64. Stephen M. Sales, "Organizational Role as a Risk Factor in Coronary Disease," *Administrative Science Quarterly* 14, 3 (September 1969): 325–337.

SUGGESTED ACTIVITIES

1. Interview a number of superintendents and principals to determine what it is about their work that either makes them feel uncomfortable or leads to a state of uneasiness. Compare the results of your interviews with the ideas presented in the section on stresses and strains.
2. Select a number of school districts in your area and seek to identify the competencies and personal and prestige traits which are associated with or which figure in appointment to administrative positions.
3. In several local school districts, make an effort to describe the procedures for assessing administrative competence. Note particularly the criteria which are used, the evidence used to establish the extent to which the criteria are being met, and the priority assigned to the various criteria.
4. Talk with a number of superintendents and attempt to find out what they regard as the sources of joy and pleasure in their work.

SELECTED READINGS

Erickson, Donald A. "The School Administrator," *Review of Educational Research* 37, 4 (October 1967): 417–431.

Gross, Edward. "Work, Organization, and Stress," in Sol Levine and Norman A. Scotch, eds., *Social Stress.* Chicago: Aldine Publishing Company, 1970, pp. 111–140.

Levinson, Harry. *Emotional Health in the World of Work.* New York: Harper & Row, 1964.

Levinson, Harry. *The Exceptional Executive: A Psychological Conception.* Cambridge, Mass.: Harvard University Press, 1968.

Levinson, Harry. *Executive Stress.* New York: Harper and Row, Publishers, 1970.

Spalding, Willard B. *The Superintendency of Schools—An Anxious Profession.* Cambridge, Mass.: Harvard University Press, 1954.

13

QUALIFYING FOR EDUCATIONAL ADMINISTRATION

In the preceding chapter we focused on the decision to become an educational administrator; our attention now shifts to the plans necessary to implement such a decision. A decision by itself is not enough; after a choice is made, the next task is to create a plan to meet the requirements implied by the decision. There are three major functions to be served by this career plan: to increase the probability of attaining the hoped-for objective, to maximize the opportunities which a person may have to qualify for a post in educational administration, and to provide a means by which the prospective administrator can evaluate his career choice. Conceivably, as he attempts to follow his plan, a person will discover that his original choice was an unwise one. By having a plan, the person may be able to determine quite early if he has made an error in judgment. With this knowledge, he can adjust his career choice accordingly and minimize the costs involved in pursuing a goal which has a low probability of attainment.

CREATING A PLAN

A classic poem reminds us that "The best laid schemes o' mice and men" often go astray. As children, we all read—but probably did not wholly comprehend—the rhyme that told of the kingdom that was lost "for want of a nail." Must we then infer that man is foolish to plan when his plans are so easily laid low? History is replete with famous men who seem to have been cast by destiny rather than self-planning into heroic or villainous roles.

Careful analysis, however, indicates that planning is far more successful than might be assumed, and is far more prevalent than might be evident. History also does not reveal to us the names of potentially great people who did not make important contributions for the lack of a plan.

Without going into detailed documentation of the need for careful planning if decisions are to be carried into reality, we shall merely state that planning seems to us to be an essential step in qualifying for educational administration. It is necessary to examine the elements of a good plan and to provide some insights into planning for a specific field—educational administration.

ELEMENTS OF A GOOD PLAN

It seems to us that planning involves clarifying purposes; defining the problem; gathering, analyzing, and interpreting facts; and deciding courses of action. This is, of course, very similar to the whole process of decision making as we defined it earlier. For our purpose here, however, it will be assumed that earlier decision-making procedures have led to a clear statement of purpose and that the problem is well defined. There will, obviously, be subpurposes and subproblems. It will be necessary to gather, analyze, and interpret facts and, certainly, to decide courses of action.

The plan should, then, be based on a clear understanding of the ultimate purpose and of the steps necessary to meet this purpose. Next comes a consideration of the qualifications required to make the steps. The basic elements of a good plan seem to be statements of purpose, of qualifications needed to meet purposes, and of the steps required to gain these qualifications. Thus, if one's ultimate purpose is to become a city superintendent, one's plan must include certification, university training, and experience. It will undoubtedly also include a principalship as a step toward the ultimate purpose, and this step will require consideration of appropriate certification, training, and experience background necessary for the principalship.

Thus both short-term and long-term goals should be included in a good plan. The short-term goals should be stated in order that sequential progress toward the ultimate goal is understood and planned. The long-term goal must be stated to provide a frame of reference as one has opportunities to change positions, to go to school, or to do both. It is the long-range goal that can help a person decide if he should stay where he is and complete, for example, the program for his master's degree.

INCLUSIVENESS OF THE PLAN

A plan such as we have been discussing cannot be too detailed, particularly as it is projected ten or even more years into the future. In addition, the plan should not be unduly specific. While, for example, it is understandable that a person might desire to be the superintendent of schools in his home town, it is not wise to restrict planning to such specific goals. The old home town can have only one superintendent at a time, and the person who clings tenaciously to this specific goal may wait in vain for an opportunity to realize it. The specifics of certification and advanced degrees are appropriate, but specifics as to geographical location of future position, exact places where nonteaching experience is to be gained, or exact salaries to be earned along the way are not.

In general, the plan should include types of positions desired, types of nonschool work or activity experiences deemed necessary, and a general picture of the economic well-being desired as the plan progresses. The prospective administrator may wait in vain for a board of education in a given school district to offer him a given job at a given salary. It is far better that a plan be developed which is sufficiently inclusive of the general progress desired than that a plan be cluttered with specific and unrealistic details.

FLEXIBILITY VERSUS VACILLATION

The above discussion makes it clear that some flexibility is desirable in a plan for the future. Earlier, when the necessity of evaluation of the basic decision to pursue a specific ultimate goal was described, it was pointed out that changes in plan may be necessary and wise. How does one tell when one is being wisely flexible and when one is being foolishly vacillatory? Generally, the most simple and basic way is to test possible changes in position or in objectives against the framework of the ultimate goal and the reasons that led to the choice of that goal.

Does experience show that some of the basic reasoning which led to the choice of the ultimate goal was in error? If so, a change in goals may be wise. Does momentary fatigue or irritation seem to demand a change in the ultimate goal? If so, such a change may be extremely unwise. Does a new position fit the requirements of the next step toward the ultimate goal even though it was not a position that was envisioned earlier as a good one? If so, accepting it may be wise. Does a new position offer financial rewards but no real progress toward the ultimate goal? If so, it may prove to be unwise both professionally and financially.

A well-made, carefully considered plan, drawn up in realistically general terms, should be discarded only for major reasons related to the ultimate goal and the basis for accepting that goal. Too many "temporary" deviations from the plan for reasons that are attractive but unsound can lead to permanent failure to reach an ultimate goal. This is the reason that long-range goals are necessary and should play an important role in reaching short-term decisions.

THE PLAN IS CREATED

We have considered the making of a decision and the creation of a plan to implement it. We need now to turn our attention to a specific plan to implement a specific decision—qualifying for educational administration. The remainder of this chapter will explore some of the specific considerations to be made as one attempts to create and follow a plan that will lead to a desired position as an educational administrator.

USING TEACHING EXPERIENCE

Many would-be administrators fail to realize and to profit from the opportunities for qualification as an administrator which are inherent in a teaching position. We have already described in some detail the role of the teacher in school administration. Undoubtedly, the fulfillment of this role will lead to increased qualification as an administrator. Certain features might well be pointed out here to relate teaching experience more specifically to qualification as an administrator. Before doing this, however, we must stress that we do not view the main function of teaching to be that of a stepping-stone to administration. The teacher who holds the attitude that teaching is only a necessary evil before entering a "real" job, will probably achieve only minor success both in teaching and in the "real" job—if, indeed, the so-called real job is ever attained. While we do want to point out that teaching experience can help qualify a person for administration, we would not want to imply that this is a major purpose of teaching.

LEADERSHIP OPPORTUNITIES

In qualifying for educational administration, the teacher should take advantage of the many first-hand opportunities which are available for gaining experience and skill in administering and leading groups. In the classroom, the processes of decision making, programing, stimulating, coordinating, and appraising should be studied and techniques improved. Not only will this lead to future qualification as an administrator, but it will lead to increased competence as a teacher. In addition, the teacher should seek opportunities for leadership in teacher organizations and in community groups. These activities will provide insight into the required skills and techniques of leadership and will provide valuable experience in their utilization.

Many teachers, for example, find themselves involved in scouting or Sunday school activities. These are organizations which provide leadership opportunities with both children and adults. When, as often happens in such activities, the teacher is sought out by other members of the community as a leader, the experience can be used both as a means of community service and as a means of developing skills in leadership.

A number of teachers gain leadership experience in local, state, and national organizations. Not only is the president of a local teachers' organization given practice as a leader, he also is provided with opportunities to observe educational administration from a closer vantage point than is usually afforded the teacher. In working on problems of teacher welfare, professional growth programs, or matters dealing with the evaluation of teaching, the association or union officer gains experience both in leadership and in the more specific areas of educational administration.

SEMIADMINISTRATIVE POSITIONS

It is difficult to draw a line and declare that certain positions are administrative while others are not. In chapter 12, we described the positions we have defined as administrative. It will be noted that such positions as department heads, athletic directors, or activity fund treasurers were not listed. For purposes of clarity, it seems best to define these and similar positions as semiadministrative positions.

There may be a number of such positions, particularly in a large high school. A high school with an enrollment of three hundred students or more might well have full-time or part-time staff members with the following semiadministrative positions: coordinator of instruction, director of activities, director of guidance, director of health and physical education, director of athletics, heads of departments, attendance supervisor, director of testing and research, director of cafeteria, and registrar. Certainly, in smaller schools, not all of these positions would be found, and probably none of them as full-time positions. In larger schools, most of them would be found, and many of them would be full-time positions. The fact is that regardless of the size of the school, these positions represent functions that need to be performed, and some arrangement of time and assignment will be developed to facilitate the performance of these functions.

In the elementary school, there is less opportunity for a teacher to gain experience in semiadministrative positions. Elementary schools are usually smaller and generally understaffed in terms of administration. The opportunities for leadership, not only for the teacher but also for the administrator, are reduced due to the heavy load of routine and clerical duties which must be assumed by the professional staff. If the elementary school teacher is to gain valuable experience through holding semiadministrative positions, he must seek committee chairmanships of both school and school district committees, such as textbook selection committees or curriculum development groups. While the position as an adviser of a student activity may sometimes not clearly fill the role of a semiadministrative position, it is more often true than not that such a position does have administrative overtones.

The acceptance of and performance in a semiadministrative position in a school or school system can aid greatly in one's attempt to qualify for educational administration. The prospective administrator often gains through such a position the chance to try his wings under the guidance of an experienced administrator.

RELATIONSHIPS WITH ADMINISTRATORS AND BOARD

Many teachers enter university courses for the preparation of educational administrators without ever observing a board of education meeting or taking a firsthand look at the work which crosses the desk of a school principal. Curricula in teacher education rarely include any courses aimed at providing the prospective teacher with some insight into such matters as school budget making, procedures of boards of education, or administrative organization of a school district. The continued pressure from many sources for increased general education, increased subject-matter preparation, and decreased professional education courses for the prospective teacher makes it unlikely that courses or units dealing with educational administration will be added in any quantity to programs for undergraduate teacher education.

Hence even a basic familiarity with such problems must be gained on the job and in graduate courses by the in-service teacher. Many teachers ignore on-the-job opportunities to learn about educational administration and thus ignore an opportunity to begin the process of qualifying for educational administration. We have, for example, observed committees dealing with teachers' salaries both neglect and refuse to become familiar with the school budget, even though the salary program they are attempting to develop may require as much as 70 to 80 percent of this budget for its implementation. We have heard teachers complain about "secrecy" or "lack of information" when even a cursory inquiry would have revealed to them that the information they desired was a matter of public record in the central office of the school district or in the office of the county superintendent of schools or of the state department of education. We have known teachers who did not know how many members were on their local school board, how they were selected, when or where they met, or what even one major duty of this board was.

In some cases, to be sure, inadequate or ineffective administrators make it difficult for teachers to observe the processes and details of educational administration in their school districts. For the most part, however, it is apathy rather than antagonism which leads to the teachers' lack of knowledge about administration. Certainly, the prospective administrator cannot afford such apathy. He needs to attend some board meetings, to study some budgets and other documents, and to inquire about administrative problems. While course work and reading may make a real contribution to the development of an administrator, there is little doubt but that the prospective administrator should also learn through observation of and participation in administering. Careful observation of administrators in action and of administrative skills, techniques, and details in the actual school setting is one way in which the teacher who is considering administration can begin to qualify for administration.

EXPANDING EXPERIENCES

Just as teaching experience when appropriately utilized can aid in qualifying for administration, so can other experiences, gained while teaching, aid in the development of a school administrator. We will not repeat in detail here the various kinds of experience which increase one's potential as an educational administrator. It does seem worthwhile to point out, however, that many teachers ignore some of the nuances of school-community relations that can be observed by the teacher. In addition to observation, there are many forms of participation available to the teacher which aid in increasing the qualifications of a prospective administrator.

Teachers can—and administrators must—study the community forces that impinge upon the school program. Teachers can pay some attention to the extent of community understandings of school problems and can analyze some of the reasons for the presence or absence of understanding. Teachers can attend P.T.A. meetings, not as reluctant back-benchers, but as interested participants in and observers of school-community relations in action. In these and many other ways the teacher who is interested in educational administration can increase his knowledge of and his competency in the area of school-community relations.

The prospective administrator can also gain experience in the area of understanding communities while teaching. What is a community? What makes this community tick? Upon what economic base does it rest? What roles do churches, service clubs, business organizations, labor groups, or farm groups play in the community?

Every teacher lives in a community. If, as we believe, one of the important qualifications of an educational administrator is the ability to recognize and understand community forces, the teacher and prospective administrator need to utilize every opportunity to gain experience in these difficult areas. There is no better place for the teacher to start developing this competency than in his local community.

Some examples might serve to point up the possibilities in this area. The teacher in a school district can often gain significant understanding of the influence of a community on the educational program in that district. Is science neglected while a trade and industry program flourishes? What elements in the community might have a bearing on this situation? Is a large industry the dominant force in the community? Is science important to this industry? To what extent do board members come from the personnel of the industrial firm? Answers to these and other questions can provide a measure of community understanding.

Or, as the teacher develops a course of study, he might well consider the ways in which community resources could be used in implementing the course of study. What possibilities for field trips exist? Are there any members of the community who might discuss certain phases of a subject with the class? To what extent will service clubs or business and labor organizations provide materials or underwrite costs of special activities? Answering questions like these will not only provide the teacher with increased understanding of his community, it can also play a major role in the improvement of the instructional program.

While the above comments emphasize experiences in the area of school-community relations, experiences in other administrative task areas are also available. The prospective administrator should be alert to such opportunities and take advantage of them as a valuable part of his preparation.

FORMAL PREPARATION

Many aspects of one's teaching experience can aid in helping one qualify for educational administration. The time must come, however, when the prospective administrator begins his formal preparation for administration, usually under the direction of an adviser from an institution accredited by the state to prepare educational administrators. The several aspects of this formal program will be considered in some detail here. It should be remembered, however, that each state has specific patterns of requirements for the administrator and that no text, article, or lecture can replace the state certification handbook as a prime source of information during the formal preparation period. By the same token, the catalog of the university or college chosen by the prospective administrator for his course work must also become a key reference book as he plans his work.

CERTIFICATION OF ADMINISTRATORS

In discussing the certification of administrators, we would stress at the outset our belief that certification requirements represent, at best, minimum requirements. Too often, an administrator-to-be gains the impression that, with certification, he is fully and perpetually prepared for any and all administrative positions. The generally low requirements for certification in most states should make it obvious that such is not the case. We believe that a master's degree is a minimum standard for administrative certification and that regular graduate work—either leading to a doctor's degree or taken as part of a post-master's nondegree program—are essential to the continuing qualification of an administrator.

Because the certification of administrators, like that of teachers, is a responsibility and an authority held by each state, requirements for certification vary from state to state.[1] In the states that grant administrative certificates, varied types are issued. These may include elementary principals' certificates, secondary principals' certificates, general principals' certificates, superintendents' certificates, and general administrative certificates. Without exception, one requirement for certification as an administrator is teaching experience, with three years of such experience being the usual requirement. In addition, many of the superintendents' or general administrative certificates require two or three years of administrative experience as a principal as a prerequisite. Almost all the states stipulate certain kinds of graduate courses for administrative certification. Generally, graduate credit is required in such areas as curriculum, supervision of instruction, and general administration, and in such specialized fields as school law or school finance. In addition to course work, many states require a master's degree for certification as an administrator.

It is also true that, regardless of certification requirements, many school boards are including the doctorate as a prerequisite for consideration as a superintendent in their districts. Furthermore, the six regional accrediting associations for secondary schools and colleges generally create standards for administrators in accredited schools that are often higher than the minimum standards for state certification.[2] Therefore, as a prospective administrator considers the steps necessary to qualify for educational administration, he must consider requirements for both certification and a graduate program.

As the administrator-to-be plans to qualify for educational administration, the question of certification must loom large. Many excellent opportunities are lost because a teacher or a principal has not taken the time and effort to be certificated for a higher administrative position. Either the state department of education or a university approved by the state to certificate administrators can supply complete details concerning certification requirements. These sources of information should be contacted early

---

1. For these state requirements, see Elizabeth H. Woellner and M. Aurilla Wood, *Requirements for Certification of Teachers, Counselors, Librarians, Administrators for Elementary Schools, Secondary Schools, Junior Colleges* (Chicago: The University of Chicago Press). This publication is revised annually.

2. The regional accrediting associations referred to are Middle States Association of Colleges and Secondary Schools, New England Association of Colleges and Secondary Schools, North Central Association of Colleges and Secondary Schools, Northwest Association of Secondary and Higher Schools, Southern Association of Colleges and Secondary Schools, and Western College Association.

in the planning phase as the prospective administrator prepares to qualify for administrative positions.

ADVANCED DEGREE REQUIREMENTS

The above discussion makes it clear that the prospective administrator must consider graduate work as he attempts to qualify for administration. In general, there are five advanced degrees which should be included in the consideration of a long-range plan: the Master of Arts, the Master of Education, the sixth-year degree or certificate, the Doctor of Education, and the Doctor of Philosophy. In discussing these degrees or certificates, it is necessary again that we remind the prospective administrator that this discussion can be only a general one and that there is no satisfactory substitute for personal contact with the degree-granting institutions as a source of specific information about the requirements for higher degrees.

The Master's Degree. The day will undoubtedly soon be here when in every state a school administrator will be required to hold a master's degree for his initial administrative position. Usually, either a Master of Arts or a Master of Education degree will be available and will be acceptable. It is difficult to say which degree should be sought. The Master of Arts degree has, in most cases, more requirements in course work outside of the specific area of professional education than does the Master of Education degree, and the former often requires a research project or thesis which may not be required for the latter degree. Many prospective administrators earn the Master of Arts degree with emphasis on their teaching field, a procedure that has much to recommend it.

Remembering that we have stressed earlier the necessity for a broad educational background and for familiarity with both educational and other social problems, techniques, and skills, the prospective administrator should study the specific requirements in the institution of his choice and make a decision in terms of the program and his own needs and plans.

The sixth-year program. Many universities have instituted a degree or certificate program that comes between the master's and doctor's degrees. The sixth-year program generally requires thirty semester hours of graduate work beyond the master's degree. Usually about one-half of this work is in the specialized area of educational administration, while the other half is in closely related supporting areas. Most of the programs require either a thesis or a report on a field project as one of the requirements for receiving the degree or certificate. In addition, one characteristic of most of these programs is a period of time the student spends in supervised field experiences. Often these programs require some period of residence as a full-time student.

In general, the student who definitely plans a doctoral program should not contemplate the sixth-year program. It is important, however, for all prospective administrators to realize that such programs do exist and, as their future plans are made, to include a consideration of these programs.

The doctoral program. While we have no figures which indicate precisely the number of all school administrators who possess doctoral degrees, for superintendents of schools Knezevich[3] has reported that in school districts of 25,000 or more pupil enrollment half of the superintendents had the doctorate. Even in districts with smaller enrollments the percentage of superintendents with doctorates is substantial and apparently on the increase. Placement offices report that the possession of a doctor's degree is becoming more common as a prerequisite listed by boards of education for major administrative positions. Certainly, the prospective college professor of educational administration needs to consider the degree as a prerequisite to the attainment of his goal.

The question of whether the Ph.D. degree or the Ed.D. degree should be sought is becoming almost an academic question. At one time, the Ph.D. degree was in no way related to preparation for engaging in any highly specialized, technical occupation. This is no longer the case. In such fields as chemistry, mathematics, or engineering, where great numbers of doctoral degrees are earned, Ph.D. programs have become specialized and professional in much the same way that an Ed.D. program represents professional training in education. Actually, there are probably more differences among various programs for these degrees than there are between the two degrees. The choice of doctoral program, then, becomes much more a matter of personal preference and specific institutional programs than of the "worth" of the degrees.

Thus the major choice that faces the prospective administrator is whether or not he should include a doctoral program in his plan. Because the doctoral program is expensive in both time and money, the candidate must be willing to make a sacrifice to secure his degree, a sacrifice borne also by his wife and children. The acknowledgment often found in a dissertation in which the student expresses gratitude for the faith, support, patience, and understanding of his wife and family is much more than a mere formality. The candidate should know where he is going and how he hopes to get there if he is able to make the commitment to a doctoral program that is necessary for success.

In making this choice, the administrator must remember that many administrative positions will never require the doctor's degree as a prerequisite, that advanced graduate work can be taken without entering a doctoral program, and that the returns to him from such a program will probably be deferred ones. On the other hand, the administrator should

3. Stephen J. Knezevich, ed., *The American School Superintendent* (Arlington, Va.: American Association of School Administrators, 1971), p. 44.

recall that many major administrative positions do require a doctor's degree, that there is much personal satisfaction in completing a difficult intellectual task, and that the completion of a doctoral program gives a person greater flexibility in seeking advanced positions. Certainly, the majority of the educational administrators in our public schols will not complete such a program. It should be considered, however, as a part of the planning to qualify for educational administration. Intellectual ability, professional goals, research interest and ability, and personal motivations will play major roles in the decision.

Timing the degree programs. The decision as to when one begins to pursue an advanced degree is one based on both professional and personal factors. In general, however, a master's degree program is not started until after at least a year's teaching experience and, for most students, is completed in from one to three years, depending on whether the course work is all summer work or done during the regular academic years. If done during the summer, the student usually accumulates three or four years of teaching experience by the time the master's degree is earned and may, therefore, be ready to assume an administrative position. Care should be taken to insure that course work taken during the master's program will meet certification requirements so that the administrator-to-be is eligible to convert the "to-be" to "is."

The post-master's program should not be delayed too long after completing the master's program. We have mentioned earlier that a doctoral program is probably best begun before the doctoral candidate reaches the age of thirty. The doctoral program usually requires at least one year of full-time residence on campus. Course work plus the completion of a doctoral dissertation will usually lengthen the doctoral program to a total of from two to five years. Two full years on a doctoral program—"full" meaning that the student is not attempting concurrently to hold a position as a full-time administrator—is, for many people, a realistic estimate of the time necessary for completion. There are a few experimental doctoral programs, such as the National Ed.D. Program for Educational Leaders at Nova University,[4] which have modified the usual residence requirements and draw their clientele from practicing administrators.

SUPERVISED FIELD EXPERIENCE

In addition to meeting degree and certification requirements, the prospective administrator should be learning about administration and learning to administer. As we stress certificates and degrees, we must also stress that the only value of either is as they represent increased professional

4. See Gerald E. Sroufe, "Nova's Ed.D. Program for Educational Leaders: Looking Backward, Looking Forward," *Phi Delta Kappan* 56 (February 1975): 402–405.

growth and knowledge. The mere possession of a degree or certificate does not guarantee excellence.

One aspect of the formal program for the preparation of educational administrators which has received particular attention in recent years is supervised field experience. In field experience programs, the prospective administrator has a chance to practice administration, usually under the joint sponsorship of university and field personnel. In this way, theory and practice are related, and the qualifications of the prospective administrator can be considerably enhanced. Supervised field experience is usually gained in one or more of three ways: as a part of class activities, in a cadet program, or in an internship program.

Field experience. There are many ways in which formal class work can be supplemented by supervised field experience. Term projects, for example, can deal with real rather than imaginary problems. Possibilities also exist during the term for field affiliations that are related to, and aid the attainment of, the objectives of a course. Students in courses that deal with school-community relations might, for example, have close relationships with local community agencies during a quarter or semester. In one such course with which we are familiar, students spent a great deal of time working on an individual basis with local Community Chest agencies on problems with educational implications. Similar possibilities exist in courses in all areas of educational administration.

Another possibility is the development of courses that revolve around field activities. Students might conduct a comprehensive educational survey in a school district and report their findings and recommendations to the board of education of the district. Or, students might survey an actual problem in that district, with the findings of the survey being examined in class sessions.

Field trips are also used in many courses. School plant and school business administration courses offer a wide variety of possibilities for field trips. While such trips offer observation rather than participation opportunities, they do create another chance for the student to see theory in action.

Another type of field experience is the social field research project, in which the students work as members of a social science research team. The students may have a major responsibility in defining, developing, and carrying out a significant administrative task in connection with the research project, or they may act as assistants to the staff that is responsible for the project. Experiences such as these provide students with opportunities to see theory in practice and to put their own theories to test in the field.

Internship programs. The internship program is primarily a university-sponsored program to provide a type of on-the-job training. The internship stresses the assumption of responsibility. In practice, the internship program in educational administration often involves placing a student or intern in an administrative position in a school district or other situation under the joint supervision of an administrator and university personnel. The intern assumes responsibility for the completion of one or more administrative tasks. Although in most cases he is at least partially paid by the school district or other agency, the emphasis is upon his learning and growth more than upon service to the employer. Such service results from the program, but it is incidental to the main purposes of the internship program.

Several dangers exist in the internship program, and several problems are present. Hooker provides an excellent cautionary statement when he indicates that:

> If the internship experience is to provide graduate students with something more than the art of being wrong with greater confidence, considerable inquiry into the professional climate of the sponsoring school district is necessary. It should be borne firmly in mind that interns are not apprentices. They are not learning the tricks of the trade nor formulae for solving problems. Under supervision they make logical deductions from basic knowledge and inference from observations.[5]

It is sometimes difficult to develop a program in which the intern assumes real rather than artificial responsibility. There may be a tendency to assign interns to positions where they are familiar with practices and problems instead of utilizing the program to fill gaps in the background of the student. While this practice usually results in greater service to the school district, it does not always serve the purposes of the intern well. The internship program is costly on all sides. The intern must devote a full year to the program, usually at a low salary. Supervision, both on the part of the university and the local district, runs high in time and money. The program usually includes a seminar on campus for interns, and travel requirements between campus and school district may become burdensome both for interns and for supervisors.

A variation of the internship program is the cadet program through which a school district attempts to select, train, and promote administrative candidates within the system. Such programs usually concentrate on the training of principals, although some school districts also use the cadet program to train central office personnel.

In general, cadet programs include some class sessions under the direction of school district personnel and assignment to various semi-administrative or administrative positions in the district under the supervision of an administrator in the system. While early cadet programs did not include university affiliations, sometimes these programs do include

---

5. Stephen B. Hencley, ed., *The Internship in Administrative Preparation* (Columbus, Ohio: The University Council for Educational Administration, 1963), p. 23.

either regular university course work or a special cadet seminar as an integral part of the plan.

The internship program is obtaining more and more recognition as a fitting climax to a program of formal preparation. In spite of the difficulties mentioned above, and others, this program appears to offer an excellent opportunity for the welding of classroom theory and field practice in the university program. The prospective administrator would do well to consider the possibility of an internship as another step in his plan to qualify for educational administration.

PLANNING THE FORMAL PROGRAM

We have now shown that the formal program for the preparation of an educational administrator will include factors involving certification, graduate study, and supervised field experiences. In any plan for a formal program, one should also consider the experience which he is gaining in teaching and plan the program to supplement and reinforce this experience. Remember too that the formal program should not result in narrow specialization. The prospective administrator should make every effort to insure that his higher education will result in his becoming a well-rounded, intellectually developed individual. It is at this point that the strengths and weaknesses of individual universities which prepare administrators should be sought out and evaluated. The kinds of programs offered, the selection procedures utilized, the kinds and scope of fellowships offered, the degrees granted, and the general reputation of higher institutions are important factors to the prospective administrator. There are certain advantages to be gained from doing graduate work in more than one university and, if this seems advisable, problems concerning the transfer of credit should be considered in advance. But, above all, as plans for the formal program are developed, the prospective administrator should remember that there are no substitutes for the written certification requirements of the state and the printed catalog of the university as authoritative and accurate sources of information concerning program requirements. And finally, the prospective administrator must always remember that his ultimate concerns are competency and professional growth. Certificates and degrees are of value only as they reflect competency in educational administration.

SEEKING THE FIRST POSITION

Formal training and experience should lead to the first administrative position for the prospective administrator. One qualification or set of qualifications which the administrator-to-be needs to consider, then, is the ability to seek and gain an administrative position.

There are several ways in which administrative positions are filled. Many principalships and assistant superintendencies and some superintendencies are filled by promotion from within a school system. When persons from outside the system are brought in, it is either by virtue of individual applications for the positions or through recommendations from commercial or university placement offices. Almost all college and university professorships are filled through placement office recommendations, while administrative positions in higher education are filled through promotion or placement office recommendation. Each of these avenues will be discussed briefly here, and then some attention will be given to selection procedures common to all of these approaches.

PROMOTION FROM WITHIN OR WITHOUT

Some large school districts fill all of their principalships by selection from the staff of the system. The assumption is made that the larger district has sufficient personnel to permit the discovery of prospective principals from within who are as well qualified as those who could be found by going outside the system.

The major danger in the process of promotion from within is "inbreeding." If all new administrators in a system are products of the same training program, new ideas and new approaches in educational administration may be scarce. This danger is not impossible to overcome, but the administrator who reaches his position by promotion from within a system should make sure that he has an open mind for ideas from outside.

One other point should be mentioned here. Sometimes those within a school system feel that it is not fair to offer administrative positions to "outsiders." The only fair policy that a board of education can follow in filling administrative positions is one which states that these positions should go to the most highly qualified applicants. The "insider" has no inherent right to such a position except as he possesses qualifications that suit him for the position better than other applicants. This implies that criteria have been developed to aid in the selection process and that these criteria are based on descriptions of the position which adequately define its duties and responsibilities.

There are two conflicting philosophies regarding the relative weight to be given an insider as opposed to an outsider. Some feel that if all other things are equal, the position should go to the insider. This feeling is based on considerations of morale of the staff, familiarity with the problems and processes of the district, and creation of an incentive for those in the system interested in administration. The other viewpoint is that if all other things are equal, the position should go to the outsider. This viewpoint is based on considerations of getting new blood and new ideas into the system, the avoidance of cliques or other human relations problems which may result from inside promotion, and the hope that more qualified people will apply for a position when this philosophy is dominant.

Each of these viewpoints has both strengths and weaknesses. The important point of the prospective administrator is that he know which of the two ideas is prevalent in his school district. Because each viewpoint can be supported on rational grounds, the prospective administrator should not feel that he is unfairly treated if the viewpoint opposite to his is the one that prevails. If he knows the situation, he can and should plan his actions accordingly.

PLACEMENT OFFICE SERVICES

A placement office is, of course, a rather dignified form of employment agency. Every university that prepares educational administrators offers placement services. These are usually free to the student, although small charges are sometimes made to cover a part of the clerical services necessary for the preparation of credentials. In addition, there are many commercial educational placement agencies. A number of these agencies are associated with the National Association of Teacher's Agencies (NATA), a voluntary organization of agencies which maintains certain minimum standards for member agencies. University placement offices also have a voluntary organization known as the National Institutional Teacher Placement Association (NITPA). Commercial agencies are probably more active in the placement of teachers than of administrators, but they do provide services in both areas. Commercial agencies have three general ways of charging for their services—a registration fee, a fee which is a percentage of the first year's income, or a combination of both. For the most part, we feel that university placement offices are more acceptable than commercial offices. The university placement personnel have a better knowledge of the candidates for positions, generally attempt to assess the position as well as the candidates in order to insure a good fit, and provide the same or better results than a commercial office, at much less cost to the candidate. It is our feeling that the profession—in this case represented by the training institutions—should provide its own placement services.

The candidate for an administrative position should take steps to see that the placement office with which he is working is aware of the types of position in which he is interested. His credentials in the placement office should be up to date and inclusive of all important data. As placement services will be utilized beyond the initial position, it is important that the administrator keep his credentials up to date while he is holding an administrative position. Many prospective and practicing administrators fail to gain new positions for which they are qualified because they have not maintained contact with a placement office. A candidate who feels that a placement agency is not serving him well may not have submitted complete records, may not have asked that recommendations for him be submitted to the agency, or may not have indicated to the agency his interest in a position. Good relations between candidate and placement office are another important part of the procedures as one attempts to qualify for and to obtain an administrative position.

INDIVIDUAL APPLICATION

The question of whether or not to apply for an administrative position on one's own in the absence of placement office or school system backing is a difficult one. The candidate, particularly for the first administrative position, must take some initiative. He must, in a real sense, be a job seeker. This fact is generally much less true as one considers administrative positions of major importance. In such cases, the job seeks the man to a much greater extent than in the case of an initial administrative position.

It is impossible to generalize about the so-called lone-wolf approach to seeking an administrative position. We do believe, however, that the approach of the position seeker to those with a position to fill is strengthened considerably if someone other than the candidate shares the candidate's confidence that he is qualified for the position. This "someone" may or may not be a placement officer, a school administrator, or a professor. In any event, the position seeker who attempts to go it alone with no recommendations of any kind will usually find the procedure a difficult one.

Thus it seems evident that the candidate for an initial administrative position should employ initiative wisely. He should be on the alert for positions in which he is interested and for which he is qualified. He should bend every effort to making his interest and his qualifications known. He should work with a placement office if possible, but he usually cannot afford to sit back and await placement. He should secure a list of people who know him and who will recommend him for a position. And—finally, but really at the head of the list—he should be sure that he is prepared for an administrative position, should one become available. The importance of being "at the right place with the right preparation at the right time" cannot be overloked.

SELECTION PROCEDURES

Let us assume that, through a placement office or through recommendation from some other source, the prospective administrator has been invited to submit a formal application for an administrative position. What can he expect as he seeks this first position? It is difficult to specify the procedures that may be used by a given district as the candidates for an administrative position are screened for selection of the ultimate appointee. Several common procedures will be discussed here, although it is not likely that many districts will use all of these procedures.

Application forms. While detailed application forms are common for teaching positions, less use of them is made in seeking candidates for administrative positions. The basic reason for this is probably that when administrators are sought, reliance is put upon the interview, a possible field investigation, and the credentials of the candidates. However, care should be taken to complete any required application forms properly, accurately, neatly, and completely. Even if not interested in the position, the candidate who is asked to apply should write a letter briefly indicating that he is not presently interested and expressing some appreciation for the invitation. This practice is more than mere courtesy, for the ignored invitation can sometimes loom large in the future.

Tests. Some school boards are using one or more tests as screening devices for the selection of administrators. Such tests include written and oral English tests, essay tests over the field or fields included in the position applied for, performance tests in which candidates are appraised in situations similar to those which might be encountered in the position, physical examinations, and objective examinations organized around such areas as general administration, curriculum, guidance, methodology, and supervision. Testing procedures are found more often in city school districts than in smaller districts, but the use of tests as a part of the selection procedure is becoming more common.

The candidate for a given administrative position should ascertain if tests are given as a part of the selection procedure for that position, if examples of questions or specific descriptions of the tests are made available to candidates, and if such tests are given individually or are given to a group at a given time and place. It is likely that the tendency for school districts to give some kind of test to candidates for administrative positions will increase in the future, and the candidate should be aware of this trend.

Interviews. After the screening process, most boards of education interview the final two or three candidates for a superintendency, or the superintendent and other central administrative personnel interview the final candidates for a principalship. Although in many cases these interviews are rather vague and general in nature, a number of districts have developed a check list of specific desired qualifications about which the interviewing team plans to gain information and make evaluations during the interview. The interview is generally used to provide the prospective employer with some indication of the appearance, poise, speaking ability, and knowledge of the candidate.

The candidate should realize that the interview is a time of mutual exploration. He is being looked at, but he is also looking at the position. Thus the interview should include some time when he can become the interviewer. He should make sure that he understands the duties and responsibilities of the position, the opportunity it offers to work toward mutually satisfying goals, and the conditions of employment. He should ask some questions about the school district and the community. Often one of the factors that an employer uses in evaluating a candidate after an interview is the nature of the questions asked. For example, the young man seeking his first principalship who asks only about tenure and retirement reveals much about himself through his questions. As he prepares for his interview, then, he should be concerned with both his answers and his questions.

Field rating. While it is not a usual procedure for the selection of a person for his first administrative position, some mention should be made of the field rating. When a list of applicants for a position is reduced to only a few, many boards of education or professional employing personnel visit the school districts in which the remaining candidates are presently employed to gain an on-the-spot evaluation. There they interview administrators, teachers, and lay citizens so that the employing officials can gain further insight into the qualifications of the candidates. There is little that a candidate can do to prepare for this procedure other than to insure that he is doing his best wherever he is. Many candidates for administrative positions have found that because they have considered their present position beneath them and have acted accordingly, they have never been able to rise to a position they consider appropriate to their ability.

THE ETHICS OF JOB SEEKING

We have already said enough about the professional nature of educational administration to make it unnecessary to dwell at great length on the ethics of seeking an administrative position. Only a few points might be mentioned here and these but briefly. As a prospective administrator, the candidate for a position should proceed through the established channels in a district rather than trying, for example, to go directly to individual board members. The subordinate who attempts to gain an administrative position by assisting in the downfall of his administrator is unethical and is establishing a precedent that may be used by his own subordinates in the future.

A candidate for an administrative position should strive to gain that position in open, ethical competition with other qualified candidates. One cannot be proud of gaining a position by manipulation or secrecy so that the employing agency does not compare his qualifications with those of others. If he is not the best-qualified person for the position, he should not have it, and he should have additional incentive to increase his qualifications.

IN REVIEW

We have pointed out that in seeking his first administrative position, the prospective administrator should become familiar with the avenues that seem to lead to the position he desires. These may involve promotions within a system or promotions to another system. The candidate should associate himself with a university placement office and insure that his credentials are in order and up to date. He should be aware that his best chance for gaining an administrative position will usually be based on recommendations from a placement office, from administrative personnel in his district, or from both, rather than only on his individual application.

As he becomes an active candidate for a given position, the prospective administrator will find himself facing several kinds of selection procedures. These may include a review of his credentials and recommendations, the submission of a formal application, participation in a testing procedure, an interview, and a field rating. Throughout the entire process, the candidate needs to remember that he is seeking a position in a highly skilled profession and that it is important to him and to the profession that all of his acts be ethical.

CONTINUED PROFESSIONAL GROWTH

Every administrator who assumes an administrative position is only partially prepared for that position. He will probably never be able to say realistically that he is completely prepared for the position he holds, and there will always be other administrative positions for which he is even less well prepared. Thus the effort to qualify for a position should not end upon its assumption.

CONTINUED ON-CAMPUS PREPARATION

Many major administrative positions, as we mentioned earlier in this chapter, now require that the incumbent possess a doctor's degree. The administrator will undoubtedly seek his first or his second administrative position before he earns this degree. This means that while he is serving as an administrator he will also be continuing his university work. Even if the doctor's degree does not become one of his goals, university graduate work should be a part of his continuing professional growth. Many workshops and seminars are planned particularly for the practicing administrator, and the insights gained on his job add value to any course he may take. Just as most salary policy statements in school districts require that the teacher return to a campus periodically for professional growth, it is important that the administrator consider this same requirement as it applies to him.

It should be noted also that the present trend in master's degree programs for educational administrators is to place less stress than formerly on specialization in administration and more stress on the broader areas of education in general. This means, in effect, that much of the course work in more advanced phases of administration is offered on the post-master's degree level and that such course work is planned for the person who has begun the practice of educational administration. In short, then, the master's degree represents minimum preparation for the educational administrator.

There are other possibilities for on-campus professional growth of the practicing administrator in addition to the course work we have stressed. Most universities hold conferences that offer opportunities for administrators to gain new understanding of their work. Many institutions and professional associations have developed one- or two-day problem-centered clinics in which twenty or thirty administrators gather with university personnel and other consultants to deal with specific problems arising in the field. There are numerous opportunities for administrators to avail themselves of university services such as consultative service for local studies, cooperative research projects, or the development of local professional growth programs. The ideal situation is one in which the relationships between universities and administrators are continuous and mutually beneficial. Often, practicing administrators make themselves available to assist in a university's pre-service preparation program and serve in a variety of ways as cooperating university staff members. Only in this way can the two groups—the practitioners and those charged with the preparation of practitioners—provide each other with the unique and important advantages and aids which each has to offer the other.

GROWTH ON THE JOB

One of the best training grounds for the administrator is an administrative position. Every day presents him with opportunities not only to serve the schools of his school district but also to increase his own professional knowledge, skills, and competence. As we have stated much earlier here, if experience is to be educative, the educational values of experience must be actively sought. As the administrator works with teachers, with other administrators, with board members, with parents, or with community leaders, he should be increasing his qualifications as a top-level, competent administrator.

A number of activities in which administrators engage are aimed at professional growth. Included among these activities are planned programs of intervisitation, development by groups of administrators of handbooks and other materials for mutual use, and group studies of skills and techniques necessary for effective performance of various administrative tasks. Some of the most valuable activities available to administrators are sponsored by the various professional organizations to which they belong. By working with colleagues for professional growth, the administrator can help to insure that his competence for his present position and his qualifications for other, more advanced positions will continue to grow. If educational administration is to grow as a profession, its practitioners must see themselves in a continual learning situation in which the aim is both their own growth and the growth of the profession.

SUGGESTED ACTIVITIES

1. Interview a number of principals and superintendents in your area and attempt to identify how they happened to get their first administrative position. From their perspective, what factors seemed to be important in their being appointed? What factors seemed unimportant?
2. Examine several university programs leading to certification as an educational administrator. What opportunities do these programs offer for connecting theory with practice and for obtaining familiarity with the world of practice?
3. Study the succession patterns of administrators in your area. When appointing people to their first administrative position, do the school districts tend to appoint insiders or outsiders? Were the administrators whom you studied insiders or outsiders when they were appointed to their first administrative position? Are there differences in the succession patterns of elementary school principals, junior high school principals, senior high school principals, and superintendents?
4. Ask your major professor or the placement director of your university to review for you the career lines of a few recent graduates from your department. Note the positions these persons have held in school districts and in other agencies.

SELECTED READINGS

Bridges, Edwin M., and Baehr, Melany E. "The Future of Administrator Selection Procedures." *Administrator's Notebook* 14, 5 (January 1971).

Briner, Conrad. "The Superintendent and the Selection of Subordinate Administrators." *Administrator's Notebook* 8, 6 (February 1960).

Campbell, Roald F., and Newell, L. Jackson. *A Study of Professors of Educational Administration.* Columbus, Ohio: University Council for Educational Administration, 1973.

Culbertson, Jack, et al. *Social Science Content for Preparing Educational Leaders.* Columbus, Ohio: Charles E. Merrill Publishing Co., 1973.

Culbertson, Jack, and Hencley, S. P. *Preparing Administrators: New Perspectives.* Columbus, Ohio: University Council for Educational Administration, 1962.

Hencley, S. P., ed. *The Internship in Administrative Preparation.* Columbus, Ohio: University Council for Educational Administration, 1963.

Howsam, Robert B., and Morphet, Edgar L. "Certification of Educational Administrators." *Journal of Teacher Education* 9, 1 (March 1958): 75–96 and 9, 2 (June 1958): 187–203.

Knezevich, Stephen J., ed. *The American School Superintendency.* Arlington, Va.: American Association of School Administrators, 1971.

March, James G. "Analytical Skills & the University Training of Educational Administrators." *The Journal of Educational Administration* 12 (May 1974): 17–44.

Woellner, Elizabeth H., and Wood, M. Aurilla. *Requirements for Certification of Teachers, Counselors, Librarians, Administrators for Elementary Schools, Secondary Schools, Junior Colleges.* Chicago: The University of Chicago Press, revised annually.

14

CHALLENGE OF ADMINISTRATION

As we reflect upon what we said about the job of administration and about the person who is to undertake such a job, we feel some need to present and amplify the challenge or challenges inherent in educational administration. This chapter, perhaps more than any other part of the book, is our credo.

We take the position that a particular kind of educative process open to all is necessary in a society that aspires to a democratic way of life. In like manner we see a public school system characterized by certain values and practices as an essential part of the educative process; and finally, we take the position that administrative leaders who meet certain requirements occupy critical roles in the public school. We shall now amplify each of these challenges.

THE DEMOCRATIC WAY OF LIFE

We believe that the democratic way of life offers the primary challenge to educational administration. To be sure, this is a challenge to all citizens of our nation, but we think that such a challenge holds unique meaning for the school administrator.

A GREAT EXPERIMENT

The democratic way of life was and is a great experiment. When, historically, America fell heir to movements that had begun to stir Europe, one of these was the Protestant Reformation, which challenged the authority of church and state. The movement placed great stress upon the responsibility of the individual for the salvation of his own soul. John Locke in England during the seventeenth century supplied some of the intellectual foundations for popular rule. Denying that kings had any divine right to rule, he placed sovereignty in the hands of the people. The founders of our government referred to him as "the great Mr. Locke" and utilized much of his thinking in formulating our federal constitution.

As Counts has so well described it, this intellectual leadership shifted later to France:

> In the eighteenth century the leadership in thought crossed the Channel to France. A galaxy of brilliant minds, with great gifts of expression, so dominated the age that it has come to be called after them and their work—the Age of Enlightenment. They proclaimed the coming victory of naturalism over supernaturalism, of science over theology, of human reason over established authority. Voltaire attacked the traditional dogmas of church and state as barriers to human advance. Montesquieu saw government, not as unchanging and sanctified by divine will, but as an expression of a people living in a particular time and place. Diderot and d'Alembert edited the great Encyclopedia which, they hoped, would bring the the best of scientific and practical knowledge to many people and arouse enthusiasm for reform and improvement. Rousseau popularized the political ideas of Locke defending with the power of genius the doctrine that only the freely expressed will of the people can render any government legitimate. Condorcet, in his *Historical Sketch of the Progress of the Human Mind,* clothed with vast learning and philosophic grasp the idea of human progress and the perfectibility of man and his institutions. These men, and others like them, prepared the way for the French Revolution and other revolutions to follow in the nineteenth century.[1]

The movement to free the common man found fertile soil in America, where, in the first place, tradition was not such a binding force. Secondly, free land was available, for almost three hundred years, to any who would settle upon it and begin its cultivation. Economic opportunity appears to have had much to do with the development of social and political democracy.

But from its inception the idea of a democratic way of life was a radical one. The thought that all men could and should read and interpret the scriptures for themselves, as advocated by Luther, was in direct contradiction to the established order of the Catholic Church. Locke's ideas of the sovereignty of the people ran counter to centuries of governmental

1. George S. Counts, *Education and American Civilization* (New York: Bureau of Publications, Teachers College, Columbia University, 1952), p. 52.

practice. Yet despite the novelty of these ideas, many of them have been put into practice in America. What success they will have one cannot yet say; the experiment goes on. The impact of the idea is still being determined, for the capacity of the common man to rise to such a role is fraught with difficulties. If one is both a common man and nonwhite the difficulties appear to be somewhat greater. But the excitement of participating in a great experiment can be experienced by any who will.

OUR HISTORICAL DOCUMENTS

Despite the uneven course of the development of the democratic way of life in America, and despite times when there has been downright despair regarding the status of the movement, our historic documents attest that, in the long view, there has been steady growth in this direction. Let us make brief reference to some of those documents.

As early as 1620 the Englishmen who had set out to plant a colony in the northern "Parts of Virginia" signed what has now become famous as the Mayflower Compact. Among other things they stated that they

> Do by these Presents, solemnly and mutually in the Presence of God and one another, covenant and combine ourselves together into a civil Body Politick, for our better Ordering and Preservation, and furtherance of the Ends aforesaid. . . .

This is a clear expression of the need to work together for the common good. Despite the conviction these people had that they must leave their own country and go to a new land where they could worship God according to their own conscience, they recognized that there must also be group action for the common good. This concern for the common good became one of the values of the new society.

More than a hundred and fifty years later, in 1776, when the Colonists felt is necessary to explain to the world their resistance to the British Crown, the Declaration of Independence was enunciated. In that document, well known to most of us, is language relevant to our purpose here:

> We hold these truths to be self evident, that all men are created equal, that they are endowed by their Creator with certain unalienable Rights, that among these are Life, Liberty, and the pursuit of Happiness. That to secure these rights, Governments are instituted among Men, deriving their just powers from the consent of the governed. That, whenever any Form of Government becomes destructive of these ends, it is the Right of the People to alter or abolish it, . . .

Let us look at two of the ideas in the above excerpt. "That all men are created equal" is a powerful concept. Men, to be sure, are not equal, physically or intellectually. But before God and the law our founders contended that they are equal. With all of our fumbling regarding civil rights, this aspect of the democratic faith has persisted—persisted until the franchise was widened, until the Emancipation Proclamation was issued, until the school desegregation decision of the United States Supreme Court was handed down in 1954, and until the voting law of 1965 was passed. While general acceptance of the idea in practice has been distressingly slow, the idea itself has conquered the armies of kings and dictators and continues to be more than a match for bigotry and sophistry.

Another concept from the Declaration of Independence is that government should serve the people who create it. And when it no longer serves the purposes which the people intended in creating it, it is to be altered or abolished. Here is legal approval for revolution. Here also is the enunciation of the idea that man is of prime importance and his institutions secondary. Man's institutions, being instrumental, are to be shaped to his needs and not his needs to the institutions, as has been attempted in totalitarian regimes.

As the various states debated the federal Constitution from 1787 to 1790, it became clear that a bill of rights would have to be appended. Thus, the first ten amendments to our Constitution became effective as of 1791. The first amendment includes these significant words:

> Congress shall make no law respecting the establishment of religion, or prohibiting the free exercise thereof; or abridging the freedom of speech or of the press; or the right of the people peaceably to assemble . . .

A reading of the McCollum,[2] Zorach,[3] Schempp,[4] and Lemon[5] cases will convince one that the injunction on religion is still a very live issue. And in hundreds of instances, our courts have affirmed freedom of speech, of press, and of assembly. These freedoms, despite their abridgment at times, have become part of the democratic doctrine.

Following the Civil War more specific language was necessary to insure the application of some of these freedoms to blacks. Thus, in 1868, the fourteenth amendment to the Constitution, part of which reads as follows, became effective:

> No State shall make or enforce any law which shall abridge the privileges or immunities of citizens of the United States. . . .

---

2. *McCollum v. Board of Education,* 333 U.S. 203.
3. *Zorach* v. *Clauson,* 343 U.S. 306.
4. *School District of Abington Township* v. *Schempp,* 374 U.S. 203.
5. *Lemon* v. *Kurtzman,* 403 U.S. 602.

These words definitely strengthened the hand of the federal government in protecting the rights of minorities from what had been discriminatory legislation in some of the states. More important, our national values were now to be policed by our *national* government.

In considering the extension of voting privileges, it seems rather shocking that it was not until 1920, with the addition of the nineteenth amendment to the Constitution, that women in all states of our nation were granted the franchise. Tardy as such action now seems, the event is further evidence that early pronouncements on the democratic way of life must receive later implementation.

Space does not permit us to continue this survey of our historical documents. We would, however, like to make reference to the now famous Brown case of 1954.[6] After suggesting the central place of public education in a nation such as ours, the U.S. Supreme Court said:

> We conclude that in the field of public education the doctrine of "separate but equal" has no place. Separate educational facilities are inherently unequal. Therefore, we hold that the plaintiffs and others similarly situated for whom the actions have been brought are, by reason of the segregation complained of, deprived of the equal protection of the laws guaranteed by the Fourteenth Amendment. . . .

This decision by the Court and many subsequent decisions appear to represent, despite what some see as a reversal in the Detroit[7] case, a movement toward full realization of democratic values.

One can quarrel with the above presentation. One could say our words as Americans are better than our deeds. They are. But we keep at it, and our deeds seem to improve. One could say that ours is essentially political democracy, and that our social democracy has not kept pace with it. Again, one might be right, but we submit that political democracy is essential if social democracy is to be achieved. Or one could say the right to vote assumes that accurate information is available to the voter, a condition which many now attempt to subvert. To be sure, this is one of our difficulties, but this very condition constitutes part of the challenge with which we are faced. In other words, what has been done and what remains to be done constitute two parts of the great experiment.

OPERATIONAL AGREEMENTS

Although our culture, as we shall note later, is far from expressing unanimity on many value questions, we do seem to have reached certain operational

6. *Brown* et al. v. *Board of Education of Topeka,* 347 U.S. 483.
7. *Milliken* v. *Bradley,* 94 S. Ct. 3112 (1974).

agreements. Some of those agreements were reflected in the words of President Johnson when he convened the Whole House Conference on Education in 1965. He said,

> . . . I want you to bring all the tools of modern knowledge—from physics to psychology—to bear on the increase of learning. And if these tools are still inadequate, then it's our job to fashion new ones and better ones.
>
> To guide discussion in this conference we are formulating a series of questions, and I hope you'll give these questions your most careful thought and your boldest imagination . . . [at] the conference. They include:
>
> How can we bring first-class education to the city slum and to the impoverished rural areas? Today the children of five million families are denied it.
>
> How can we stimulate every child to catch the love of learning so that he wants to stay in school? One million children now drop out of schools each year.
>
> How do we guarantee that new funds will bring new ideas and techniques to our school system—not just simply expand the old and the outmoded?
>
> How can local and state and federal government best cooperate to make education . . . the first among all the nation's goals?[8]

Reference to *Goals for Americans,*[9] the work of the President's Commission on National Goals, at an earlier time, is also illuminating. This commission emphasized that opportunity for individual development must remain a primary concern; that discrimination on the basis of religion, sex, or race was morally wrong; that the degree of effective liberty available to the people is the ultimate test; and that the development of the individual and the nation demands that education at every level be improved.

It seems possible to arrive at the value positions noted above from different philosophical orientations. For that reason we are stressing here our *operational* agreements rather than our philosophical differences. This we must do, in any culture as diversified as that in America, if there is to be a common ground for action.

In light of such a position, we wish to set forth a set of values which we think gives meaning to what we have been calling a democratic way of life. First, there is implied a *belief in people.* This, as we have already indicated, is much harder to live than to say. Nevertheless, our history and our action, even though the latter has at times been tardy, suggest

---

8. Subcommittee on Education of the Committee on Labor and Public Welfare, United States Senate, *White House Conference on Education* (Washington, D.C.: U.S. Government Printing Office, 1965), p. 17.

9. Report of the President's Commission on National Goals, *Goals for Americans* (Englewood Cilffs, N.J.: Prentice-Hall, 1960), pp. 3–6.

that most of us place people above institutions. For most of us this means all people, without regard to race, color, religion, economic circumstance, or national background. In particular, we believe that educational opportunity should not be denied any person.

A second value characteristic of the democratic way of life is a belief in *cooperation for the common good.* True, some cry out against the welfare state, but when the nation has been threatened, even as early as the Mayflower Compact, we have been willing to join together, to submerge individual desires when necessary, to foster the welfare of the group. This tendency received special impetus during the era of the New Deal, but it is noteworthy that Republican administrators have repealed little of the New Deal legislation. Actually, both political parties act this way because we as people adhere to this principle.

Three, our nation believes in *freedom of the press, of speech, and of religious expression.* This was the substance of the first amendment to our federal Constitution. Again, we have abridgment and abuses of these rights, but in the end our courts and the public stand up for these freedoms. To be sure, we have had to learn that freedom is a relative matter and that it must be accompanied by responsibility. The relative nature of freedom does not mean that any one of us is free to pursue his own interests to the detriment of the group. This balance between personal freedom and the social good is the thing we are working to achieve.

Finally, our people accept *the method of intelligence* as an approach to problem-solving. Some of us, as Broudy[10] has suggested, may be temporarily enamoured with the new humanism which seems to stress feeling more than thought. Yet there seems to be a conviction on the part of most Americans that we can, by giving thought, solve many of the problems with which we are faced. Moreover, we have a conviction that this ability to think is not the possession of just the few, but the heritage of the many.

CHALLENGES TO THE DEMOCRATIC WAY

There are both challenges *to* and challenges *of* the democratic way of life. Let us deal with the first of these. Briefly, the challenges to the democratic way might be categorized as outside and inside challenges. The chief outside challenge, as is now clear to most of us, is world communism. Communism in its Russian or Chinese expression is a far cry from what Karl Marx, its founder, visualized. To be sure, Marx advocated a militant movement, but the ends he sought seem to many to be in keeping with the Hebraic-Christian ethic to which we ourselves subscribe. He wanted an abundant life for the individual, the elimination of the exploitation of man, and the establishment of a world-wide regime of peace and brotherhood.

10. See Harry S. Broudy, *The Real World of the Public Schools* (New York: Harcourt Brace Jovanovich, Inc., 1972), p. 75.

It has now become clear that communism in practice exalts the state above the individual, that the ruling hierarchy is straining to perpetuate autocracy, and that any challenge to the system will be quelled by force. It may have taken such events as the Hungarian rebellion of 1956 and the invasion of Czechoslovakia in 1968 to convince many people, but most of us now see world communism for what it is. Clearly, we do not wish to be dominated by such a system.

There is also a challenge to democracy from within. In spite of our optimism about what we believe to be long-term gains in the achievement of the democratic way, there are definite schizophrenic symptoms in our culture. Brameld has listed them as follows:

> Self-interest versus social-interest.
> Inequality versus equality.
> Planlessness versus planning.
> Nationalism versus internationalism.
> Absolutism versus experimentalism.
> Man-against-himself versus man-for-himself.[11]

An examination of each of these issues will convince one that at both the verbal and the operational levels of American life there are adherents of each of the contrasting approaches. Unfortunately, the perpetuation of these dichotomies obscures the point that, in many cases, it is not an either-or proposition. There may be, for instance, an enlightened self-interest that is consistent with social interest.

This analysis of our cultural conflicts suggests that our society is a dynamic one, that its direction may not always be clear, and that in the arena of ideas a good many battles are still ahead of us. This struggle is the inside challenge to the democratic way.

CHALLENGE OF THE DEMOCRATIC WAY

There is also the challenge *of* the democratic way of life. Let us examine briefly a few aspects of this part of the problem. The first of these is perhaps the challenge of accurate information. If the average citizen is to participate in his economic, social, or political destiny, he must be informed. This has always been a difficult expectation. In our early history it was a question of teaching people to read and to understand, and then of making written documents widely available.

In recent decades the process has been complicated by the tremendous development of the mass media, notably radio and television, and by the great competition for the mind of man that has evolved. As a matter of fact, the money spent annually on advertising in this country ap-

11. Theodore Brameld, *Philosophies of Education in Cultural Perspective* (New York: Dryden Press, 1955), pp. 53–62.

proximates that spent for the operation of all the schools and colleges in the nation. In advertising, of course, the motive is not primarily to inform but rather to sell.

The appeal of advertising to the conscious man seems serious enough, but recently, with the rise of motivation research (M-R), there is also planned, large-scale appeal to man's subconscious.[12] The application of M-R to the selling of automobiles may seem somewhat amusing, but when the same techniques are applied to presidential elections, as they were in recent campaigns, one can become cynical about the "information" made available to the average elector.

A second challenge *of* the democratic way is that of concern about public affairs. A number of studies suggest that in most communities, about 50 percent of the people are uninformed and apathetic about public questions.[13] Some social critics go so far as to suggest that this indifference reflects a twilight period in our political system.[14] In any case this condition represents two potential dangers. There is first the possibility that the leadership group of a community will go unchecked. Such a course of action may mean that the leaders cease in time to represent the values and programs of their constituents. The second danger inherent in apathy is found in the possibility that citizens with no facts at hand may become prey to those who seek personal advantage and who do not hesitate to use emotional and biased approaches. In both of these dangers the challenge of how to create concern in people is clearly exemplified.

Along with the challenges of providing information and of creating concern, there is the challenge of action. How Americans exercise their voting privileges may serve to illustrate our point. In recent presidential elections only about two-thirds of the persons of voting age in the nation cast their ballots. In some states between 70 and 80 percent of the potential voters cast their ballots, while in other states only 30 to 50 percent voted. If voting is indicative of other action on the part of citizens concerning the common good, and we fear it is, there is little wonder that organized efforts to thwart projects designed to foster the general welfare do succeed.

THE EDUCATIVE PROCESS

The second challenge to educational administration is the educative process. We contend, moreover, that without an educative process of the

12. See Vance Packard, *The Hidden Persuaders* (New York: David McKay Company, 1957). See also Joe McGinniss, *The Selling of the President, 1968.* (New York: Trident Press, 1969).

13. See *Supplementary Papers—Cincinnati School Survey* (Chicago: Midwest Administration Center, University of Chicago, 1968), pp. 9-24–9-54.

14. For instance, see Robert Nisbet, "The Decline of Academic Nationalism," *Change* (Summer 1974).

kind we shall describe, the democratic way of life is an impossibility. In other words, if the great experiment to which we have alluded is to succeed, a genuine opportunity for learning must be available to all.

MEANING OF THE EDUCATIVE PROCESS

The educative process of which we speak is much broader than schooling. Actually, much of what we have learned was not acquired in school. Our schooling seems to have relatively little to do, perhaps unfortunately, with how we vote, how we spend our leisure, and the ways by which many of us make our living. Without in any sense deprecating the school, it sharpens our discussion to recognize that education and schooling are not synonymous.

Upon reflection one soon decides that the total culture is involved in teaching and learning. Perhaps we can see this point more easily in cultures other than our own, described in the writings of the anthropologists.[15] For instance, Benedict speaks of the Zuñi Indians as a ceremonious people. She says that grown men spent most of their waking hours in ceremonial observance, for which a staggering amount of word-perfect ritual has to be memorized.

The teaching-learning potential of our own culture has been dealt with in dramatic terms by Bloom.[16] After a comprehensive synthesis of the research in human development, he concludes that, with the exception of school achievement, the most rapid period of development is in the first five years of life. Thus, physical growth, intelligence, language development, and other characteristics are more than 50 percent determined by the home and its surrounding culture by the time the child enters the school.

In this educative process, or cultural adaptation, what are the important steps? As we see it, they are three in number: (1) acquiring of a feeling of being at home in one's culture, (2) learning about one's culture, and (3) contributing to one's culture. Let us look at each of these.

The first step of coming to feel at home in one's culture appears to be largely emotional in character. The affection extended to the new baby by the parents and other members of the family are part of it. The trial and error of age-mates as they learn to play together, whether in a nursery school or on the street, represent an important potential in the process. The great need for peer approval found in most adolescents and the need which all of us have for recognition on the part of other adults are also involved. Somehow we must feel that we belong.

But we must feel that we belong to the larger culture, not merely

---

15. For example, see Margaret Mead, *Coming of Age in Samoa* (New York: W. Morrow & Company, 1928) and Ruth Benedict, *Patterns of Culture* (Boston: Houghton Mifflin, 1934).

16. Benjamin S. Bloom, *Stability and Change in Human Characteristics* (New York: Wiley, 1964).

to some minority group within it. This point has particular relevance today for those who grow up in the slums of our central cities. The feelings of hopelessness and alienation of youth in slum neighborhoods has been depicted by Conant.[17]

But alienation is found not only in the slums. We see manifestations of alienation among privileged youth in our high schools and on our college campuses. Keniston has argued that alienation from American society is fostered by stresses flowing from the unquestioned primacy of technology in our society.[18] According to his analysis the supremacy of technology de-emphasizes human values and needs and creates conditions such as chronic social change, fragmentation in society, discontinuities between childhood and adulthood, and value conflicts, which alienate us all to some extent and totally alienate certain especially sensitized individuals. We cannot pass from this topic without noting that, in addition to the adverse effects of technology, another source of alienation among our youth in recent years has been the increasingly obvious contradictions between our society's ideals and its practices, especially with respect to racial equality.

But the educative process cannot stop with belonging; there is also the necessity for understanding. This places great demands upon all of us. How can we learn about the social and physical world in which we live? Much can be gained from observation, but we soon find a need for trained observation, and observation, without reference to some conceptual scheme, may be relatively pointless. Regardless of the field of study, we soon learn that we need to consider the observations, the feelings, and the reflections of others. This process would seem to constitute the beginning of scholarship, whether in or out of an organized school.

But there is still another aspect of the educative process. Feeling at home in and knowing about one's culture ought to lead one to contribute to that culture. Contributions, to be sure, will vary greatly in nature and in quality; and ways of improving the culture will be apparent only to those who have the capacity to examine critically the cultural practices now extant.

The challenge of the educative process to equip people to reflect critically about the conditions of life around them and to project possible improvements is, we believe, the aspect of the educative process most important to the survival of the democratic idea. Unfortunately, those who attempt to examine our way of life critically, in an attempt to make improvements, are often misunderstood and sometimes even called subversive. Many people fail to recognize the value and importance of this critical examination, and ignorantly use words of abuse to describe people who, through their criticisms, are contributing toward the improvement of our way of life.

---

17. James B. Conant, *Slums and Suburbs* (New York: McGraw Hill, 1961).

18. Kenneth Keniston, *The Uncommitted: Alienated Youth in American Society* (New York: Dell Publishing, 1965).

MANY INSTITUTIONS CONTRIBUTE

Many institutions make contributions to the educative process. The home, despite the suggestion of some that it has reached a point of declining influence, still seems to be the most important educative agency we have. Our basic personality characteristics, including such simple matters as friendliness or distrust, are in large part a product of the home. Our attitudes toward religion, government, sex, and learning itself reflect the home environment. To be sure, the home also tends to reflect the biases of the culture of which it is a part. The home, as any social worker or psychiatrist can testify, is a significant influence in whatever a person learns.

For most people the church, too, is an important agency in the educative process. That segment of our population that affiliates with a church and participates in church activities is subject to an educative influence of considerable magnitude. For instance, the attitudes of these people toward marriage, toward childbearing, toward authority, and toward social behavior are greatly influenced by the church. For those people who belong to no church, the influence of the church may be less direct, but it is nonetheless significant. The nonchurchgoer as well as the churchgoer is affected by the Hebraic-Christian tradition as it has found expression in our ethics and in our law.

Also important is the street corner or the play group of one's peers. Beginning at about age eight or ten and continuing through adolescence, most young people feel great need for acceptance by their peers. Often it takes expression in the clothes that are worn. If leather jackets are the thing, then leather jackets there must be. Woe to any parent who has the temerity to suggest that there is a satisfactory substitute. Many times status with one's fellows is acquired by doing those things which the gang has decided to do. Dragracing with souped-up cars, for instance, in some communities among certain youngsters has become a prestige activity. Anyone not joining in the activity is labeled "chicken." Clearly, then, these peer groups have great influence with young people and are thus potent educative influences.

Nor should we stop with young people. Riesman early made the point that our culture is becoming more and more other-directed.[19] In other words, the sanctions one feels, which influence one's behavior, have their origins in the group to which one belongs rather than in one's upbringing as reflected in one's conscience. Whyte makes a similar point when he speaks of the organization man.[20] For all of us, the group or groups with which we affiliate, particularly in our work, seem to be decisive forces in determining our family life, our goals for educating our children, our dress, our leisure, and our values in general.

---

19. David Riesman et al., *The Lonely Crowd* (New Haven: Yale University Press, 1950).
20. William H. Whyte, Jr., *The Organization Man* (New York: Simon & Schuster, 1956), chap. 3.

All of this gives some support to Jencks[21] who contends that family background is the most important determinant of educational attainment. Even if we accept this point, we should not overlook the fact that the school has a unique role in the educative process, as we shall soon see. May we conclude this section by emphasizing the point that an educative process that is comprehensive, understanding, and permissive within limits is essential to the democratic way of life. This means that the educative role of many institutions in our society should be recognized. It means, too, that each institution should exercise its role with some recognition that other influences and agencies are and must be at work in our kind of society. Finally, it means that class barriers should be sufficiently flexible so that one's place and position in society can be altered through the educative process.

THE PUBLIC SCHOOL

The third challenge to education administration is found in the public school itself. Despite the breadth of the educative process, as suggested above, we hold that the public school has a unique, indeed an indispensable, part to play in that process. Let us examine such an idea.

CHARACTERISTICS

About 90 percent of the children and youth in this country attend public schools.[22] Without deprecating the role of the private school in American education, it seems clear that a great part of the task of providing formal schooling is placed squarely upon the public school.

The significance of the percentage of total school enrollment found in the public school is not entirely a matter of numbers. The pupil populations of the public schools tend, by and large, to be more heterogenerous than the pupil populations of the private schools. Although this circumstance has its problems, it also provides opportunities, for the public school becomes a prototype of society itself. The diversity of our nation socially, economically, politically, religiously, racially, and academically is well reflected in the public school.

We do not wish to overdo this matter. We are well aware of the fact that many individual public schools, particularly in urban and suburban areas, have pupil populations with relatively less diversity than suggested

21. Christopher Jencks et al., *Inequality: A Reassessment of the Effect of Family and Schooling in America* (New York: Basic Books, Inc., 1972), p. 158.

22. *Statistical Abstract of the United States, 1974* (Washington, D.C.: U.S. Government Printing Office, 1969), p. 109.

above. Indeed, some suburban communities have segregated exclusive schools and central cities tend to have segregated slum schools. It now seems clear that there must be deliberate social planning of both housing and school attendance areas if most youngsters in the public schools are going to have the opportunity to find out how the other half lives.

In this diversity, once common and now harder to attain, the public school pupil has an opportunity to acquire a sense of realism as to what people are like; he can note the variety of contributions that its various members make to the group; and he can learn much about relating himself to many kinds of people. These skills are essential in our kind of culture.

The public school has still another opportunity. More than any other nonschool community agency, and possibly more than most private schools, the public school can be the most impartial institution in our culture. Business, labor, and farm organizations have great difficulty in viewing all sides of a controversial issue, particularly if the issue affects them in any way. Most churches must approach problems within a particular framework. Thus, useful as these organizations are for some purposes, they alone cannot nurture adequately the person with an inquiring mind who wishes to weigh the evidence on all sides of a tough problem and come to his own decision.

We recognize that some teachers in the public schools are not adequately prepared to guide objective inquiry, but we still maintain that the opportunity for such inquiry is present in the public school and that it is being admirably exploited in some instances. Moreover, we have found that thoughtful members of special interest groups such as business, labor, and agriculture are expecting the public school to exercise its role of impartiality.

THE SCHOOL'S UNIQUE ROLE

With this brief consideration of what the public school is like, actually and potentially, we shall next turn to the unique role of the public school. This is a difficult task, for over the years public schools have gradually taken on more and more functions, usually as a result of public demand. Moral education on one hand, and driver training on the other, are two cases in point. Sometimes it seems that relatively little examination of the appropriateness of the new functions being placed in the public school has been made either by the public or by the school people. Perhaps, in some cases, other agencies in society are better equipped to meet these new demands than is the school. We believe that the transfer of certain child-rearing functions from the home to the school is a case in point.

Another reason it is difficult to delimit the public school's role is the concomitant character of learning. As a child learns to read and write he is also learning many other things. He may be learning to like or dislike school. He may be learning to like or dislike teachers. He may find in his acquiring of skill with words that the doors to ideas have been unlocked, or he may find reading a wearisome task, never to be pursued except under duress. We cannot ignore or be unconcerned about these concomitants.

Despite the difficulties inherent in depicting the unique role of the school, we shall attempt such a task. Our concern is that the public school recognize some sort of priority in what it does, so that those things which are essential to the democratic way of life and to the educative process shall not be left undone. We are not offering objection to the fact that other functions can and in many cases should be performed. Moreover, we recognize that the school shares with other institutions responsibility for helping the young acquire constructive beliefs and attitudes. We do hope, however, that as the demands placed upon the public school increase, the financial resources to meet such demands will be proportionately increased.

The first task we would place upon the public school is teaching for literacy. To read, to write, and to figure are old, old expectations of what the school is to do. We recognize that with the advent of mass media reading has come to seem relatively unimportant to some people. Moreover, literacy alone may simply make people prey to those who control what is to be read. However, this is an unlikely result of literacy in a free country, and it is clear that all citizens of a nation such as ours need skills in reading, writing, and numbers.

The fact that literacy is a matter of acquiring certain skills—skills that are helpful in developing certain understandings and appreciations—might cause some to suggest that those understandings and appreciations were the *sine qua non* of education, and that the skills were only instrumental to their achievement. Much as we recognize the logic of this position, we still think there are practical reasons for the public school to consider its first indispensable task to be that of teaching for literacy.

If the public school does not do the job of teaching for literacy, it will not be done. For most people the private school cannot do it. Relatively few parents are equipped to do it. Other agencies in society are even less able to step into such a role. Literacy on the part of most citizens is indispensable to our way of life, and the public school is indispensable to providing this literacy.

The teaching of critical thinking is, we think, the second unique task of the public school. This is really the purpose that the founders of our public schools had in mind when they spoke of the need of intelligence on the part of all people. Note a part of what Caleb Mills had to say to the legislature of Indiana in 1846:

> The true glory of a people consists in the intelligence and virtue of its individual members, and no more important duty can devolve upon its representatives in their legislative capacity than the devising and perfecting of a wise, liberal, and efficient system of popular education. . . . It is, indeed, a favorable circumstance that appropriate and efficient action on this subject will

> awaken no sectional jealousies, alarm no religious prejudices, subserve the interests of no political party. It is emphatically a topic which, ably discussed and wisely disposed of, will benefit every part of the State, improve every class in the community, give permanence to our civil and religious institutions, increase the social and literary capital of our citizens, and add materially to the real and substantial happiness of everyone. Such a system of improvement ought surely to require no logrolling to secure its adoption by the representatives of an intelligent people, nor will the burden its operation may occasion be reluctantly borne by a community that scorns the repudiation of a debt incurred for the construction of railroads and canals.[23]

Mills and others may not have appreciated fully what it takes to get people to behave intelligently, but there was no question in their minds about the need for such behavior. Nor did those early champions of the public school foresee the age of propaganda, the rise of mass media, and the intensity of the struggle for the mind of man. Yet the objective they had for public education still stands, even though its achievement has been beset with new difficulties.

What do we mean by critical thinking? We mean simply the ability to define a problem, to seek the relevant facts having to do with it, to weigh the evidence, and to make decisions based upon the evidence. In short, we are talking of problem-solving or the scientific method. Literacy, as we have discussed it above, is a necessary tool to most problem-solving, but literacy alone is not enough. Also necessary are the ability to suspend judgment until the evidence is in, and the ability to analyze the evidence so as to detect when personal bias or privileged position has obscured, slanted, or selected the facts. There is, finally, the courage to accept the position supported by the evidence even in face of preconceived notions.

This is a big order. The capacity of people to learn critical thinking, even with the best of tutelage, varies just as it does with other kinds of learning. The public school must provide opportunity and encouragement for such learning. We have already indicated that the public school can be the most objective institution in our society. Such objectivity must be exploited by teachers if children are to learn critical thinking.

Perhaps Thelen has given us a cue as to how critical thinking is to be fostered when he says:

> . . . inquiry involves firsthand activity in real situations. In most cases, the inquiring student is aided by working close to some adult with whom he can identify—some adult he would like to be like, perhaps, but at the least an adult he can easily trust. This adult must be without ulterior motives in dealing with the students. He has a job to do; he helps define the role of the student on the

23. Quoted in Ellwood P. Cubberley, *Readings in Public Education in the United States* (Boston: Houghton Mifflin, 1934), p. 192.

> job, and the demands the student has to meet come either from the nature of the task or from the nature of the social conditions obviously required to get the work done. In other words, I want the student to transact his business directly with the work and the work environment; I want him to discover that there are realities outside of his own personal desire or those of "authorities," for it is only within such a stable framework of action that his own behavior can be assessed unequivocally by himself. It is only thus that he can discover and learn to depend on his abilities and that he can face up to weaknesses, because they cannot be blamed on other persons.[24]

The White House Conference on Education in 1956 highlighted the third unique task we shall suggest for the public school, the facilitation of social mobility. A part of the Report reads:

> The schools have become a major tool for creating a Nation without rigid class barriers. *It is primarily the schools which allow no man's failure to prevent the success of his son.* [italics in original][25]

To be sure, other institutions in our society contribute to social mobility. For some the ladder is supplied by business, for others by the military, and for others by the church. But the schools seem to be the chief agency in society that can and should accept as one of its prime tasks the providing of opportunity for the upward (or downward) mobility of its students. Again, the relative inclusiveness of public school enrollments is a pertinent matter. For many people the public school can and does discover and encourage ability, notwithstanding the position of Jencks[26] on the relative impotence of the school. When the school accepts this as one of its major functions, those who live "across the tracks" have an opportunity to rise in the world.

To suggest that the school should contribute to social mobility opens up a larger question. While we believe that the primary purpose of the school is educative in nature, the school is also an instrument of social policy. Havighurst[27] maintained that the program of the school was the most powerful factor contributing to the decision of middle-income people to live in the central city or the suburbs, or to live in one section of the city or another. In a very real sense one can say that as go the schools so goes the city. Boards of education and school workers fail, at times, to recognize the social import of their decisions; indeed, they occasionally rebel at the social

---

24. Herbert A. Thelen, *Education and the Human Quest* (New York: Harper & Brothers, 1960), p. 107.

25. The Committee for the White House Conference on Education, *A Report to the President* (Washington: U.S. Government Printing Office, 1956), p. 9.

26. Christopher Jencks et al., *Inequality.*

27. Robert J. Havighurst, *The Public Schools of Chicago* (Chicago: Board of Education, 1964), p. 28.

role they are required to play. We see no alternative. Education has become a powerful social factor and those who are charged with its governance cannot escape their social role.

This whole matter of the need for social mobility and the part the public school might play in such a process takes on a new urgency in a technological society. Workers are needed in most skilled and professional occupations. A major source of supply of these workers is found in the unskilled workers and the children of unskilled workers. If these children are to enter new jobs and acquire new social status, they must have more schooling. For most people the extent of upward mobility in a single generation is probably limited, but the need for such mobility and the role of the school in the process should be clear.

To summarize, if the public school is to fulfill its unique role in the educative process necessary to our way of life, it must teach literacy, stimulate critical thinking, and provide opportunity for those with ability to rise occupationally and socially. We need to recognize that as the school performs these functions it also serves as a powerful instrument of social policy. At the same time, we note that the school shares important educative functions with other institutions. We are aware that the basic purposes of the school are continually under examination and as society changes the schools unique and supporting roles may also change.[28]

ADMINISTRATIVE LEADERSHIP

The fourth challenge that we see, perhaps the pivotal one as far as this book is concerned, is the challenge confronting administrative leaders in the public schools. Or, to put it differently, an indispensable condition necessary for the public school to perform adequately its unique role is the type of administrative leadership we shall now describe. When we speak of administrative leaders, we refer to appointed or official leaders in the school system, such as principals, supervisors, directors, and superintendents. It is the challenge confronting them as official or status leaders with which we are concerned.

We do not wish to minimize the roles played by classroom teachers as the public schools attempt to meet their obligations. Teaching and learning go on only through the teachers. At the same time, teachers and researchers alike have repeatedly indicated that a good part of what any school does is dependent upon the administrative leadership given to that school. The principal, for instance, has a key role in setting the tone, establishing the conditions, and providing stimulation for the kind of living and learning in his school. It is the challenge inherent in such a role that we wish to discuss here.

28. For instance, see James S. Coleman et al., *Youth: Transition to Adulthood* (Chicago: University of Chicago Press, 1974).

As suggested in Chapter 7, each administrator finds himself related to certain major reference groups. In each of these relationships there is a challenge to administrative leadership. We shall, therefore, examine the nature of that challenge with respect to the community, the board of education, the teaching staff, and the pupils.

THE COMMUNITY CHALLENGE

Since we are speaking of administration in the public schools, obviously the public or the community is a major reference group with which any school administrator must work. Most people see this clearly as it applies to the superintendent of schools. For the school principal, however, such recognition is not as general. As a matter of fact, some principals have almost no relationships with the citizens of their respective attendance areas or school communities. This condition seems most undesirable to us. We think every superintendent and every principal in the public schools must deal extensively with the public. While supervisors and directors may deal somewhat less with the public, we are convinced that they, too, must be involved in some public relationships.

The public is not monolithic in nature. Actually, there are many publics. The school administrator may stand alone among other administrators in the great number of publics to whom he feels responsible. Moreover, let us point out that these publics are more than local in nature. Often decisions affecting local school districts are made at county, state, and national levels. This very condition suggests one aspect of the challenge. It is necssary that the administrator ascertain for his school or school district who these publics are and how they believe and act with respect to school matters.

Thus it is necessary that communication with the many publics of a school community be a two-way process. The old business of selling, or telling, or interpreting the schools just will not suffice. Just as the problems, the achievements, and the shortcomings of the public schools must be explained, the feelings, the beliefs, and the aspirations of the people who make up the various publics must also be ascertained. There is, then, the need for listening as well as telling; the need for assessment as well as projection. Hearing what people say in our pluralistic society is no simple task. There are many conflicting voices particularly in our large urban centers. Moreover, some of the voices once submerged are now loud and vociferous. Blacks and other minorities are insisting upon participation in educational matters whether they be related to the curriculum or to the organization and control of the schools. In many places these new demands are caught up in the term "community control."

The real challenge to the administrative leader in dealing with the many publics of the school community comes in what he does with the feelings, beliefs, and aspirations of the people. Ordinarily, he cannot accept these data alone as providing the basis for charting courses of action, any more than he can impose his own professional values on a community without consideration of the factors existing in the particular situation. In other words, the administrator finds out what people think, what they value, and what they want in order to determine where to begin or to determine what are the reasonable limits beyond which action cannot go.

The excitement comes in finding and helping arrange ways by which people get new ideas, gradually come to accept new values, and come to have more realistic expectations of the public school. Or it may be that in the diversity of ideas and aspirations among the publics of a school community, ways can be found by which a greater degree of agreement can be reached so that the course of school operation can go forward at a higher level.

We are not suggesting that the administrator can be all-wise in this situation, nor that his task is simply one of ingenious manipulation. Actually, the administrator may be no wiser than other leaders in his school community. He would do well to relate himself to people in such a way that he might learn from them as well as influence them. We do suggest, however, that the administrator needs professional knowledge, and values that include a conviction that the democratic way of life is important and that the public school has a significant role to play in the realization of that way of life. With that as his prime motivation, he can keep a focus without offending by insisting upon patterned behavior.

In the end the community must take action for public education. This may involve the selection of wise school board members, the passing of bond issues, and the approval of operating levies. Important and necessary as these separate acts are, the continuous voice of the community as it gives expression to what schools ought to be, and as it reacts both favorably and unfavorably to what schools are, may be even more indicative as to how well the community challenge is being met.

THE BOARD CHALLENGE

Public schools in America are controlled through legally constituted boards of education. These boards have been given broad grants of power by the respective state legislatures. In most states the board members are publicly elected to their offices, and while they are assumed to be representative of the people of the school district, the courts have actually declared them to be state officers.

School board members are usually selected from the professional and managerial groups of society, though in rural areas they are often farm owners. This fact has caused some to conclude that boards would be strong defenders of the status quo. Studies of board performance indicate that that interpretation is too simple an explanation and in many cases not warranted. Actually, most board members are seriously concerned with their responsibility and welcome professional help in interpreting and implementing this responsibility.

Clearly, the board of education is the major reference group with which the superintendent must deal. In most school districts the superintendent of schools, as the chief school administrator, will be most directly concerned with the board of education. On occasions, however, superintendents will ordinarily involve other administrators in the board relationship, and board opinions, board action, and board policies are always significant to administrators.

The superintendent of schools has two major roles to play if he is to meet the challenge of working with the board of education. First, he is the chief executive of the board. This may involve helping a board decide what its legislative and judicial functions are, and what the executive functions of the superintendent are. Even after such definition there may be the continuing necessity of clarifying the board-superintendent relationship. This clarification may be even more necessary as new members come on the board.

Assuming that reasonable agreement concerning the board-superintendent relationship can be reached, the superintendent still has the challenge of the executive function. Can he and his staff develop an adequate instructional program? Can he and his staff secure competent personnel? Can he and his staff develop a satisfactory building program? Can he and his staff project accurately the financial needs of the district? Can he and his staff expend efficiently the available funds, and account accurately for them? These represent some of the major expectations most boards of education hold for their superintendents.

In addition to being the chief executive officer of the board of education, the superintendent has a second role as chief educational adviser to the board. In this role the superintendent helps the board form basic policy for school district operation. It is in this role that he brings professional knowledge to board deliberation, and that he broadens the understanding of board members so that they function with greater intelligence as the chief policy-makers for a school district. Zeigler[29] contends that board members not only expect their superintendents to implement board decisions, but they have permitted superintendents to become the chief policy makers as well, a position which probably underplays the board role.

For the superintendent to serve as chief educational adviser to the board, certain conditions are necessary. As in the case of the community, the superintendent must bring to his task force professional understanding and convictions. Moreover, he will find it necessary to work closely with his staff so as to reflect the best possible insights to the board of education at a particular time and place.

---

29. L. H. Zeigler et al., *Governing American Schools* (North Scituate, Mass.: Duxbury Press, 1974).

THE STAFF CHALLENGE

Another major reference group for any school administrator is the school staff. We use the word "staff," at this point, to designate all certified personnel within a school system, including teachers, pupil personnel workers, and administrators. Much of what we shall say about the certified personnel also applies, of course, to the noncertificated personnel of a school system. The staff represents another challenge to administrative leadership, the nature of which we need to examine.

The first chalenge is that of building and maintaining a staff that is thoroughly equipped to do the job of the public schools. If the district is a sizable one, there must be a staff for the central office. For any school district there is the problem of building the staff for each school building, whether there is one or a hundred. These circumstances make it clear that building a staff is the obligation of the chief administrator assisted by his entire administrative staff, including each of the building principals.

There are also other aspects to the staff challenge. While the overall shortage of teachers characteristic of recent decades seems to be at an end, there remains a shortage in certain fields and for certain types of schools. The appropriate involvement of staff members already in a school or school system in the selection of new staff members is also a part of the challenge being suggested here. For instance, some superintendents have not yet learned how to use their building principals in getting teachers well suited for the positions that are open.

There is also the challenge of evaluating the work of staff members. Ascertaining the competence of teachers or administrators is a very difficult matter. Establishing criteria of competence is essentially a valuing procedure and may vary from district to district. The collection of evidence on teaching or administrative performance is difficult when criteria are clear and practically useless when criteria are nonexistent or confusing. Thus, it is understandable that superintendents and principals are, at times, a little hazy on the matter, and no wonder at all that the problem is even more dimly perceived by the lay mind. Despite these difficulties, there are ways of checking the performance of any prospective teacher and administrator in order to get at least a rough measure of how well he fits the job description. By employing these ways and keeping a record of his batting average, any practicing administrator can increase his power of discrimination regarding personnel selection.

May we emphasize the critical nature of each staff selection! The school system may actually work years with a relatively incompetent teacher in order to help him reach a better level of performance. A better selection in the first place would have saved hundreds of hours of effort on the part of the principal and the supervisors. Or the selection of an inadequate principal may mean that for years the program and atmosphere of an entire building, often with hundreds of youngsters involved, may be seriously handicapped. To secure for each position the most competent available person is a continuing challenge to administrative leadership.

Assuming the administrators of a school system have been able to build a competent staff, there is still the challenge of keeping the staff productive. In too many school systems one can find teachers and even administrators and supervisory personnel who, once vigorous, stimulating, and effective people, have now settled into a dull routine of doing what has to be done but with no zest for the task as it now exists or as it might be altered. The factors contributing to such a situation are undoubtedly complex. They may include low salaries, which force many teachers to take a second job and thus become part-time teachers. They may include a seeming lack of opportunities for promotion, particularly within the teaching ranks. But we suspect that other factors of importance lie within the control of administrators and thus constitute a part of the challenge to their leadership.

As further challenge to administrators, teachers and other staff members have become increasingly militant in recent years. Teachers' organizations, whether union or association, are no longer willing to be treated paternalistically by the superintendent or the board of education, no matter how benevolent such action might be. More and more, school managers are faced with annual negotiating sessions with teachers in which the procedures developed in private industry are being adapted to the school situation.

At least a partial understanding of this situation may be found in some of the studies on administrative behavior. Halpin found that staff members preferred their superintendents to be strong both in consideration and in the initiating of structure in group interaction.[30] Research clearly supports the concept that organizations have both a normative and a personal dimension, and that both of these must be taken into account to explain organization behavior.[31] In fact, no proposition in administration has been as well documented as the one that effective administrators perform above the mean in *two* major areas of behavior. The first is consideration or adequate human relations. The second is the initiation of structure or the development of understanding concerning roles and responsibilities of people within an organization.

The evidence suggests clearly that it is not enough for an administrator to be concerned with human relations only. Personal concern on the part of the administrator for each member of his staff is necessary and appropriate. In addition, the administrator must be able to help a staff develop goals and a plan of action, he must be able to help each staff member see where he can make his particular contribution to the total effort, and he must

30. Andrew W. Halpin, *Theory and Research in Administration* (New York: Macmillan, 1966), chap. 3.

31. Jacob W. Getzels, James M. Lipham, and Roald F. Campbell, *Educational Administration as a Social Process* (New York: Harper & Row, 1968).

stimulate each staff member to make his contribution the best of which he is capable.

THE PUPIL CHALLENGE

Another major reference group with which administrators must deal is composed of the pupils—the children and youth who are enrolled in school. In a sense all challenges to administrative leadership have their focus here, because the pupils are the immediate consumers of the school program. School-community agreements, school board action, and staff efforts culminate in what happens to youngsters. These more remote and instrumental programs, no matter how pretty they appear on paper, are of no avail unless they make a difference in the programs of instruction and services to pupils. This is the whole purpose of educational administration, as was suggested in Chapter 4.

Of all administrators and supervisors within a school system, the building principal is nearest to the teaching-learning situation. His influence in that situation is a strategic one. As a matter of fact, what central office people can do to influence instruction must, for the most part, be expressed through the building principal. In better schools the principal, more than any other person, can see that teacher assignments are appropriate, that necessary pupil personnel services are made available, and that extra-class activities are made significant experiences for youngsters.

The principals of most school buildings will wish some direct contact with pupils, but there are limitations to such activity. Effective principals recognize that their chief work group is the faculty and that most of their influence with pupils will be expressed through the faculty and through the programs of the school.

In working with his staff to build and to implement a school program the principal must recognize three aspects of such a program: the classroom instruction, the pupil personnel services, and the extra-class activities. There is always the question of how each of these parts should fit into the total offering. Continually, there is the need to keep classroom instruction stimulating and challenging. Often with the extra-class activities, particularly at the secondary level, there is the problem of keeping them educative and not exploitative or simply commercial. With respect to pupil services, there is the need of providing those services, whether in health, guidance, or some other area, which will contribute to the total development of each youngster or permit his learning to go on more effectively. Trying to provide the best possible program for each pupil enrolled is the tremendous challenge to public education. As the principal deals with instruction, with services, and with extra-class activities, he, like other school workers, needs to be aware of the social role the school is playing.

As noted earlier, increasing numbers of students today are showing signs of alienation in our high schools as well as on our college campuses. This development, plus a more general and widespread sense of discontentment among youth regarding the nature and relevance of conventional high school education, constitutes a very serious and important new dimension to the pupil challenge. Students today are not reluctant to tell us when they believe we have not achieved the goals we discussed in the foregoing paragraph. Indeed, a growing number of young people are contending that the social climate of most high schools today is impersonal, dehumanizing, and authoritarian and that the educational programs are sterile, irrelevant, and deadening. Some critics also add that the social role of the schools in fact seems to be to produce unreflective passive consumers who fit narrow slots in a mechanistic and exploitive society. Moreover, students today not infrequently back up or accompany their complaints or "demands" with strikes or other kinds of protests. The great challenge for administrators here is to try to create open and responsive communication channels among students, themselves, and the faculty and also vehicles for the collective reformation of those aspects of the social climate or educational programs which, upon examination, prove to be in need of change.[32]

A FINAL WORD

We began this chapter by presenting challenges to educational administration. We said that our first challenge, the democratic way of life, is dependent upon an educative process open to all, in which the contributions of many agencies are recognized. While we noted that the educative process is much broader than that provided by the public schools, we maintained that the public schools of this nation perform a role that is an indispensable part of that process. Finally, we took the position that the public schools cannot perform adequately except as administrative leaders in those schools give appropriate direction to the enterprise.

Now let us reverse the process. If the administrative leaders of the public schools of this nation can visualize the crucial place of the public schools, and if they can bring adequate understanding and skill to their task, the public schools can contribute substantially to the development of the people's capacity to do critical thinking. People with such capacity can, and we think will, take steps to preserve that which should be preserved in our culture and to change that which needs to be improved. These people will function through numerous community agencies, and thus the programs of those agencies will reinforce and complement the efforts of the public schools. This effort will perpetuate and extend the democratic way of life. To the educational administrator is given the privilege of participating significantly in this whole endeavor.

32. For a succinct analysis and set of proposals on this topic, see Edwin M. Bridges, "Student Unrest and Crisis Decision-Making," *Administrator's Notebook* 18, 4 (December 1969).

Index

Abbott, Max G., 189–190, 199
Abington Township v. *Schempp,* 46–47
Academy, 43
Administration (*see also* Systems approach):
  approaches to, 87–94
    behavioral science, 92–94, 99
    coordination, 90
    democratic, 99
    human relations, 89–92, 94, 99
    job analysis, 87–89, 97–99
    social process, 183–184
  concept of, 22–24, 113–114
  development of, 85–87
    educational, 94–97
    hierarchy of relationships, 184, 187
    three periods, 94
  developments in field, 99–102
  educational:
    complex functions, 109
    crucial to society, 107–108
    emergence of, 53–54
    key questions, 107
    levels of operation, 106–107
    major functions, 102–103
    necessary relationships, 110
    professionalization, 110–111
    public visibility, 108–109
    six continua, 107–111
    unique aspects, 106–111
  overview, 102–106
  politics and, 86
  problems (samples), 3–20
  process of, 98–99, 183–184
  scholars of, 97–99
  types of, 23
Administration Industrielle et Generale (Fayol), 88–89, 158–159
Administrative behavior:
  concept of success, 306–310
  factors affecting, 290–292
  major areas, 386–387
  perception of others, 292–293
    managing change, 295–297
    rule enforcing, 294–295
    supervision, 293–294
  perception of self, 297–301
    perceived control, 299–301
  values and beliefs, 301–306
    role of authority, 302–303
    role of educational administrator, 305–306 (*see also* Educational administrator)
    role of school, 303–305
Administrative Behavior (Simon), 93
Administrative leadership:
  challenges to, 381–388
    from board of education, 383–384
    from community, 382–383
    from pupils, 387–388
    from staff, 385–387
Administrative tasks, 116–157
Administrator (*see also* Educational administrator):
  authority, 302–303
  characteristics, 268–272
  conflicting expectations, 204–208
  in complex world, 104–106
  influencing, 268, 273–278
    modes, 274–279
  influences on, 279–287
  label for, 21–22
  as leader, 267–279, 302–303
  mission, 268–271
  mission failure, 272
  power of, 203
  recipient of action, 279–287
    against will, 279, 282–283
    by choice, 279, 280–281
    without knowledge, 79, 284–287
  resolving conflict, 207–208, 218–219
  specialist vs. generalist, 104
Adult education, 37, 43
Age of Enlightenment, 365

"Agency shop," 77
Alienation of youth, 374, 387–388
American Federation of Teachers (AFT), 74–76, 262
Appraisal *See* Evaluation
Authority, 248
organizational or normative, 250
two-way flow, 249

Bargaining: (*see also* Collective bargaining)
scope of, 179
Bargaining agent, 261–262
Barnard, Chester, 92–93, 99
Barnard, Henry, 38
Behavioral change, 111 (*see also* Administrative behavior)
locus of causation, 297
Belief, 301
Bible reading, 46 (*see also* Religious freedom; Religious instruction)
Bill of Rights *See* U. S. Constitution
Binding arbitration, 264
Black population, 51, 367
Boards of education:
authority, 70, 105, 151, 248, 283
in bargaining, 262
duties, 152
employing teachers, 137
link with community, 105
membership, 70–71, 383–384
in policy making, 384
pressure on, 72–74
school superintendent and, 71–72, 95, 103, 105, 151–152, 199–202, 384
Bobbitt, Franklin, 98, 99
Boston Latin Grammar School, 27, 43
Brown et al. v. *Board of Education of Topeka, Kansas,* 368
Budget:
building, 126
control record, 148
line-item, 220
program, 220
Building needs, 129
Business manager, 148, 159

Cadet training program, 353–354
Capital outlay, 142
Career crisis, 337
Career plan:
creating 340–343
expanding experiences, 346–347
formal preparation, 347–354
using teaching experience, 343-346
Carnegie Foundation, 66
Catholic Church, 365
Center for Educational Policy and Management, 101
Center for the Advanced Study of Educational Administration (CASEA), 101
Central office position, 319–320 (*see also* Personnel)
Certificated personnel, 133, 149, 385 (*see also* Staff personnel)
Child employment, 35
Church, 375
Church schools *See* Parochial schools
Citizen participation, 27, 40–41 (*see also* Boards of education; Community control)
Class barriers, 376, 380
Clinical supervision, 137
Cocking, Walter D., 99
Coleman, James S., 51–52
Coleman report, 51, 52
Collective bargaining, 75, 222, 251–252
administrator and, 282
nature of the process, 263
resolving impasse, 263–264
teacher participation, 261–264
College Entrance Examination Board (CEEB), 65–66
Commanding, 159, 277–278
Commercial employment agencies, 356
Common good, 366, 370
Communication, 155–156, 169–170
community-school, 382
face to face, 208
of manager, 174
Communism, 370–371
Community control, 52, 80–81, 382
Community-school relations *See* School-community relations
Competition for the mind, 371–372, 379
Compulsory attendance law, 35, 36
Condorcet, 365
Contract (*see also* Collective bargaining):
agent of change, 265
negotiations, 5–9, 135
Controlling, 159–160
Cooperative Program in Educational Administration, 99–100
Coordination, 90, 163, 170–171
Fayol concept, 159
Coordinator role, 22, 159
County superintendent, 54

Creative Experience (Follett), 89–90
Crisis in the Classroom (Silberman), 123
Critical Path Method (CPM), 226–230
Curriculum:
- changes, 253–254, 388
- decisions about, 81
- instruction and, 122–129
  - appraising instruction, 127–129
  - determining program, 124–125, 387–388
  - national curriculum programs, 125–126
  - objectives, 123–124
- selection of materials, 126–127

d'Alembert, 365
Decision making: 164–165
- organizational, 161–162, 166–168
- personnel decisions, 337–338
- role of administrator, 177–179, 218–219
- under crisis, 337

Declaration of Independence, 366–367
Democracy:
- administrative leadership in, 381–388
- challenges of, 371–372
- challenges to, 370–371
- continuing experiment, 364–366
- education in, 372–376
- historical documents, 366–368
- operational agreements, 368–370
- public schools in, 376–381 (*see also* U. S. schools)

Designing, 278
Dewey, John, 114
Diderot, 365
Disputes, 78
District board of education, 40 (*see also* Boards of education)
Disturbance handler, 178

Ecological control, 278
Economic Opportunity Act, 62
Education:
- in colonial America, 27–30
- function of, 303–305
- ideal in United States, 120–121
- an investment, 62–64
- state responsibility, 30–33, 38–39, 105 (*see also* entries under "State," e.g. State board of education)

Educational administration:
- as a career, 313–339
  - competencies required, 323–329
  - judging success, 327–329
  - personal traits, 324–325
  - positions available, 314–323 (*see also* titles, e. g. Principal; Superintendent; U. S. Office of Education)
  - prestige traits, 324–327
  - qualifying for, 340–363
    - career plan, 340–343
    - expanding experiences, 346–347
    - formal preparation, 347–354
    - professional growth, 360–362
    - seeking first position, 354–360
    - using teaching experience, 343–346

Educational administrator:
- administrative process concept, 158–163
  - applied to educational administration, 163–165
- advanced degree requirements, 349–351
- conflicting demands, 204–208
- crucial activities, 163–164
- leadership role, 265, 305–306
- managing time, 180–181 (*see also* Network analysis)
- process, 165–173
  - appraising, 171–173
  - coordinating, 170–171
  - decision making, 166–168, 218, 246–247, 256
  - programming, 168–169
  - stimulating, 169–170
- supervised field experience, 351–354
- systems analysis, 211–215
- systems perspectives and, 210–231
- work of, 158–182

Educational expertise, 248–249
Educative process, 372–376
Effectiveness, 93
Efficiency, 93, 98
Einstein, Albert, 112
Elementary and Secondary Education Act, 46, 62, 67–68, 322
Elementary schools, 344
Emancipation Proclamation, 367
Employment:
- application, 357, 358
- in public schools, 314–315

Employment—*cont.*
in secondary schools and colleges, 322–323
Encyclopedia (Diderot and d'Alembert), 365
Enrollment data, 129–130
Entrepreneurial role, 178
Equal educational opportunity, 37, 41, 48–49, 53, 120, 370
Evaluation, 171–173
process, 128, 164
Extra-class activities, 387

Fact finding, 264
Family Educational Rights and Privacy Act, 68, 131
Fayol, Henri, 88–89, 93, 98, 99, 158–169, 163
Federal support to schools, 146–147
categorical, 42
expenditures, 67
grants, 41–42
oversight of federal programs, 68
Federalists, 86
Federally sponsored courses, 127
Feedback mechanisms, 189–190
Figurehead role, 175–176
Follett, Mary Parker, 89–90, 93, 99
Ford Foundation, 66, 101
Foreign language instruction, 36
French intellectuals, 365
French Revolution, 365
Functional management principle, 88
Functions of the Executive, The (Barnard), 92

Gardner, John W., 123
Getzels, Jacob W., 183–184, 186, 187, 194, 198, 199
Grammar schools, 28, 43
Gregg, Russell T., 164
Griffiths, Daniel E., 164–165
Group membership, 375
Guba, Egon G., 183, 194, 203
Gulick, Luther, 160–161, 163

Hamilton, Alexander, 86
Harvard University, 27
Hawaii, 32, 40
Hawaiian cases, 30
Hawthorne studies, 91–92, 169
High schools, 43, 44, 242, 388
positions in, 344
Higher Education Act, 322
Higher Education Facilities Assistance Act, 322
Historical Sketch of the Progress of the Human Mind (Condorcet), 365
Home, 375

Idiographic dimension of activity, 184, 186–187, 203
Idiographic style of leadership, 195
Immigrants, 48
Information, 176–177
role of, 208
system, 220
Input-output analysis, 215–219
Institutional role, 184, 185, 188
Instruction *See* Curriculum; Teacher; Teaching
Internship programs, 352–354

Jefferson, Thomas, 34, 86
Jensen, Arthur, 52
Job description, 136, 240
Johnson, Lyndon B., 300–301, 369

Kalamazoo case, 44
Kellogg Foundation, 99–100
Kettering Foundation, 66

Leader:
abilities, 22
authority, 302–303
role, 176, 193–194, 267–268
Leadership opportunity, 343–344
Leadership style, 195–196
Liaison role, 176
Line and staff, 154, 237, 238–239
Litchfield, Edward H., 162, 172
Literacy, 378
Local support to schools, 146, 147
Locke, John, 365
Luther, Martin, 365

Man: A Course of Study, 127
Management:
elements of, 89, 158–159, 215
work of, 173–180
Managerial control principle, 88
Mann, Horace, 38

Marx, Karl, 370
Massachusetts Colony, 28
Massachusetts Law of 1827, 43
Mastery learning, 218
Mayflower Compact, 366, 370
Mayo, Elton, 90–92, 93, 99
Mayors, 79
Mediation, 264
Mediator role, 202–204
Mills, Caleb, 378–379
Minority groups, 48–49
  pressures on, 52–53
  rights of, 368
Monitor role, 176
Montesquieu, 365
Motivation, 163, 187
  case for study, 9–14
Motivational research, 372
Mott Foundation, 66

National Advisory Commission on Civil Disorders, 61
National Association of Teachers' Agencies (NATA), 356
National Conference of Professors of Educational Administration (NCPEA), 99
National Defense Act, 65
National Defense Education Act, 67, 322
National Educational Association, 74–77, 262
National foundations, 66
National Institutional Teacher Placement Association (NITPA), 356
National Merit Scholarship Program, 65
National Program for Educational Leadership, 101
National School Boards Association, 77
National Science Foundation, 65, 125, 127
Need dispositions, 186, 373
Negotiating procedures, 76–77 (*see also* Collective bargaining; Contract)
Negotiator role, 179
Network analysis, 226–230
New England common school, 27–28, 43
Nomothetic dimension of activity, 184–187, 203
Nomothetic style of leadership, 195
Noncertificated personnel, 133, 144, 148–149, 240, 385 (*see also* Personnel, central office)
Northwest Territory, 31

Occupational stress, 333–334
  among school executives, 334–336
  physical disorders and, 332–333
  stressful conditions, 336–338
Ordinance of 1787, 31
Oregon case, 29, 30
Organization:
  administrative, 153–155
  formal, 150–151
  horizontal/vertical, 155
  informal, 93, 150
  principles of, 90
  span of control, 155
  structure, 149
  systems of, 94
Organization chart, 159, 246
Organizational development (O.D.) 222–226
Out-organization relationships, 197–198

Parent and neighborhood groups, 78
Parochial schools, 28–29, 44–45
Participation, 155–156
  planned staff, 254–265
Pauper schools, 29–30, 34, 37
Peer approval, 373, 375
Pennsylvania Free School Act, 34
Perception of self, 297–301
  awareness of self, 297–299
  control of others, 300–301
  control of self, 299–300
Personality, 186, 188, 291
Personality conflict, 194–195
Personnel (*see also* Pupil personnel; Staff personnel):
  central office:
    coordination, 239, 259–261
    participation, 257–258
    resource people, 239–240
    roles of, 235–240
    specialists, 237–235
  criteria of competence, 385
  decisions, 337–338
  development, 234–235
  ethics, 359
  policy building, 255–257, 385
  promotion, 355–356
  selection procedures, 357–359, 385–386
    field rating, 359
Physical plant, 140–143
Piece-rate principle, 87
Placement office services, 356–357

Planned staff participation, 254–265
 patterns, 257–261
Planning, 163
Planning-programming-budgeting system (PPBS), 145, 219–222
Planning vs. performance, 87–88
 Fayol's planning, 159–160
Plessy v. *Ferguson,* 49
Policy-making process, 82–83
 board of education and, 152–153, 384
Population shifts, 51, 57
POSDCoRB, 160–161
Preparation for Decision v. Taking Final Action, 165
Preschool learning, 373
Preschool programs, 38
President's Commission on National Goals, 369
Principal, 96, 331
 attitude of, 1
 authority, 243–244
 competency, 329, 244, 387
 in decision making, 256
 functions, 96–97, 106, 315–316
 key roles, 125, 240–244, 335
 leadership, 193–194, 196, 381
 personal traits, 327–328
 prestige traits, 326, 328
 salary, 330
Principles of Scientific Man, The (Taylor), 87
Private schools, 29, 30, 34
Problem analysis, 166
Problem solving, 379
Professional associations, 361
Professor of educational administration, 323
Program Evaluation Review Technique (PERT), 226–230
Programming, 168–169
Project TALENT, 216
Property tax, 82
Protestant Reformation, 365
Public Laws 874, 815, 147
Public school:
 characteristics, 376–377
 concomitant learning, 377–378
 employer, 314–315
 instrument of social policy, 380–381
 social role, 388
Pupil control, 132–133
Pupil personnel, 129–133
 accounting system, 130–131
 discipline policy, 132
 inventory and organization, 129–130
 services to, 131–132, 387

Racial tensions, 61
Rate-bill, 36–37
"Released time," 46
Religion, 44–47 (*see also* Parochial schools)
Religious freedom, 45
Religious instruction, 44, 46, 47
Resource allocator, 178–179
Retirement, 337
Revenue sharing, 42
Rewarding, 277
Rewards, 329–332
Role, defined, 185
Role conflict, 193–194, 334–336
Role expectations, 185, 186, 190, 191
 conflicting, 205, 334
Role overload, 336, 338
Role/personality conflict, 191–193

Salaries, 330
School:
 attendance, 35–36
 basic responsibility, 120–121
 climate, 21
 decentralization, 27, 33, 41, 238, 258–259
  building principal's responsibility, 258
  v. centralization, 154
   coordinated planning, 259–261
 desegregation, 49–50, 51–52, 367, 377
  court decisions, 68–69
 finance, 81–82
  budget making, 144–145, 148 (*see also* Budget)
  eligibility for federal funds, 147 (*see also* Federal support to schools)
  expenditures, 148
  securing revenue, 145–147, 378
 local autonomy, 26
 setting, 56–84
 as a social system, 183–209
  extensions and limitations of theory, 197–202
  feedback mechanisms, 189
   implications for practice, 202–208
  leadership style, 195–196

School—*cont.*
as a social system—*cont.*
model, 187–190
normative dimension, 184–186
personal dimension, 184, 186–187
personality conflict, 194–195
role/personality conflict, 191–193
selective perception, 187, 190–191, 201
School committee, 95
School-community relations, 117–122, 346–347, 382–383
character of community, 117–118
desires of citizens, 118–119
informing the community, 119–120
role of other community agencies, 121–122
role of schools, 120–121
School district, 32–33, 40, 41, 105
character of, 117–118
School district superintendent, 319–320
School elections, 118
School handbook, 246
School population, 64, 96, 142, 376
School suppliers, 64–65
School surveys, 97
Schools for handicapped, 36
Scientific methods-of-work principle, 88
Sears, Jesse B., 98–99, 163, 164
Selective perception, 187, 190–191, 201
Self-perception *See* Perception of self
Semiadministrative positions, 344–345
Sensitivity training, 225–226
Separate but equal, 49–50, 368
Separation of church and state, 30, 44–47
Settings for learning, 142
Simon, Herbert A., 93, 113, 161–162
Social field research, 352
Social mobility, 380–381
Social system, defined, 184
Span of control, 155
Special purpose districts, 33
Specialists, 131–132
Spindler, George, 199
Spokesperson role, 177
Staff officers, 237–238
selecting personnel, 385–386
Staff personnel:
appraising, 138–139, 385
mediator role 202–204
policies, 133–135
seeking personnel, 135–137, 385–386
supervising personnel, 137–138
Standard Metropolitan Statistical Areas, 57
State board of education, 38, 39, 147
certification of administrators, 347–349
requirements for administrators, 347, 354
State certification handbook, 347
State constitutions, 45–46
State educational agencies, 320–321
State superintendent of public instruction, 321
State superintendent of schools, 38
State support of schools, 146, 147
State teachers associations, 39
State university, 44
Stimulation, 163–164, 169–170
Student activism, 61, 69, 133 (*see also* Alienation of youth; Pupil personnel services)
case for study, 14–17
in high schools, 133, 388
Student counseling:
case for study, 14–17
Student promotion:
case for study, 3–5
Student rights, 69
Success, 308–309
concept of, 306–310
need of feedback, 307–308
gasing, 308–309
response to, 309–310
in school administration, 327–329
Superintendent of schools, 95, 97, 331
advanced degrees, 350
board of education and, 71–72, 77, 103, 105, 152, 199–202, 384
delegation of work, 232–233
functions, 106, 153, 320, 384
in selecting staff, 234
generalist, 233–234
leadership style, 196, 233, 235
problems, 79–80
qualifications, 95–96, 326
role of, 232–235, 319–320
role conflict, 334–336
salaries, 330
Supervisory positions, 317–318
System, defined, 211
Systems analysis, 211–215, 236–237 (*see also* Input-output analysis)
components, 214–215
defining objectives, 212
demands for services, 213–214
describing environment, 212–213

Systems analysis—*cont.*
  identifying resources, 214, 215
  management, 215

Taxpayer support, 36, 82, 146
  case for study, 17–20
  taxation legislation, 43–44
Taylor, Frederick, 87–88, 89, 93, 97–99, 113
Teacher:
  administrative authority and, 248–250
  appraising programs, 252–253
  in curriculum change, 253–254
  in decision making, 250–254, 256
  evaluating, 138–139
  in-service education, 253
  job rewards, 245 (*see also* salaries)
  position in hierarchy, 246–248
  role in organization, 244–250
  salaries, 330, 336, 360
Teacher organizations, 74–78, 135, 249
  in collective bargaining, 251–252, 261–264, 386
  lobby, 205
Teacher strikes, 75, 76
Teachers College, Columbia University, 100
Teachers' contract, 134, 251–252, 264
Teaching critical thinking, 378–380, 388
Teaching experience, 343–346, 348, 351
Teaching for literacy, 378
Technology, 374
Thelen, Herbert A., 379–380
Theory, 112–114
Time-study principle, 87
Tinker v. *Des Moines Independent Community School District,* 69, 133
Transactional style of leadership, 195, 196
Transportation service, 143

United Federation of Teachers, 75, 76
United States:
  economic growth, 58–59
  median family income, 59
  personal income, 58
  socioeconomic diversity, 59–60
  tensions in, 60–61
  urbanization, 57–58
United States Constitution, 31, 41
  amendments, 49, 69
  Bill of Rights, 31, 68, 367
  court decisions, 367–368
  First Amendment, 45, 46–47, 367, 370
  Fourteenth Amendment, 367
  Nineteenth Amendment, 368
United States Office of Education, 66, 67, 101, 126
  employment by, 315, 322
United States school system:
  basic responsibility of, 120–121
  continuing education, 43–44
  as employer, 314–315
  federal expenditures, 67
  gederal participation, 41–42, 62, 64, 66–67
  free education, 36–38
  historical themes, 33–53
  local (district) schools, 39–41
    control, 80–81
    shaping educational policy, 69–79
      participants, 70–79, 80
      process of, 82–83
  melting pot influence, 48–53
  nationalizing influences, 65–69 (*see also* Democracy)
  religion and, 44–47
  in southern states, 49–50
  state responsibility, 30–33, 38–39
  universal education, 33–36
United States Supreme Court:
  decisions affecting education, 49–50, 68–69, 367
University Council for Educational Administration (UCEA), 100–101
University of Oregon, 101

Values, 301
  and beliefs, 301–306
  concept of, 199–202
  conflicts, 374
  democratic, 369–370
Voltaire, 365
Voting law of 1965, 367
Voting privileges, 368–372
Voucher system, 47

White flight, 52
White House Conference on Education, 120, 369, 380
Wilson, Woodrow, 86
Women:
  in administration, 324–326
  voting right, 368
Work permits, 130–131